THEORY CULTURE & SOCIETY

Explorations in Critical Social Science
Volume 5, Numbers 2–3, June 1988

SPECIAL ISSUE ON POSTMODERNISM

CONTENTS

Articles

In Pursuit of the Postmodern:
An Introduction

Mike Featherstone

Any reference to the term 'postmodernism' immediately exposes one to the risk of being accused of jumping on a bandwaggon, of perpetuating a rather shallow and meaningless intellectual fad. One of the problems is that the term is at once fashionable yet irritatingly elusive to define. As the *Modern-day Dictionary of Received Ideas* confirms 'This word has no meaning. Use it as often as possible' (*The Independent*, 24 December 1987). Over a decade earlier, in August 1975, another newspaper anounced that 'postmodernism is dead', and that 'post-post-modernism is now the thing' (Palmer, 1977: 364). If postmodernism is an ephemeral fashion then some critics are clear as to who are responsible for its prominence: 'To-day's paid theorists surveying the field from their booklined studies in polytechnics and universities are obliged to invent movements because their careers — no less than those of miners and fishermen — depend on it. The more movements they can give names to, the more successful they will be' (Pawley, 1986). For other critics these strategies are not just internal moves within the intellectual and academic fields; they are clear indicators and barometers of the 'malaise at the heart of contemporary culture'. Hence, 'It is not difficult to comprehend this cultural and aesthetic trend now known as Postmodernism — in art and architecture, music and film, drama and fiction — as a reflection of . . . the present wave of political reaction sweeping the Western world' (Gott, 1986). But it is all too easy to see postmodernism as a reactionary, mechanical reflection of social changes and to blame the academics and intellectuals for coining the term as part of their distinction games. Even though certain newspaper critics and para-intellectuals use the term in a cynical or dismissive manner, they confirm that postmodernism has sufficient appeal to interest a larger middle-class audience. Few other recent academic terms can claim to have enjoyed such popu-

Theory, Culture & Society (SAGE, London, Newbury Park, Beverly Hills and New Delhi), Vol. 5 (1988), 195–215

196 Theory, Culture & Society

larity. Yet it is not merely an academic term, for it has gained impetus from artistic 'movements' and is also attracting wider public interest through its capacity to speak to some of the cultural changes we are currently going through.

Before we can look at the means of transmission and dissemination of the concept, we need a clearer notion of the range of phenomena which are generally included under the umbrella concept postmodernism. We therefore need to take account of the great interest and even excitement that it has generated, both inside and outside the academy, and to ask questions about the range of cultural objects, experiences and practices which theorists are adducing and labelling postmodern, before we can decide on its political pedigree or dismiss it as merely a short swing of the pendulum.

In the first place the broad range of artistic, intellectual and academic fields in which the term postmodernism has been used, is striking. We have music (Cage, Stockhausen, Briers, Holloway, Tredici, Laurie Anderson); art (Rauschenberg, Baselitz, Mach, Schnabel, Kiefer; some would also include Warhol and 1960s pop art, and others Bacon); fiction (Vonnegut's *Slaughterhouse Five*, and the novels of Barth, Barthelme, Pynchon, Burroughs, Ballard, Doctorow); film (*Body Heat, The Wedding, Blue Velvet, Wetherby*); drama (the theatre of Artaud); photography (Sherman, Levine, Prince); architecture (Jencks, Venturi, Bolin); literary theory and criticism (Spanos, Hassan, Sontag, Fielder); philosophy (Lyotard, Derrida, Baudrillard, Vattimo, Rorty); anthropology (Clifford, Tyler, Marcus); sociology (Denzin); geography (Soja). The very names of those included and excluded in the list will doubtless strike some as controversial. To take the example of fiction, as Linda Hutcheon (1984: 2) argues, some would wish to include the novels of García Márquez and even Cervantes under the heading of postmodernism and others would want to refer to them as neobaroque and baroque. Scott Lash, writing in this issue, would want to regard Dada as postmodernism *avant la lettre*. There are those who work and write unaware of the term's existence and others who seek to thematize and actively promote it. Yet it can be argued that one of the functions of the interest in postmodernism on the part of critics, para-intellectuals, cultural intermediaries and academics has been to diffuse the term to wider audiences in different national and international contexts (this is one of the senses in which one can talk about the globalization of culture); and to increase the speed of interchange and circulation of the term between the various fields in the academy and the arts, which now want to, and have to, pay more attention to developments in their neighbours. In this sense it is possible that some greater agreement on the meaning of the term might eventually emerge as commentators in each particular field find it necessary to recapitulate and explain the multiplex history and usages of the term in order to educate new, academic audiences.

To work towards some preliminary sense of the meaning of postmodernism it is useful to identify the family of terms derived from 'the postmodern' and these can best be understood by contrasting them to those which derive from 'the modern'.

modern	postmodern
modernity	postmodernity
modernité	postmodernité
modernization	postmodernization
modernism	postmodernism

If 'the modern' and 'the postmodern' are the generic terms it is immediately apparent that the prefix 'post' signifies that which comes after, a break or rupture with the modern which is defined in counterdistinction to it. Yet the term 'postmodernism' is more strongly based on a negation of the modern, a perceived, abandonment, break with or shift away from the definitive features of the modern, with the emphasis firmly on the sense of the relational move away. This would make the postmodern a relatively ill-defined term as we are only on the threshold of the alleged shift, and not in a position to regard the postmodern as a fully fledged positivity which can be defined comprehensively in its own right. Bearing this in mind we can take a closer look at the pairings.

Modernity–Postmodernity
This suggests the epochal meaning of the terms. Modernity is generally held to have come into being with the Renaissance and was defined in relation to Antiquity, as in the debate between the Ancients and the Moderns. From the point of view of late nineteenth- and early twentieth-century German sociological theory from which we derive much of our current sense of the term, modernity is contrasted to the traditional order and implies the progressive economic and administrative rationalization and dif-

ferentiation of the social world (Weber, Tönnies, Simmel): processes which brought into being the modern capitalist–industrial state
and which were often viewed from a distinctly anti-modern perspective.

Consequently, to speak of postmodernity is to suggest an epochal
shift or break from modernity involving the emergence of a new
social totality with its own distinct organizing principles. It is this
order of change that Douglas Kellner, in his paper 'Postmodernism
and Social Theory' detects in the writing of Baudrillard, Lyotard,
and to some extent, Jameson. Both Baudrillard and Lyotard
assume a movement towards a post-industrial age. Baudrillard
(1983) stresses that new forms of technology and information become central to the shift from a productive to a reproductive social
order in which simulations and models increasingly constitute the
world so that the distinction between the real and appearance
becomes erased. Lyotard (1984) talks about the postmodern society, or postmodern age, which is premised on the move to a post-
industrial order. His specific interest is in the effects of the 'computerization of society' on knowledge and he argues that the loss of
meaning in postmodernity should not be mourned, as it points to a
replacement of narrative knowledge by a plurality of language
games, and universalism by localism. Yet Lyotard, like many users
of the family of terms, sometimes changes register from one term to
the next and switches usages, preferring more recently to emphasize
that the postmodern is to be regarded as part of the modern. For
example, in 'Rules and Paradoxes or Svelte Appendix' he writes
' "postmodern" is probably a very bad term because it conveys the
idea of a historical "periodization". "Periodizing", however, is still
a "classic" or "modern" ideal. "Postmodern" simply indicates a
mood, or better a state of mind' (Lyotard, 1986–87: 209). The other
interesting point to note about Lyotard's use of postmodernity in
The Postmodern Condition, is that where he talks about the changes
in knowledge accompanying the move to the post-industrial society
he still conceives this as occurring within capitalism, adding weight
to Kellner's argument that the move to the postmodern society is
undertheorized in Lyotard's work. Although the move is assumed
at some points, it is easier to avoid the accusations of providing a
grand narrative account of the move to postmodernity and the
eclipse of grand narratives, by insisting on a more diffuse notion of
'mood' or 'state of mind'. Fredric Jameson (1984) has a more
definite periodizing concept of the postmodern, yet he is reluctant

to conceive of it as an epochal shift, rather postmodernism is the cultural dominant, or cultural logic, of the third great stage of capitalism, late capitalism, which originates in the post-World War Two era.

Lyotard's invocation of a postmodern mood or state of mind points us towards a second meaning of modernity–postmodernity. The French use of *modernité* points to the experience of modernity in which modernity is viewed as a quality of modern life inducing a sense of the discontinuity of time, the break with tradition, the feeling of novelty and sensitivity to the ephemeral, fleeting and contingent nature of the present (see Frisby, 1985a). This is the sense of being modern associated with Baudelaire which, as Foucault (1986: 40) argues, entails an ironical heroicization of the present: the modern man is the man who constantly tries to invent himself. It is this attempt to make sense of the experience of life in the new urban spaces and nascent consumer culture, which developed in the second half of the nineteenth century, which provided the impetus for the theories of modern everyday life in the work of Simmel, Kracauer and Benjamin discussed by David Frisby (1985b) in his *Fragments of Modernity*. The experience of modernity also forms the subject matter of Marshall Berman's (1982) book *All That is Solid Melts into Air* in which he looks at the visions and idioms accompanying the modernization process which he pulls together under the term 'modernism'. Berman discusses the modern sensibility that is manifest in a wide range of literary and intellectual figures from Rousseau and Goethe in the eighteenth century to Marx, Baudelaire, Pushkin, Dostoevsky in the nineteenth.

Apart from the confusing use of modernism to take in the whole of the experience and the culture that accompanied the modernization process, Berman and many of those who are currently trying to delineate the equivalent experience of postmodernity focus upon a particularly restrictive notion of experience: that which appears in literary sources and is so designated by intellectuals. But we have to raise the sociological objection against the literary intellectual's license in interpreting the everyday, or in providing evidence about the everyday lives of ordinary people. Of course, some intellectuals may have articulated well the experience of the shocks and jolts of modernity. Yet we need to make the jump from modernity or postmodernity as a (relatively restricted) subjective experience to outlining the actual practices and activities which take place in the everyday lives of various groups. Certainly the descriptions of subjective experience may make sense within intellectual practices, and within aspects of the practices of particular audiences educated to interpret these sensibilities, but the assumption that one can make wider claims needs careful substantiation.

To take an example of the alleged experience of postmodernity (or *postmodernité*), we can refer to Jameson's (1984) account of the onaventure Hotel in Los Angeles. Jameson gives an interesting interpretation of the experience of the new hyperspace of postmodern architecture, which, he argues, forces us to expand our sensorium and body. Yet we get little idea of how individuals from different backgrounds actually experience the hotel, or better still, how they incorporate the experience into their day-to-day practices. Perhaps for them to interpret the experience as postmodern they need guidelines to make sense of things they may not fully notice, or view through inappropriate codes. Hence, if we want to understand the social generation and interpretation of the experience of postmodernity we need to have a place for the role of cultural entrepreneurs and intermediaries who have an interest in creating postmodern pedagogies to educate publics. The same can be said for two other features of postmodern culture identified by Jameson: the transformation of reality into images and the fragmentation of time into a series of perpetual presents. Here we can take an example which encompasses both features: the media, which tends to be central to many discussions of the postmodern sensibility (one thinks for example of Baudrillard's simulational world, where 'TV is the world'). Yet for all the alleged pluralism and sensitivity to the Other talked about by some theorists one finds little discussion of the actual experience and practice of watching television by different groups in different settings. On the contrary theorists of the postmodern often talk of an ideal-type channel-hopping MTV (music television) viewer who flips through different images at such speed that she/he is unable to chain the signifiers together into a meaningful narrative, she/he merely enjoys the multiphrenic intensities and sensations of the surface of the images. Evidence of the extent of such practices, and how they are integrated into, or influence, the day-to-day encounters between embodied persons is markedly lacking. Thus while learned references to the characteristic experiences of postmodernity are important we need to work from more systematic data and should not rely on the readings of intellectuals. In effect we should focus upon the actual cultural practices and changing power balances of those groups engaged in the production, classification, circulation and consumption of postmodern cultural goods, something which will be central to our discussion of postmodernism below.

Modernization–Postmodernization
On the face of it, both terms seem to sit unhappily amidst discussion of modernity–postmodernity, modernism–postmodernism. Modernization has been regularly used in the sociology of development to point to the effects of economic development on traditional social structures and values. Modernization theory is also used to refer to the stages of social development which are based upon industrialization, the growth of science and technology, the modern nation state, the capitalist world market, urbanization and other infrastructural elements. (In this usage it has strong affinities with the first sense of modernity we discussed above.) It is generally assumed, via a loose base–superstructure model that certain cultural changes (secularization and the emergence of a modern identity which centres around self-development) will result from the modernization process. If we turn to postmodernization it is clear that a concomitant detailed outline of specific social processes and institutional changes has yet to be theorized. All we have is the possibility of deriving the term from those usages of postmodernity which refer to a new social order and epochal shift mentioned above. For example, Baudrillard's (1983) depiction of a postmodern simulational world is based upon the assumption that the development of commodity production coupled with information technology have led to the 'triumph of signifying culture' which then reverses the direction of determinism, so that social relations become saturated with shifting cultural signs to the extent that we can no longer speak of class or normativity and are faced by 'the end of the social'. Baudrillard however does not use the term 'postmodernization'.

The term does, however, have the merit of suggesting a process with degrees of implementation, rather than a fully fledged new social order or totality. One significant context for the utilization of the term postmodernization is the field of urban studies, exemplified in this issue in the contributions of Philip Cooke and Sharon Zukin. For Cooke, postmodernization is an ideology and set of practices with spatial effects which have been notable in the British economy since 1976. Zukin also wants to use postmodernization to focus on the restructuring of socio-spatial relations by new patterns of investment and production in industry, services, labour markets and telecommunications. Yet, while Zukin sees postmodernization as a dynamic process comparable to modernization, both she and Cooke are reluctant to regard it as pointing to a new stage of society, for it is held to take place within capitalism. They both share the merit of focusing on processes of production as well as consumption and the spatial dimension of particular cultural practices (the redevelopment of downtowns and waterfronts, development of urban artistic and cultural centres, and the growth of the service class and gentrification) which accompany them.

Modernism–Postmodernism
As with the pairing modernity–postmodernity, we are again faced with a range of meanings. Common to them all is the centrality of culture. In the most restricted sense, modernism points to the styles we associate with the artistic movements which originated around the turn of the century and have dominated the various arts until recently. Figures frequently cited are: Joyce, Yeats, Gide, Proust, Rilke, Kafka, Mann, Musil, Lawrence and Faulkner in literature; Rilke, Pound, Eliot, Lorca, Valéry in poetry; Strindberg, Pirandello and Wedekind in drama; Matisse, Picasso, Braque, Cézanne and the Futurist, Expressionist, Dada and Surrealist movements in painting; Stravinsky, Schoenberg and Berg in music (see Bradbury and McFarlane, 1976). There is a good deal of debate about how far back into the nineteenth century modernism should be taken (some would want to go back to the bohemian avant-garde of the 1830s). The basic features of modernism can be summarized as: an aesthetic self-consciousness and reflexiveness; a rejection of narrative structure in favour of simultaneity and montage; an exploration of the paradoxical, ambiguous and uncertain open-ended nature of reality; and a rejection of the notion of an integrated personality in favour of an emphasis upon the destructured, dehumanized subject (see Lunn, 1985: 34ff). One of the problems with trying to understand postmodernism in the arts is that many of these features are appropriated into various definitions of postmodernism. The problem with the term, as with the other related terms we have discussed, revolves around the question of when does a term defined oppositionally to, and feeding off an established term, start to signify something substantially different?

According to Köhler (1977) and Hassan (1985) the term postmodernism was first used by Federico de Onis in the 1930s to indicate a minor reaction to modernism. The term became popular in the 1960s in New York when it was used by young artists, writers and critics such as Rauschenberg, Cage, Burroughs, Barthelme, Fielder, Hassan and Sontag to refer to a movement beyond the 'exhausted' high modernism which was rejected because of its institutionalization in the museum and the academy. It gained wider usage in architecture, the visual and performing arts, and music in the 1970s and 1980s and then was rapidly transmitted back and forth between Europe and the United States as the search for theoretical explanations and justifications of artistic postmodernism shifted to include wider discussions of postmodernity and drew in, and generated an interest in, theorists such as Bell, Kristeva, Lyotard, Vattimo, Derrida, Foucault, Habermas, Baudrillard and Jameson (see Huyssen, 1984). Amongst the central features associated with postmodernism in the arts are: the effacement of the boundary between art and everyday life; the collapse of the hierarchical distinction between high and mass/popular culture; a stylistic promiscuity favouring eclecticism and the mixing of codes; parody, pastiche, irony, playfulness and the celebration of the surface 'depthlessness' of culture; the decline of the originality/genius of the artistic producer and the assumption that art can only be repetitious.

There is also a wider usage of the terms modernism and postmodernism which refers to broader cultural complexes: i.e. modernism as the culture of modernity, and postmodernism as the emergent culture of postmodernity. Daniel Bell (1976) takes up this position in which he sees the fundamental cultural assumption of modernity, the ideal of the autonomous self-determining individual, as giving rise to the bourgeois entrepreneur in the economic realm and the artistic search for the untrammelled self (which finds its expression in modernism) in the cultural realm. For Bell modernism is a corrosive force, unleashing an adversarial culture which in conjunction with the hedonistic culture of mass consumption subverts traditional bourgeois values and the Puritan ethic. Bell's analysis is based on the notion of the disjunction of the three realms, the polity, culture and economy, so there is no sense in looking for a base-superstructural model in his work in which a shift in the economy, or socioeconomic order such as to the post-industrial society would give rise to a new culture of postmodernism. Rather, postmodernism is perceived as a heightening of the adversarial tendencies of modernism with desire, the instinctual, and pleasure unleashed to carry the logic of modernism to its furthest reaches (Bell,

1980), exacerbating the structural tensions of society and disjunction of the realms. Jameson (1984) too uses postmodernism to refer to culture in the broader sense and talks about postmodernism as a cultural logic, or cultural dominant, which leads to the transformation of the cultural sphere in contemporary society. While Jameson shows some reluctance in adopting the view of periodization which assumes a sudden shift and transformation of all aspects of culture, he follows Mandel (1975) and links the stages of modernism to monopoly capitalism and postmodernism to post-World War Two late capitalism. This suggests that he uses a form of the base-superstructural model. Yet he also goes part of the way along the same route as Baudrillard, without referring to him, to argue that postmodernism is based upon the central role of reproduction in the 'de-centred global network' of present-day multinational capitalism which leads to a 'prodigious expansion of culture throughout the social realm, to the point at which everything in our social life . . . can be said to have become "cultural"' (Jameson, 1984: 85–7).

There is one further point that needs to be taken up from the work of Bell and Jameson before going on to look at the use of postmodernism as a cipher for fundamental cultural changes as well as the possible expansion of the significance of culture in contemporary western societies. In his paper on 'Religion and Postmodernism' John O'Neill argues that both Bell and Jameson adopt a nostalgic reaction to postmodernism, and are united against postmodernism in their 'will to order', their desire to renew the threatened social bond via religion (Bell) or the Marxist utopia (Jameson). Both have the merit or flaw, depending on where you stand, of wanting to totalize: to depict postmodernism in its degrees of connectedness and disjunction to the contemporary social order. They also want to judge postmodernism as negative; they have a distaste for it — a response which has not passed unnoticed on the part of those critics who welcome the playfulness and pluralistic, 'democratic' spirit of postmodernism, and would see Jameson (and by association, Bell) as nostalgically bemoaning the loss of authority of the intellectual aristocracy over the population (see Hutcheon, 1986–7; During, 1987).

For those who welcome postmodernism as a mode of critical analysis which opens up ironies, inter-textuality and paradoxes, attempts to devise a theory of postmodern society or postmodernity, or delineate the role of postmodernism within the social order, are essentially flawed efforts to totalize or systemize. In effect they

are authoritarian grand narratives which are ripe for playful deconstruction. Critics are, for example, quick to point out this apparent
inconsistency in Lyotard's *Postmodern Condition*. In this issue Kellner argues that Lyotard's notion of postmodernity itself entails a
master narrative, that we can't have a theory of the postmodern
without one. It should be added that in the interview, which also
appears in this issue, Lyotard is quick to move away from what he
sees as the misunderstanding of his book as an example of totalizing
reason. For those who take seriously the implications of postmodernism as a mode of critical theorizing or cultural analysis, the
attempt to produce a sociological understanding must necessarily
fail as it cannot avoid totalizations, systematizations and legitimation via the flawed grand narratives of modernity: science, humanism, Marxism, feminism etc. Sociological synthesis must be abandoned for playful deconstruction and the privileging of the aesthetic
mode. A postmodern sociology so-conceived would abandon its
generalizing social science ambitions and instead parasitically play
off the ironies, incoherencies, inconsistencies and inter-textuality of
sociological writings. There are, of course, lessons to be learned
from a postmodern sociology: it focuses attention on the ways in
which theories are built up, their hidden assumptions, and questions the theorists' authority to speak for 'the Other', who as many
researchers are finding out, is now often actively disputing both the
account and the authority of the academic theorist. Yet if we are to
attempt to make sense of the emergence of postmodernism and the
changes taking place in the culture of contemporary western
societies we need to move beyond the false oppositions of foundationalism and relativism, of single epistemology and plural ontology, and investigate specific social and cultural processes and the
dynamics of the production of particular funds of knowledge. In
effect we must relinquish the attractions of a postmodern sociology
and work towards a sociological account of postmodernism (see
Featherstone, 1988).

To follow such an approach would entail focusing on the inter-
relationship between three aspects or meanings of the culture of
postmodernism. In the first place we can consider postmodernism
in the arts and in the academic and intellectual fields. Here we could
usefully employ the field approach of Bourdieu (1971, 1980) and
focus upon the economy of symbolic goods: the conditions of supply
and demand for such goods, the processes of competition and
monopolization, and the struggles between the established and

outsiders. We could, for example direct attention to the act of *naming* as an important strategy of groups engaged in struggles with other groups; the use of new terms by outsider groups who have an interest in destabilizing existing symbolic hierarchies to produce a reclassification of the field more in line with their own interests; the conditions which are breaking down the barriers between subfields of the arts and academic subjects; the conditions which dictate changes in the demand for particular types of cultural goods by various state agencies, consumers, audiences and publics.

To adequately deal with the last areas, indeed to adequately conceptualize all the above areas, would take us outside the specific analysis of particular artistic and intellectual fields and their inter-relationship. Here we would need to consider postmodernism in terms of a second 'level' of culture, what is often called the cultural sphere, and consider the means of transmission and circulation to audiences and publics and the feedback effect of the audience response in generating further interest amongst intellectuals. To focus on this second area we need to look at artists, intellectuals and academics as specialists in symbolic production and consider their relationship to other symbolic specialists in the media, and those engaged in consumer culture, popular culture and fashion occupations. Here we need to focus on the emergence of what Bourdieu (1984) calls 'new cultural intermediaries', who rapidly circulate information between formerly sealed-off areas of culture, and the emergence of new communication channels under conditions of intensified competition (Crane, 1987). We also need to consider the competition, changing balances of power and interdependencies between specialists in symbolic production and economic specialists (c.f. Elias, 1987) within conditions of a growth in the former group's power potential as producers and consumers accompanying the growth of mass and higher education in western nations in the postwar era. We need to examine some of the processes of demonopolization and dehierarchization of previously established and legitimate cultural enclaves which has brought about a phase of cultural declassification in the western world (DiMaggio, 1987). Finally, in addition to considering these changes on an intra-societal level we need also to consider the processes of intensified competition on an inter-societal level which is shifting the balance of power away from western intellectuals and artists and their right to speak for humanity, as well as the emergence of genuine global cultural questions through what Roland Robertson (forthcoming) has called 'globalization'. These processes point to changes within the broader cultural sphere which are worthy of investigation in their own right; processes which, it can be argued, the concept of postmodernism has served to sensitize us to.

The concept of postmodernism is not however, merely an empty sign which can be manipulated by artists, intellectuals and academics as part of the power struggles and interdependencies within their particular fields. Part of its appeal is that it speaks to the above changes and also purports to illuminate changes in the day-to-day experiences and cultural practices of broader groups in society. It is here that the evidence is weakest and the possibility of simply relabelling experiences as postmodern which were formerly granted little significance, is most obvious. It is here that we face the problem of an adequate definition of postmodernism and find a good deal of loose conceptual confusion with notions of 'the loss of a sense of historical past', 'schizoid culture', 'excremental culture', 'the replacement of reality by images', 'simulations', 'unchained signifiers' etc., multiplying. Scott Lash, in his paper 'Discourse or Figure?' has endeavoured to move to a tighter definition of postmodernism as involving de-differentiation and the figural, which are held to be central to postmodern regimes of signification; yet here too we possess little systematic evidence about day-to-day practices, and we need information in terms of the stock sociological questions 'who? when? where? how many?' if we are to impress colleagues that postmodernism is more than a fad. Yet there is also a sense in which postmodernism proceeds under its own steam, with the changes in the cultural sphere we have hinted at above, leading to the formation of new audiences and publics interested in postmodernism. Such audiences and publics may eventually adopt postmodern practices and become attuned to postmodern experiences under the guidance of pedagogues produced by cultural intermediaries and para-intellectuals. Such 'feed-back' could lead to postmodernism becoming translated into reality.

To summarize, before proceeding to the next section in which we will take a closer look at some of the 'postmodern' theories, practices and regimes of signification discussed in this issue: there is, as yet, no agreed meaning to the term postmodern — its derivatives, the family of terms which includes postmodernity, postmodernité, postmodernization and postmodernism are often used in confusing and interchangeable ways. We have attempted to outline and discuss some of these meanings. Postmodernism is of interest to a wide range of artistic practices and social science and humanities disciplines because it directs our attention to changes taking place in contemporary culture. These can be understood in terms of a) the artistic, intellectual and academic fields (changes in modes of theorization, presentation and dissemination of work which cannot be detached from changes in specific competitive struggles occurring in particular fields); b) changes in the broader cultural sphere involving the modes of production, consumption and circulation of symbolic goods which can be related to broader shifts in the balance of power and interdependencies between groups and class fractions on both inter- and intra-societal levels; c) changes in the everyday practices and experiences of different groups, who as a result of some of the processes referred to above, may be using regimes of signification in different ways and developing new means of orientation and identity structures. It is apparent that the very existence of this journal has been premised upon the upsurge of interest in the issue of culture. Culture once on the periphery of social science disciplines, particularly in sociology, has now been thrust increasingly towards the centre of the field (Featherstone, 1988). We can understand this in terms of two processes which must be interrelated: firstly, the way in which culture has shifted in the arsenal of social science concepts from something which is essentially explicable in terms of other factors to broader metacultural questions concerning the cultural underpinning, or 'deep' cultural coding of the social (see Robertson, 1988); secondly, the way in which the culture of contemporary western societies seems to be undergoing a series of major transformations which must be investigated in terms of intra-societal, inter-societal and global processes. It should be apparent that this is one reason for the rise of interest in postmodernism, and a further reason why as cultural theorists and researchers we should be interested in it.

As Huyssen (1984) and others have argued postmodernism originated among artists and critique in New York in the 1960s and was taken up by European theorists in the 1970s, one of them being Jean-François Lyotard whose *La Condition postmoderne* appeared in 1979. This book which together with the subsequent essay, 'An Answer to the Question What is Postmodernism?' (placed as an appendix to the 1984 English translation), became a key text in the diffusion of postmodernism in the English-speaking world. In the first, Lyotard (1984: 31ff) attacks the grand narratives, or legitimating myths of the modern age, the progressive liberation of humanity through science and the idea that philosophy can restore unity to learning and develop universally valid knowledge for humanity. (One of the targets here is Habermas, and a number of 'debates', largely instigated and developed by third parties developed around this time on the question of the conservative nature of French poststructuralist and postmodernist social theory [see Bernstein, 1985; Richters, forthcoming]). Postmodern theory became identified with the critique of universal knowledge and antifoundationalism. As Lyotard points out in the interview in this issue, our age can no longer talk about a totalizing idea of reason for 'there is no reason, only reasons'. In his 'Introduction to Lyotard', Dick Veerman elaborates Lyotard's point to argue that after Auschwitz, Solidarity, May '68, the Prague Spring, we cannot continue to subsume critical reason under the ideal of a natural teleology, all these events are evidence of complex incommensurable teleologies, of heterogeneity in social, society and aesthetic experience. In their paper Nancy Fraser and Linda Nicholson provide an interesting and elegant account of the implication of such a postmodernist critique of metanarratives for feminism, yet argue that while the lessons of this approach point to the dangers of using universalist categories such as 'women' and 'female gender identity', feminist theory should continue to strive to use more historically specific categories in conjunction with the analysis of social macrostructures.

The Lyotard interview is interesting in the light it throws on the development of his work from *Discours/figure* down to his recent *Le Différend*, and the elaboration on themes in the essay 'An Answer to the Question: What is Postmodernism?' in which he discusses in detail the relationship between aesthetics and politics.

The interview also contains some insights on his differences with Derrida and Rorty. Fraser and Nicholson, like many commentators link Rorty's antifoundational stance with postmodernism. Yet it is by no means clear how far he would wish to be included amongst those he has recently dubbed 'posties' (Rorty, 1987). Richard Shusterman, in his piece on 'Postmodern Aestheticism', is in no doubt that the label should apply and that Rorty follows the postmodernist aestheticization of ethics and the advocacy of an ethics of taste which is largely 'a re-hash of fin-de-siècle aestheticism, which shares the same feverish anxious lust for pleasurable novelty and the same weary and faithless scepticism we postmoderns claim as our own'.

Rorty's emphasis upon an aesthetic of taste and the quest to acquire more and more experiences, new pleasures and new sensations, points to a decentred self which is merely a bundle of 'quasi-selves'. This is similar to some of the characteristics of the postmodern identity which Jonathan Friedman discusses in his paper. It also, as Shusterman points out, is similar to the type of 'ideal self' promoted by consumer culture.

In his paper 'Discourse or Figure?' Scott Lash makes a strong case for considering contemporary culture as involving both de-differentiation and figural tendencies. De-differentiation is seen as reversing the process of differentiation which was held to be integral to the process of modernization. Lash's notion of the figural entails a contrast discourse/figural derived from the work of Lyotard, which is used to suggest that postmodern cultural forms are figural in their emphasis upon: visual images over words; primary processes against the secondary processes of the ego; the preference for the immersion rather that the distantiation of the spectator. Susan Sontag, one of the earliest writers to endorse postmodernism in New York in the 1960s, is seen as an exemplar of the figural and de-differentiation approach, in advocating an aesthetics of the body and sensation, in which the work of art is seen as a sensory thing. The work of the painter, Francis Bacon also provides a good example of the figural work of art with his aleatory paintings which communicate the feeling of raw meat. As Roy Boyne tells us, in his discussion in 'The Art of the Body', Bacon has remarked that 'narratives are meant to get in the way of sensation' and therefore refuses to provide any commentary on his work. Lash also discusses postmodernism in the cinema, which, he argues, is the main figural cultural form as images signify through 'iconicity' and articulate meaning and desire in a way that words do not. The postmodern cinema attempts to problematize the real, as Norman Denzin suggests in his analysis of the film *Blue Velvet*, which proved to be one of the most acclaimed and controversial films of 1987; bringing a mass of contradictory critical assessments ranging from pornography, religious art, gothic, trash, mindless, junk, murder mystery to dream film, comedy and surrealism. Denzin argues that the range of postmodern qualities the film embodied accounts for the perplexity and fascination it aroused amongst critics and the public.

For Gillian Rose, in her tightly argued paper 'Architecture to Philosophy — the Postmodern Complicity', the term 'postmodern' is of dubious value. It represents the false importation into philosophy and social theory of an over-simple periodization of twentieth century as modernist and post-sixties as postmodernist architecture. For Rose the modern has always involved internal contestations. Essentially the reception of postmodernism in architecture and philosophy, which presents it as offering a genuine opening, disavows previous openings. Instead of these strained periodizations and analogies, she argues that we need the development of a sociological analysis to cover architecture. As we have mentioned earlier the contributions by Cooke and Zukin which discuss postmodernization and developments in urban form, provide the basis for understanding the emergence of postmodern architecture and urban spaces. For Sharon Zukin postmodern architecture points to the new neo-classical buildings and historical re-creations which were constructed in American and European cities in the early 1970s and the rebuilding of downtowns and waterfronts for high-class business and cultural consumption. Here the term postmodernism is used to point to real changes in culture and society, and we need to give attention to the structural forces, the political, economic and cultural institutions which have made them possible. We need to integrate the social production of cultural products with cultural producers and cultural consumers. Postmodern urban forms provide the liminal spaces for a new range of cultural meanings to be played out to an enlarged public of cultural 'connoisseurs'. The contemporary city, then is more a centre of consumption, and postmodern architecture becomes both the object of the tourist gaze and provides the spaces for an accumulation of spectacles. Here we think of the Edmonton shopping mega-mall with its 64-acre entertainment centre, with an indoor golf course, water park and 'Fantasyland' fun fair and most spectacular of all a 2.5-acre indoor salt-water lake containing dolphins, reproduction Spanish galleons and mini-submarines (Shields, 1987: 9). As John Urry (1988) has argued in his paper on changes in holiday-making and tourism, such changes can be associated with the rise of the 'service class'. This broad group, or what some would call the new middle class, or new petite bourgeoisie, which includes the new cultural intermediaries, (Bourdieu 1984; Featherstone 1987a, 1987b) merits further investigation. The growth of what has been referred to as 'postmodern museum culture' with its 'post-tourists' who move through the liminal urban spaces in search of spectacles in the simulational world of shopping malls, theme parks, department stores and museums therefore provides examples of new spatial forms, social processes and inter-group relationships which call for more detailed investigation. As Roberts argues in his paper 'The Museum and Montage', the museum has changed its function to provide a less rigorous classification of culture which is no longer based upon the idea of progress. Rather the past and present become epistemologically equal, with a spatialization of the future, the past and the present to cater for a pluralization of reception of taste on the part of less coherent audiences. While such cultural developments are interesting, one might even use Baudrillard's phrase 'seductive', we should be careful about how far along the road towards the 'simulational world' we let them take us. As Michael Ryan argues in his review article of recent books on post-modernism, 'Post-Modern Politics', such models of development from non-simulational modern to simulational postmodern social orders hides the fact that 'The real never became simulational: it always was constructed as a rhetoric of shapes, forms, arrangements of dispositions. . . . Power has always been simulational and material.' This should direct us towards investigating the social process and changing power balances between groups and class fractions which have helped to produce the changes we have just described.

  One key group involved in the production of postmodern cultural goods is, of course, the intellectuals and it is argued by Zygmunt Bauman that postmodernism articulates the experience of the intellectuals who face a status and identity crisis as a result of the decline in demand for their services with the state no longer having any need for their legitimations. The state has also, he argues, relinquished control over culture, so that culture is no longer seen by the educated intellectual elite as their own private property. With the widening and pluralizing of the market for cultural goods the authority and purpose of their universalist education project is diminished leaving them with the lesser role of interpreters, who can only play with, or immerse themselves in, or translate for others, the multiplicity of life-worlds, traditions and language games. This loss of authority and shift in the position of the intellectuals is also commented on by Lyotard who tells us that today's intellectuals cannot speak in the name of an 'unquestionable' universal authority as, for example Zola or Sartre were able to. This, he remarks, 'is because the modern intellectual was an enlightenment figure, and all intellectuals, no matter what side they were on . . . found their legitimacy, the legitimacy of the public speech through which they designated the just cause and made themselves the spokespersons, in the grand metanarrative of emancipation'. With the collapse of the global idea of history developing towards a natural end, which entailed the emancipation of humanity from poverty, ignorance and pain, we have the collapse of their authority. Today all they are left with is to argue for the respect of natural rights or to resist established thought through their activity of writing, literature, painting, architecture — to resist in the field of culture, which is often called 'postmodernism'.

In one sense then 'postmodernism' has been used to articulate changes in the intellectuals' social position; the secularization of their ideal of progress and enlightenment has resulted in a loss of authority and sense of mission. This process can be connected to the rise of para-intellectuals, cultural intermediaries, who effectively circulate the intellectuals' views and lifestyles to a wider audience and devalue the currency of their symbolic goods (Featherstone, 1988). The growth of a mass culture and consumerism, makes it difficult to maintain their distinctive high culture, which according to Stauth and Turner lead to responses of nostalgia and resentment. We can add that there is a strong inter-societal dimension to this process. As Mary Douglas (1986) has argued, intellectuals may turn inward to nihilism and relativism through their inability to contribute to the solution of problems. In effect their incapacity to command or unify society heightened their sense of powerlessness and retreat into scepticism. She tells us that the nineteenth-century nihilism amongst the Russian intelligentsia can be seen as a reaction to their inability to do anything about the plight of the wretched peasants; the same, she speculates may be the case with western intellectuals, who from the northern hemisphere survey with guilt the misery and poverty of the oppressed in the southern hemisphere. This can also be related to a more general global shift in the balance of power between the west and other nations which has forced them to consider the possibility that the other (the non-western cultures, civilizations and traditions) could be a mutual partner in a dialogue. As Jonathan Friedman argues, cultural pluralism may be the western experience of the real postmodernization of the world, the ethnic and cultural pluralization of a dehegemonizing and de-homogenizing world incapable of its former enforced politics of assimilation. An argument which resonates with Gianni Vattimo's statement that we now are in the age of the end of the Eurocentric perspective, on the threshold of a truer dialogue between different cultures in which hermeneutics promises to become dominant, the koine of the current age.

Note

I would like to thank Josef Bleicher, Roy Boyne, Philip Cooke, Mike Hepworth, Scott Lash, Doug Kellner, Willem van Reijen and Bryan Turner for their help and support in putting together this issue.

References

Baudrillard, J. (1983) *Simulations*. New York: Semiotext(e).

Bell, D. (1976) *The Cultural Contradictions of Capitalism*. London: Heinemann.

Bell, D. (1980) 'Beyond Modernism, Beyond Self' in *Sociological Journeys*. London: Heinemann.

Berman, M. (1982) *All That is Solid Melts into Air*. New York: Simon and Schuster.

Bernstein, R. (ed.) (1985) *Habermas and Modernity*. Oxford: Polity.

Bourdieu, P. (1971) 'Intellectual Field and Creative Project' in M. Young (ed.) *Knowledge and Control*. London: Collier-Macmillan.

Bourdieu, P. (1980) 'The Production of Belief: Contribution to an Economy of Symbolic Goods', *Media, Culture and Society* 2 (3): 261–93.

Bourdieu, P. (1984) *Distinction*. London: Routledge.

Bradbury, M. and McFarlane, J. (eds) (1976) *Modernism, 1890–1930*. Harmondsworth: Penguin.

Crane, D. (1987) 'Avant-Gardes, Popular Culture and Cultural Change', paper presented to the American Sociological Association, Annual Meeting, Chicago.

Di Maggio, P. (1987) 'Classification in Art', *American Sociological Review* 52 (4).

Douglas, M. (1986) 'The Social Preconditions of Radical Scepticism', in J. Law (ed.) *Power, Action and Belief*. London: Routledge.

During, S. (1987) 'Postmodernism or Post-colonialism Today', *Textual Practice*, 1 (1).

Elias, N. (1987) 'The Retreat of Sociologists into the Present', *Theory, Culture & Society* 4 (2–3): 223–47.

Featherstone, M. (1987a) 'Lifestyle and Consumer Culture', *Theory, Culture & Society* 4 (1): 55–70.

Featherstone, M. (1987b) 'Postmodernism and the New Middle Class'. Paper presented at the ISLP Conference on Postmodernism, Lawrence, Kansas.

Featherstone, M. (1988) 'Towards a Sociology of Postmodern Culture', in H. Haferkamp (ed.) *Culture and Social Structure*. Berlin and New York: De Gruyter.

Foucault, M. (1986) 'What is Enlightment?' in P. Rabinow (ed.) *The Foucault Reader*. Harmondsworth: Penguin.

Frisby, D. (1985a) 'Georg Simmel: First Sociologist of Modernity', *Theory, Culture & Society* 2 (3): 49–67.

Frisby, D. (1985b) *Fragments of Modernity*. Oxford: Polity.

Gott, R. (1986) 'The Crisis of Contemporary Culture', *Guardian* 1 Dec: 10.

Hassan, I. (1985) 'Postmodern Culture', *Theory, Culture & Society* 2 (3): 119–31.

Hutcheon, L. (1984) *Narcissistic Narrative: The Metafictional Paradox*. London: Methuen.

Hutcheon, L. (1986–7) 'The Politics of Postmodernism', *Cultural Critique* 5.

Huyssen, A. (1984) 'Mapping the Postmodern', *New German Critique* 33.

Jameson, F. (1984) 'Postmodernism or the Cultural Logic of Late Capitalism', *New Left Review* 146.

Köhler, (1977) 'Postmodernismus: Ein begriffsgeschichter Überblick', *America Studies* 22 (1).

Lunn, E. (1985) *Marxism and Modernism*. London: Verso.

Lyotard, J.F. (1984) *The Postmodern Condition*. Manchester: Manchester U.P.

Lyotard, J.F. (1986–7) 'Rules and Paradoxes or Svelt Appendix', *Cultural Critique* 5.

Mandel, E. (1975) *Late Capitalism*. London: New Left Books.

Palmer, R.E. (1977) 'Postmodernity and Hermeneutics', *Boundary 2* 22.

Pawley, M. (1986) 'Architecture: All the History that Fits', *Guardian* 3 Dec: 10.

Richters, A. (forthcoming, 1988) 'Habermas and Foucault', *Theory, Culture & Society* 5 (4).

Robertson, R. (1988) 'The Sociological Significance of Culture: Some General Considerations', *Theory, Culture & Society* 5 (1): 3–23.

Robertson, R. (forthcoming) *Globalization*. London: Sage.

Rorty, R. (1987) 'Review of Habermas's *Philosophical Discourse of Modernity*', *London Review of Books* 3 Sept.

Shields, R. (1987) 'Social Spatialization and the Built Environment: The West Edmonton Mall', Sussex University, (mimeo).

Urry, J. (1988) 'Cultural Change and Contemporary Holiday-Making', *Theory, Culture & Society* 5 (1): 35–55.

HANDBOOK OF SOCIOLOGY

Edited by **Neil J Smelser**,
University of California, Berkeley

The publication of the **Handbook of Sociology** heralds a new age of sociological thought and practice. This long awaited volume synthesizes the field. It provides an original and comprehensive look at this vital discipline - which has not had a new Handbook in 25 years...years in which sociology as a field of study and practice has undergone significant change. Top scholars representing both micro and macro perspectives combine their expertise to address the diversity, growth, and new developments which characterize the field of sociology today.

Smelser, one of the leading sociologists of our time, introduces the **Handbook** with a reflective and incisive essay on the historical developments within the field, the status of sociology as a discipline, and the future of the profession. Eminent contributors from all subfields of the discipline provide chapters on theoretical and methodological issues; bases of inequality in society; major institutional and organizational settings; and social processes and change. Offering incomparable depth and breadth, the **Handbook of Sociology** effectively synthesizes the complex and controversial issues which surround the discipline of sociology.

October 1988 ● approx 800 pages
Cloth (8039-2665-0) £75.00
(Pre-publication price of £65 until September 30th)

SAGE Publications Ltd
28 Banner Street, London EC1Y 8QE
SAGE Publications Inc
2111 West Hillcrest Drive, Newbury Park, CA 91320, USA

Is There a Postmodern Sociology?

Zygmunt Bauman

Why do we need the concept of 'postmodernity'? On the face of it, this concept is redundant. In so far as it purports to capture and articulate what is novel at the present stage of western history, it legitimizes itself in terms of a job which has been already performed by other, better established concepts — like those of the 'post-capitalist' or 'post-industrial' society. Concepts which have served the purpose well: they sharpened our attention to what is new and discontinuous, and offered a reference point for counter-arguments in favour of continuity.

Is, therefore, the advent of the 'postmodernity' idea an invitation to rehash or simply replay an old debate? Does it merely signify an all-too-natural fatigue, which a protracted and inconclusive debate must generate? Is it merely an attempt to inject new excitement into an increasingly tedious pastime (as Gordon Allport once said, we social scientists never solve problems; we only get bored with them)? If this is the case, then the idea of 'postmodernity' is hardly worth a second thought, and this is exactly what many a seasoned social scientist suggests.

Appearances are, however, misleading (and the advocates and the detractors of the idea of 'postmodernity' share the blame for confusion). The concept of 'postmodernity' may well capture and articulate a quite different sort of novelty than those the older, apparently similar concepts accommodated and theorized. It can legitimize its right to exist — its cognitive value — only if it does exactly this: if it generates a social-scientific discourse which theorizes different aspects of contemporary experience, or theorizes them in a different way.

I propose that the concept of 'postmodernity' has a value entirely of its own in so far as it purports to capture and articulate the novel experience of just one, but crucial social category of contemporary society: the intellectuals. Their novel experience — that is, their

Theory, Culture & Society (SAGE, London, Newbury Park, Beverly Hills and New Delhi), Vol. 5 (1988), 217–37

reassessment of their own position within society, their reorientation of the collectively performed function, and their new strategies.

Antonio Gramsci called the 'organic intellectuals' of a particular class the part of the educated elite which elaborated the self-identity of the class, the values instrumental to the defence and enhancement of its position within society, an ideology legitimizing its claims to autonomy and domination. One may argue to what extent Gramsci's (1971) 'organic intellectuals' did in fact answer this description; to what extent they were busy painting their own idealized portraits, rather than those of their ostensible sitters; to what extent the likenesses of all other classes represented (unknowingly, to be sure) the painters' cravings for conditions favourable and propitious for the kind of work the intellectuals had been best prepared, and willing, to do. In the discourse of 'postmodernity', however, the usual disguise is discarded. The participants of the discourse appear in the role of 'organic intellectuals' of the intellectuals themselves. The concept of 'postmodernity' makes sense in so far as it stands for this 'coming out' of the intellectuals.

The other way of putting it is to say that the concept of 'postmodernity' connotes the new self-awareness of the 'intellectuals' — this part of the educated elite which has specialized in elaborating principles, setting standards, formulating social tasks and criteria of their success or failure. Like painters, novelists, composers, and to a rapidly growing extent the scientists before them, such intellectuals have now come to focus their attention on their own skills, techniques and raw materials, which turn from tacitly present means into a conscious object of self-perfection and refinement and the true and sufficient subject-matter of intellectual work.

This implosion of intellectual vision, this 'falling upon oneself', may be seen as either a symptom of retreat and surrender, or a sign of maturation. Whatever the evaluation of the fact, it may be interpreted as a response to the growing sense of failure, inadequacy or irrealism of the traditional functions and ambitions, as sedimented in historical memory and institutionalized in the intellectual mode of existence. Yet it was this very sense of failure which rendered the ambitions and the functions visible.

'Postmodernity' proclaims the loss of something we were not aware of possessing until we have learned of the loss. This view of past 'modernity' which the 'postmodernity' discourse generates is made entirely out of the present-day anxiety and uneasiness, as a model of a universe in which such anxiety and uneasiness could not arise (much like the view of 'community', of which Raymond Williams (1975) said that it 'always has been'). The concept of 'modernity' has today a quite different content from the one it had before the start of the 'postmodern' discourse; there is little point in asking whether it is true or distorted, or in objecting to the way it is handled inside the 'postmodern' debate. It is situated in that debate, it draws its meaning from it, and it makes sense only jointly with the other side of the opposition, the concept of 'postmodernity', as that negation without which the latter concept would be meaningless. The 'postmodern' discourse generates its own concept of 'modernity', made of the presence of all those things for the lack of which the concept of 'postmodernity' stands.

The anxiety which gave birth to the concept of 'postmodernity' and the related image of past 'modernity' is admittedly diffuse and ill-defined, but nevertheless quite real. It arises from the feeling that the kind of services the intellectuals have been historically best prepared to offer, and from which they derived their sense of social importance — are nowadays not easy to provide; and that the demand for such services is anyway much smaller than one would expect it to be. It is this feeling which leads to a 'status crisis'; a recognition that the reproduction of the status which the intellectuals got used to seeing as theirs by right, would now need a good deal of rethinking as well as the reorientation of habitual practices.

The services in question amount to the provision of an authoritative solution to the questions of cognitive truth, moral judgment and aesthetic taste. It goes without saying that the importance of such services is a reflection of the size and importance of the demand for them; with the latter receding, their *raison d'être* is eroded. In its turn, the demand in question draws its importance from the presence of social forces which need the authority of cognitive and normative judgments as the legitimation of their actual, or strived-for domination. There must be such forces; they must need such legitimation; and the intellectuals must retain the monopoly on its provision. The 'status crisis', or rather that vague feeling of anxiety for which it can serve as a plausible interpretation, can be made sense of if account is taken of the undermining of the conditions of intellectual status in, at least, three crucial respects.

First of all — the advanced erosion of that global structure of domination, which — at the time the modern intellectuals were born — supplied the 'evidence of reality' of which the self-confidence of the West and its spokesmen has been built. Superiority of the West over the rest remained self-evident for almost three centuries. It was not, as it were, a matter of idle comparison. The era of modernity had been marked by an active superiority: part of the world constituted the rest as inferior — either as a crude, still unprocessed 'raw material' in need of cleaning and refinement, or a temporarily extant relic of the past. Whatever could not be brought up to the superior standards, was clearly destined for the existence of subordination. Western practices defined the rest as a pliable or malleable substance still to be given shape. This active superiority meant the right of the superior to proselytize, to design the suitable form of life for the others, to refuse to grant authority to the ways of life which did not fit that design.

Such superiority could remain self-evident as long as the denied authority showed no signs of reasserting itself, and the designs seemed irresistible. A historical domination could interpret itself as universal and absolute, as long as it could believe that the future would prove it such; the universality of the western mode (the absoluteness of western domination) seemed indeed merely a matter of time. The grounds for certainty and self-confidence could not be stronger. Human reality indeed seemed subject to unshakeable laws and stronger ('progressive') values looked set to supersede or eradicate the weaker ('retrograde', ignorant, superstitious) ones. It was this historically given certainty, grounded in the unchallenged superiority of forces aimed at universal domination, which had been articulated, from the perspective of the intellectual mode, as universality of the standards of truth, judgment and taste. The strategy such articulation legitimated was to supply the forces, bent on universal and active domination, with designs dictated by universal science, ethics and aesthetics.

The certitude of yesteryear is now at best ridiculed as naïvety, at worst castigated as ethnocentric. Nobody but the most rabid of the diehards believes today that the western mode of life, either the actual one or one idealized ('utopianized') in the intellectual mode, has more than a sporting chance of ever becoming universal. No social force is in sight (including those which, arguably, are today aiming at global domination) bent on making it universal. The search for the universal standards has suddenly become gratuitous; there is no credible 'historical agent' to which the findings could be addressed and entrusted. Impracticality erodes interest. The task of establishing universal standards of truth, morality, taste does not seem that much important. Unsupported by will, it appears now misguided and irreal.

Secondly — even the localized powers, devoid of ecumenical ambitions, seem less receptive to the products of intellectual discourse. The time modern intellectuals were born was one of the great 'shake-up': everything solid melted into air, everything sacred was profaned . . . The newborn absolutist state did not face the task of wrenching power from old and jaded hands; it had to create an entirely new kind of social power, capable of carrying the burden of *societal* integration. The task involved the crushing of those mechanisms of social reproduction which had been based in communal traditions. Its performance took the form of a 'cultural crusade'; that is, practical destruction of communal bases of social power, and theoretical delegitimation of their authority. Faced with such tasks, the state badly needed 'legitimation' (this is the name given to intellectual discourse when considered from the vantage point of its power-oriented, political application).

Mais où sont les croisades d'autant? The present-day political domination can reproduce itself using means more efficient and less costly than 'legitimation'. Weber's 'legal–rational legitimation' — the point much too seldom made — is, in its essence, a declaration of the redundancy of legitimation. The modern state is effective without authority; or, rather, its effectivity depends to a large extent on rendering authority irrelevant. It does not matter any more, for the effectivity of state power, and for the reproduction of political domination in general, whether the social area under domination is culturally unified and uniform, and how idiosyncratic are the values, sectors of this area may uphold.

The weapon of legitimation has been replaced with two mutually complementary weapons: this of *seduction* and that of *repression*. Both need intellectually trained experts, and indeed both siphon off, accommodate and domesticate an ever growing section of educated elite. Neither has a need, or a room, for those 'hard-core' intellectuals whose expertise is 'legitimation', i.e. supplying proof that what is being done is universally correct and absolutely true, moral and beautiful.

Seduction is the paramount tool of integration (of the reproduction of domination) in a consumer society. It is made possible once the market succeeds in making the consumers dependent on itself. Market-dependency is achieved through the destruction of such skills (technical, social, psychological, existential) which do not entail the use of marketable commodities; the more complete the destruction, the more necessary become new skills which point organically to market-supplied implements. Market-dependency is guaranteed and self-perpetuating once men and women, now consumers, cannot proceed with the business of life without tuning themselves to the logic of the market. Much debated 'needs creation' by the market means ultimately creation of the need of the market. New technical, social, psychological and existential skills of the consumers are such as to be practicable only in conjunction with marketable commodities; rationality comes to mean the ability to make right purchasing decisions, while the craving for certainty is gratified by conviction that the decisions made have been, indeed, right.

Repression stands for 'panoptical' power, best described by Foucault (1977). It employs surveillance, it is aimed at regimentation of the body, and is diffused (made invisible) in the numerous institutionalizations of knowledge-based expertise. Repression as a tool of domination-reproduction has not been abandoned with the advent of seduction. Its time is not over and the end of its usefulness is not in sight, however overpowering and effective seduction may become. It is the continuous, tangible presence of repression as a viable alternative which makes seduction unchallengeable. In addition, repression is indispensable to reach the areas seduction cannot, and is not meant to, reach: it remains the paramount tool of subordination of the considerable margin of society which cannot be absorbed by market dependency and hence, in market terms, consists of 'non-consumers'. Such 'non-consumers' are people reduced to the satisfaction of their elementary needs; people whose business of life does not transcend the horizon of survival. Goods serving the latter purpose are not, as a rule, attractive as potential merchandise; they serve the needs over which the market has no control and thus undermine, rather than boost, market dependency. Repression reforges the market unattractiveness of non-consumer existence into the unattractiveness of alternatives to market dependency.

Seduction and repression between them, make 'legitimation' redundant. The structure of domination can now be reproduced, ever more effectively, without recourse to legitimation; and thus without recourse to such intellectuals as make the legitimation discourse their speciality. Habermas's (1976) 'legitimation crisis' makes sense, in the final account, as the intellectual perception of 'crisis' caused by the ever more evident irrelevance of legitimation.

The growing irrelevance of legitimation has coincided with the growing freedom of intellectual debate. One suspects more than coincidence. It is indifference on the part of political power which makes freedom of intellectual work possible. Indifference, in its turn, arises from the lack of interest. Intellectual freedom is possible as political power has freed itself from its former dependence on legitimation. This is why freedom, coming as it does in a package-deal with irrelevance, is not received by the intellectuals with unqualified enthusiasm. All the more so as the past political patronage made a considerable part of intellectual work grow in a way which rendered it dependent on the continuation of such a patronage.

What, however, more than anything else prevents the intellectuals from rejoicing is the realization that the withdrawal of the government troops does not necessarily mean that the vacated territory will become now their uncontested domain. What the state has relinquished, is most likely to be taken over by the powers on which the intellectuals have even less hold than they ever enjoyed in their romance with politics.

The territory in question is that of culture. Culture is one area of social life which is defined (cut out) in such a way as to reassert the social function claimed by the intellectuals. One cannot even explain the meaning of the concept without reference to human 'incompleteness', to the need of teachers and, in general, of 'people in the know' to make up for this incompleteness, and to a vision of society as a continuous 'teach-in' session. The idea of culture, in other words, establishes knowledge in the role of power, and simultaneously supplies legitimation of such power. Culture connotes power of the educated elite and knowledge as power; it denotes institutionalized mechanisms of such power — science, education, arts.

Some of these mechanisms, or some areas of their application, remain relevant to the repressive functions of the state, or to the tasks resulting from the state role in the reproduction of consumer society (reproduction of conditions for the integration-through-seduction). As far as this is the case, the state acts as the protector-cum-censor, providing funds but reserving the right to decide on the tasks and the value of their results. The mixed role of the state rebounds in a mixed reaction of the educated elite. The calls for more state resources intermingle with the protests against bureaucratic interference. There is no shortage of the educated willing to serve; neither is there a shortage of criticisms of servility.

Some other mechanisms, or some other areas of their application, do not have such relevance. They are, as a rule, 'underfunded', but otherwise suffer little political interference. They are free. Even the most iconoclastic of their products fail to arouse the intended wrath of the dominant classes and in most cases are received with devastating equanimity. Challenging the capitalist values stirs little commotion in as far as the capitalist domination does not depend on the acceptance of its values. And yet freedom *from* political interference does not result in freedom *for* intellectual creativity. A new protector-cum-censor fills the vacuum left by the withdrawal of the state: the market.

This is the third respect in which the intellectual status is perceived as undermined. Whatever their other ambitions, modern intellectuals always saw culture as their private property; they made it, they lived in it, they even gave it its name. Expropriation of this particular plot hurts most. Or has it been, in fact, an expropriation? Certainly intellectuals never controlled 'popular' consumption of cultural products. Once they felt firmly in the saddle, they saw themselves as members of the circle of 'culture consumers', which, in the sense they would have recognized, was probably significant, if small. It is only now that the circle of people eager to join the culture consumption game has grown to unheard of proportions — has become truly 'massive'. What hurts, therefore, is not so much an expropriation, but the fact that the intellectuals are not invited to stand at the helm of this breath-taking expansion. Instead, it is gallery owners, publishers, TV managers and other 'capitalists' or 'bureaucrats' who are in control. The idea has been wrested out of the intellectual heads and in a truly sorcerer's apprentice's manner, put to action in which the sages have no power.

In another sense, however, what has happened is truly an expropriation, and not just 'stealing the profits'. In the early modern era intellectual forces had been mobilized (or self-mobilized) for the gigantic job of conversion — the culture crusade which involved a thorough revamping or uprooting of the totality of heretofore autonomously reproduced forms of life. The project was geared to the growth of the modern absolutist state and its acute need of legitimation. For reasons mentioned before, this is not the case anymore. Native forms of life have not, however, returned to autonomous reproduction; there are others who manage it — agents of the market, this time, and not the academia. No wonder the old gamekeepers view the new ones as poachers. Once bent on the annihilation of 'crude, superstitious, ignorant, bestial' folkways, they now bewail the enforced transformation of the 'true folk culture' into a 'mass' one. Mass culture debate has been the lament of expropriated gamekeepers.

The future does not promise improvement either; the strength of the market forces continues to grow, their appetite seems to grow even faster, and for an increasing sector of the educated élite the strategy 'if you cannot beat them, join them' gains in popularity. Even the areas of intellectual domain still left outside the reach of the market forces are now felt to be under threat. It was the intellectuals who impressed upon the once incredulous population the need for education and the value of information. Here as well their success turns into their downfall. The market is only too eager to satisfy the need and to supply the value. With the new DIY (electronic) technology to offer, the market will reap the rich crop of the popular belief that education is human duty and (any) information is useful. The market will thereby achieve what the intellectual educators struggled to attain in vain: it will turn the consumption of information into a pleasurable, entertaining pastime. Education will become just one of the many variants of self-amusement. It will reach the peak of its popularity and the bottom of its value as measured by original intellectual-made standards.

The three developments discussed above go some way, if not all the way, towards explaining this feeling of anxiety, out-of-placeness, loss of direction which, as I propose, constitutes the true referent of the concept of 'postmodernity'. As a rule, however, intellectuals tend to articulate their own societal situation and the problems it creates as a situation of the society at large, and its, systemic or social, problems. The way in which the passage from 'modernity' to 'postmodernity' has been articulated is not an exception. This time, however, those who articulate it do not hide as thoroughly as in the past behind the role of 'organic intellectuals' of other classes; and the fact that they act as 'organic intellectuals of themselves' is either evident or much easier to discover. Definitions of both 'modernity' and 'postmodernity' refer overtly to such features of respective social situations which have direct and crucial importance for the intellectual status, role and strategy.

The main feature ascribed to 'postmodernity' is thus the permanent and irreducible *pluralism* of cultures, communal traditions, ideologies, 'forms of life' or 'language games' (choice of items which are 'plural' varies with theoretical allegiance); or the awareness and recognition of such pluralism. Things which are plural in the post-modern world cannot be arranged in an evolutionary time-sequence, seen as each other's inferior or superior stages; neither can they be classified as 'right' or 'wrong' solutions to common problems. No knowledge can be assessed outside the context of culture, tradition, language game etc. which makes it possible and endows it with meaning. Hence no criteria of validation are available which could be themselves justified 'out of context'. Without universal standards, the problem of the postmodern world is not how to globalize superior culture, but how to secure communication and mutual understanding between cultures.

Seen from this 'later' perspective, 'modernity' seems in retrospect a time when pluralism was not yet a foregone conclusion; or a time when the ineradicability of pluralism was not duly recognized. Hence the substitution of one, 'supra-communal', standard of truth, judgment and taste for the diversity of local, and therefore inferior, standards, could be contemplated and strived for as a viable prospect. Relativism of knowledge could be perceived as a nuisance, and as a temporary one at that. Means could be sought — in theory and in practice — to exorcize the ghost of relativism once and for all. The end to parochialism of human opinions and ways of life was nigh. This could be a chance — once real, then lost. Or this could be an illusion from the start. In the first case, postmodernity means the failure of modernity. In the second case, it means a step forward. In both cases, it means opening our eyes to the futility of modern dreams of universalism.

The reader will note that I am defining 'modernity' from the perspective of the experience of 'postmodernity', and not vice versa; all attempts to pretend that we proceed in the opposite direction mislead us into believing that what we confront in the current debate is an articulation of the logic of 'historical process', rather than re-evaluation of the past (complete with the imputation of a 'telos' of which the past, in as long as it remained the present, was not aware). If the concept of 'postmodernity' has no other value, it has at least this one: it supplies a new, and external, vantage point, from which some aspects of that world which came into being in the aftermath of Enlightenment and the Capitalist Revolution (aspect not visible, or allotted secondary importance, when observed from inside the unfinished process) acquire saliency and can be turned into a pivotal issue of the discourse.

The reader will note also that I am trying to define both concepts of the opposition in such a way as to make their mutual distinction independent of the 'existential' issue: whether it is the 'actual conditions' which differ, or their perception. It is my view that the pair of concepts under discussion is important first and foremost (perhaps even solely) in the context of the self-awareness of the intellectuals, and in relation to the way the intellectuals perceive their social location, task and strategy. This does not detract from the significance of the concepts. On the contrary, as far as the plight of 'western culture' goes, the way the two concepts are defined here presents them as arguably the most seminal of oppositions articulated in order to capture the tendency of social change in our times.

The change of mood, intellectual climate, self-understanding etc. implied by that vague, but real, anxiety the proposition of the 'advent of postmodernity' attempts to capture, has indeed far-reaching consequences for the strategy of intellectual work in general — and sociology and social philosophy in particular. It does have a powerful impact even on 'traditional' ways of conducting the business of social study. There is no necessity whatsoever for the old procedures to be rescinded or to grind to a halt. One can easily declare the whole idea of 'postmodernity' a sham, obituaries of 'modernity' premature, the need to reorient one's programme non-existent — and stubbornly go where one went before and where one's ancestors wanted to go. One can say that finding the firm and unshakeable standards of true knowledge, true interpretation, defensible morality, genuine art etc. is still a valid, and the major, task. There is nothing to stop one from doing just that. In the vast realm of the academy there is ample room for all sorts of specialized pursuits, and the way such pursuits have been historically institutionalized renders them virtually immune to pressures untranslatable into the variables of their own inner systems; such pursuits have their own momentum; their dynamics subject to internal logic only, they produce what they are capable of producing, rather than what is required or asked of them; showing their own, internally administered measures of success as their legitimation, they may go on reproducing themselves indefinitely. This is particularly true regarding pursuits of a pronouncedly philosophical nature; they require no outside supply of resources except the salaries of their perpetrators, and are therefore less vulnerable to the dire consequences of the withdrawal of social recognition.

Even with their self-reproduction secure, however, traditional forms of philosophizing confront today challenges which must rebound in their concerns. They are pressed now to legitimize their declared purpose — something which used to be taken (at least since Descartes) by and large for granted. For well-nigh three centuries relativism was the *malin génie* of European philosophy, and anybody suspected of not fortifying his doctrine against it tightly enough was brought to book and forced to defend himself against the charges the horrifying nature of which no one put in doubt. Now the tables have been turned — and the seekers of universal standards are asked to prove the criminal nature of relativism; it is they now who are pressed to justify their hatred of relativism, and clear themselves of the charges of dogmatism, ethnocentrism, intellectual imperialism or whatever else their work may seem to imply when gazed upon from the relativist positions.

Less philosophical, more empirically inclined varieties of traditional social studies are even less fortunate. Modern empirical sociology developed in response to the demand of the modern state aiming at the 'total administration' of society. With capital engaging the rest of the society in their roles of labour, and the state responsible for the task of 're-commodifying' both capital and labour, and thus ensuring the continuation of such an engagement — the state needed a huge apparatus of 'social management' and a huge supply of expert social-management knowledge. Methods and skills of empirical sociology were geared to this demand and to the opportunities stemming from it. The social-managerial tasks were large-scale, and so were the funds allotted to their performance. Sociology specialized therefore in developing the skills of use in mass, statistical research; in collecting information about 'massive trends' and administrative measures likely to redirect, intensify or constrain such trends. Once institutionalized, the skills at the disposal of empirical sociologists have defined the kind of research they are capable of designing and conducting. Whatever else this kind of research is, it invariably requires huge funds — and thus a rich bureaucratic institution wishing to provide them. Progressive disengagement of capital from labour, falling significance of the 're-commodification' task, gradual substitution of 'seduction' for 'repression' as the paramount weapon of social integration, shifting of the responsibility for integration from the state bureaucracy to the market — all this spells trouble for traditional empirical research, as state bureaucracies lose interest in financing it.

The widely debated 'crisis of (empirical) sociology' is, therefore, genuine. Empirical sociology faces today the choice between seeking a new social application of its skills or seeking new skills. Interests of state bureaucracy are likely to taper to the management of 'law and order', i.e. a task aimed selectively at the part of the population which cannot be regulated by the mechanism of seduction. And there are private bureaucracies, in charge of the seduction management, who may or may not need the skill of empirical sociology, depending on the extent in which the latter are able, and willing, to reorient and readjust their professional know-how to the new, as yet not fully fathomed, demand.

To sum up: if the radical manifestos proclaiming the end of sociology and social philosophy 'as we know them' seem unfounded — equally unconvincing are the pretentions that nothing of importance has happened and that there is nothing to stop 'business as usual'. The form acquired by sociology and social philosophy in the course of what is now, retrospectively, described as 'modernity' is indeed experiencing at the moment an unprecedented challenge. While in no way doomed, it must adjust itself to new conditions in order to self-reproduce.

I will turn now to those actual, or likely, developments in sociology which do admit (overtly or implicitly) the novelty of the situation and the need for a radical reorientation of the tasks and the strategies of social study.

One development is already much in evidence. Its direction is clearly shown by the consistently expanding assimilation of Heideggerian, Wittgensteinian, Gadamerian and other 'hermeneutical' themes and inspirations. This development points in the direction of sociology as, above all, the skill of interpretation. Whatever articulable experience there is which may become the object of social study — it is embedded in its own 'life-world', 'communal tradition', 'positive ideology', 'form of life', 'language game'. The names for that 'something' in which the experience is embedded are many and different, but what truly counts are not names but the inherent pluralism of that 'something' which all the names emphasize more than anything else. Thus there are *many* 'life-worlds', *many* 'traditions' and *many* 'language-games'. No external point of view is conceivable to reduce this variety. The only reasonable cognitive strategy is therefore one best expressed in Geertz's (1973) idea of 'thick description': recovery of the meaning of the alien experience through fathoming the tradition (form of life, life-world etc.) which constitutes it, and then translating it, with as little damage as possible, into a form assimilable by one's own tradition (form of life, life-world etc.). Rather than proselytizing, which would be the task of a cross-cultural encounter in the context of 'orthodox' social science, it is the expected 'enrichment' of one's own tradition, through incorporating other, heretofore inaccessible, experiences, which is the meaning bestowed upon the exercise by the project of 'interpreting sociology'.

As interpreters, sociologists are no more concerned with ascertaining the 'truth' of the experience they interpret — and thus the principle of 'ethnomethodological indifference' may well turn from the shocking heresy it once was into a new orthodoxy. The only concern which distinguishes sociologists-turned-interpreters as professionals is the correctness of interpretation; it is here that their professional credentials as experts (i.e. holders of skills inaccessible to lay and untrained public) are re-established. Assuming that the world is irreducibly pluralist, rendering the messages mutually communicable is its major problem. Expertise in the rules of correct interpretation is what it needs most. It is badly needed even by such powers that are not any more bent on total domination and do not entertain universalistic ambitions; they still need this expertise for their sheer survival. Potential uses are clear; the users, so far, less so — but one may hope they can be found.

As all positions, this one has also its radical extreme. The admission of pluralism does not have to result in the interest in interpretation and translation, or for that matter in any 'social' services sociology may offer. Release from the often burdensome social duty sociology had to carry in the era of modernity may be seen by some with relief — as the advent of true freedom of intellectual pursuits. It is, indeed, an advent of freedom — though freedom coupled with irrelevance: freedom *from* cumbersome and obtrusive interference on the part of powers that be, won at the price of resigning the freedom to influence their actions and their results. If what sociology does does not matter, it can do whatever it likes. This is a tempting possibility: to immerse oneself fully in one's own specialized discourse inside which one feels comfortably at home, to savour the subtleties of distinction and discretion such discourse demands and renders possible, to take the very disinterestedness of one's pursuits for the sign of their supreme value, to take pride in keeping alive, against the odds, a precious endeavour for which the rest, the polluted or corrupted part of the world, has (temporarily — one would add, seeking the comfort of hope) no use. It is one's own community, tradition, form of life etc. which commands first loyalty; however small, it provides the only site wherein the intrinsic value of the discourse can be tended to, cultivated — and enjoyed. After all, the recognition of futility of universal standards, brought along by postmodernity, allows that self-centred concerns treat lightly everything outside criticism. There is nothing to stop one from coming as close as possible to the sociological equivalent of *l'art pour l'art* (the cynic would comment: nothing, but the next round of education cuts).

The two postmodern strategies for sociology and social philosophy, discussed so far, are — each in its own way — internally consistent and viable. Looked at from inside, they both seem invulnerable. Given their institutional entrenchment, they have a sensible chance of survival and of virtually infinite self-reproduction (again, barring the circumstances referred to by the cynic). Whatever critique of these strategies may be contemplated, it may only come from the outside, and thus cut little ice with the insiders.

Such a critique would have to admit its allegiance to ends the insiders are not obliged to share. It would have to cite an understanding of the role of sociology the insiders have every reason to reject, and no reason to embrace. In particular, such a critique would have to declare its own value preference, remarkable above all for the supreme position allotted to the *social relevance* of sociological discourse.

The critique under consideration may be launched in other words only from the intention to preserve the hopes and ambitions of modernity in the age of postmodernity. The hopes and ambitions in question refer to the possibility of a reason-led improvement of the human condition; an improvement measured in the last instance by the degree of human emancipation. For better or worse, modernity was about increasing the volume of human autonomy, but not autonomy which, for the absence of solidarity, results in loneliness; and about increasing the intensity of human solidarity, but not solidarity which, for the absence of autonomy, results in oppression. The alternative strategy for a postmodern sociology would have to take as its assumption that the two-pronged ambition of modernity is still a viable possibility, and one certainly worth promoting.

What makes a strategy which refuses to renounce its modern ('pre-postmodern'?) commitments a 'postmodern' one, is the bluntness with which its premises are recognized as assumptions; in a truly 'postmodern' vein, such a strategy refers to values rather than laws; to assumptions instead of foundations; to purposes, and not to 'groundings'. And it is determined to do without the comfort it once derived from the belief that 'history was on its side', and that the inevitability of its ultimate success had been guaranteed beforehand by inexorable laws of nature (a pleonasm: 'nature' *is* inexorable laws).

Otherwise, there is no sharp break in continuity. There is a significant shift of emphasis, though. The 'meliorative' strategy of social science as formed historically during the era of modernity had two edges. One was pressed against the totalistic ambitions of the modern state; the state, in possession of enough resources and good will to impress a design of a better society upon imperfect reality, was to be supplied with reliable knowledge of the laws directing human conduct and effective skills required to elicit a conduct conforming to the modern ambitions. The other was pressed against the very humans modernity was bent on emancipating. Men and women were to be offered reliable knowledge of the way their society works, so that their life-business may be conducted in a conscious and rational way, and the casual chains making their actions simultaneously effective and constrained become visible — and hence, in principle, amenable to control. To put the same in a different way: the 'meliorative' strategy under discussion was productive of two types of knowledge. One was aimed at rationalization of the state (more generally: societal) power; the other — at rationalization of individual conduct.

Depending on the time and the location, either one or the other of the two types of knowledge was held in the focus of sociological discourse. But both were present at all times and could not but be co-present — due to the ineradicable ambiguity of ways in which any information on social reality can be employed. This ambiguity explains why the relations between social science and the powers that be were at best those of hate-love, and why even during the timespans of wholehearted cooperation there was always more than a trace of mistrust in the state's attitude toward sociological discourse; not without reason, men of politics suspected that such a discourse may well undermine with one hand the self-same hierarchical order it helps to build with the other.

Inside the postmodern version of the old strategy, however, the balance between the two types of knowledge is likely to shift. One circumstance which makes such a shift likely has been already mentioned: the drying up of the state interest in all but the most narrowly circumscribed sociological expertise; no grand designs, no cultural crusades, no demand for legitimizing visions, and no need for models of centrally administered rational society. Yet the effect of this factor, in itself formidable, has been still exacerbated by the gradual erosion of hope that the failure of the rational society to materialize might be due to the weaknesses of the present administrators of the social process, and that an alternative 'historical agent' may still put things right. More bluntly, the faith in a historical agent waiting in the wings to take over and to complete the promise of modernity using the levers of political state — this faith has all but vanished. The first of the two types of knowledge the modern sociological discourse used to turn out is, therefore, without an evident addressee — actual or potential. It may be still used: there are, after all, quite a few powerful bureaucracies which could do with some good advice on how to make the humans behave differently and more to their liking. And they will surely find experts eager to offer such advice. We did discuss such a possibility in the context of strategies which refuse to admit that 'postmodernity' means new situation and calls for rethinking and readjustment of traditional tasks and strategies. For the strategy aimed at the preservation of modern hopes and ambitions under the new conditions of postmodernity, the question *who* uses the administrative knowledge and for what *purpose* is not, however, irrelevant. It would recognize such knowledge as useful only if in the hands of a genuine or putative, yet rationalizing agent. From the vantage point of the political power all this reasoning is redundant anyway. Having lost their interest in its own practical application of sociological knowledge, the state will inevitably tend to identify the totality of sociological discourse with the second of its traditional edges, and thus regard it as an unambiguously subversive force; as a problem, rather than a solution.

The expected state attitude is certain to act as a self-fulfilling prophecy; rolling back the resources and facilities the production of the first type of knowledge cannot do without, it will push the sociological discourse even further toward the second type. It will only, as it were, reinforce a tendency set in motion by other factors. Among the latter, one should count an inevitable consequence of the growing disenchantment with the societal administration as the carrier of emancipation: the shifting of attention to the kind of knowledge which may be used by human individuals in their efforts to enlarge the sphere of autonomy and solidarity. This looks more and more like the last chance of emancipation.

So far, we have discussed the 'push' factors. There is, however, a powerful 'pull' factor behind the shift: a recognition that the task of providing men and women with that 'sociological imagination' for which C.W. Mills (1959) appealed years ago, has never been so important as it is now, under conditions of postmodernity. Emancipation of capital from labour makes possible the emancipation of the state from legitimation; and that may mean in the long run a gradual erosion of democratic institutions and the substance of democratic politics (reproduction of legitimation having been the political democracy major historical function). Unlike the task of reproducing members of society as producers, their reproduction as consumers does not necessarily enlarge the political state and hence does not imply the need to reproduce them as citizens. The 'systemic' need for political democracy is thereby eroded, and the political agency of men and women as citizens cannot count for its reproduction on the centripetal effects of the self-legitimizing concerns of the state. The other factors which could sponsor such reproduction look also increasingly doubtful in view of the tendency to shift political conflicts into the non-political and democratically unaccountable sphere of the market, and the drift toward the substitution of 'needs creation' for 'normative regulation' as the paramount methods of systemic reproduction (except for the part of the society the market is unable or unwilling to assimilate). If those tendencies have been correctly spotted, knowledge which provides the individuals with an accurate understanding of the way society works may not be a weapon powerful enough to outweigh their consequences; but it surely looks like the best bet men and women can still make.

Which leads us into an area not at all unfamiliar; some would say traditional. The third of the conceivable strategies of sociology under the postmodern condition would focus on the very thing on which the sociological discourse did focus throughout its history: on making the opaque transparent, on exposing the ties linking visible biographies to invisible societal processes, on understanding what makes society tick, in order to make it tick, if possible, in a more 'emancipating' way. Only it is a new and different society from the one which triggered off the sociological discourse. Hence 'focusing on the same' means focusing on new problems and new tasks.

I suggest that a sociology bent on the continuation of modern concerns under postmodern conditions would be distinguished not by new procedures and purposes of sociological work, as other postmodern strategies suggest — but by a new *object* of investigation. As far as this strategy is concerned, what matters is that the society (its object) has changed; it does not necessarily admit that its own earlier pursuits were misguided and wasted, and that the crucial novelty in the situation is the dismissal of the old ways of doing sociology and 'discovery' of new ways of doing it. Thus to describe a sociology pursuing the strategy under discussion one would speak, say, of a 'post-full-employment' sociology, or a 'sociology of the consumer society', rather than of a 'post-Wittgensteinian' or 'post-Gadamerian' sociology. In other words, this strategy points toward a sociology of postmodernity, rather than a postmodern sociology.

There is a number of specifically 'postmodern' phenomena which await sociological study. There is a process of an accelerating emancipation of capital from labour; instead of engaging the rest of society in the role of producers, capital tends to engage them in the role of consumers. This means in its turn that the task of reproducing the capital-dominated society does not consist, as before, in the 're-commodification of labour', and that the non-producers of today are not a 'reserve army of labour', to be tended to and groomed for the return to the labour market. This crucial fact of their life is still concealed in their own consciousness, in the consciousness of their political tutors, and of the sociologists who study them, by a historical memory of society which is no more and will not return. The new poor are not socially, culturally or systemically an equivalent of the old poor; the present 'depression', manifested in the massive and stable unemployment, is not a later day edition of the 1930s (one hears about the poor losing their jobs, but one does not hear of the rich jumping out of their windows). 'The two nations' society, mark two, cannot be truly understood by squeezing it into the model of mark one.

'The two nations, mark two' society is constituted by the opposition between 'seduction' and 'repression' as means of social control, integration and the reproduction of domination. The first is grounded in 'market dependency': replacement of old life skills by the new ones which cannot be effectively employed without the mediation of the market; in the shifting of disaffection and conflict from the area of political struggle to the area of commodities and entertainment; in the appropriate redirecting of the needs for rationality and security; and in the growing comprehensiveness of the market-centred world, so that it can accommodate the totality of life business, making the other aspects of systemic context invisible and subjectively irrelevant. The second is grounded in a normative regulation pushed to the extreme, penetration of the 'private' sphere to an ever growing degree, disempowering of the objects of normative regulation as autonomous agents. It is important to know how these two means of social control combine and support each other; and the effects their duality is likely to have on the tendency of political power, democratic institutions and citizenship.

One may guess — pending further research — that while control-through-repression destroys autonomy and solidarity, control-through-seduction generates marketable means serving the pursuit (if not the attainment) of both, and thus effectively displaces the pressures such a pursuit exerts from the political sphere, at the same time redeploying them in the reproduction of capital domination. Thus the opposite alternatives which determine the horizon and the trajectory of life strategies in the postmodern society neutralize the possible threat to systemic reproduction which might emanate from the unsatisfied ambitions of autonomy and solidarity.

Those alternatives, therefore, need to be explored by any sociology wishing seriously to come to grips with the phenomenon of postmodernity. Conscious of the postmodern condition it explores, such a sociology would not pretend that its preoccupations, however skilfully pursued, would offer it the centrality in the 'historical process' to which it once aspired. On the contrary, the problematics sketched above is likely to annoy rather than entice the managers of law and order; it will appear incomprehensible to the seduced, and alluring yet nebulous to the repressed. A sociology determined to tread this path would have to brace itself for the uneasy plight of unpopularity. Yet the alternative is irrelevance. This seems to be the choice sociology is facing in the era of postmodernity.

References

Foucault, Michel (1977) *Discipline and Punish*. Harmondsworth: Allen Lane.
Geertz, Clifford (1973) *The Interpretation of Culture*. New York: Basic Books.
Gramsci, Antonio (1971) *Selections from the Prison Notebooks*. London: Lawrence & Wishart.
Habermas, Jürgen (1976) *Legitimation Crisis*. London: Heinemann.
Mills, C. Wright (1959) *The Sociological Imagination*. Oxford: Oxford University Press.
Williams, Raymond (1975) *The Country and the City*. St Albans: Paladin.

Zygmunt Bauman is Professor of Sociology at the University of Leeds. His latest book, *Legislators and Interpretors: On Modernity, Post-Modernity and the Intellectuals*, was published by Polity Press in 1987.

Postmodernism as Social Theory: Some Challenges and Problems

Douglas Kellner

Introduction

Discussions of postmodernism began in the field of cultural theory as indicators of new forms of 'postmodern' culture in the domains of architecture, literature, painting, and so on, which specified a set of cultural artifacts which allegedly broke with the forms and practices of modernist art. As opposed to the seriousness of 'high modernism', postmodernism exhibited a new insouciance, a new playfulness, and a new eclecticism embodied above all in Andy Warhol's 'pop art' but also manifested in celebrations of Las Vegas architecture, found objects, happenings, Nam June Paik's video-installations, underground film, and the novels of Thomas Pynchon. In opposition to the well-wrought, formally sophisticated, and aesthetically demanding modernist art, postmodernist art was fragmentary and eclectic, mixing forms from 'high culture' and 'popular culture,' subverting aesthetic boundaries and expanding the domain of art to encompass the images of advertising, the kaleidoscopic mosaics of television, the experiences of the post-holocaust nuclear age, and an always proliferating consumer capitalism. The moral seriousness of high modernism was replaced by irony, pastiche, cynicism, commercialism, and in some cases downright nihilism.

Consequently, while modernism was becoming a part of the pantheon and canon of 'high art', postmodernism exhibited a populist 'anything goes' aesthetic visible in pop art but also in the architecture, film and literature of the period. While much modernist art exhibited a frenzy for the new, was future-oriented, and celebrated innovation and novelty, postmodernist art mixed nostalgia for the old and fascination with the new in eclectic combinations of styles, forms and genres extracted from the entire history of art.

Theory, Culture & Society (SAGE, London, Newbury Park, Beverly Hills and New Delhi), Vol. 5 (1988), 239–69

And while at least the political avant-garde of the modernist move-ment celebrated negation and dissidence, and called for a revolu-tion of art and life, postmodernist art often took delight in the world as it is and happily co-existed in a pluralism of aesthetic styles and games (Jameson, 1984a; Huyssen, 1984).

In philosophy as well, claims began to emerge that a new post-modern philosophy was needed to replace the bankrupt tradition of philosophy established in the Cartesian–Lockean–Kantian tradi-tions (Bernstein, 1985; Baynes et al., 1987). It was claimed that this tradition of modern philosophy was destroyed by its vacuous and impossible dreams of a foundation for philosophy, an absolute bedrock of truth that could serve as the guarantee of philosophical systems (Derrida, 1976; Rorty, 1979). Others claimed that there were fundamental problems with the basic metaphysical presup-positions of western philosophy; Derrida, for example, argued that modern philosophy was vitiated by its system of binary thinking, its logocentrism, and its privileging of speech over writing. For Der-rida and others the binary metaphysical system ensnared its victims in hopeless metaphysical traps requiring a thoroughgoing decon-struction of philosophy and radically new philosophical practice. Precursors of the postmodern critique of philosophy were found in Nietzsche, Heidegger, Wittgenstein and Dewey, and in more mar-ginal writers like Sade, Bataille and Artaud (Foucault, 1970; Rorty, 1979).

By the late 1970s, new postmodern social theories began appear-ing. Jean Baudrillard (1983a and 1983b) describes a postmodern society in which radical semiurgy produces simulations and simulac-ra that create in turn new forms of society, culture, experience and subjectivity, while Jean-François Lyotard (1984a) describes a 'post-modern condition' that marks the end of the grand hopes of mod-ernity and the impossibility of continuing with the totalizing social theories and revolutionary politics of the past. Attempting to pre-serve precisely such marxizing social theories and politics, Fredric Jameson (1984) argues that postmodernism should be interpreted as the 'cultural logic of late capitalism' thus promoting totalizing marxian theories as the grand narratives — or the most inclusive social theories — of the present age, while relativizing postmodern-ism itself as a mere cultural logic within a new stage of capitalism. Arthur Kroker and David Cook (1986), however, in *The Postmod-ern Scene* describe contemporary society as a new 'panic' scene which eludes the categories and social theories of the past, and which requires new theorizing and abandonment of previous social theory.

Other social theorists like Habermas (1987) reject the claims for a postmodern break in history and attack postmodernism as a form of neo-conservative ideology. In view of these disputes, it is time to sort out the differences between the most significant articulations of postmodernism *as social theory* and to distinguish the central positions, insights and limitations in the new postmodern social theories. In these reflections, I shall specify some of the problems that I see emerging in postmodern social theory and will point to some of the differences between varying theoretical paradigms and to some tasks for a future postmodern social theory.

Before beginning, it should be pointed out that postmodern social theory exalts in exploding boundaries between previous academic disciplines and thus puts in question the very field or discipline of social theory. For some postmodernists — as for the supradisciplinary Critical Theorists of the so-called Frankfurt School — disciplinary fragmentation and abstraction is a symptomatic expression of an academic division of labour that is unable to conceptualize fundamental trends of social development or to demonstrate interrelations between the economy, state, society and culture (Kellner, 1988a). Postmodernists, like Critical Theorists, thus tend to subvert boundaries between disciplines and draw upon a sometimes bewildering variety of disciplines, discourses and positions. All postmodern social theory thus puts into radical question the previous discipline and boundaries of social theory, and some — like Baudrillard (1983b) — have even questioned whether 'the social' exists any longer and whether social theory is even possible or desirable.

It should also be pointed out in advance that there is nothing like a unified 'postmodern social theory'. Rather one is struck by the diversities between theories often lumped together as 'postmodern'. One is also struck by the inadequate and undertheorized notion of the 'postmodern' in various social theories which call themselves 'postmodern', or are identified in such terms. Consequently, in this paper, I shall sort out some of the most prominent varieties of contemporary postmodern social theory, and shall focus on their periodizations of the transition from modernity to postmodernity, their characterizations of the postmodern, and their challenges to traditional social theory while also pointing to some of their limitations.

Baudrillard, Postmodernism and the End of the Social

While discussions of postmodernism in the arts began in the United States, the first works which presented themselves as postmodern social theory originated in France in the late 1970s and drew upon earlier French cultural and social theory. Anticipations of later postmodern social theories of Baudrillard, Lyotard, Deleuze/ Guattari and others are found in Roland Barthes' (1957) explorations of mythologies and popular culture; in the rediscovery of Ferdinand de Saussure and the intense explorations of language in the 1960s and 1970s (Jameson, 1972; Coward and Ellis, 1977); in Henri Lefebvre's (1971) explorations of everyday life, in Guy Debord's (1970) critiques of 'the society of the spectacle', and in the powerful criticisms of established philosophy and the 'human sciences' by those associated with 'poststructuralism' (Derrida, Foucault, *Tel Quel*, the later Barthes, etc.).

Jean Baudrillard was perhaps the first to organize these interventions into a postmodern social theory. Although Baudrillard does not adopt the term postmodernism until the 1980s when it became *the* fashion in some circles, his late 1960s/early 1970s work contained many proto-postmodernist themes focusing on the consumer society and its proliferation of signs, the media and its messages, environmental design and cybernetic steering systems, and contemporary art and sign culture (Baudrillard, 1968, 1970, 1972 discussed in Kellner, 1988b). His work from the mid-1970s to the present — which began with *Symbolic Exchange and Death* (1976) and continued in *In the Shadow of the Silent Majorities* (1983b) and *Simulations* (1983a) — can be read as a proto-postmodernist social theory. Baudrillard's narrative concerns the end of the era of modernity dominated by production and industrial capitalism, and the advent of the era of a postindustrial postmodernity constituted by 'simulations,' 'hyperreality,' 'implosion' and new forms of technology, culture and society (see Kellner, 1987, 1988b).

Whereas modernity was characterized by the explosion of commodification, mechanization, technology, exchange and the market, postmodern society is the site of an *implosion* of all boundaries, regions and distinctions between high and low culture, appearance and reality, and just about every other binary opposition maintained by traditional philosophy and social theory. For Baudrillard, this signifies the end of all the positivities, grand referents and finalities of previous social theory: the Real, Meaning, History, Power, Revolution, and even the Social itself (Baudrillard, 1983a and 1983b; see the argument below on this latter point). Thus while modernity could be characterized as a process of increasing differentiation of spheres of life (Max Weber as interpreted by Habermas, 1984 and 1987) with attendant social fragmentation and alienation, postmodernity could be interpreted as a process of *dedifferentiation* (Lash, 1988) and attendant implosion.

Furthermore, while production for Baudrillard was the key to modern industrial society, in the postmodern society 'simulations' come to dominate the social order as models precede 'the real' and come to constitute society as a 'hyperreality' (Baudrillard, 1983a). In this condition, 'the very definition of the real becomes: *that of which it is possible to give an equivalent reproduction — the real is not only what can be reproduced, but that which is always already reproduced, the hyperreal*' (Baudrillard, 1983a: 146). From this perspective, track suburban houses, interior design manuals, exercise video-cassettes, Dr Spock's childcare prescriptions, and other simulation models precede 'the real' and are endlessly reproduced in a hyperreal society where the distinction between real and unreal is no longer apparent or valid and where simulacra constitute and count as 'the real'.

The first sketch of this new social situation is found in 'The Orders of Simulacra' published in French in *L'Echange symbolique et la mort* (1976) and collected in *Simulations* (1983a). This study contains a historical sketch of various orders of simulacra culminating in the society of simulations, while another study, 'The Precession of Simulacra' (also collected in *Simulations*) contains a series of analyses of some of the ways that simulations have come to dominate contemporary society and have produced a new kind of hyperreal social order.

'Simulacra' for Baudrillard are representations or copies of objects or events, while the 'orders of simulacra' form various stages in the 'orders of appearance', in the relationships between simulacra and 'the real'. Baudrillard presents his theory of how simulacra came to dominate social life both historically and phenomenologically. In a historical sketch of the order of simulacra — heavily influenced by Foucault's genealogies of knowledge (1970) — Baudrillard claims that simulacra first appeared as a constituent organizing principle when the Renaissance broke with the fixed feudal-medieval hierarchy of signs and social position by introducing an artificial and democratized world of signs that valorized artifice (stucco, theatre, fashion, baroque art, political democracy), and thus exploded fixed medieval hierarchies and order (Baudrillard, 1983a: 83–92). Yet a 'natural law of value' dominated these stages in which simulacra (from art to political representation) were held to represent nature or embody 'natural' rights or laws.

The 'second order' of simulacra appeared during the Industrial Revolution when infinite reproducibility was introduced into the world in the form of the industrial simulacrum or series (Baudrillard, 1983a: 96ff.). Production is mechanized and turns out series of mass objects: exact replicas can be infinitely produced and reproduced by assembly line processes and eventually automation. Baudrillard illustrates the difference between these orders of simulacra with a comparison between an automaton which mechanically imitates human beings, and a robot which simulates and replaces human labour power (Baudrillard, 1983a: 92–3). At this point, an 'industrial law of value' reigns where technology itself and mechanical reproduction come to constitute a new reality.

In the 'third order of simulacra', we are no longer in the world 'of the counterfeit of an original as in the first order, nor that of the pure series as in the second' (Baudrillard, 1983a: 100–1). This is the stage of 'simulation' proper when simulation models come to constitute the world. Now 'the structural law of value reigns' and models take precedence over things and: 'serial production yields to generation by means of models . . . Digitality is its metaphysical principle . . . and DNA its prophet. It is in effect in the genetic code that the "genesis of simulacra" today finds its most accomplished form' (Baudrillard, 1983a: 103–4). Society thus moves: 'From a capitalist-productivist society to a neo-capitalist cybernetic order that aims now at total control' (Baudrillard, 1983a: 111).

Baudrillard presents this theory in terms of suggestive analogies between language, genetics and social organization. Just as language contains codes or models that structure how we communicate — and our cells contain genetic codes, DNA, that structure how we experience and behave — so too does society contain codes and models of social organization and control which structure the environment and human life. That is, urban, architectural and transportation models structure within certain limits how cities, houses and transportation systems are organized and used. Within 'model homes', codes of design, decoration and taste, childcare books, sexual manuals, cook books, and magazines, newspapers and broadcast media all provide models that structure various activities within everyday life.

Models and codes thus come to structure everyday life, and modulation of the code comes to constitute a system of differences and relations in the society of simulations. Thus, urban planners modulate codes of city planning and architecture in creating urban systems, as television producers modulate TV codes to produce programming. The codes send signals and continually test individuals, inscribing them into the simulated order. Responses are structured in a binary system of affirmation or negation: every ad, fashion, commodity, television programme, political candidate and poll presents a test to which one is to respond: Is one for or against? Do we want it or not? Are we for X or Y? In this way, one is mobilized in a coded system of similarities and dissimilarities, of identities and programmed differences.

The triumph of cybernetics: everything is reduced to a binary system whose supposedly two dominant poles (i.e. political parties, world superpowers, seemingly opposing forces or principles, etc.) cancel out their differences and serve to maintain a self-regulating, self-same, self-identical system. In his writings from the mid-1970s to the present, Baudrillard provides example after example to support these hypotheses. The political upshot of his analysis seems to be that everything in the system is subject to cybernetic control and that what appears to be oppositional, outside of, or threatening to the system are really functional parts of a society of simulations.

In a text first published in 1978, *In the Shadow of the Silent Majorities*, Baudrillard puts in question previous theories of the social and of class and class conflict, arguing that these distinctions have imploded in the society of simulations. Consequently, traditional theories of politics, the social, class conflict, social change, etc. are obsolete if they posit individuals, classes or masses as capable of social action. Instead, in an era of 'hyperconformity' the masses solely concern themselves with spectacle: 'Messages are given to them, they only want some sign, they idolize the play of signs and stereotypes, they idolize any content so long as it resolves itself into a spectacular sequence' (Baudrillard, 1983b: 10).

Baudrillard proliferates a series of metaphors to capture the nature of the masses whom he describes as that 'spongy referent, that opaque but equally translucent reality, that nothingness'; 'a statistical crystal ball . . . swirling with currents and flows', 'in the image of matter and the natural elements'; an 'inertia', 'silence', 'figure of implosion', 'social void', and — what is probably his favourite metaphor — an 'opaque nebula whose growing density absorbs all the surrounding energy and light rays, to collapse finally under its own weight. A black hole which engulfs the social' (Baudrillard, 1983b: 1–4). This 'black hole' absorbs all meaning, information, communication, messages etc. and renders it meaningless, refusing to accept and produce 'meaning', indifferent and apathetic in the face of the messages which bombard it and which it refuses.

The main force in rendering the masses an apathetic silent majority seems to be the proliferation of information and media (Baudrillard, 1983b: 25–6, passim, and the critique in Kellner, 1987). Yet it is not until the postmodern craze of the 1980s that Baudrillard explicitly takes up the term 'postmodern' in relation to his own work. In an article 'On Nihilism' (1984b), he describes 'modernity' as 'the radical destruction of appearances, the disenchantment of the world and its abandonment to the violence of interpretation and history'. Modernity was the era of Marx and Freud, the era in which politics, culture and social life were interpreted as epiphenomena of the economy, or everything was interpreted in terms of desire or the unconsciousness. These 'hermeneutics of suspicion' employed depth models to demystify reality, to show the underlying realities behind appearances, the factors that constituted the facts.

The 'revolution' of modernity was thus a revolution of meaning grounded in the secure moorings of the dialectics of history, the economy, or desire. Baudrillard scorns this universe and claims to be part of a 'second revolution, that of the twentieth century, of postmodernity, which is the immense process of the destruction of meaning, equal to the earlier destruction of appearances. Whoever lives by meaning dies by meaning' (Baudrillard, 1984b: 38–9). The postmodern world is devoid of meaning; it is a universe of nihilism where theories float in a void, unanchored in any secure harbour or mooring. Meaning requires depth, a hidden dimension, an unseen substratum; in postmodern society, however, everything is visible, explicit, transparent, obscene. The postmodern scene exhibits signs of dead meaning, dissection and transparency, excremental culture, frozen forms mutating into new combinations and permutations of the same. Accelerating proliferation of signs and forms, growing implosion and inertia. Growth beyond limits, turning in on itself. The secret of cancer (and AIDS?): 'Revenge of excrescence on growth, revenge of speed in inertia' (Baudrillard, 1984b: 39).

Acceleration of inertia, the implosion of meaning in the media; the implosion of the social in the mass; the implosion of the mass in a dark hole of nihilism and meaninglessness — such in the Baudrillardian postmodern scene — or absence of a scene. Fascinated by this void and inertia, Baudrillard privileges the scene of nihilism over the phantasy of meaning arguing that — and this is as good an expression of his postmodern position as any:

> If being nihilist is to privilege this point of inertia and the analysis of this irreversibility of systems to the point of no return, then I am a nihilist.
>
> If being nihilist is to be obsessed with the mode of disappearance, and no longer with the mode of production, then I am a nihilist. Disappearance, aphanisis, implosion, Fury of the *Verschwindens*'. (Baudrillard, 1984b: 39)

Baudrillard's nihilism is without joy, without energy, without hope for a better future: 'No, melancholy is the fundamental tonality of functional systems, of the present systems of simulation, programming and information. Melancholy is the quality inherent in the mode of disappearance of meaning, in the mode of volatilization of meaning in operational systems' (Baudrillard, 1984b: 39). In fact, Baudrillard's postmodern mind-set exhibits a contradictory amalgam of emotions and responses ranging from despair and melancholy, to vertigo and giddiness, and nostalgia and laughter. Analysis of the 'mode of disappearance' constitutes a rather original contribution to contemporary social theory and indeed Baudrillard has been faithful to this impulse.

In an interview 'Game with Vestiges', Baudrillard (1984a) again describes his thought in terms of postmodernism, and continues to describe the disappearance of the central items in previous social theories. After the destruction of meaning and all the referentials and finalities of modernity, postmodernism is described as a response to emptiness and anguish which is oriented toward 'the restoration of a past culture' that tries

> to bring back all past cultures, to bring back everything that one has destroyed, all that one has destroyed in joy and which one is reconstructing in sadness in order to try to live, to survive. . . . All that remains to be done is to play with the pieces. Playing with the pieces — that is post-modern. (Baudrillard, 1984a: 24)

Baudrillard claims — rather contentiously — that all art — and presumably theory, politics, individuals — can do is to recombine and play with the forms already produced. As he puts it at the end of the interview:

> Post-modernity is neither optimistic nor pessimistic. It is a game with the vestiges of what has been destroyed. This is why we are 'post' — history has stopped, one

is in a kind of post-history which is without meaning. One would not be able to find any meaning in it. So, we must move in it, as though it were a kind of circular gravity. We can no longer be said to progress. So it is a 'moving' situation. But it is not at all unfortunate. I have the impression with post-modernism that there is an attempt to rediscover a certain pleasure in the irony of things, in the game of things. Right now one can tumble into total hopelessness — all the definitions, everything, it's all been done. What can one do? What can one become? And post-modernity is the attempt — perhaps it's desperate, I don't know — to reach a point where one can live with what is left. It is more a survival among the remnants than anything else. [Laughter!] (Baudrillard, 1984a: 25)

Baudrillard's postmodern social theory takes place on a high level of theoretical abstraction. It now appears that he is trying to invent his own social theory with its own distinctive language, positions, style and idiosyncrasies. He posits — without really defining or justifying — an absolute break between the previous historical epoch and the postmodern one, and offers a new theory to attempt to conceptualize the new historical era. In my forthcoming study of Baudrillard (Kellner, 1988b), I shall criticize in more detail his postmodern social theory and his surprising turn to metaphysics in his 1980s' writings. For now suffice it to point out that Baudrillard tends to take tendencies in the current social situation for finalities, trends for finished states. His theory is arguably good science fiction but poor social theory. Lacking adequate contextualization, his theory tends to be abstract, one-sided, and rather blind to a large number of continuities between modernity and postmodernity, and to a large number of depressing realities and problems of the present age. The first high-tech social theorist, Baudrillard reproduces certain trends of the present age which he projects into a simulation model of postmodernism as the catastrophe of modernity.

Lyotard and *The Postmodern Condition*

Jean-François Lyotard explicitly takes up the challenge of providing a postmodern social theory in *The Postmodern Condition*. Subtitled *A Report on Knowledge*, the text was commissioned by the Canadian government to study

the condition of knowledge in the most highly developed societies. I have decided to use the word *postmodern* to describe that condition. The word is in current use of the American continent among sociologists and critics; it designates the state of our culture following the transformations which, since the end of the nineteenth century, have altered the game rules for science, literature, and the arts. (Lyotard, 1984a: xxiii)

For Lyotard, the 'postmodern' concerns developing a new epistemology responding to new conditions of knowledge, and the main focus of the book concerns the differences between the grand narratives of traditional philosophy and social theory, the practice and legitimation of contemporary science, and what he calls 'postmodern science' which he defends as a preferable form of knowledge to traditional and contemporary philosophical and scientific forms.

This project influences his definition of terms and focus. Modernity for Lyotard is more a form of knowledge than a condition of society (as it was for Baudrillard). Lyotard by contrast writes:

I will use the term *modern* to designate any science that legitimates itself with reference to a metadiscourse ... making an explicit appeal to some grand narrative, such as the dialectics of Spirit, the hermeneutics of meaning, the emancipation of the rational or working subject, or the creation of wealth. (Lyotard, 1984a: xxiii)

From this perspective the '*postmodern*' is defined 'as incredulity toward metanarratives', the rejection of metaphysical philosophy, philosophies of history and any form of totalizing thought — be it Hegelianism, liberalism, Marxism or whatever. Postmodern knowledge, by contrast, 'refines our sensitivity to differences and reinforces our ability to tolerate the incommensurable. Its principle is not the expert's homology, but the inventor's paralogy' (Lyotard, 1984: xxv).

Although Lyotard's main focus is epistemological, he also implicitly presupposes a social theory of the postmodern condition writing: 'Our working hypothesis is that the status of knowledge is altered as societies enter what is known as the postindustrial age and culture enters what is known as the postmodern age' (Lyotard, 1984a: 3). Like Baudrillard, Lyotard thus associates the postmodern with the trends of so-called 'postindustrial society'. Postmodern society is thus for Lyotard the society of computers, information, scientific knowledge, advanced technology, and of rapid change due to new advances in science and technology. Indeed, he seems to agree with theorists of post-industrial society concerning the primacy of knowledge, information and computerization — describing postmodern society as 'the computerization of society'.

For Lyotard, as for theorists of 'postindustrial society' (Bell, 1976), technology and knowledge become principles of social organization. On the other hand, Lyotard does not — like Bell and others — claim that his postmodern society is a post-capitalist one stressing early in his study how the flow and development of technology and knowledge follow 'the flow of money' (Lyotard, 1984a: 6). Yet Lyotard does not adequately analyse the relations between technology, capital and social development and really cannot in principle do this because of his rejection of a macro-theory of capital — a point that I shall expand below.

Lyotard adopts a language games approach to knowledge proposing that we conceive of various discourses as language games with their own rules, structure and moves. Different language games are thus governed by different criteria and rules, and none is to be privileged: 'All we can do is gaze in wonderment at the diversity of discursive species, just as we do at the diversity of plant or animal species. Lamenting the "loss of meaning" in postmodernity boils down to mourning the fact that knowledge is no longer principally narrative' (Lyotard, 1984: 26). Yet Lyotard wants to privilege precisely this plurality of language games, and rejects all modes of philosophical discourse which would legislate between the various validity claims, values, positions, etc. affirmed in the various discourses which circulate through society. Rather than engaging in totalizing social theory and critique, Lyotard wants more localized, heterogeneous microanalysis with 'little narratives' (Lyotard, 1984a: 60ff.). He writes:

> A recognition of the heteromorphous nature of language games is a first step. . . . The second step is the principle that any consensus on the rules defining a game and the 'moves' playable within it *must* be local, in other words, agreed on by its present players and subject to eventual cancellation. (Lyotard, 1984a: 66)

Language games for Lyotard (1984a: 10ff.) are indeed the 'social bond' which holds society together, and he characterizes social interaction primarily in terms of making a move in a game, playing a role and taking a part in various discrete language games. In these terms, he characterizes the self as the intersection of all the language games which it participates in:

> A *self* does not amount to much, but no self is an island; each exists in a fabric of relations that is now more complex and mobile than ever before. Young or old, man or woman, rich or poor, a person is always located at 'nodal points' of specific communication circuits, however tiny these may be. Or better: one is always located at a post through which various kinds of messages pass. (Lyotard, 1984a: 15)

Yet participation in language games involves struggle and conflict for Lyotard; he claims that 'the first principle underlying our method as a whole' is that 'to speak is to fight, in the sense of playing, and speech acts fall within the domain of a general agonistics' (Lyotard, 1984a: 10). Lyotard's model of a postmodern society is thus one in which one struggles within various language games in an agonistic environment characterized by diversity, conflict and the difficulty — even undesirability and impossibility — of an unforced consensus. Furthermore, postmodern knowledge for Lyotard involves knowledge of local terrains, and tolerance of a variety and diversity of different language games.

It also involves the search for paralogisms, for new discoveries which destabilize and disturb existing forms of knowledge: 'Postmodern science — by concerning itself with such things as undecidables, the limits of precise control, conflicts characterized by incomplete information, *'fracta*, catastrophes, and pragmatic paradoxes — is theorizing its own evolution as discontinuous, catastrophic, non-rectifiable and paradoxical' (Lyotard, 1984a: 60). Yet it is not clear at this point if Lyotard is claiming that this analysis of 'postmodern science' — which builds on Bachelard's and Althusser's notions of epistemological breaks, Foucault's notion of episteme, and Kuhn's notion of paradigm shifts — describes what he thinks contemporary scientists are actually doing, or whether he is simply prescribing or recommending this model as a normative ideal for postmodern theory today.

If Lyotard actually believes that scientists today are searching for paralogisms and seeking destabilization, then his account is subject to strong counter-arguments, thus his notion of postmodern science is probably better interpreted as a normative ideal for postmodern theory. On the other hand, Lyotard seems to believe that certain aspects of contemporary science point to the need for a 'postmodern' view of the world to replace the modern view which he associates with Newtonian physics (as well as the Enlightenment, grand narratives, etc.). He claims that modern science (i.e. relativity theory, quantum mechanics, Godel's incompleteness theorem, Heisenberg's uncertainty principle, etc.) overthrows the idea of a stable universe, and suggests that knowledge must be constantly modifying itself, and must be tentative, probabilistic, and revisible in principle. This vision of the universe supposedly invalidates not only Newtonian scientific theories but metanarratives which claimed to grasp the truth and which purported to offer a universalistic and totalizing account of history, society or whatever. Lyotard writes:

> In contemporary society and culture — postindustrial society, postmodern cul-
> ture — the question of the legitimation of knowledge is formulated in different
> terms. The grand narrative has lost its credibility, regardless of what mode of
> unification it uses, regardless of whether it is a speculative narrative or a narrative
> of emancipation. (Lyotard, 1984a: 37)

Lyotard repeatedly claims that postmodernism involves 'incredulity toward' grand narratives, the 'breaking up' of grand narratives, and delegitimation of all metanarratives without describing in
any detail *how* and *why* this theoretical collapse took place, and *why*
he is himself polemicizing against these discourses. In other words,
his rejection of metanarratives and account of the transition from
modern to postmodern knowledge is undertheorized and underdeveloped and his own notion of postmodern knowledge is likewise
underconceptualized. Lyotard's one somewhat developed polemic
against what he calls 'narratives of the legitimation of knowledge'
concerns a critique of the French-Napoleonic and German-
Humboldtian politics of education and their 'narratives of legitimation' with some closing swipes at a Marxian narrative and Martin
Heidegger's infamous Rector speech where he linked German
education to fascism (Lyotard, 1984a: 31ff.). But surely because
some 'narratives of legitimation' are highly dubious, politically
suspect, and not very convincing does not entail that we should
reject *all* grand narratives — that is, all of traditional philosophy
and social theory which has systematic and comprehensive aims.

Lyotard's work points to an overlooked aporia in certain French
theories of postmodernism. He concludes the appendix to the English version of *The Postmodern Condition* with the programmatic
proviso: 'Let us wage a war on totality; let us be witness to the
unpresentable; let us activate the differences and save the honour of
the name' (Lyotard, 1984a: 82). Lyotard is thus rejecting totalizing
social theories which he describes as master narratives that are
somehow reductionist, simplistic and even 'terroristic' (i.e. providing legitimations for totalitarian terror, and suppressing differences
in unifying schemes). Indeed, Lyotard joins at this juncture the
so-called 'new philosophers' who attempted to associate totalizing
thought with totalitarianism tout court, replaying an ideologically
loaded argument about the theoretico-historical route from Hegel
and Marx to the Gulag.

Yet Lyotard himself is offering a theory of the postmodern condition which presupposes a dramatic break from modernity. Indeed,
does not the very concept of postmodernism, or a postmodern

condition, presuppose a Master Narrative, a totalizing perspective, which envisages the transition from a previous stage of society to a new one? Doesn't such theorizing presuppose *both* a concept of a period of modernity, or phenomenon of modernism, and a presupposition of a radical break, or rupture within history, that leads to a totally new condition which justifies the term *post*modern? Therefore, does not the very concept 'postmodern' seem to presuppose both a 'master narrative' and some notion of totality, or some notion of a periodizing and totalizing thought — precisely the sort of epistemological operation and theoretical hubris which Lyotard and others want to oppose and do away with.

Against Lyotard, we might want to distinguish between 'master narratives' that attempt to subsume every particular, every specific viewpoint, and every key point into one totalizing theory (as in some versions of Marxism, feminism, Weber, etc.) from 'grand narratives' which attempt to tell a Big Story, such as the rise of capital, patriarchy or the colonial subject. Within grand narratives we might want to distinguish as well between metanarratives that tell a story about the foundation of knowledge and macro social theory that attempts to conceptualize and interpret a complex diversity of phenomena. We might next distinguish between synchronic narratives that tell a story about a given society at a given point in history, and diachronic narratives that analyse historical change, discontinuities and ruptures. Lyotard tends to lump all 'grand narratives' together and thus does violence to the diversity of theoretical narratives in our culture.

My key point is that while Lyotard resists grand narratives, it is impossible to discern how one can have a theory of postmodernism without one. Rejecting grand narratives, I believe, simply covers over the theoretical problem of providing a narrative of the contemporary historical situation and points to the undertheorized nature of Lyotard's theory of the postmodern condition — which would require at least some sort of rather large narrative of the transition to postmodernism — a rather big and exciting story one would think.

The problem of the undertheorized nature of Lyotard's analysis of postmodernism is compounded with the highly superficial and theorically problematic appendix to his report, 'Answering the Question: What is Postmodernism?' The title would seem to promise an answer but his response is most disappointing and unpromising. After discussing some recent demands in the cultural world for a return to realism in the arts, Lyotard (1984a: 81) defends artistic experimentation and the avant-garde, and then defines postmodernism as:

> The postmodern would be that which, in the modern, puts forward the unpresentable in presentation itself; that which denies itself the solace of good forms, the consensus of a taste which would make it possible to share collectively the nostalgia for the unattainable; that which searches for new presentations, not in order to enjoy them but in order to impart a stronger sense of the unpresentable. A postmodern artist or writer is in the position of a philosopher: the text he writes, the work he produces are not in principle governed by preestablished rules, and they cannot be judged according to a determining judgment, by applying familiar categories to the text or to the work. Those rules and categories are what the work of art itself is looking for. The artist and the writer, then are working without rules in order to formulate the rules of what *will have been done*. Hence the fact that work and text have the characters of an *event*; hence also, they always come too late for their author, or, what amounts to the same thing, their being put into work, their realization *mis en oeuvre* always begin too soon. *Postmodern* would have to be understood according to the paradox of the future (*post*) anterior (*modo*).

But is this not the very definition of modernism (or modernity) which is constantly revolutionizing cultural (and all other) forms, reacting against tradition and what came before it in order to create something new? Lyotard (1984a: 79) himself seems to admit this: 'Postmodernism thus understood is not modernism at its end but in the nascent state, and this state is constant.' Postmodernism for Lyotard is thus ultimately an intensification of the sort of dynamism, restless quest for novelty, experimentation, and constant revolutionizing of life that is associated with modernity. In other words he doesn't really have much of a postmodern social theory, ending up with a modernist aesthetic, post-industrial social theory, and what he calls postmodern knowledge.

Lyotard is also inconsistent in calling for a plurality and heterogeneity of language games, and then excluding from his kingdom of discourse those grand narratives which he suggests have illicitly monopolized the discussion and proferred illegitimate claims in favour of their privilege. One is tempted to counter Lyotard's move here with an injunction to 'let a thousand narratives bloom' — though one would need to sort out some differences between these narratives, and perhaps — à la Habermas — distinguish between better and worse narratives in order to provide a critical position towards conservative, fascist, idealist and other theoretically and politically objectionable narratives.

Furthermore, it seems like a more promising venture to make explicit, critically discuss, take apart, and perhaps reconstruct and rewrite the grand narratives of social theory rather than to just prohibit them and exclude them from the terrain of narrative and theory. It is likely — as Fredric Jameson argues — that we are condemned to narrative and that the narratives of social theory will continue to operate in social analysis in any case (Jameson, Foreword to Lyotard 1984a: xii). If this is so, it would seem preferable to bring to light the narratives of social theory so as to critically examine and dissect them rather than forcing them underground to escape censure by Lyotard's Thought Police. It also seems better to highlight and develop the narrative component of social theory in general and to be aware of the extent to which narrative is an important and arguably indispenable aspect of social theory.

In sum, Lyotard does not offer us a new theoretical paradigm for postmodern society — indeed he argues that it is impossible to do so, that we should abandon the project of developing a theory of society which inevitably involves the construction of a grand narrative. Yet he does offer us a new paradigm for the practice of theory: just gaming (Lyotard and Thébaud, 1985). Indeed, this is an attractive and compelling proposal for it is both exciting and pleasurable to intervene in a wide variety of different sorts of language games, to make moves in a plurality of debates or discussions, and to oppose the moves and positions of other players while advancing one's own positions. Gaming in this way is much easier than doing social research, than constructing theoretical models, than trying to develop a theory of society. But is gaming enough to do radical social theory? Do we not also need theoretical models and more systematic social theory and criticism.

Another problem: when one does not specify and explicate the specific sort of narrative of contemporary society involved in one's gaming, there is a tendency to make use of the established narratives at one's disposal. For example, in the absence of an alternative theory of contemporary society, Lyotard uncritically accepts theories of 'postindustrial society' and 'postmodern culture' as accounts of the present age (Lyotard, 1984a: 3, 7, 37, passim). Yet he presupposes the validity of these narratives without really defending his model and without developing an adequate social theory which would delineate the transformation suggested by the 'post' in 'postindustrial' or 'postmodern'. Furthermore, he places himself within the camp of postindustrial theory by failure to more closely and critically examine this rather grand narrative which he himself makes use of.

Generalizing from the lacunae and aporia in Lyotard's 'theory,' one could argue that a properly postmodern social theory — that is, an adequate account of postmodern society or culture — must satisfy several key demands. First, one must historize or periodize one's theory. If one wishes to claim that a transition from modern to postmodern society has occurred, one must provide an account of the features of the previous social order (modernity), the new social condition (postmodernity), and the rupture or break between them.

Furthermore, one should also indicate both continuities and discontinuities between the old and the new, the previous and the current social order. Michel Foucault — despite problematical interpretations of his work to the contrary — constantly engaged in such dialectical analysis. And Jacques Derrida — sometimes celebrated as the voice of rupture, break, otherness, difference — warns us: 'I do not believe in decisive ruptures, in an unequivocal "epistemological break", as it is called today. Breaks are always, and fatally, reinscribed in an old cloth that must continually, interminably be undone' (Derrida, 1981: 24).

Neither Foucault nor Derrida have produced postmodern social theories, however, and neither Baudrillard nor Lyotard have adequately theorized what is involved in a break or rupture between the modern and the postmodern. Baudrillard dramatically proclaims a fundamental break in history and the end of a historical era with the advent of a new postmodern era without providing a clear account of the transition to postmodernity and without seeing or specifying the continuities between the previous era and the allegedly new one. And Lyotard in principle is prohibited from producing a postmodern social theory of this kind by his postmodern epistemology.

Consequently, the first discussions of postmodernism in social theory are vitiated by the failure to clearly distinguish between modernity, postmodernity, and to specify what produces the rupture in society and history that produces the postmodern condition or postmodern society. Such an operation would require both rigorous and detailed theoretical analysis, and a historical account or narrative that would tell the story of how modernity metamorphosized into the postmodern condition. Theorists who reject master narratives, or historical/diachronic, periodizing social theory, are naturally going to have difficulty producing such a narrative, and thus find themselves in an aporetic situation.

Poststructuralist theory produces some other problems for would-be postmodern social theorists which are evident in Baudrillard and Lyotard. Poststructuralists problematize reference, representation, and the very concept of 'reality' or 'the real' as they like to refer to IT. Yet theories of postmodernism presuppose an access to 'the real', to social reality, and thus to some 'ground' of reference, in order to make claims about postmodern society. That is, the very statements about contemporary social reality made by a Baudrillard or a Lyotard presuppose that they are actually telling us something new or important about society or social theory today, that their statements are accurately describing some phenomena, that they are illuminating at least some domain of social reality. This raises the issue of whether commitments to poststructuralism and theories of postmodernism are compatible.

Baudrillard and Lyotard dramatize different sides of the poststructuralist critique. As noted, Baudrillard problematizes the concept of 'the real' and representation in postmodern society yet makes many claims about contemporary social conditions. Lyotard seems comfortable with the concepts 'reality' and 'society', yet consistent with his prohibitions against totalizing narratives takes the poststructural critique of representation seriously and rarely attempts to represent postmodern society as a whole — and thus fails to develop a social theory of his own while uncritically adopting many aspects of postindustrial social theory.

Moreover, there isn't really too much social critique in Lyotard. His focus — like much poststructural and postmodernist theory — is on critique of metatheory, philosophy and knowledge. Consequently, as a social theory, Lyotard's theory and critique are underdeveloped and do not really provide much of a critical theory of society. Fredric Jameson, however, has attempted to develop a postmodern social theory that would meet these challenges and overcome the weaknesses and limitations of previous attempts while developing a synchronic and diachronic postmodern social theory which synthesizes some of the insights found in previous theories with new theoretical perspectives and reflections on what is involved in producing a postmodern social theory.

Jameson's Theory of Postmodernism as the Cultural Logic of Capitalism

Fredric Jameson's writings on postmodernism can be read as an attempt to meet the challenges to radical social theory posed by poststructuralist and postmodernist theorists like Baudrillard and Lyotard which both provides an alternative model of a postmodern social theory while appropriating their insights and contributions. Like Baudrillard and Lyotard, Jameson argues that there is a fundamental break in social development, and thus something like a postmodern condition, yet he believes that it can be theorized within the framework of a neo-Marxian social theory (Jameson, 1984a). Unlike his predecessors, he attempts to delineate the epistemological issues involved in providing a new postmodern social theory.

In his article 'Postmodernism — or the Cultural Logic of Late Capitalism', Jameson (1984a) attempts to provide an account of the features, contours, genesis and possibilities of a contemporary postmodern culture. In a panoramic sweep, Jameson presents postmodernism as the 'cultural logic of late capitalism' which constituted both a new 'cultural dominant' and a new socioeconomic stage of capitalism; his studies expand the discussion concerning postmodernism to include a wide range of cultural, social, economic and political phenomena. Jameson thus moves the postmodernism debate out of the arenas of cultural theory and metatheory into the field of social theory.

For Jameson — as for Ernst Mandel (1975) upon whom he draws — contemporary capitalism is an even purer, more developed, more realized, form of capitalism than those earlier stages described by Marx's critique of market capitalism and Lenin's theory of imperialism. On this account, contemporary capitalism has colonialized and penetrated ever more domains of life, and commodification and capitalist exchange relations have penetrated the spheres of information, knowledge, computerization, and consciousness and experience itself to an unparallelled extent. Jameson thus proposes correlating postmodernism as the cultural logic of a new type of capitalist society.

Jameson gives a fairly precise periodization of postmodern culture and a detailed account of its differences from the culture of high modernism. Yet while he is prepared to postulate the existence of a new stage of society in terms of important new developments within capitalism, he does not provide a detailed narrative of the transition from the stages of capitalism described by Marx, Lenin and earlier Marxists, relying on a rather brief synopsis of Mandel instead of providing a more detailed analysis. In fact, by limiting postmodernism to the domain of culture, Jameson limits the relevance of postmodernism for social theory, although his discussion implies that social theory must cognitively map the new socio-economic and political conditions of which postmodern culture is a part.

Despite these limitations, Jameson provocatively poses the challenges to postmodern social theory that I specified above in terms of periodization and characterization of the postmodern. Furthermore, Jameson's account suggests that the seemingly fragmented, chaotic, non-representable nature of the postmodern world presents new challenges to social theory, art and radical politics. To begin, we need cultural maps of the new terrain, and Jameson (1984a, 1988) calls for a theoretics, aesthetics and politics of what he calls *cognitive mapping*. Citing difficulties of orientation and mapping in postmodern cities and architecture, Jameson suggests that:

> Disalienation in the traditional city, then, involves the practical reconquest of a sense of place, and the construction or reconstruction of an articulated ensemble which can be retained in memory and which the individual subject can map and remap along the moments of mobile, alternative trajectories. (Jameson, 1984a: 89)

Such cognitive mapping is precisely one of the functions of theory and Jameson calls for new theories of 'the larger national and global spaces' of the postmodern world which both theory and art could provide.

Then, presumably, once we've mapped and begun to understand the new cultural and socio-political field we can devise radical cultural politics and other political strategies. In the concluding discussion of 'the need for maps', Jameson (1984a) suggests in his 'Postmodernism' article that progressive art in the postmodernist era would be pedagogical and didactic, and would presumably involve new representational and mapping strategies to provide critical perceptions in the postmodern world. Jameson does not presume to provide any examples there, but in an article published in *Social Text* from the same period (1986), he presents some third-world novels as examples of how novels might serve to provide cognitive maps for their nations. In particular, he reads Lu Xun's *Diary of a Madman* and Sembene Ousmane's *Xala* as allegor-

ies. of national identity which combine the personal and the political, and the fates of the individual and the nation in ways that
illuminate the place of the individual in relation to her or his society
and to the political demands posed in a particular society in a given
era; and in another article (1986), he sketches out some of the ways
that 'magical realist' novels and films provide mapping functions.

In another article related to Jameson's work on postmodernism,
'Cognitive Mapping' (1988), he spells out more of what is included
in a postmodern aesthetic of cognitive mapping. The term seems to
derive from Brecht scholar Darko Suvin's emphasis on the cognitive
function of art and aesthetics, Kevin Lynch's attempt to map out
images of the city, and Althusser's theory of ideology as 'the Imaginary representation of the subject's relationship to his or her
Real conditions of existence'. Just as Jameson argued in *The Political Unconscious* (1981) that narrative was a fundamental function of
human being, he now seems to argue that individuals need some
sort of image or mapping of their society and the world as a whole.
'Cognitive mapping' thus involves the task of individuals, artists and
theorists in providing orientation, a sense of place, and a theoretical
model of how society is structured. Jameson claims that this sort of
mapping is of crucial importance for both social theory and politics
for 'the incapacity to map socially is as crippling to political experience as the analogous incapacity to map spatially is for urban
experience. It follows that an aesthetic of cognitive mapping in this
sense is an integral part of any socialist political project.'

Jameson is thus attempting to answer the poststructuralist/
postmodernist critique of representation by stressing that we need
representations of our society, however imperfect, to get about in
the world. As a theoretical model, Jameson's own sketches can be
taken as cognitive maps of postmodern space, and from this perspective he poses the challenge to social theory to provide novel
cognitive mapping of the allegedly new postmodern society. Indeed, in a Hegelian–Marxian fashion, Jameson is in effect providing
a defence of the concept of totality against postmodern and poststructuralist attacks, and is offering his own totalizing theory of the
present age — precisely the traditional function and important
contribution of Hegelian Marxism. Jameson points to the debilitat-
ing effects of living in the fragments and just gaming with the
remnants, and argues that new cognitive mapping is needed to
contextualize and critique our present postmodern condition. One
might question, however, whether a theory of the present historical

moment, the totality of the present age, is best derived from reading off of cultural phenomena, as Jameson does in the essays so far examined. Here, one might compare his method in the postmodernism essay with his studies of the 1960s in the anthology *The '60s Without Apology* (Jameson, 1984b).

In his article 'Periodizing the 60s', Jameson defends a totalizing and periodizing attempt to globally characterize an entire epoch, this time the 1960s, against attacks on such totalizing procedures. In this essay, however, Jameson begins with analysis of salient *political* and *historical* origins and features of the epoch, moving from discussions of its 'Third World Beginnings', its politics, the fate of philosophy, transformations in culture, and the connections of political, cultural and social developments with economic developments. In this article, Jameson privileges the political in ways that he privileges the cultural in his postmodernism study. Both essays attempt to ground their analyses in developments of the economy and both conceptualize changes in politics, society and culture in terms of changes in the mode of production (utilizing Ernst Mandel's *Late Capitalism* for a theory of both the historical stages of capitalism and a theory of the present stage of multinational capitalism). The analysis of the relationship between the new stage of the economy and culture, and the failure to say much about the supposed new stage of multinational capitalism is, arguably, the weakest part of Jameson's analysis — i.e. he does not provide adequate mediations between the economic and the cultural and political in these essays. However, Jameson's studies raise the question of whether theories of the present age should be developed as theories of postmodernism or as a new reconfiguration of capitalism to be characterized by the term 'multinational capitalism' or some other concept.

Finally, Jameson's article on the 1960s reveals the extent to which he remains committed to a classical Marxian class politics which most postmodernists reject. He concludes his study with a political prognosis of the future:

> With the end of the 60s, with the world economic crisis, all the old infrastructural bills then slowly come due once more; and the 80s will be characterized by an effort, on a world scale, to proletarianize all those unbound social forces which gave the 60s their energy, by an extension of class struggle, in other words, into the farthest reaches of the globe as well as the most minute configurations of local institutions (such as the university system). The unifying force here is the new vocation of a henceforth global capitalism, which may also be expected to unify

the unequal, fragmented, or local resistances to the process. And this is finally also the solution to the so-called 'crisis' of Marxism and to the widely noted inapplicability of its forms of class analysis to the new social realities with which the 60s confronted us: 'traditional' Marxism, if 'untrue' during this period of a proliferation of new subjects of history, must necessarily become true again when the dreary realities of exploitation, extraction of surplus value, proletarianization and the resistance to it in the form of class struggle, all slowly reassert themselves on a new and expanded world scale, as they seem currently in the process of doing'. (Jameson, 1984b: 209)

It remains to be seen whether the oppressive realities of contemporary capitalist societies are producing a new proletarianization of the underlying population, or whether the glitzy joys of its culture and consumerism will continue to entrap the majority of the underlying population in its massified and commodified pleasures, and its simulated politics. In any case, one sees how, against Lyotard, Jameson employs the form of a grand narrative, of a totalizing theory of society and history that makes specific claims about features of postmodernism — which he interprets as 'the cultural logic of capital' rather than as a code word for a new (post)historical condition — as do Lyotard and Baudrillard (however much they reject totalizing thought). Obviously, Jameson wishes to preserve Marxism as *the* Master Narrative and to relativize all competing theories as sectoral or regional theories to be subsumed in their proper place within the Marxian Master Narrative. (Jameson performs a similar operation in *The Political Unconscious* (1981) where he assigns all competing literary and cultural theories to their proper place as elements that may be of some use in some contexts with the grand narrative of Marxian theory.)

Furthermore, Jameson wants to hold onto fundamental distinctions between social classes, base/superstructure, Left/Right, Progressive/Reactionary, etc. etc. that Baudrillard and other postmodernists claim have been imploded. Jameson also wants to utilize and advance a multidimensional, dialectical narrative that is both diachronic and synchronic, that holds together both the moments of the present, and that provides an optic that allows us to see the movement from the past to the present into the future. His strategy is to conceptualize postmodernism as a moment within the new stage of capitalism rather than as an autonomous demi-urge which produces a new (post-capitalist?) social order.

Habermas, Critical Theory and Postmodernism

Jameson's project parallels the 1930s trajectory of Critical Theory which attempted to develop a supradisciplinary theory of the new stage of capitalism which they saw emerging (see Kellner, 1988a). His studies replicate Critical Theory's Hegelian–Marxian and Lukácsian attempt to provide a theory of the totality of contemporary capitalism which Jameson contrasts with earlier forms of culture, society and experience in capitalist societies. A completely different strategy was undertaken in the intervention into the postmodernism debate by Jürgen Habermas and his followers.

By the 1980s, the debate over 'postmodernism' eventually engaged the second and third generation of the Frankfurt School. Whereas the first generation of the Critical Theorists — Horkheimer, Marcuse, Adorno, etc. — had attempted to update and revise the Marxian theory in response to the new social conditions, the response of Habermas and his followers to the discourse of postmodernism was defensive and hostile. In an article on 'Das Moderne — ein unvollendes Projekt', translated in *New German Critique* as 'Modernity versus Postmodernity', Habermas (1981) argued that the various theories of postmodernism were a form of attacks on modernity which had their ideological precursors in various irrationalist and counter-Enlightenment theories. In a series of succeeding *Lectures on the Philosophical Discourse of Modernity*, Habermas (1987) continued to attack the (primarily French) theories of postmodernism. He used standard methods of ideology critique suggesting that the French theories of postmodernism which had their roots in Nietzsche and Heidegger were aligned with the counter-Enlightenment, and exhibited disturbing kinship with fascism. Against theories of postmodernism, Habermas defended 'the project of modernity' that he believed was 'an unfinished project' which contained unfulfilled emancipatory potential.

Habermas begins by indicating that from as early as the classical period until recently, 'the modern' signified 'the new', designating the present epoch as distinct from the past, from 'antiquity'. In the Enlightenment, the 'modern' came to take on significations of science, technology and industry, while the 'aesthetic modernity' of the nineteenth century equated the modern with innovations in art and aesthetic novelty. Aesthetic modernity took to an extreme rebellion against tradition and valorized highly charged aesthetic experiences of novelty, dynamism, singularity and intense presence.

Habermas cites some sources who claim that this aesthetic modernity is dead, and then raises the question of whether this decline in the sphere of culture signals 'a farewell to modernity' and the 'transition to a broader phenomenon called postmodernity' (Habermas, 1981: 6). He next makes a distinction between aesthetic modernity and societal modernization which he interprets in the Enlightenment (and Weberian) sense of a process of cultural differentiation. In particular, Habermas defends the differentiation of cultural spheres and development of autonomous criteria of rationality and universality in the fields of knowledge, morality, law and justice, and art (Habermas, 1981: 8). He refers to this as the 'project of modernity' which he interprets

> as the efforts to develop objective science, universal morality and law, and autonomous art, according to their inner logic. At the same time, this project intended to release the cognitive potentials of each of these domains to set them free from their esoteric forms. The Enlightenment philosophers wanted to utilize this accumulation of specialized culture for the enrichment of everyday life, that is to say, for the rational organization of everyday social life. (Habermas, 1981: 9)

While the project of modernity resulted in part in the colonization of the life-world by the logic of scientific-technological rationality and domination by a culture of experts and specialists, it also for Habermas has unrealized potential in increasing social rationality, justice and morality. He defends the project of modernity by citing what he considers some failed aesthetic revolts (i.e. surrealism) and then defends a type of modern art which he believes could illuminate conditions in the life-world and provide progressive cognitive and moral effects (his example here is Peter Weiss; Habermas, 1981: 10–12).

From the standpoint of this qualified defence of modernity, Habermas then criticizes what he considers to be 'false programs of the negation of culture', or overly negative attacks on modernity, which fail in his view to recognize its positive contributions and potential. Here he distinguishes (not very successfully) between the antimodernism of the young conservatives, the premodernism of the old conservatives, and the postmodernism of the neoconservatives. Here he categorizes Bataille, Foucault and Derrida as critics of modernity who capitulate to the experience of aesthetic modernity and reject the modern world as 'young conservatives' — a procedure that has elicited spirited controversy (see Bernstein, 1985; Benhabib, 1984; Ryan, 1988).

Habermas concludes with expression of a fear that 'ideas of anti-modernity, together with an additional touch of premodernity, are becoming popular in the circles of alternative culture', and advances his own defence of modernity in opposition to these tendencies (Habermas, 1981: 14) — a position that became central to his *Lectures on the Philosophical Discourse of Modernity* (1987).

Habermas's attack on theories of postmodernism and defence of modernity is ambivalent. His attacks on the discourses of postmodernism frequently assume a guilt by association (with Nietzsche, Heidegger and fascism), and his defences of modernity, the Enlightenment and the universalist heritage of philosophy and reason, often fail to answer the strongest critiques of these discourses by Foucault, Derrida, Lyotard, Baudrillard and others. In addition, Habermas's Adornoesque use of ideology critique as negation fails to redeem in a Benjaminian redemptive hermeneutic those positive contributions found in New French Theory which Critical Theory might make use of (compare Habermas, 1979).

Indeed, Critical Theory has previously distinguished itself by being at the cutting edge of radical social theory, by conceptualizing new social conditions, practices and experiences, and by rethinking radical social theory and politics in the light of these new socio-historical conditions. Critical Theory always presented itself as a dialectical and historical social theory which attempts to capture and conceptualize historical changes in terms of its theories and concepts, and to appraise the impact of such changes for the socialist project and possibilities of human emancipation (Kellner, 1988a).

If it is the case that new socio-historical conditions, forms and experiences have emerged, then Critical Theory today should obviously analyse, criticize and conceptualize these phenomena, and should develop and rethink radical social theory and politics in the light of these changes. Most Critical Theorists, however, have not really confronted these challenges, and have either attacked postmodernist culture en masse from traditional Critical Theory positions (mostly Adorno's), or like Habermas have presented ideology critiques of the theories of postmodernism while defending modernity (see Kellner, 1988a). This is unfortunate for Critical Theory provides the framework, methodology and positions which could be used to develop a theory of the new social conditions which postmodern social theory points to without, arguably, adequately theorizing.

Indeed, there are important similarities and lines of contact between Critical Theory and postmodernist New French Theory.

Both Critical Theory and New French Theory agree, by and large, in their critiques of the boundaries of the academic division of labour, of traditional philosophy, and of ideology, though Critical Theory generally wants to draw and defend some boundaries, some categorical distinctions, which some postmodernists reject (I'm thinking here of Baudrillard's critiques of many categories of radical social theory that the Critical Theory would want to hold onto — class, dialectics, emancipation-domination etc. — or various French critiques of Habermas's lust for categorical distinctions, systematization and totalizing takes on history and society.) And Habermas and other Critical Theorists tend to reject the borderline between modernity and postmodernity that many New French theorists are eager to defend (i.e. Lyotard, Baudrillard and others). Indeed, Baudrillard at least would argue that changes in contemporary postmodern society obliterate in a series of implosions the boundaries that are central to critical theory (nature and history, the economic and political, true and false needs, high and low culture, emancipation and domination, left and right, etc. etc.). At stake, then, in confronting Critical Theory with New French Theory are *both* the fundamental categories and distinctions of radical social theory and the historical representation of the present age and its relation to the past and a possible future.

Conclusions, Problems, Tasks

The Critical Theory of the Frankfurt School therefore has yet to develop a theory of postmodernism beyond its denunciations of postmodern social theory and culture. Yet it remains an open question for radical social and cultural theory today as to whether the alleged rupture in history asserted by postmodernists is great enough to justify development of a postmodern social theory, or whether the whole discourse of postmodernism is itself ideological and reactionary. And if one assumes that new social conditions and developments are sufficiently comprehensive and significantly different to justify the claims for a rupture in history that one calls postmodernism, then one needs to choose between competing paradigms of postmodern social theory or to create a new one.

  Although there has been both a faddish embrace of the new theories of postmodernism and an equally fervent rejection of these theories — frequently predicated, I suspect, on reluctance to spend the time reading some difficult theoretical works which may subvert one's previous theoretical positions — I imagine that the postmodernism debate will be with us for a long time to come. There is a sense in many disciplines of the end of an era and there are equally compelling searches for new paradigms, new politics, and new theories (see Baynes, et al., 1987, for some of the efforts in the domain of philosophy). The postmodernism debate poses in a dramatic way the issue of competing paradigms for social theory and the need to choose paradigms that are most theoretically and practically applicable to social conditions in the present era. The debate also highlights the importance of social theory for a wide variety of debates within the arts, philosophy, politics and society. Although one wing of postmodernism wants to jettison, or dramatically revise, social theory, on the whole I think that the postmodernism debate highlights precisely the importance of social theory for a variety of disciplines and problems.

My own feeling is that while postmodern social theory is articulating real problems and posing important challenges to radical social theory and politics today, it is exaggerating the break, rupture and alleged novelty in the contemporary socio-historical epoch and is downplaying, and even occluding, the continuities. Adopting a term of Max Horkheimer, I would prefer to speak of a 'society in transition' rather than a completely new postmodern social formation. On the other hand, postmodern social theory is analysing some of the fundamental trends and future possibilities of our era and is confronting issues that require at least dramatic revision and updating of previous social theories (whether Marxian, Weberian, structural-functionalist, neo-conservative or whatever). While I do not believe that we should jettison all the grand theories of the past we certainly have to be careful in applying previous paradigms to contemporary conditions.

Finally, in light of the continued vitality and destructiveness of capitalism I would prefer to situate and analyse postmodernism in terms of a theory of techno-capitalism that would present the current social order in the capitalist countries as a synthesis of new technologies and capitalism that is characterized by new technical, social and cultural forms combining with capitalist relations of production to create the social matrix of our times (Kellner, 1988a). This move points to continuities with the social theories of the past (i.e. Marxism) and the need to revive, update, expand and develop previous theories in the light of contemporary conditions. Analysing the new configurations of capitalism and technology would allow emphasis on the new role of information, media, consumerism, the implosion of aesthetics and other themes stressed by post-modernists while situating these developments within a larger socio-historical frame. Theories of techno-capitalism would also allow specification of a radical politics as both anti-capitalist and cognizant of new technologies, social movements and political challenges. Radical politics could thus be at once macro and micro, and concerned to provide links between existing radical movements and to demonstrate the links between the existing problems of the present age. For utopia and catastrophe are both part of the post-modern scene and if hope in a better future is to be rationally justified it must be grounded in a theory of both the possibilities and dangers of the present age.

References

Barthes, Roland (1957) *Mythologies*. Paris: Editions du Seuil; translation, New York: Hill and Wang, 1962.

Baudrillard, Jean (1968) *Le Système des objects*. Paris: Denoel-Gonthier.

Baudrillard, Jean (1970) *La Société de consommation*. Paris: Gallimard.

Baudrillard, Jean (1972) *Pour une critique de l'économie politique du signe*. Paris: Gallimard; translated as *For a Critique of the Political Economy of the Sign*. St Louis: Telos Press, 1981.

Baudrillard, Jean (1976) *L'Echange symbolique et la mort*. Paris: Gallimard.

Baudrillard, Jean (1983a) *Simulations*. New York: Semiotext(e).

Baudrillard, Jean (1983b) *In the Shadow of the Silent Majorities*. New York: Semiotext(e).

Baudrillard, Jean (1984a) 'On Nihilism', *On the Beach* 6 (spring): 38–9.

Baudrillard, Jean (1984b) 'Game with Vestiges', *On the Beach* 5 (winter): 19–25.

Baynes, Kenneth, Bohman, James and McCarthy, Thomas (eds) (1987) *After Philosophy. End or Transformation?*. Cambridge, Mass.: MIT Press.

Bell, Daniel (1976) *The Coming of Post-Industrial Society*. New York: Basic Books.

Benhabib, Seyla (1984) 'The Epistemologies of Postmodernism', *New German Critique* 33: 103–26.

Bernstein, Richard (1985) *Philosophical Profiles: Essays in a Pragmatic Mode*. Cambridge: Polity Press.

Coward, Rosalind and Ellis, John (1977) *Language and Materialism*. London: Routledge & Kegan Paul.

Debord, Guy (1970) *The Society of the Spectacle*. Detroit: Black and Red.

Derrida, Jacques (1976) *Of Grammatology*. Baltimore: Johns Hopkins Press.

Derrida, Jacques (1981) *Positions*. Chicago: University of Chicago Press.

Foster, Hal (ed.) (1983) *The Anti-Aesthetic: Essays on Postmodern Culture*. Port Townsend, Washington: Bay Press.

Foucault, Michel (1970) *The Order of Things*. New York: Random House.

Foucault, Michel (1972) *The Archaeology of Knowledge*. New York: Harper and Row.

Habermas, Jürgen (1979) 'Consciousness-Raising or Redemptive Criticism', *New German Critique* 17: 30–59.

Habermas, Jürgen (1981) 'Modernity versus Postmodernity', *New German Critique* 22: 3–14.

Habermas, Jürgen (1984) *Theory of Communicative Action, Vol. 1*. Boston: Beacon Press.

Habermas, Jürgen (1987) *Lectures on the Philosophical Discourse of Modernity*. Cambridge, Mass.: MIT Press.

Huyssen, Andreas (1984) 'Mapping the Postmodern', *New German Critique* 33: 5–52.

Jameson, Fredric (1972) *The Prison House of Language*. Princeton: Princeton University Press.

Jameson, Fredric (1981) *The Political Unconscious*. Ithaca: Cornell University Press.

Jameson, Fredric (1984a) 'Postmodernism, or the Cultural Logic of Late Capitalism', *New Left Review* 146: 53–93.

Jameson, Fredric (1984b) 'Periodizing the '60s', in Sohnya Sayres et al. (eds) *The '60s Without Apology*. Minneapolis: University of Minnesota Press.

Jameson, Fredric (1986) 'Third-World Literature in the Era of Multinational Capitalism', *Social Text* 15.

Jameson, Fredric (1988) 'Cognitive Mapping', in Cary Nelson and Lawrence Grossberg (eds), *Marxism and the Interpretation of Culture*. Urbana and Chicago: University of Illinois Press.

Kellner, Douglas (1987) 'Baudrillard, Semiurgy and Death', *Theory, Culture & Society* 4 (1): 125–46.

Kellner, Douglas (1988a) *Critical Theory, Marxism, and Modernity: Development and Contemporary Relevance of the Frankfurt School*. Cambridge: Polity Press.

Kellner, Douglas (1988b) *Jean Baudrillard: From Marxism to Postmodernism and Beyond*. Cambridge: Polity Press.

Kroker, Arthur and Cook, David (1986) *The Postmodern Scene*. New York: Saint Martin's Press.

Lefebvre, Henri (1971) *Everyday Life in the Modern World*. New York: Harper and Row.

Lyotard, Jean-François (1971) *Discours, figure*. Paris: Klincksieck.

Lyotard, Jean-François (1984a) *The Postmodern Condition*. Minneapolis: University of Minnesota Press.

Lyotard, Jean-François (1984b) *Driftworks*. New York: Semiotext(e).

Lyotard, Jean-François and Thébaud, Jean-Loup (1985) *Just Gaming*. Minneapolis: University of Minnesota Press.

Mandel, Ernst (1975) *Late Capitalism*. London: New Left Books.

Rorty, Richard (1979) *Philosophy and the Mirror of Nature*. Princeton: Princeton University Press.

Ryan, Michael (1988) *Culture and Politics*. London: Macmillan.

Douglas Kellner is Professor of Philosophy at the University of Texas at Austin. His latest books *Critical Theory, Marxism and Modernity* and *Jean Baudrillard* will soon be published by Polity Press.

Introduction to Lyotard

Dick Veerman

We can subdivide the writings of the French philosopher Jean-François Lyotard (born 1924, Versailles) into two main periods. The doctoral thesis *Discours, figure* (1971) opens the first period. *Economie libidinale* (1974) closes it. In the intervening period Lyotard published *Dérive à partir de Marx et Freud* and *Des Dispositifs pulsionnels* (both 1973), two collections of essays written between 1968 and 1973. From 1975 onwards we can speak of the second period. Amongst its most important articles and books I count the following: *Instructions païennes* (1977), *Au juste* (1979, conversations with Jean-Loup Thébaud), *The Postmodern Condition* (1979), 'Answering the Question: What is Postmodernism?' (1982), 'Judicieux dans le différend' (1982, published 1985), *Le Différend* (1983), *L'Enthousiasme, la critique kantienne de l'histoire* (1986), 'Grundlagenkrise' (1986), 'Sensus communis' (1987), 'L'Intérêt du sublime' (1987) and *Que peindre?* (1987) (for complete references, see the interview).

I shall try to summarize Lyotard's intellectual development in a few lines. From 1954 to 1964 he had been a member of the critical Marxist group *Socialisme ou barbarie*. In 1964 he joined another group, *Pouvoir ouvrier*, which he left only two years later. It would mean the end of his direct political commitment and the starting point of his brilliant philosophical career.

In *Discours, figure* Lyotard develops the metaphysics of a kind of truth without negation. 'Truth' means here the real truth as it exists in itself. The word does not refer to the relational notion of truth (truth as a successful correspondence between word and world, i.e. as an *adaequatio rei et intellectus*). Lyotard shows that we cannot possibly found the meaning and/or reference of a proposition ontologically and at the same time see the clear meaning of the foundational act. If we persist in trying to find ontological rock bottom, we shall inevitably lose the capacity to distinguish between truth

Theory, Culture & Society (SAGE, London, Newbury Park, Beverly Hills and New Delhi), Vol. 5 (1988), 271–75

and falsehood: 'falsehood' will have to correspond to something which is positively true in the world 'out there'.

Lyotard develops his metaphysics by criticizing Merleau-Ponty (especially *Le visible et l'invisible*, 1964) and by modelling his criticism after the death instinct of Freud's *Beyond the Pleasure Principle* (1920). The result does away with dichotomy. Oppositions collapse in what the idiom of *Economie libidinale* calls 'la grande pellicule éphémère'. In this book we find a much more exclusive interest in *Beyond the Pleasure Principle*; Merleau-Ponty's influence is apparently absent.

In *Economie libidinale* the metaphysics Lyotard had set out in *Discours, figure* turns out to imply a deadly critique of the ethico-social truths of Marxist political theory. This is because no criterion, no proposition stating this and not that, can possibly be true (or false). Since Marxist political theory appeals to the truth of a historical ideal it finds itself in a predicament. The truths which supposedly legitimize Marxist political action are no better than the falsehoods it would wish to combat. The political — or in fact anti-political — upshot of the metaphysics of Lyotard's first period is this: we cannot take one political stand rather than another, since the correct one cannot be decided.

Nevertheless, there is a problem. In *Au juste* Lyotard argues that his earlier metaphysics did not adequately deal with the problem of justice. For example: person A thinks that x means a whereas person B thinks it means b. Who is right? This is not just a theoretical question. Its impact is profoundly important in social life: A would like to oblige B to act according to interpretation a while B would want to make A act according to b. Here we have a question to which the first Lyotard would have to respond that x means both a and b since we cannot make a difference between them. We are obliged to dwell upon the problem, yet we *need* a decision, we have to judge a or b since human actions are discriminate and since A might do injustice to B or vice versa. The first Lyotard, however, cannot decide the problem.

What gives A (or B) the right to let his judgment prevail? We are asking for the legitimacy of his judgment. Outside the field of ontology, Kant had tried to establish precisely the kind of legitimacy needed to help us out here. Kant's critical philosophy of the faculties of the human mind defines validity (and not the 'successful correspondence' and most certainly not the 'truth', in the ontological sense) of judgments in terms of Human Interest (which necessarily imply distinctions of the kind between *a* and *b*: we in order to desire anything we must be able to point it out). In doing so, Kant comes up with a model. Judgments are legitimate if they correspond to a valid judgment in the model. The question is, of course: why is the model valid? That, according to Lyotard in the more recent writings of his second period, is precisely the question Kant deals with in his third *Critique* and in the so-called historical and political texts (e.g. 'What is Enlightenment?', 'Idea for a Universal History with Cosmopolitan Intent', 'Eternal Peace'). The model is valid, i.e. legitimate, not because it is produced by the interests of subjective reflexivity but because empirical data can confirm — though never prove — the product of subjective reflexivity.

Both the structure and aims of Kant's argument as Lyotard interprets it are rather complex. I can only try to be as clear as possible in this short sketch. Let us start from what we already know: in the end only a teleology of human interest can explain why we think, do and feel the way we do. Thinking, doing and feeling are the respective topics of the *Critique of Pure Reason*, the *Critique of Practical Reason* and the *Critique of Judgment*. As is well known, the workings and objects of the three critical reasons are very much different. Lyotard says they are 'incommensurable' (or 'heterogeneous'). The famous and crucial example is presented by the difference between Kantian Intellect (*Verstand*, which centres on the objective data presented to it by *Anschauung*) on the one hand and Kantian Reason (*Vernunft*, which, being autonomous and self-productive, deals solely with subjectivity) on the other.

Thus far, Lyotard goes along with Kant's dictum: 'It is not possible to throw a bridge from the one realm to the other.' He turns away from Kant, criticizing him with his own analytical tools, at the point where the third *Critique* seeks to bridge the gap anyhow — in order to guarantee the validity of the model for valid judgments critical philosophy presents us — thus violating the incommensurable realms of the critical reasons.

Lyotard criticizes Kant for his tendency to forget his critical rigour when he writes:

> In accordance with the concept of freedom the effect is the final end which (or the manifestation of which in the sensible world) is to exist and this presupposes the condition of the possibility of that end in nature (that is in the nature of the subject as a being of the sensible world, or man). It is so presupposed *a priori*, and without regard to the practical, by judgment. This faculty, with the concept of the finality of nature, provides us with the mediating concept between concepts of

nature and the concept of freedom — a concept that makes possible the transition
from the pure and theoretical [laws of understanding] to the pure practical [laws
of reason] and from conformity to law in accordance with the former to final ends
according to the latter. For through that concept we conceive of the possibility of
the final end that can only be actualized in nature and in harmony with its laws.
(Kant, 1970: 411)

However, critical philosophy cannot allow the actual reality of the
teleology of the final human goal implied here by Kant. Kant,
Lyotard reminds us, can only succeed 'as-if', as his own tools make
clear. He cannot subsume the whole lot of critical reasons under the
concept (in fact the ideal) of a natural teleology for that subsumption does not obtain in the way the schematism of *Verstand* subsumes data under a concept (the categories), that is by a determining judgment. Judgments rendered by the faculty of judgment
moulding data to the ideal of a natural end can only be reflective,
'as-if': only *regulated* by an ideal, *not determined* by a concept.

That is not all Lyotard has to say on Kant. The historical facts of
our century can no longer corroborate the (regulative) philosophy
of history Kant's teleology demands in order to be legitimate.

Kant tries to make plausible his philosophy of history in the
historical and political texts. The European peoples of the eighteenth century had met the French Revolution with enthusiasm.
'Liberté, fraternité, égalité' — the ideal of the universal unity of
mankind — had been appealing even to those who likely would not
benefit from the 1789 implementation of this catch-phrase. For
Kant this revolutionary enthusiasm had been a 'sign' of the kind he
indicated in his *Contest of Faculties*, the *signum historicum*. Since it
is indicative of the fact that the empirical (but Interest-related)
world corroborates the goals for which the autonomous subject is
striving, the sign tells us that we may have confidence that unity is
actually forthcoming. But *we* cannot cling to this corroborated
ideal, Lyotard says. 'Auschwitz' provokes a horror-enthusiasm
against unity. 'Solidarity' (the Polish trade union), 'May 1968', 'The
Prague Spring' probably confront the philosopher of history with
positively tuned signs of the same *sentiment* — a sentiment corrob-
orating the fact that history is not the product of a unifying teleology
but rather of many complex and incommensurable teleologies. That
is why Lyotard takes up the case for 'incommensurability' and
'heterogeneity' in science, society and aesthetic experience. He
cannot, however, impose his views, he cannot tell us who is right.
And that is precisely what he wants to make clear, for the same

thing goes for others and for this clarifying point itself. The right thing to do is a question we must not expect to provide an easy answer.

To conclude, I should like to add two short remarks on Lyotard's relation toward Habermas and Rorty. The German philosopher and sociologist Jürgen Habermas, as Lyotard reads him, clings to the very regulative unity which Lyotard no longer thinks appropriate for our times. Now that we experience heterogeneity, what could possibly make plausible the ideal of the political Enlightenment? Lyotard discusses this point at length in *L'Enthousiasme*.

Richard Rorty thinks we ought to give up 'Philosophy'. Philosophers are to cooperate with historians, sociologists, literary critics etc. in order to produce 'great big pictures'. Why? 'In order to get something done', Rorty answers. In the case of persons A and B, we cannot go on discussing who is 'right' for ever. This pragmatist line of argument does not seem to interest Lyotard. He would rather renew the question at the point where Rorty abolishes it: if we decide in favour of A, will we also have done justice to B? What about the justice rendered? Probably the question between Rorty and Lyotard is the following: even if it is hard to come by answers, can we decide to stop doing Philosophy? We can at least question justice. Anyhow, it is the best thing we can do in order to respect the problem of justice. The problem is legitimacy, not practical need. How else are we to arm ourselves against the needs of others, is the question Lyotard proposes.

Reference

Kant, I. (1970) ' "Introduction" to the *Critique of Judgement*', in A. Zweig (ed.) *The Essential Kant*. New York: Mentor.

Dick Veerman teaches Philosophy at the University of Utrecht.

Society, Culture, and Urbanization

S N Eisenstadt and **A Shachar** *Hebrew University of Jerusalem*

Eisenstadt and Shachar provide new insights into the ways in which the process of urbanization has taken place over time and across different cultures and societies. It is the first comparative analysis of cities and urban hierarchies to be undertaken jointly by a sociologist and a geographer. The authors believe that it is not only possible, but necessary, to combine the different approaches and analytical tools of sociology and geography into a common analytical framework.

Society, Culture and Urbanization presents a broad comparative study of the historical context within which modes of spatial organization and urbanization develop. It challenges and enlarges the boundaries by which we understand the evolution of cities over time, space, and within vastly different social and cultural environments.

Readership

Researchers and graduate students in urban studies, sociological theory, comparative analysis of civilizations, macrosociology, cultural anthropology, and architectural historians

April 1987 ● 392 pages
Cloth (8039-2478-X)

Sage Publications Ltd
28 Banner Street, London EC1Y 8QE
Sage Publications Inc
2111 West Hillcrest Drive, Newbury Park CA 91320, USA

An Interview with Jean-François Lyotard

Willem van Reijen and Dick Veerman

Q. 1: Monsieur Lyotard, as you have said several times (Lyotard, 1985a: 229; 1986a: 37, 45) you now think that you have moved beyond the language-game approach of The Postmodern Condition *(1979a); speaking of* Le Différend *(1984a), you have said that this is 'your book of philosophy'. Do you think that the polemic stirred up by your association with* The Postmodern Condition *has distracted attention from your other writings, and in particular from* Le Différend?

A. 1: Has *The Postmodern Condition* effaced or occluded *Le Différend*? The answer is yes. The former book effectively provoked a number of polemics. I did not expect that; nor was it what I was looking for. But, on reflection, it is understandable. I mean that, having been presented with the usage of this term, borrowed, as I explained, from American literary criticism and the crisis of modernism in the arts, especially architecture and painting, one might have expected that on that side at least there might be some reaction. The reason for this is that I take the term in a sense which is completely different from that which is generally accepted in these matters, from its designation as the end of modernism. I have said and will say again that 'postmodern' signifies not the end of modernism, but another relation to modernism. On the other hand, if we turn to the philosophers, *The Postmodern Condition* was received by them rather as a book which sought to put an end to philosophical reflection as it had been established by Enlightenment rationalism. But what is certain is that *The Postmodern Condition* is not a book of philosophy. It is rather a book which is very strongly marked by sociology, by a certain historicism, and by epistemology. These were the subjects which were imposed on me by the task of providing a report on the actual state of the sciences in the advanced countries. The philosophical basis of the report could not be elabo-

Theory, Culture & Society (SAGE, London, Newbury Park, Beverly Hills and New Delhi), Vol. 5 (1988), 277–309

rated there; and, besides, I explained that in my small introduction to the book. I think that the philosophical basis of *The Postmodern Condition* will be found, directly or indirectly, in *Le Différend*. As to the latter book, I developed it at length, very slowly, starting on it immediately after the publication of *Economie libidinale* (so it took me ten years), and resuming there the philosophical readings of the great tradition because these readings appeared to me to be indispensable. These readings only appear to a very limited extent in *The Postmodern Condition*.

Q. 2: You ascribe to certain American and, especially, German philosophers (Lyotard, 1984b: 81) a rationalist or consensualist terror. These philosophers, in their turn, reproach you for being irrationalist and for betraying the positive side — this hard-won baby did not have to be thrown out with the dirty bath-water — of the Enlightenment and the 1789 revolution. What do you think about these allegations of irrationalism, and of the stigmatization that accompanies them?

A. 2: I think that, in effect, a part of the attack against the position developed in *The Postmodern Condition* — my critics generally not having read the other works — bears the marks of a summary and totalizing idea of reason. I would oppose them simply with the following principle (which seems to me much more rationalist than they think): there is no reason, only reasons. And here I can draw support from the example, from the model, if I may put it that way, of Kant. I can follow the line of Kantian thought, and also, to a very large extent, that of Wittgensteinian thought. Finding or trying to elaborate the rules which make the discourse of knowledge, for example, possible — rules which we know to be under a general regime where truth or falsehood is at stake — is not the same thing as trying to elaborate the rules of a discourse, for example ethics, whose regime is one where good or evil, justice or injustice are at stake; nor is it the same thing for the discourse of aesthetics whose field of play is defined by the question of beauty or ugliness (or, at least, lack of beauty).

These rules are quite different. By 'quite different' I mean that the presuppositions which are necessary, which are accepted as prerequisites for successful participation in one field or another, their *a priori* conditions — by this I mean the *a priori* conditions of, let us call them, in a very wide sense, phrases (we could also call them acts of language, although this seems to me even more confusing than 'phrase') — are not the same. This is what Kant shows when he passes from the first to the second *Critique*. It is clear that reason in its, as Kant puts it, theoretic or theoretical usage is quite different from reason in its practical usage. It is not the same thing, on the one hand, conceptually to subsume the sensible given which is already preformed, or if you prefer, preschematized by the sensibility, which is to say by the imagination, as it is; and on the other hand, to hold oneself accountable to the demands of the moral law, that is to say, to be obliged, without interest, to allow this law to prescribe, in principle, those objects of interest which are defined as good, whether as phrases or acts — at the same time as, in actual fact, the definition of those acts or phrases as good remains, as you know, dependent on the reflexive judgment. And if one takes the example of aesthetics, one would have no difficulty in showing that the regime of phrases concerning beauty and non-beauty is again quite different for Kant, since it is here a question of, as he puts it, a state of mind, which is to say of a sentiment, an elementary form, one might say, of the reflexive judgment.

As we think through this side of Kant's thought (and it is also possible to find an analogue in the late work of Wittgenstein), it is easy to show that it is never a question of *one* massive and unique reason — that is nothing but an ideology. On the contrary, it is a question of *plural* rationalities, which are, at the least, respectively, theoretical, practical, aesthetic. They are profoundly heterogeneous, 'autonomous' as Kant says. The inability to think this is the hallmark of the great idealist rationalism of nineteenth-century German thought, which presupposes without any explication that reason is the same in all cases. It is a sort of identitarianism which forms a pair with a totalitarianism of reason, and which, I think, is simultaneously erroneous and dangerous.

Let me add two further things to this first reply. The first is that the rationalism of the Enlightenment and of the 1789 revolution was infinitely more subtle than my critics recognize. If I examine, for example, the thought of someone like Diderot, who in my view is probably the most eminent of French Enlightenment thinkers, perhaps more so than Rousseau, it is extremely evident that his 'rationalism' is infinitely complex. I cannot enlarge upon this here and now — it is one of the projects that I have always had in mind, and I do not know if the gods will grant me the time to pursue it properly. But my intention would be to show both the complexity of this rationalism and how it incorporates elements — that is to say those elements of rationality which do not subordinate their arguments to the end of *consensus* — which are totally excluded from the current American-German version.

The other thing that I would wish to add, and we remain here on the same territory, is that today there is a generally recognized 'crisis' of what is called reason in the sciences. I am speaking of the hard sciences. The names of Kuhn and Feyerabend come to mind in connection with this crisis. I am probably not in agreement with the whole scheme of thought of these celebrated epistemologists; but, since the middle of the nineteenth century, the question of what is rational in mathematics and the sciences of animate and inanimate nature is an open one. This question has such force that it even affects the nature, whether rational or non-rational, of space and time. What has been called 'the crisis of the foundations' is not something that can be neglected today to the pretended advantage of a consensus of arguments, when this consensus is precisely what is missing from the interior of the, let us say physical, sciences. And far from suppressing the possibility, contrary to what might be thought, this absence of consensus has, on the contrary, only worked to allow a more rapid and more impressive development of the sciences. I am thinking, for example, of the discussion between Einstein, who was in a certain way a classical rationalist, a Leibnizian we might say, and the Danes, who showed themselves to be very adventurous in these matters, or, again, with Louis de Broglie.

What conclusions can we draw, bearing in mind that I am not competent to go any further in this direction? I would say one thing, which is that the crisis of reason has been precisely the bath in which scientific reason has been immersed for a century, and this crisis, this continual interrogation of reason, is certainly the most rational thing around. In the deepest sense, it is there, in this 'critical' — in the two senses of the term — movement, that I would like to situate my thought.

(Coup didactique, I)

Van Reijen and Veerman: In your 1985 interview with Bernard Blistène, you accept the qualification that he makes of you as a philosopher who shows something (Lyotard, 1985b: 62). Since Discours, figure (1971) and the essays which surround that intricate book, you seem to appear as an aesthetician rather than a philosopher; you present something to the senses instead of trying to recover and articulate that which isn't said in what you say. Three years ago, you yourself remarked on the continuity which exists from your first to your most recent writing (Lyotard, 1984d: 17), notably between the figural of Discours, figure *and the has-it-happened-yet which is introduced in* Le Différend. *Your writings could be summed up by saying that they all bear witness to the monster of truth and of good which exists outside of discourse and its oppositional values, outside of our languages, whether denotative or axiological, and the criteria which define them, but that a refusal of articulation is achieved by a discursive skewing. This monstrosity — which is nothing other than being — has access to the discourse at the critical moment, which is to say at the moment that the discourse cannot manage to sustain and continue itself out of its own resources. Thus we have the 'line', the figure of* Discours, figure: *is it a place of intensity (a notion fundamental to* Economie libidinale *(1974) or a place within the discourse of ontico-ontological being (completely destroying it, which is to say crushing it under its enormous weight); thus we have the has-it-happened-yet: isn't this the uncertain but inescapable moment which precedes the chaining (up) of one phrase to another, and which is characterized by the anguishing embarrassment of choice with regard to the kind of discourse which will fix the regime of the phrase with which I am now confronted, and to which I must fasten myself?*

It is here that the possibility of articulating being is arrested, at the point which precedes its articulation and which is never itself articulated. And it is here that we discover that, at the most, we can bear witness for being, and for the revolution that it implies; to articulate it is to have lost it. Now, with his notion of the sublime, Kant tried to think within the world, as it were, what could not be presented there, in other words, what could not be recovered and therefore articulated and demonstrated. Kant's mode of thought here is symbolic; it is a question of alluding to something impresentable. In the text which clearly parodies the title of Kant's piece on the Enlightenment — 'Answering the question: what is postmodernism' (Lyotard, 1984c) — you indicate that from the time of the Enlightenment two paths are open. The symbolic stress may be placed on the powerlessness of the faculty or presentation, and therefore on nostalgia for what is absent. It may, on the other hand, be placed on the power of the faculty of imaginative understanding, which results in a 'growth of being' accompanied by 'jubilation' — which is simultaneously an expression of delight and anguish — at the creative achievement of the imagina-

tion, at its invention of new ideas and symbolic presentations, which is to speak of, in your Kantian-Wittgensteinian idiom, 'new rules of the game, pictural, artistic, or whatever'. These remarks betray the interest which you have maintained since the late seventies in the aesthetic reflections of the Critique of Judgement.

If we restrict ourselves to the Kantian vocabulary — to which, in part, a brief remark in 1977 (Lyotard, 1977: 36) and the dialogues of Au juste *(Lyotard, 1979b) mark your manifest passage for the first time — you must opt for the second path, and bear witness for the unthought, for the difference from what has been thought, for the other (should we write Other?) of thought. It will not be a question of dealing with what comes along in so far as it is articulable, but of giving sensible form to what is there before discursive thought. It will be as a witness for the ineffable (in a sense which may be neither nostalgic nor melancholic) nature of the ontological and essential ground of discourse.*

The writings of your 'first period' which run from Discours, figure *to* Economie libidinale *inclusively provide parallel evidence. The 'line' in the former book and the 'tensor' in the latter relate to a point of arrival, an event (in the sense of* ereignen[1]*), without which that which has arrived can never be presented, receding before its moment of demonstration. As in* Le Différend, *you are not looking to recover this ontological thing, whatever it may be. In* Discours, figure, *you write with a feeling of regret which is different to the melancholia and nostalgia which defines the first Kantian path: 'This book is not an honest book, it remains within the field of signification; deconstruction [which assumes the burden of ontological difference — D.V.] does not take place here directly, it is signified' (p. 18). In* Economie libidinale, *in a more radical, even ecstatic vein, it is said, straight away: 'No need to criticise metaphysics ... since such criticism presupposes and continually recreates that very theatricality [of the representation which tries to recover the "thing" — D.V.], better to be inside and forget it.' (p. 11)*

We would like to cite several passages from Le Différend, *which is at the centre of your 'second period', in order to show the analogy — non-melancholic but sensitive — between your first and most recent writings, in respect of which the common aim is defined as, following your formulation in 'Sensus communis' (Lyotard, 1987b), the undoing of the mind.*

As to what remains unarticulated:

113. Can we specify the presentation comprised in the phrase *being*? But this is a presentation, or: what in the case of a phrase is the case ... Not being, but a being, once only.

114. ... The phrase which ... presents [being] itself comprises a presentation that it does not present. Can it even be said that it escapes, or differs from itself? That would presuppose that it is the same over several phrases....

126. ... In ... addressing [the absolute presentation comprised by a phrase] you present it. That is why the absolute is not presentable. With the sublime ... Kant was always right over Hegel. The sublime persists, not beyond, but in the heart of the *Aufgehobenen*.

As to the confusing force of the ontological difference which results from this:

136. To link or chain together is necessary, a series is not ...

147. From one phrase regime (descriptive, cognitive, prescriptive, evaluative, interrogative ...) to another, a connection may not always be relevant. It is not appropriate to connect *Open the door* with *You have laid down a prescription* or *What a beautiful door!* ... The type of discourse fixes the rule for the linking of phrases ... This may provide the opportunity for irrelevant connections so as to produce such and such an effect. Teleology begins with the genres of discourse ...

150. The error implied in the last judgment: *After this I will say, there is nothing more to say* — But you say it! ...

151. ... We can never know about the *Ereignis*. What idiom does this phrase come from, from what regime? The mistake is always to anticipate, that is to say, to forbid.

Jean-François Lyotard: I would like to make some observations on this *coup didactique* before passing to the next question. I admire its precision, and, if I may say, the svelteness of your argument. Overall, I find myself in agreement with what you say. I would simply like to make some points more precise.

I really do not use, in the way you suggest, the word 'revolution' in the phrase '*it is here that we discover that, at the most, we can bear witness for being, and for the revolution that it implies*'. I do not see exactly what you understand by this word, but I will not discuss it now.

A second observation is inspired by the following phrase: '*Kant's mode of thought here is symbolic; it is a question of alluding to something unpresentable.*' I know that I have often used this term; it appears in the title of a text to which I have signed my name. But the title: 'Presenting the Impresentable' (Lyotard, 1982) was made up by the American revue, *Artforum*, it was not my title, and I could never have written it. 'Unpresentable' is a Kantian term, but I should like to make a comment, itself Kantian, about it.

In the third *Critique*, Kant observed that it is always necessary to distinguish between two sorts of presentation, or exposition, as he put it. It is not only necessary to differentiate between two forms of exposition, but also between two forms of absence (Kant, 1970: 19, para 57, note 1).

Firstly, with regard to exposition, Kant says that it is important to see that there are two styles of exposition. One of them is argumentation, and he calls this the *modus logicus*, or simply the mode (or method), and this is, in the final analysis, a procedure of connection which employs the operations of rational logic. But there is, he says, another form of exposition, which he calls the *modus estheticus* or the 'manner' (Kant, 1970: para 57). Kant says that presentation can proceed by focusing on manner, through an exposition centred on the form and not on the concept to be displayed. In this case, he explains, the unity to be exposed finds itself in the spatio-temporal organization of the exposition itself. This is the open gateway into the arts, whose modes of exposition, seen in this way, and while without doubt not at the same level as the philosophico-logical method, must in every case be taken into account when addressing the unpresentable.

Turning now to the second distinction, which is also Kantian, but which does not seem to be properly attended to in your commentary. It is a question of the distinction between ideas of the imagination and ideas of reason. For example, when you speak of '*the creative achievement of the imagination, of its invention of new ideas and symbolic presentations*', I think you cover over too quickly the distinction that I have in mind. The ideas of reason are truly indemonstrable — I use the Kantian term — in the sense that one cannot show the intuitions corresponding to them. We agree about this. But the ideas of the imagination are, on the contrary, inscribed in the presentation. They are suggested by the presentation itself, or they are immanent to it and are there for all that, and such is their mode of absence, inexplicable as Kant writes: they cannot be articulated logically (thus it is that we must return to the *modus estheticus* or 'manner').

I think that this distinction is important because it makes us reconsider with more precision the very notion of the unpresentable. The way in which an idea of reason, say liberty or the absolute, is unpresentable is not the same as the 'manner' of an idea of the imagination, which is a sort of type or monogramme (these terms are equally Kantian), which, if it can be put this way, expresses itself in the arrangement of sensible materials through creative forms — it is not the same therefore as the 'manner' in which this idea is suggested in the work of art or in the natural landscape. You see that the unpresentable there is not to be taken in the sense of the 'indemonstrable', which is to say unshowable by reason, or at least unshowable by the intuition in accordance with reason, but that it is a question of the unpresentable as inexplicable in at least the sense that it cannot be rationally articulated.

My third remark concerns the use you make of the notion of an *'ontological and essential ground of discourse'*. I should tie this to the critique of the usage of the term *Grund* in the very citations from *Le Différend* that you have happily provided. Numbers 113 and 114, with some others, precisely distance themselves from the notion of a ground which would be ineffably the same, the unthought as a unity which thought could never attain. I think that it is important to keep one's distance from such a notion of the unthought, whose being would be singular. We have no means of sustaining the thesis that its being is singular. Except that in naming being as such, we already, so to speak, employ the singular; and we forget that singularity denotes plurality, as I have explained in *Le Différend* (p. 9).

I think that it is important, at least to distinguish between the usage which would precisely universalize the singular (or its definite article), *the being*, and a usage which is on the contrary singularizing: *this being, this time*. But I think that, above all, it would be preferable not to use the term being very much at all. In consequence, with regard to your *'ontological and essential ground of discourse'*, I would object at once that 'ontological' and 'essential' are not appropriate to qualify the term. The situation may be entirely contrary. Above all it is a question of withdrawing from the very possibility of an ontology.

Q. 3: How do you establish today the relationship which exists between the positive sensibility of the authentic ontological force, at the heart of which you used to appeal to the 'line', and that which you call, in 'Judicieux dans le différend', the ontological well-being of the second path of the sublime, which, to read you, is the properly

Kantian result of the 'critique of critique'? This question contains another, which, if you will permit us, we will add straight away.

We refer here to your evidence for the other of discourse. This other is present but ineffable, absenting itself from the product of the discursive process. In an interview in 1970 (Lyotard, 1970: 228–9), entirely in the style of Discours, figure, *you criticize the Derridean notions of 'trace' and 'archi-writing' for being unable to take any account of the positive presence of the other in relation to discourse. It seems to us that, for example, your comment on Kant's critical aesthetic: '. . . the critical aesthetic, at the same time as it is wound up with the decline of metaphysics, opens and reopens the way to ontology.' Lyotard (1986b: 13) makes the same point. Of course, we do not forget that the point of departure of* Discours, figure *was linguistic (on page 11 of that book, we read, 'We must start from where we are: in the heart of words'); but given that the approach of your recent work puts the emphasis on 'phrases' rather than on ontology, and that because of this it has become more rigorously 'discursive', isn't there a danger of your arriving at an ontology of absence such as you found in Derrida?*

A. 3: I do not really understand the first part of this question, but would repeat the reservations which I have with regard to the usage of the term 'ontological', and would also refer to the two paths of the sublime with which I have been concerned for some years now, and, as you remind me, appear to me to stand in need of re-examination today. Let me pass rather to the last part of your question; it is a very good question, and raises difficult matters. To get straight to the point, the question concerns my relation to Derrida's thought. You ask whether I run the risk of committing myself to the kind of ontology of absence that is found in Derrida. Obviously I must begin by explaining my reservations with regard to this ontology.

I think that the notion of absence is itself deconstructed in and by Derrida's thought; it is rendered undecidable there. That any being whatever may be absent, and this applies all the more strongly to being itself, is in my view an idea that is much too simple, for at least the absence of being is present, being presents itself *in absentia*, and if it is absent, this is *in presentia* (to the extent that these terms still retain some meaning in Derridean thought). If there is a variation between my thought and Derrida's, it is expressed in the extension given to the idea of difference.

It seems to me that Derrida brings difference into play over all genres, all phrases, all linkages, as I would put it — excuse me for employing a vocabulary which is mine rather than his; I do this to make myself understood to my questioners. To make difference cover everything, to show or exhibit the difference in all kinds of linkages, in all kinds of phrases, there is a risk (I speak of *risk*, which is also a courting of difference) of being accused of scepticism. In any event, I do not regard such accusations as well founded. It is not that it would be wrong, *a priori*, to be sceptical; there is no need to tremble before such an accusation. Rather it is necessary to examine if it is right to make that accusation: how well has it been argued? Here I will open a parenthesis which will recall an intervention which Derrida made — in an open letter, for he was absent — at the International College of Philosophy on the occasion of a paper given by Karl-Otto Apel. Derrida was indignant, in any event he jibbed, against the lack of care in reading which characterized most of our critiques. Against this eagerness to locate us among such cases, to label us, to fix our place among those families of thought which are openly and mutually hostile, and which will therefore at once go on to the attack, all the evidence, once it is surveyed, shows that what is said is not at issue. It is fantasies which are attacked, not the *texts themselves* which ought to have been read. I close the parenthesis.

To return to the question of my relationship to Derrida's thought, I would say that the notion of difference mainly rests upon, it seems to me, an idea of time which comes from the transcendental deduction of the first *Critique* as it was deployed by Heidegger from his book on Kant to his essay on Husserl's 'Internal Time-consciousness'. This notion of time — which can be shown, following Heidegger, to come down to the place of the subject, a subject which, as Derrida has never failed to stress, is evidently never given in itself, but perpetually lacks and differs from itself — is assuredly the schema of all schemas, that is to say the form of all internal syntheses of the given. Now this form of the synthesis of the given is elaborated in the *Critique of Theoretical Reason*; it is subordinated to a language-game, let us say, in which truth and falsehood are at stake. If we examine the question of temporality in the second *Critique*, for example, that is to say ethical temporality, difficulties of quite another kind are immediately encountered; they concern the time of obligation.

But in the third *Critique*, it is very clear that the minute examination of the syntheses at play in the aesthetic sensibility, in taste, without speaking of the Analytic of the sublime, bring us to the conclusion that temporality there is completely different again from the first *Critique*. Here it is not at all a matter of a self which is perpetually different from itself. Rather it is a question of something like a suspension of the kinds of temporal syntheses examined in the first *Critique* — I refer to three kinds of synthesis, those of apprehension, reproduction and recognition — owing to the fact that in the aesthetic judgment it can be a question neither of recognition nor even of reproduction. I would add that apprehension itself is understood in a most rudimentary and minimal way, at least in the Analytic of the sublime, where the comprehension of the given seems like a request which is beyond the synthetic capacities of the imagination. And so one is led to 'conceive', for the beautiful as well as for the sublime (even though totally different in the two cases), an aesthetic temporality which would not at all be of the order of difference, which would defer not to the *durchlaufen* of the first *Critique*, but to a state of time which, in comparison with that of difference, would appear as a suspension or an 'interdiction', which would be in sum a sort of 'interruption' of difference itself.

I would say one thing more, to try and make myself understood quickly (and badly as a result). This refers to what I have been able to write in recent works concerning the visual arts, especially painting (but sketched out earlier in regard to the cinema (Lyotard, 1978)). It seems to me that precisely what is important in aesthetic time is what can be called 'presence'. Not in the sense of the present, nor in the sense of what is there, but in that sense in which, on the contrary, the activity of the very minimal synthesis of the given into the very forms which are free (forms properly speaking, not merely schemas) is suspended. It would be a question of a kind of, let us say, spasm or stasis (it does not matter which word of that genre) which has a relation, I think, with a 'direct' access not to the meaning of the situation (which is the case with the forms), but to the material. One would be on this side of the synthetic activity by means of forms, in a relation with the great X, to use the Kantian term, with that enigmatic *Mannigfaltigkeit*, that diversity, that *poikilon*. — I have wondered for a long time why the material is always presented as a diversity, a mixture, but it is obviously on account of the obsession to safeguard the unifying activity of mind. In the 'strongly' aesthetic moments (but what does that mean? They are at the same time the weakest moments for mind seen as a power of synthesis), it would perhaps be a matter of a non-mediated relationship with the material, without even the most elementary synthetic activity.

This is not so enigmatic. It is very clear that the usage made of colour, by someone like Barnett Newman, the great, postwar American painter (labelled an expressionist although one wonders why), or someone like your compatriot, Karel Appel (also a very great painter, although very different), shows that what is important to both is not the form within which colour is held captive, like a material which depended on its form to be made presentable, but very much to the contrary it is a question of material-colour having in itself a power to suspend the formative activity of mind. This sort of painting calls to mind what musicians call *timbre*. You know that when they speak of timbre, musicians happily use metaphors borrowed from the visual arts. We can speak of the colour or the chromatism of a sound — independent of the note or the duration or intensity of the sound — as it is produced by this or that instrument, even, I would say in general, by this or that impact, or percussion in the wide sense.

One of the current aims of my work is to show that there is, I would not say an ontology, but a mode of relation to something which is very certain within the given, but which also transcends those very empty forms within which the given is habitually synthesized. It is there that I would find presence, in short, a kind of stupefaction or stupidity suspending the activity of mind. This 'stupefaction' should be understood in relation to what I have called elsewhere 'obedience' or 'soul' (the latter term being employed by Kant). Nevertheless, it remains the case that this presence, which cannot be a presence since truly the mind is absent from it, is not a theme which is compatible with Kant, except perhaps in certain passages of the text on the sublime. At least, the time of the sublime, of its presence, is neither accountable nor appreciable in terms of the apperceptive synthesis; the latter's deferrals are not to be found there.

(Coup didactique, II)
Van Reijen and Veerman: In Le Différend, *No. 126, you criticize Kant's melancholic presentation of totality. The force of his critique would result only in failure, as you say in arguing against Gérard Raulet. The critique would consist in the oscillation of judgments 'on the line of division between genres' (Lyotard, 1986a: 110). Your*

'reply' explains that there is a difference between the aesthetic of the sublime, in the sense of the first path — which according to Kant is a mode of presentation of the existent, or in the case of the absolute totality, of being — and a postmodern sublime which allows being outside of being presented and unpresentable, indeed this is a being which never ceases producing more. Thus we find you often producing variations on the theme of the work of anamnesis in the modern plastic and visual arts. This process is taken, as you have explained (Lyotard, 1986a: 125), in the sense of psychoanalytic therapy. The work of Cézanne, Picasso, Delaunay, Kandinsky, Klee, Mondrian, Malévitch and 'finally Duchamp' would be like a gliding through[2] which elaborated an initial moment of forgetfulness. The phrase 'and finally' indicates a displacement. The movement of return, anagogic and anamorphic, the process of 'ana-', would pass; this seems to us to be your thesis, which concerns the work of a forgetfulness and of a destruction of the — let us say, naive — sensible, which operates to develop the forgotten presupposition in the naive work of forgetfulness. And, in fact, there will always be presuppositions, the least reflection will be a moving on and a moving from. This last point suggests that the work of reflection will never be finished; it is without doubt to say that the aesthetic withdraws from the sensible but always remains there. So Duchamp, on account of his reflexive work, would be closer to postmodern than to modern. This complex of ideas evokes a complex of questions.

Firstly:
Q. 4: What is the relation between the two sublimes, that of the first path, which is modern and which moves naively to and from a sensible loss, and that of the second, postmodern, path which perlaborates the very work of perlaboration? And, since you suggest that there is a transition from one to the other, where is this located?

A. 4: First let me make a comment on your second *coup didactique*. The least that I can say is that what you make me think appears acceptable to me, and I am grateful for the numerous things that I have learnt from what is a beautiful and useful piece of elaboration. But your question troubles me. You tell me that there are two sorts of sublime, that of the first path which is a sublime in some way nostalgic about the impossibility of presentation, and that of the second path, a postmodern sublime, which consists simply in putting back into an endless play the presuppositions which are at work in all work. And next you tell me that the first path perlaborates naively a loss of the sensible. I would not say that the loss is one of sensibility, unless we give that phrase an almost British meaning; what is in question is perhaps a loss of meaning. It is above all the understanding that something gives us the material-sensible, and this something can never be reached.

I am reminded here of what Bettina von Arnim wrote, in regard to Hölderlin, in a 'letter' in the *Günderrode*: 'And we, we who have not been put to the test, will we ever see the day?' 'To see the day' that would be precisely to have access to that 'thing' (a term that I prefer to 'being'), that resonous, visual, timbrous, chromatic, nuanced, etc., matter. I use the phrase as a kind of inscription, although it is not my normal practice, in my *Que peindre?* (Lyotard, 1987a).

When you ask me where the transition from one sublime to the other takes place, I wonder if I understand this 'where' properly, because it seems very clear to me (but perhaps I am mistaken) that what you are asking for is a sort of periodization of the passage from an aesthetic of the nostalgic sublime to an aesthetic of a joyful sublime. This is a direction I pointed toward in, for example, 'The Sublime and the Avant-Garde' (Lyotard, 1984e) or 'Answering the question: what is postmodernism?' However, I believe that I am always cautious as far as periodizing this passage is concerned. Rather I have shown, in several examples, even if I have never truly analysed any one of them, that examples of both forms of sublime can be found — in the *writing* (in the widest possible sense of the term), that is to say in the mode of inscription which, whatever its historical conditions and surface form, will always dictate what cannot be expressed — let us leave it at that — in no matter what epoch of the history of literature, or of art, or of ideas. Thus I do not think that, correctly speaking, periodization is possible.

I would take for today, if you would like, not a transition but a sort of opposition between something like the Suprematism of Malévich and the 'expressionism' of Karel Appel. The former's work would be seen in the sense of a rarefaction of presentation aimed at giving expression to the thing which cannot present itself; the latter's on the contrary would be taken in a completely opposite sense of chromatic superabundance, and of a heedlessness, both voluntary and involuntary, of the form in which the colours are put together. In doing this, Appel tries to show moreover, but in a style which is, if I may say, rich (in reality this richness is also a poverty as the examination of both his works and their accompanying texts shows), the operation of a 'thing' which is completely different from Malévich's 'thing'.

Secondly:
Q. 5: The sophisticated development of the artistic conditions which characterize the postmodern arts (as you define them) functions to explode established discursive and conceptual truths. In the rather more political context of 'Judicieux dans le différend' you say: 'The clear task of the critical observer is continually to dissipate illusion, the situation is made obscure, however, because this dissipation may itself be illusory' (Lyotard, 1985a: 235). The Kantian idiom is here used, so to speak, against itself, against the a priori, *and the rules that it seeks to establish. The facility, if such it is, which enables you to draw your disunifying and shattering conclusions is the faculty (a notion whose illusory unity you have criticized (Lyotard, 1986c: 112–14)) of judgment. The question, then, is this: given that it is learnt in the preface to the* Critique of Judgement *that the faculty of judgment makes possible the way toward agreement, which, at bottom, is the unifying concordance between the first two* Critiques *and not the bursting apart of the well-defined fruits of critical thought, does not your readiness to fragment these products of critical thought constitute a betrayal of the faculty of judgment?*

A. 5: I would like to make two observations. The first is a sort of parenthesis, although essential, which bears on Kant's particular usage of the term faculty in the expression, 'faculty of judgement', but also certainly in that of 'faculty of presentation' and so on. You tell me that I have written in *L'Enthousiasme* that the very notion of a faculty introduces the illusion of a unity. You ask me if in engineering the fragmentation of thought I am not betraying the 'faculty of judgement' itself. My first observation bears on the notion of faculty, and my second on this question of fragmentation.

I must unhappily be brief as far as the notion of faculty is concerned. It is a very large problem that I have tackled in a recent text entitled *L'Intérêt du sublime*. The notion of faculty is that of the Aristotelian *dynamis*. It is a 'power of mind' as Kant puts it, especially in the second *Critique*. The mind has several powers which, as I have just said, respond to practical conditions, to the different functions according to which it is a question of judgments of truth or justice or beauty. What is awkward in the notion of faculty is that it is often taken as a metaphysics of power and action as may be found in Aristotle, or else in a weaker hypothesis, largely of Platonic origin, as part of a sort of metapsychology. The former connotation is often to be found in Kant's work. It is on that that I have worked, with respect to the notion of interest, in the third *Critique*. There must be an interest for the faculty to actualize itself, and there must be an interest which the empirical mind has in actualizing the power of the said faculty. There is therefore a double interest which operates in one sense as in the other, and this does not go without saying. A form of economy is necessarily introduced with these notions of faculty and act. For 'interest' is an economic term, whether libidinal or not. This economy, for Kant, is ultimately a practical economy. And I think that the privilege that Kant accords to the practical resides just there. For to have some interest in an object is always to want it. A faculty 'wants' its own actualization. Each faculty is under the regime of a 'metawill', of a 'drive' towards actualization. This metaphysic of power and action is the direction taken by the third *Critique*. Prudently, this direction is only made subject to a hypothetical idea, for which, according to Kant, there is no demonstrable proof available within the sensible world. This hypothetical idea is the idea of nature. It is an extremely important idea. It is not a simple question of a nature outside the subject, but of a nature 'within' the subject. The third *Critique* cannot be understood unless one develops fully this hypothesis which belongs, I repeat, to a metaphysics of power and of the act, and to an economy of faculties.

If, so far as the usage of the term 'faculty' is concerned, one wants to avoid the hypothesis of a metaphysic of nature which derives from Aristotle, a weaker hypothesis is taken. It is then a question of a sort of metaphysical psychology which will evidently have the merit of drawing nearer to what interests us under the name, for instance, of 'language game'. But here still the question which arises is how, according to Plato (rather than Aristotle this time), the three instances of the Platonic mind or the three faculties of the Kantian mind can co-exist. You can see that this is very much a question of the unity of the subject rather than of the metaphysic of nature. In fact these two hypotheses, the natural metaphysic and the subjective metaphysic, are tightly interwoven in Kant, even though Aristotle and Plato are in profound divergence on the matter.

Let me pass to the question of fragmentation. Does my work

betray the faculty of judgment in advocating fragmentation? I am not the one who advocates this. It is the critical method itself which insists upon the differentiation between the regimes of judgment according to which it is a question of truth, or of beauty, or of the good. It is from this point that Kant finds himself confronted with the problem of reconstructing the subject as if the regimes of judgment were perfectly autonomous. What he finds, at the end of his diverse 'deductions', that is to say these legitimations of the demand that judgment be considered valid for the beautiful, for the good, or for the true, are principles which are heterogeneous with respect to each other. This is the whole of the problem of the constitution of the unity of the subject which is posed after that, and which Kant poses, in effect, in the preface to the third *Critique*. Kant tries to resolve this problem *by* the third *Critique* itself, by opening a possible passage between reason in its theoretical usage and reason in its practical usage. As you know, he has the greatest difficulty in succeeding in this. For finally the passage itself cannot be traced, it is open only by virtue of a general hypothesis of a natural finality, of nature as pursuing, both within human beings and outside of them, the supreme end of the development of its powers of liberty which have a 'primacy' over that of the power of knowledge. All this amounts to the fact that the question which you ask me is much more embarrassing for Kant than it is for me. For, as far as I am concerned, I am in the situation of thought today, and this is marked, shall we say, by the critique of the subject. This critique does not mean that we can dispense with the subject. It does mean that in every way that we relate to the notion of the subject, we carry the Kantian and Wittgensteinian heritage with us, and that we cannot continue to think under the general regime of the *cogito*. The evidence for the 'I think' is for us as scarce as it could possibly be. This is a point of severe disagreement with Karl-Otto Apel, and perhaps with the whole of phenomenology.

I would add that Heidegger's conclusions in the *Kantbuch* do not allow us to think ourselves free of the crisis of the critique of the subject in contemporary thought. For, once again, these considerations only relate to the evanescence, if I may put it like this, of the knowing subject in the time of knowing. We have to deal with a crisis of the subject which is much more serious. It concerns the unification of the heterogeneous or autonomous regimes of judgment, that is to say the regimes of different phrases. Can we think without the subject? There again it is necessary to add something, which is that even the considerable contribution that psychoanalysis, especially in its Lacanian form, has been able to contribute to the elaboration of this question does not seem to us philosophers to be sufficient (I say 'us' because I believe that I am far from alone in thinking this). This also arises in so far as, in one way or another, but principally in (re)introducing the capitalized Other, Lacanian thought reconnects with a certain idea of the unity of 'sense'. Obviously, I am well aware that it is a unity of sense of the singular unconscious, and that this sense remains a problem concerning the communicability of the different unconsciences governed by the *grands A* which are in principle heterogeneous each from the others. Nevertheless, the properly theoretical aspect of Lacanian thought (at the beginning, at least) seems to me to resort more to a very profound and very subtle renewal of Platonic thought as a way of taking serious consideration of the crisis of the subject after Kant.

Thirdly, a little more complex:
Q. 6: It is in answering the question of what is at stake in modern art and the postmodern arts that it seems to you opportune to parody 'An answer to the question: "What is enlightenment?"' We know that the bearing of this famous Kantian text is upon the political; it is counted, and you do not contest this in any way, among Kant's historico-political texts. It does not treat aesthetic or artistic issues. It could be said that he speaks about religion when speaking of the political class,[3] but that would make the general view mistaken. The actual choice of subject matter is arbitrary in comparison with the essentially political nature of Kant's concerns. He writes: 'I have portrayed matters of religion as the focal point of enlightenment, i.e. of man's emergence from his self-incurred immaturity. This is firstly because our rulers have no interest in assuming the role of guardians over their subjects so far as the arts and sciences are concerned, and secondly, because religious immaturity is the most pernicious and dishonourable variety of all' (Kant, 1970: 57). The religious issue only obscures the fact that the text is essentially political. Therefore, since you parody the title of Kant's text, and since your own text aims at providing a critique of the political thought of Habermas, that defender of the Enlightenment tradition, what is it that makes your aesthetic reflections political? It seems to us that there are two sub-questions here.
First, in what way is the aesthetic political?
Second, does the transformation of the aesthetic, about which you

have spoken, have implications with respect to the form of politics that we could tentatively call 'postmodern', or has a kind of reversal taken place whereby the 'political' has become 'aesthetic'? It will be useful to cast our minds back in this connection. You have said about politics, understood here as that consideration of creativity which has been at the core of modern philosophical reflection: 'What is striking is that I have been required to abandon [the task of constructing a theory of history] and have made an enormous detour [the reference here is to the aesthetics of Discours, figure *— D.V.] which has displaced the initial object.' And it is certainly in reasserting the bond with your active political past that you follow on to say: 'Basically, what interests me is, in effect, to return to practical critique and to the theory of practical critique: to see what politics can be' (Lyotard, 1972: 19). In the 1985 interview with Blistène, you evince the same objective throughout. How do we make a politics when we are confronted with politics which manifestly (Stalin, the Prague Spring, Solidarity (see Lyotard, 1977: 19; 1984a: No. 257)) do not work? — There are your reasons for leaving the critical Marxism of* Socialisme ou barbarie, *first of all, and then leaving* Pouvoir ouvrier, *and, at the same time, always the same question: 'What is to be done when there is no horizon of emancipation; where do we resist?' (Lyotard, 1985b: 69). Aesthetics or politics, that is to say: does philosophy bring something into view, or is it reflection? Or, perhaps, this dichotomy is obsolete?*

A. 6: If you will allow me, I will take these questions together. I will reply as to how the aesthetic is political. Aesthetics in the Western tradition has always been political in the sense that politics has always been aesthetic. I would refer you to an unpublished thesis by Philippe Lacoue-Labarthe, titled *La Fiction du politique*, which is a totally remarkable consideration of aesthetics and politics in the work of Heidegger. To speed things up, and I make my apologies to Philippe Lacoue-Labarthe for this, the essential point can be put very briefly (not that briefly, for I do not wish what I say to falsify what I mean); what he shows very clearly is that at least since Plato, all politics has obeyed a politics of fashioning. You know that the Greeks called that *to plattein*, and that the Sophists made a word-play on *Platon* and *plattein*. It is a question of fashioning and refashioning the city of fashion to make it appropriate to a metaphysical paradigm which would be precisely that of the good arrangement of the three instances, the *logos*, the *thumos*, and the *eputhimetikon*, so that they will be accurately mirrored in the copy constituted by the well-fashioned city. This idea of having to fashion the human community is fundamentally an aesthetic idea. It is a question of making a work. And this is clearly what Jean-Luc Nancy (1986) presupposes when he writes of an idle community. What he seeks to show is that we are kept in check by this traditional connotation of the political to the aesthetics of the work.

I am well aware that Plato has not reigned supreme right up to the present day without opposition. But I think it can be shown that even after or during the Enlightenment, where however great a rupture with Platonism Kant shows to have occurred, it is possible to continue to think of fashioning as being the secret of politics. I mean that while it is certainly not a question of fashioning with eyes fixed on a metaphysical paradigm already constituted in the heaven of ideas, it is a question of fashioning in accordance with what Kant calls an idea of reason, that is to say a concept, but one which is not presented in the intuition. One finds oneself therefore in the familiar paradox of modern societies (more than one, with Leo Strauss, has exposed and denounced the rest), which is that a community moulded on an idea which has no reference mark in the sensible world (the idea of liberty is such an idea), that is to say an idea which cannot be demonstrated (in the sense used just now), an ideal of political design, whether it is the work of the left or of the right, will always remain contestable with regard to its legitimacy. To the extent that, in the case of Platonism, the model is in principle present in everyone's mind, and therefore all can judge whether the political organization of the city conforms to it or not, and to the extent that, after the Enlightenment [if one does not take account of the re-establishment of a certain Platonism which is clearly inscribed in Hegel, and even in Nietzsche], the idea of liberty is *ex hypothesi* singularly unavailable to any possible sensible intuition, then, to that extent, political fashioning will always be suspect.

It is as a result of this that modern politics constructs itself as suspicion and conflict interior to the community. This conflict may assume exorbitant proportions, even to the point of civil war. It is too easy to show that all modern wars differ from classical wars in that the former are always civil wars, whether internal or external, that is to say that they are wars over the legitimacy of one form or another of the political modelling of human communities. You see that we come back here to the problem of nature, which can clearly be found in what are called natural rights, in the fundamental freedoms which prescribe the limits of social fabrication. It can be seen that ultimately the legitimacy of the resistance to Nazism was located just there, to the extent that the 'natural order' invoked by Nazism did not seem to respect (this is the least that can be said) these rights. But these rights are only the minima whose violation takes us into the very heart of suspicion. I mean that if one abandons the observation of these rights, one is in a certain way absolutely condemnable, obviously evil, but on the other hand respect for rights does not guarantee that the political fabrication will properly correspond to it. It is not enough then to observe these rights in order to say that a good political order has been constructed.

We have to deal here with an entire problematic which, in a certain sense, remains 'aesthetic'. This no longer refers to the aesthetic of the beautiful as defined by Plato, but rather to an aesthetic of the sublime, rational in the sense that it is a question of shaping human communities according to an idea of reason, which is however not presentable. Does it follow that there is a reversal of the relation between politics and aesthetics? I do not think so. I would simply say this (with respect to the last part of your question): that it is necessary to distinguish between what is aesthetical and what is political, and what would be interesting is not pursuing the idea of fabrication with an obsessive regard for developing the aesthetic aspect under the heading of the political work, but developing the dissociation between what is at stake in the aesthetic and the political, in the way that I have already indicated but also (please excuse the comparison) as already indicated by Kant and Wittgenstein. This is a work of critique and of critique alone. For why must the social or human (an unimportant distinction for the moment) community not only be good but beautiful? And how would the fact that it was beautiful guarantee that it was good?

I am well aware that Greek tradition had it that the *kalos kagathos* was at once beautiful and good, and that Kant admitted an analogy between the beautiful, as a symbol, and the good. But Kant explained also that, even though the analogy is possible, nevertheless nothing authorizes the conclusion that the analogy is a substitute for a rational deduction. 'If beautiful, then good' cannot be said. There is a sort of privilege of the aesthetic over the political in the tradition which has in effect come down to us from Greece. This primacy seems to me to stand in need of being broken, and I think that this is the moment. Briefly, I would say that politics in itself is not a rule-bound enterprise, that it is much more complex than a *genre*. It is that, as I tried to show at the end of *Le Différend*, politics combines discursive genres (but also phrase–regimes) which are totally heterogeneous. Within the political there are interrogative genres and affirmative or assertive genres; there are questions which imply descriptions and questions which imply prescriptions; there is the aesthetic and poetic use of discourse in parliamentary rhetoric, or in the equivalent politics of publicity like propaganda. And certainly the use of reflective judgment must be added to this, when people ask themselves how they should vote, or what should be done in a particular situation, when the question cannot be disposed of under the rule of a single judgment.

Politics is not a free-standing genre of discourse; it is a profoundly unstable combination (although it may be relatively stabilized in the countries we call democratic) because it is subject to the instability of the 'polygon of forces' in which different discursive genres are combined. It can be said that the situation today is characterized by the fact that these genres concern areas, 'objects', which are more and more numerous. In a certain sense, everything has become political, as we used to say although it is a bad expression. Rather it is politics which has become invested in territories and in relation to objects which formerly were held to be outside of it. I am thinking here particularly about problems like those of health or those of destruction, although the latter may be more classically associated with the political; but they are assuming such proportions in contemporary physics and chemistry, that it is evidently science itself which has become a political affair. All we refer to as the 'cultural' has acquired a hegemony in the combination of different genres which constitutes politics; and the 'cultural' is not the aesthetic.

To get right to the heart of it, what I want to point to again is that, having admitted this plurality of genres articulated together in politics today, an essential philosophical task will be to refuse the aesthetic its two thousand year-old privilege, which in one sense was given its 'final' particularly disquieting expression by Nazism. This is nothing other than the complete aestheticization of the political. It would be desirable to rethink the political rather than set out from the disquieting appeal to 'doing good', in other words, we should rather begin from the Kant of the second *Critique* or from the thought of Levinas. That would allow at least — I do not say that this hypothesis can take us very far, I am not qualified to see so far — the avoidance of the understanding of politics in terms of fabrication and fashioning.

Q. 7: In Au juste *you say that the problem of injustice has caused you to reconsider the libidinal-figural philosophy of* Discours, figure *and, more especially, the theorizing of intensities of* Economie libidinale *(Lyotard, 1985c: 90).* Le Différend *is the most wide-sweeping result of this reconsideration. What exactly is the problem and how does* Le Différend *remedy it?*

A. 7: This is a simple enough question. In *Economie libidinale*, the aim was the elimination of the game of good/evil in favour of that of intensities. The only criterion taken into account was the event itself. Now the event cannot be a criterion because it never stops retreating, because it is never there. Expressed in the terms of the philosophy of desire or of energy (I would rather say energetics) the event is construed as intensity. The few readers of *Economie libidinale* (you know that the book was very badly received) were shocked by this position, and this is not the worst that was said about the book. I think these readers did not appreciate the aspect of despair in the book, a desperation which appeared clear to me when I reread it (I do not usually reread my books, but I am obliged to when precise questions are put to me about them, as was the case recently with David Carroll in the United States). It is a book of desperation. It cannot be understood, or supported, except from the basis of the crisis I was going through at the time, and I was not alone (otherwise the book would have had no public interest at all). The crisis pertains to the ending of all the attempts to moralize politics which were incarnated in Marxism. The source of *The Postmodern Condition*, of the theme that is referred to as the crisis or the end of the great metanarratives, is found in *Discours, figure* (you have been perceptive in speaking of the nostalgic tone of that book). It is a theme which seeks to find affirmative expression in *Economie libidinale* (under the obvious influence of Nietzsche, and of a certain Freud). This position has since led me towards, *mutatis mutandis*, Diderot's *Rameau's Nephew*. It is certain that there is no rationalism, understood in Habermas's sense, which does not pass through that terrible moment of nihilism or complete scepticism. *Economie libidinale* represented for me that moment, or rather the return of that moment for I believed I had already passed through it and rid myself of it. It was, on the historico-social scale, perhaps even ontological.

Le Différend remedies the shortcomings of *Economie libidinale*; it is an attempt to try and say the same things, but without unloading problems so important as justice. On the one hand in *Le Différend*, what is specifically at stake is the re-establishment of justice under the form of the ethical (in the part which is entitled 'Obligation'), on the other hand, in the total scheme of the book, *Le Différend* re-establishes what is at stake in justice as *Au juste* had summarily but not — even though I now see that the arguments were full of doubts and objections — falsely indicated. In *Le Différend*, it is said that there is an inevitable difficulty with respect to the possibilities of enchaining arising out of each phrase, out of each event by means of other phrases, because only a single phrase is possible at any one time (and therefore the others are for the moment different and not 'actualized'). In spite of the ineluctable nature of this problem, the demand remains. Properly speaking, the demand is not moral — I think that I examined moral exigency in the section entitled 'obligation' — when I now speak of an exigency which hangs over the whole of the book, it is to respect as much as possible the has-it-happened-yet. It is that *thing* that the event is even before signification, before connotation, its *quiddity* whether determined or determinable. This determination is precisely the enchainment which will be made out of it, which will say it and, therefore, make it.

As to a politics of justice, you tell me that this interest in the event reduces political philosophy to almost nothing, to an ontological attitude, and that this is because of respecting or listening for the has-it-happened-yet. My response is that it is not so simple. I want to say at least two things. First, it is probable that now and for the foreseeable future we, as philosophers, as much as we may be concerned by politics (and inevitably we are so concerned), are no longer in a position to say publicly: 'Here is what you must do.' I developed this theme particularly in the *Tombeau de l'intellectuel* which, all the same, did not mean following Maurice Blanchot's idea that the intellectual is dead and must be buried. You know that *'tombeau'* is also a term which, in French, designates a literary or musical genre, a sort of memorial movement. The *'tombeau'* of the intellectual is also the memorial of the intellectual. So we are *in memoriam*. This is not to say that there are no longer any intellectuals, but that today's intellectuals, philosophers in so far as they are concerned by politics and by questions of community, are no longer able to take up obvious and pellucid positions; they cannot speak in the name of an 'unquestionable' universality as, for example, Zola or Sartre were able to. Sartre was the limit of this because he is clearly mistaken in the positions he defends. But why has this period ended? It is because the modern intellectual was an Enlightenment figure, and all intellectuals, no matter what side they were on (except, of course, the Nazis) found their legitimacy, the legitimacy of the public speech through which they designated the just cause and made themselves its spokespersons, in the grand metanarrative of emancipation. It was possible to disagree about how to proceed, about how to work toward emancipation. But always the intellectuals had the authority of this kind of speaking in common, and it was founded on the general idea of a history developing toward its 'natural' end, which was the emancipation of humanity from poverty, ignorance, prejudice and the absence of enjoyment.

Now we do not have the resource of the emancipatory metanarrative(s). What we have left is the minimum required for, what I call, a politics of resistance. What does resistance mean? What are the points of resistance? They are, on the other hand, the points about which I just spoke with regard to the respect for natural rights, in other words those liberties which are said to be elementary (and our clear duty there is to intervene when they are at stake), but on the other hand there is a resistance that is perhaps more secret and more specific, at the same time moreover as being more pertinent to the contemporary political condition which, as we have just been saying, is invested in the field of culture as well. I am talking about resistance in and through writing as, in the sense just outlined, inscription which attends to the uninscribable. The real political task today, at least in so far as it is also concerned with the cultural (and we should surely not forget, even though we may maintain a prudent silence on the subject which is nevertheless very important, at least in so far as it is also 'just simply' capital), is to carry forward the resistance that writing offers to established thought, to what has already been done, to what everyone thinks, to what is well-known, to what is widely recognized, to what is 'readable', to everything which can change its form and make itself acceptable to opinion in general. The latter, you understand, always works with what is taken for granted and with what is forgotten as such — for it grants no place to anamnesis. It is prejudiced. 'Culture' consists, as 'activity' and 'animation', in introducing all that into the order of writing, in the wide sense, into literature, painting, architecture and so on. The name most often given to this is 'postmodernism'.

I think that we have to resist. In the section of *Le Postmoderne expliqué aux enfants*, entitled 'Glose sur la résistance', I cited the very important example — Claude Lefort has also developed this —

of Winston in Orwell's *1984*. The line of resistance there is traced by the writing of the journal, and by the anamnesis that this writing demands of Winston in those circumstances. This example is a kind of model. I can take as well the artists and writers whom I hold to be (and you understand why I value them so much), in their various ways, models of resistance (they may hate to be so described but that is quite another problem). Perhaps they lock themselves away, apart from everyone, unknown to the general public; I would say that in one sense that does not matter, for they do not owe this resistance to the community directly but to thought. Whether it is in a century or in six months that the community realizes the necessity of what they have done is another question. Their essential task is above all to write, to paint, and so on, and to do this here and now in response (and responsibility) to that question: what is writing, painting?

Q. 8: The special issue of Critique, *entitled 'La traversée de l'Atlantique' (1985) contains texts from yourself and Richard Rorty, and amounts to a 'discussion' between you. In spite of the profound differences that you note between you, you do not appear to disapprove too much of what he has to say since you describe his exposition as 'excellent'. However, it seems to us that there is a radical difference between your conclusions and those which Rorty draws in 'The End of Philosophy'. He thinks that we can and must abandon philosophy, and that amounts to turning away from that source of philosophy to which you have always remained faithful, that source being the question, the questioning of everything, even the question itself. It seems to us that you continue to do philosophy, but radically. A quick indication of this would be your conversation with Derrida on 'France–Culture' printed in* Le Monde *under the title of 'Plaidoyer pour la métaphysique' (1984f)). From this perspective, is your description of Rorty's thought as 'excellent' an acceptance of his ultimately non-philosophical point of view, with all the machinery of 'enlightened' bourgeois North American values which are uncritically accepted there, realizing that it is precisely in this latter respect that Rorty's thought looks ill when faced with your continually questioning and honestly philosophical refusal of emancipatory thought?*

A. 8: You are referring to the discussion which we had at Johns Hopkins some two and a half years ago. You suggest that I was very generous in describing Rorty's presentation as excellent, and you have the feeling that there is, on the contrary, a radical divergence between his thought and mine. If I described his discourse in this way, it is because it was an excellent exposition of his thesis. It is a homage that should be paid to an interlocutor, whether an adversary or not, in recognition that everything has been made understandable. Now, such was the case with Richard Rorty (without taking any account of my sympathy for the man himself). As to the divergence between our tendencies, I agree with you that this is radical. In support of your interpretation, you cite the publication in *Le Monde* of a radio interview between Derrida and myself. The title — 'Metaphysics: the Case for the Defence' — was given to it by the newspaper. I would not have chosen it. I certainly do not think that it might be time for a return to metaphysics as has been suggested by some of my young French colleagues. I would have preferred that the title referred to the defence of *philosophy*, because no one knows exactly what that marvellous term means (if it is only a discursive genre in pursuit of its own rule, there can be no certainty in regard to its pronouncements; it does not have the dominion over itself to be assured that what is said provides an effective plea for its own defence).

Let us go back to my relation with Rorty. There is something very powerful, but sophisticated, in his rhetoric. He says, 'we should drop all foundationalism, as it is put in the United States; it is without interest since it is indecidable. Only one thing is decidable, that is whether we do or do not speak together'. Conversation becomes the absolute safeguard of the rationalist heritage. It is absolute because it is so minimal that it is totally incontestable. It is not even a question of 'opening a dialogue', taking that term in its highest sense, of pursuing a hermeneutic of the kind elaborated by Ricoeur, Gadamer or Buber. No, it is simple conversation, the fact that we talk to each other. This is a pragmatist minimalism which can distinguish itself by recovering the essential heritage of the Enlightenment in so far as it truly concerns the 'practice' of democracy. It demands that instead of killing, or putting in prison, or effacing, or eliminating in whatever way, or using those critical methods which rely on exclusion, one listens to the other and constitutes the other through speech as an interlocutor. Rorty's thesis of generalized interlocution can avail itself of a rationalism, which I would say is neither bourgeois North American, as you suggest, nor anaemic, but of a rationalism conscious of that which comprises what is absolutely discussable, which rationalism is not itself discussable, since it is both it and what makes it possible. This is the clear opposition between Rorty and Karl-Otto Apel or even with Habermas. The only true problem is whether discussion can take place. It is not a question of looking for the foundation behind, at the source, underneath or at the root of what is said; but it is a matter of what lies ahead of conversation, in a future which can only be that of interlocution. All conversation, even if it results in the greatest dissension (which was the case at the time of my public discussion with Rorty at Baltimore), nevertheless attests to the work of interlocution. This is where Rorty's sophistication lies: even if we do not agree, this disagreement implies that there is still an accord over the necessity of talking to each other. There is, if you will, a pragmatic *Mitsein* which in Rorty's view is the only essential thing to preserve, all the attempts to arrive at a semantic *consensus* being doomed to failure or at least always subordinated to this pragmatic *Mitsein*. It is what Rorty (1985) calls 'solidarity'. This is a powerful thesis.

That said, it is also an 'imperialist' thesis, as I objected to him. The notion of an interlocution, as a passage or circulation of speech in the first person — from *I* to *you*, and from *you* to *I* — firstly does not guarantee that the *I* and *you* must make a *We* (and moreover Rorty comes up against a difficult problem with the enigma of the *We*). Secondly, and above all, it is not certain and it seems to me even very improbable that this pragmatic relationship of interlocution may be constitutive of our relations with language. I am prepared to argue the thesis that, in the case of ethical obligation for example, there is no interlocution. If I follow the way in which Kant or Levinas have analysed obligation, what strikes me is that being obliged is a relation with the law, a law which does not above all focus on the *I*, but rather on the *you*: 'You will do this', 'You must act in such and such a way', 'You will listen to me', 'You must listen' (I revive these terms which are those of Kant, of Levinas, of the Jewish tradition). Are others implicated by conversational address through my relation to the law? Neither for Kant, nor for Levinas. According to Levinas, this is because the relationship is one of hostage-taking and not at all one of interchange. The Other takes me hostage, and hostage-taking, as I understand it, is neither exactly conversational nor a matter of interlocution. It is violence. There is violence exercised by the law over its subject. In Kant's case, it is said that the maxim of my action must be able to be extended to the entire human (reasonable–practical) community. And it is the case that this is what Kant tells us that the law demands. 'Act in such a way that' or 'Act as if the maxim of your will could be established as the principle of a universal law', as a law valid for the totality of reasonable, practical, finite beings that we are. But it is up to me to judge, in the solitude of my seizure by the law, that my intention of doing or that my judgment (which comes to the same thing) is in effect universalizable. If we now take the case of the critique of aesthetic judgment, it can be seen that the aesthetic judgment, 'This is beautiful', is singular, and, even if it contains a pretension to universality, i.e. to communicability (and it is in order to found this that Kant elaborates the notion of a *sensus communis*, and for no other reason), it still is the case that aesthetic judgment is equally exempt from the dominion of conversation. Even if my taste for a work or for a landscape leads me to discuss it with others (taking that last term in the sense, this time, of an empirical group), it is no less true that any assent that I can obtain from them has nothing to do with the validity of my aesthetic judgment. For the conditions of validity of this judgment are transcendental, and are clearly not subject to the opinions of any others whatsoever. The communicability, and even, to speak rigorously, the communion of aesthetic sentiments, cannot be obtained *de facto*, empirically, and much less by means of conversation. At this point conversation encounters the antinomy of *La Faculté de juger*, which is that there must certainly be some promise of universality, which creates the need for argumentation, but, at the same time, aesthetic judgment does not proceed through concepts, it cannot be validated by argumentative consensus. That does not mean that we do not talk to each other; we certainly do. But the question is about knowing if such conversation is constitutive of aesthetic judgment, of taste.

In putting forward the principle of interlocution, Rorty carries — and this is neither a shortcoming nor an error, I would say rather an 'illusion', and not only his today — the pragmatic relation to a transcendental level. It is as if the *I/you* relationship marked by the exchangeability of letters between persons or empirical individuals were a transcendental condition of philosophy, of history, of progress, of Enlightenment, in short of those things that he is concerned with (and I am certainly not scornful of them). But to accord oneself the privilege of the pragmatic, even under the most minimal form given by interlocution, even under the cloak of the greatest modesty (simple 'solidarity'), is finally to get the essential on the cheap. Although it might seem otherwise, his position does not really pose the question of the other as such. It is as if the thought about constitution (let us say, so as not to go too far, in the sense of it elaborated by Husserl in his *Cartesian Meditations*) had not run aground on the problem of the constitution of others. Now, it is clear that it did come to grief, and we know very well why. It is because the other in its empiricity, in its pretended 'presence' as the interlocutor with whom I can exchange speech, does not constitute a transcendental figure in the strict sense of the term. The transcendental figures are the 'either/ors', either the true or the false, either the just or the injust, either the beautiful or the not-beautiful, but *not* either the other or the not other. Let me note besides something which seems to me quite fascinating, which is that Kant always refers to others, in a more or less explicit way (less so in the first *Critique*, more so in the second and third), in the constitution of universality. Thus while it arises in a response to the question of the what-is-otherwise, it is not an answer, only a reference to them. The empirical other(s) is not a transcendental figure. Now Rorty treats other(s) as not only the single transcendental figure, since either solidarity or the invalidity of philosophy, and since if solidarity then the other(s) as interlocutor, but also takes it to be the case that the question thereby posed is already resolved: 'we' talk to each other. I think that on this point the divergence between our positions is profound. I think moreover that it would be interesting to see if a *Critique of Altruistic Reason* could be written. This would be essential because what we would confront at this point, whether under the form of Apel's foundationalism, or of Habermas's communicationalism, or of Rorty's non-foundationalist and strictly interlocutory pragmatics, is finally the acceptance without examination (I would rather say, if you will allow it, without anamnesis) of the idea of others as the principal figure of contemporary thought. Now, whether others can be properly spoken of as a figure is problematic, as would be its 'constitution'; and whether it might be the principal figure, I very much doubt.

Translated by Roy Boyne

Notes

This interview was originally recorded in April 1987 in Paris and Utrecht. The original French text has been published in the Social Philosophy/Philosophical Anthropology Group Reprint Series, No. 1, 1987, Department of Philosophy, University of Utrecht and in *Les Cahiers de philosophie*.

1. See Martin Heidegger (1972: 19) 'What determines both, time and Being, in their own, that is, in their belonging together, we shall call: *Ereignis*, the event of appropriation. *Ereignis* will be translated as Appropriation or event of Appropriation. One should bear in mind, however, that "event" is not simply an occurrence, but that which makes any occurrence possible' [translator's note].

2. The word used here, which I have translated here as *gliding through* is *perlaboration*. This word appears to be a neologism in the French language, and there is no directly comparable word in English (the word 'perlaboration' does not appear in the *OED*). The word is derived from the Latin: *perlabor*, an intransitive verb meaning to move on, to glide along, to pass through. Sometimes it has been possible to translate the usage in the text in the way that I have done here; but at other points, its usage is determined not only by its Latin root, but also by its close relation to the word 'elaboration', and where this has happened, I have allowed the term (in both noun and verb form) to stand as an acceptable neologism in English [translator's note].

3. Kant writes, 'But should not a society of clergymen, for example an ecclesiastical synod or a venerable presbytery (as the Dutch call it), be entitled to commit itself by oath to a certain unalterable set of doctrines, in order to secure for all time a constant guardianship over each of its members, and through them over the people?' Immanuel Kant (1970: 57).

References

Critique (1985) Special issue 'La traversée de l'Atlantique', 456.

Heidegger, M. (1972) *On Time and Being*. New York: Harper and Row.

Kant, I. (1970) 'An Answer to the Question "What is Enlightenment?" ', in H. Reiss (ed.) *Kant's Political Writings*. Cambridge: Cambridge University Press.

Lyotard, J.-F. (1970) 'Sur la théorie' (Interview with B. Devismes), in J.-F. Lyotard *Dérive à Partir de Marx et Freud*. Paris: 10/18.

Lyotard, J.-F. (1971) *Discours, figure*. Paris: Klincksieck.

Lyotard, J.-F. (1972) 'En finir avec l'illusion de la politique' (Interview with Gilbert Lascault), *La Quinzaine litteraire* 1, 15 May.

Lyotard, J.-F. (1974) *Economie libidinale*. Paris: Minuit.

Lyotard, J.-F. (1977) *Instructions païennes*. Paris: Galilée.

Lyotard, J.-F. (1978) 'L'Acinéma' in cinéma théorie, lectures'. Paris: Klincksieck; reprinted in *Les Dispositifs pulsionnels*. Paris: 10/18.

Lyotard, J.-F. (1979a) *La Condition postmoderne*. Paris: Minuit.

Lyotard, J.-F. and J.-L. Thébaud (1979b) *Au juste*. Paris: Christian Bourgeois; translated as *Just Gaming*. Manchester University Press.

Lyotard, J.-F. (1982) 'Presenting the Impresentable', *Art forum*.

Lyotard, J.-F. (1984a) *Le Différend*. Paris: Minuit.

Lyotard, J.-F. (1984b) 'Appendice svelte à la question postmoderne', in *Tombeau de l'intellectuel*. Paris: Galilée.

Lyotard, J.-F. (1984c) 'An Answer to the Question "What is Postmodernism?" ', appendix to *The Postmodern Condition*. Manchester University Press.

Lyotard, J.-F. (1984d) 'Interview' (with G. van den Abbeele), *Diacritics* 14 (3).

Lyotard, J.-F. (1984e) 'The Sublime and the Avant-Garde', *Art forum* 22.

Lyotard, J.-F. (1984f) 'Plaidoyer pour la métaphysique' (Conversation with Derrida), *Le Monde*, 28–29 September.

Lyotard, J.-F. (1985a) 'Judicieux dans le différend', in *La Faculté de juger*. Paris: Minuit.

Lyotard, J.-F. (1985b) 'Kunst Heute', in *Immaterialität und Postmoderne*. Berlin: Merve.

Lyotard, J.-F. (1985c) *Just Gaming*. Manchester University Press (translation of 1979b).

Lyotard, J.-F. (1986a) *Le Postmoderne expliqué aux enfants*. Paris: Galilée.

Lyotard, J.-F. (1986b) 'Argumentation and Presentation: the Crisis of Foundations', *Neue Hefte für Philosophie* 26.

Lyotard, J.-F. (1986c) *L'Enthousiasme — la critique Kantienne de l'histoire*. Paris: Galilée.

Lyotard, J.-F. (1987a) *Que peindre?* Paris: Editions de la différence.

Lyotard, J.-F. (1987b) 'Sensus communis', *Le Cahier* 3.

Nancy, Jean-Luc (1986) *La Communauté desoeuvrée*. Paris: Christian Bourgeois.

Rorty, R. (1985) 'Solidarity or Objectivity', in J. Rachman and C. West (eds) *Post-Analytic Philosophy*. New York: Columbia University Press.

Discourse or Figure?
Postmodernism as a 'Regime of Signification'

Scott Lash

Some of the very best and sharpest critics of postmodernism have put forward a strikingly similar, yet quite powerful, argument against the claim that we live in some important sense in a postmodern era.[1] Analysts such as Anderson (1984), Frisby (1985) and Callinicos (1985) have thus aggressively disputed Lyotard's famous pronouncement that the contemporary scepticism before 'meta-narratives' has been midwife to the birth of the postmodern condition. Such analysts point out such a refusal of the 'great narratives' and the 'foundationalisms' took place, not in the past decade or two, but were integral to the very rise of modernism itself. Thus Baudelaire, arguably the godfather of aesthetic modernism, broke with the foundationalist assumptions of realism to celebrate the transitory, the fleeting, the contingent. And Nietzsche, well before the turn of the century, castigated foundationalisms not just in the aesthetic realm, but similarly refused the certainties of notions of unconditional ethics and realist, mirror-of-nature epistemologies. Indeed a recent collection of essays shows a remarkable convergence of opinion among contributors supporting the propositions that Max Weber himself had an eminently post-Enlightenment and 'post-metanarrative' idea of modernity (Whimster and Lash, 1987).

It is helpful in the understanding of the modernist, late nineteenth-century departure from foundationalisms, if we think in terms of the traditional sociological, structural–functional model which features the process of differentiation. Let us however confine this process of differentiation to only the cultural realm. In this sense the non-referential and anti-realist nature of for example modernist painting and literature can be seen in terms of the differentiation of aesthetic forms from the real world. And the modernist critique of realist epistemologies (present for example in

Theory, Culture & Society (SAGE, London, Newbury Park, Beverly Hills and New Delhi), Vol. 5 (1988), 311–36

Durkheim's 'sociologistic epistemology') is a matter of the differentiation of the 'theoretical realm' from the real world. The differentiation of fact from value, of the ethical from theoretical spheres, is similarly evidenced in Weber's work, and in the work of English philosophers such as Moore and Stephenson (MacIntyre, 1981).

This process of differentiation is integral to the process of 'modernization'. Modernization conceived as differentiation is of course the linchpin of Parsonian sociology, but can be traced back through the work of Weber and even of Lukács to the aesthetic writings of the mature Hegel (Kätz, 1982). And if modern*ism* is the result of a stage of differentiation whose onset is proper to the late nineteenth and early twentieth centuries, then modern*ity* is the product of a much earlier stage of this differentiation process. On this account the Renaissance would document the differentiation of cultural from religious realism, and, as Hegel underscored, the differentiation of the aesthetic realm from the social. It makes sense perhaps then to speak in terms of an 'early' modernity of the Renaissance and the Enlightenment, and a 'late' or at least later modernity co-extensive with the much later rise of aesthetic modernism. Both of these would be products of a continued modernization process based on a principle of cultural differentiation.

The critics of postmodernism are thus correct in their contention that what Lyotard takes to be postmodernity is in fact part and parcel of modernism. This however does not entail that postmodern culture does not exist. Indeed I think it does exist, but that Lyotard has not got it quite right. I think that if modernism and modernity result from a process of differentiation, or what German social scientists call *Ausdifferenzierung*, then postmodernism results from a much more recent process of de-differentiation or *Entdifferenzierung*. There has been in this sense de-differentiation in the postmodernist attempt to drain the aura from the work of art. De-differentiation is also present in the postmodernist refusal to separate the author from his or her oeuvre or the audience from the performance; in the postmodernist transgression of the boundary (with no doubt greater or lesser success) between literature and theory, between high and popular culture, between what is properly cultural and what is properly social.

In an earlier article I illustrated this characteristic de-differentiation (though at the time I did not understand it to be de-differentiation) in conceiving of postmodernity in terms of the notion of 'desire' (Lash, 1985). Here, 'modernist' Freudian theory would conceive of the psyche as differentiated into two spheres — of desire, on the one hand, and the conscious mind on the other. Postmodern psychotherapy, in contradistinction, could no longer speak in terms of such differentiation. Desire instead would have to be on the very 'surface' of a now largely de-differentiated psychic apparatus. Similarly, the no longer representational, modernist painting would correspond to the formal principles of rationality of the secondary process, while the postmodernist painting of, say, Francis Bacon, would break with such principles of formal rationality and show again desire on the canvas's surface (Deleuze, 1981).

In what follows I should like further to work through the implications of conceiving of postmodernism in terms of de-differentiation. This time I want to concentrate on what might be called the postmodern mode of signification, or a postmodern 'semiotics'. In the earlier article that was just mentioned above I argued that a postmodernist culture that foregrounded 'desire', signalled somehow a renunciation of signification. This resulted in a sort of 'naturalism', which relegated signification and semiotics to the ranks of the merely modern, with whose possible political implications I am not entirely happy. In what follows I shall claim that postmodern cultural forms do indeed signify, only that they signify differently. I shall argue that modernist culture signifies in a largely 'discursive' way, while postmodernist signification is importantly 'figural'. The terms 'discourse' and 'figure' of course are taken from Lyotard. My conception of postmodernist de-differentiation via an aesthetics of desire was also in large part dependent on Lyotard's work. Little of this work draws on Lyotard's *Postmodern Condition* (1979), on which so much ink of secondary analysis, has been split, and which, as indicated above I think is largely misconceived. The work in which Lyotard is the most valuable about postmodernism is, I think, his earlier work, in which he does not directly address the topic at all.

The body of this paper will then attempt to construct as contrasting ideal-types a 'discursive' modernist sensibility with a 'figural' and postmodernist sensibility. In this context the discursive 1) gives priority to words over images; 2) valuates the formal qualities of cultural objects; 3) promulgates a rationalist view of culture; 4) attributes crucial importance to the *meanings* of cultural texts; 5) is a sensibility of the ego rather than of the id; 6) operates through a distancing of the spectator from the cultural object. The 'figural' in contradistinction: 1) is a visual rather than a literary sensibility; 2) it devalues formalisms and juxtaposes signifiers taken from the banalities of everyday life; 3) it contests rationalist and/or 'didactic' views of culture; 4) it asks not what a cultural text 'means', but what it 'does'; 5) in Freudian terms it advocates the extension of the primary process into the cultural realm; 6) it operates through the spectator's immersion, the relatively unmediated investment of his/her desire in the cultural object.

This contrast of the two, discursive and figural, 'regimes of signification', will be addressed via rather theoretical considerations first, of Susan Sontag's contrast of an (I think, postmodernist) aesthetics of sensation with a (modernist) aesthetics of interpretation, and second, briefly, through Lyotard's more systematic distinction of 'discourse' and 'figure'. Then I turn to the (in large measure postmodern) avant-garde of the 1920s and examine how surrealism worked through the opposition between an image-centred culture, associated with the unconscious, and a formalist, word-centred culture, associated with the conscious mind. Finally cinema, and the cinematic experience, is addressed in a similar vein. Here it is noted that even in mainstream cinema, narrative content is increasingly losing centrality and giving way to a more image-centred 'spectacular' cinema. It is then argued further that in non-mainstream, critical cinema, a new image-centred mode of signification, based on an alternative 'regime of pleasure' may come increasingly to displace the most pervasive type of critical cinema which is modernist, discursive and intellectualist.

Sensation versus Interpretation
The new postmodern sensibility was perhaps first given systematic articulation by the critic Susan Sontag in the middle 1960s. Sontag counterposed an aesthetics of sensation to what she described as an aesthetics of 'interpretation'. She claimed that, 'in a culture whose already classical dilemma is the hypertrophy of the intellect at the expense of energy and sensual capability, interpretation is the revenge of the intellect upon art'. 'It is simultaneously,' she (Sontag, 1967: 7) continued, 'the revenge of the intellect upon the world. To interpret is to impoverish, to deplete the world — in order to set up a shadow of "meanings".' Sontag's attack on interpretation was two-pronged and aimed at both works of art and art criticism. Her attack on any notion of art as 'expressive' was generalized into an opposition to works of art whose main effect on an audience lies in

their 'meaning'. She thus had little use for cinema which gave great weight to symbolism, and unfavourably contrasted symbolist poetry to the work of poets like Ezra Pound whose work operated, not through meaning, but through the 'direct impact of words'. For Sontag, who contrasted an 'erotics of art' with 'hermeneutics of art', a work of art should be, not a 'text', but another 'sensory' thing in the world (Sontag, 1967: 165–7).

What Sontag saw as the 'new sensibility' was clearly not a literary sensibility, but foregrounded a 'cooler art' with 'less content'; it favoured not the novel, but music, dance, architecture, painting, sculpture. She discussed in this context who she saw as the twentieth century's two most influential analysts of theatre, Brecht and Antonin Artaud. Sontag (1967: 21) advocated, against Brecht's 'theatre of dialogue', an Artaudian 'theatre of the senses', whose driving force would be, not the playwright, but the director. This sort of theatre was not literature but was visual, its effects created through sounds and images. To the Brechtian 'didactic theatre' or 'theatre of the intelligence' was opposed the 'theatre of magic, of gesture, of "cruelty"' (Sontag, 1967: 173).

Sontag's postmodernist aesthetic was formed in opposition to contemporaneous 'hermeneutic' criticism, which for her foisted Marxian and/or Freudian interpretations onto the meanings of literature. However, her main opponent here was what has come to be known as the cultural conservatism among New York's intelligentsia, purveyed today by writers such as Daniel Bell and Irving Howe, but whose perhaps most influential figures were Lionel Trilling and Clement Greenberg. Cultural conservatives privileged the auratic work of art, whether realist or high modernist, either on grounds of the significance of its meaning, or on Apollonian grounds of its formal qualities. By contrast Sontag's postmodern criticism aggressively disputed such a separation of text and life. She (1967: 300) broke with such an implicitly Arnoldian view of art as a 'criticism of life' and instead endorsed a Nietzschean aesthetic in which even ideas should function as 'sensory stimulants' and in which art is an extension of or a 'supplement' to life.

Jean-François Lyotard provides a theoretical grounding to Sontag's distinction between a modernist hermeneutics and a postmodern aesthetics of sensation in his counterposition of 'discourse' and 'figure'. Lyotard's 'discursive' is the Freudian secondary process, the ego operating in terms of the reality principle. The figural, by contrast, is the primary process of the unconscious which operates according to the pleasure principle (Lyotard, 1971; 1973; 1984). Words arise from a particular set of oppositions between the secondary and primary processes, which are formulated partly as a critique of Lacan's dictum that the unconscious is structured like a language. He holds that we can best understand the nature of the unconscious through examining precisely how it is *not* structured like a language, that the most important criterion of demarcation of the unconscious from the ego lies in the ways that the former does not operate as does language. This has crucial implications for Anglo-American and Continental Culture Studies, whose Lacanian impulse has arguably prevented the establishment of important distinctions between cultural forms. We should note here that Lyotard does not maintain that the unconscious does not *signify*, but only that it does not signify like a language.

Lyotard's (1984: 69) understanding of 'the discursive' is rooted in his understanding of language as a means by which the ego discharges energy according to the reality principle. That is, in the secondary process energy is discharged 'through activities of transformation and verbalization'. In the primary process, by contrast, energy is discharged (and desire is fulfilled) through cathexis; through investment in 'perceptual memories'. Lyotard further clarifies this distinction in discussion of fantasies and hallucinations. He observes that fantasies operate like the primary process in that they 'fulfil desire' without the transformation of external reality but instead through the cathexis of, for example, the perceptual memory (image) of an organ. And hallucinations resemble the primary process in that again energy is discharged through investment in perceptual memories, through the displacement of energy from what Lyotard (1984: 57–68) calls the 'verbal-motor' end of the psychic apparatus to the perceptual end. Lyotard then has initially defined 'discourse' and 'figure' as two alternative means for the discharge of psychic energy. Discourse discharges energy through the transformation of the external world, while 'figures' are perceptual memories through which psychic energy is straightaway discharged by investment in them.

There is another important way secondary and primary processes are for Lyotard characterized through the language/image opposition. This, again relates to Lyotard's focus on *perception* in the unconscious, which derives from the influence of Merleau-Ponty's phenomenology of perception on his work. Here the secondary process does not just operate through discourse, but is structured like discourse, while the primary process does not only discharge energy through the use of perceptual memories, but is structured like a 'perceptual field'. That is, the unhindered mobility of the eye in the 'continuous and asymmetrical visual field' resembles the 'unhindered mobility of cathexis' in the primary process. Discourse, on the other hand, does not have the same unhindered mobility. It must proceed according to a set of obstacles, a set of rules, that is, through a 'process of selection and combination of language', which itself is more bound than mobile in language's articulated and differential nature. Similarly, in the secondary process the invest-ment of energy is canalized by rules, by obstacles, that the defense mechanisms of the ego construct, which subordinate the possibility of energy discharge to the 'transformation of the relationship be-tween the psychic apparatus and the external world' (Lyotard, 1984: 58; Dews, 1984).

Lyotard has thus asserted the existence of two alternative econo-mies of desire. In the first, the discursive, the secondary process makes inroads into the primary process. For example Lyotard considers Freud's 'talking cure' itself to promote a discursive eco-nomy of desire through the colonization of the unconscious by discourse; through the subversion of the primary process by lan-guage and the transference (Lyotard, 1984: 106). What he prefers of course is a figural economy of desire; he wants a sensibility, a culture and a politics in which the primary process 'erupts' into the secondary process like 'the application of a force to a text' (Dews, 1984: 47) Lyotard's (1984: 60–1) aesthetics is an aesthetics of Freu-dian 'unconscious space', which (i) permits condensation and other contradictions; (ii) permits the mobility of cathectic energies and hence displacement and which (iii) severs temporality from rule-boundedness. This figural aesthetics is a doctrine which opposes the subordination of the image to the dictates of narrative meaning or representation; to language like rule-bound formalisms (hence his preference for Cage over Schoenberg); or (in his (1984: 80) example of advertising images) to the dictates of capitalism and the law of value.

What both Sontag and Lyotard have endorsed is an effectively postmodernist aesthetics based on a paradigm of cultural de-differentiation. Sontag was arguing in the context of intellectual New York of the early 1960s. Then, as, arguably, now the terrain of debate was partly structured by the polarization of a serious and moral 'uptown' high modernist culture versus a more self-consciously populist and 'funky' yet equally elite, 'downtown' culture. Sontag argued against what was in effect the differentiated mode of signification implicit in the assumptions of uptown culture. This was the thrust of her attack on 'hermeneutics', whether the latter be of Arnoldian, Freudian or (reformist) Marxist complexion. Her attack on hermeneutics was an advocacy of de-differentiation in three important senses. First her challenge to the primacy of 'meaning' and support of 'cool' rather than an 'expressive' aesthetic assumptions was at the same time an advocacy of the collapse of some sort of deep level of the signified into the signifier. Second, her refusal of the counterposition of text and reality and determination to see the work of art as a 'sensory thing', was simultaneously an insistence that this already overloaded signifier was in fact not very different from a referent. Third, her dispute with 'interpretation', which is for her also a dispute with any kind of critical theory, is due to the assumptions of cultural differentiation built into the former and latter. In both there is a differentiated level of criticism standing over and above both art and life. Sontag counterposes to critical theory, casting adrift from both Marx and Freud, a de-differentiated Nietzschean aesthetics of affirmation, in which aesthetic analysis would be a supplement to art and art a supplement to life.

Lyotard similarly has proposed a de-differentiated semiotics. Arguing in the very different Parisian intellectual climate of the early 1970s, he assimilates assumptions of differentiated signification to Lacanian and orthodox Freudian psychoanalysis, to the commodity form in capitalism, to the ordered temporality of narrative realism and to the formalism of Adornian aesthetic rationality. Unlike Lacan, Lyotard very rigorously distinguishes between the image-based (in perceptual memories) signification of the unconscious and the discursive signification of the ego. His subsequent endorsement of the former, figural signification is an endorsement of cultural de-differentiation in two important senses. First, in the sense that unlike words or utterances, images signify iconically, i.e. through resemblance, and hence are less different from referents than properly linguistic signifiers. And second his promotion of the colonization of the secondary process by primary process in art and in psychoanalysis is also a rejection of the psyche rigidly hierarchized into levels for one in which desire is no longer an underlying 'essence'. Instead desire is present on the very surface of social and cultural practices.

Let us move now from the level of cultural theory to cultural 'practice'. We will find here, in the case of surrealism a not dissimilar state of affairs. In arguing, in what follows, that surrealism also exemplifies de-differentiated signification I will be *eo ipso* arguing that surrealism exemplifies postmodernism.

Surrealism: The Real Become Signifier

Surrealism was self-consciously 'figural' in its foregrounding of the visual. André Breton, self-styled 'pope' of the surrealist movement contrasted a high modernist aesthetic in which all art would be based on a musical model with the surrealist (and, in the present context, postmodern) idea that all art should partake of a visual mode. And indeed the reflections on art by modernists such as Flaubert, Klee and Auguste Macke did argue that literature and painting should be like music in a quest for the attainment of formal qualities and in a departure from realist notions of representation. Breton, on the other hand juxtaposed the 'savage eye' with the 'educated ear' and celebrated the immediacy of the visual (Krauss, 1985: 93). Surrealist écriture automatique, grounded in a Freudian unconscious structured through free association and perceptual memories, presented vision itself as a written form, a 'cursive' rather than a discursive flow, which Breton understood to be, not representational, but immediate.

Semiotics has conventionally spoken in terms of a tripartite model of signifier, signified and referent, in which the signifier is often a word or statement, the signified is a concept or a thought and the referent an object in the real world to which both signifier and signified connect. In the postmodern and figural aesthetic suggested by Lyotard, we saw above, that the image took the place of the word as signifier. In the surrealist movement, by contrast, it was the, equally figural, *referent*, the real itself, which becomes the signifier. Thus Rosalind Krauss can argue that photography is the quintessential surrealist art form. Photographs, she (1985: 110) observes, are like death masks, like footprints in the sense of being 'imprints of the real'. Breton compared the camera with psychic automatism in that both for him were processes of mechanical recording. Surrealist photographers indeed developed techniques which self-consciously addressed this juxtaposition of the real as signifier and the signifier as real. This was the case in their technique of writing or drawing on photos, or photographing bits of reality — like J.A. Boiffard's telescopically enlarged shot of a big toe (*Le Gros Orteil*)

— which seem primarily to be signifiers. It is also illustrated in the 'doubling' technique of using double exposures in which the first shot is read, not photographically, but as a signifying element whose referent is the second shot. The point here is that not only did surrealists see art as being composed of signifying elements drawn from the real, but understood reality to be composed of signifying elements. Thus Naville enthused that we should get pleasure from the streets of the city in which kiosks, autos and lights were in a sense already representations, and Breton spoke of the world itself as 'automatic writing'.

This thematic of the real, or the referent, as signifier is essential to the surrealist strategy which Walter Benjamin understood in terms of 'allegory'. Surrealist allegory would be based on, in Breton's words, 'the bringing together of two more or less distant realities', these realities forming 'an aggregation based on elective affinities' (Kuspit, 1983: 58). The point here is that the surrealist signifiers in 'allegory' are real, are *already* referents. Further, surrealist allegory for Benjamin is a method in which these figural signifiers are taken from 'the petrified and insignificant', from what Breton spoke of as the 'dresses of five years ago' (Sontag, 1979: 26). This bringing together of 'two more or less distant realities' creates the surreal *point sublime*. The latter is a 'profane illumination', a 'poeticization of the banal' and was a matter for Breton, not just of painting, literature and photography, but also of life and love, the latter arising in no small portion from an 'intoxication' in connection with the things of the beloved. There is surely a significant thematic of Benjaminian allegory in surrealist painting, in the young De Chirico's and Ernst's, not to mention Dali's, poeticization of petrified figures, or even in De Chirico's later, more kitsch method of juxtaposing scenes from Antiquity with the banal present (Dell'Arco, 1984: 82). De Chirico himself, upon arriving in New York in the mid-1930s, compared its architecture with his metaphysical paintings as a 'homogeneity and harmonic monumentality formed by disparate and heterogeneous elements'. Such surrealist allegory mirrors the process of displacement and condensation in dreams and in the primary process more generally.

Benjamin (1979: 226) wrote of the surrealist movement that 'life only seemed worth living where the threshold between waking and sleeping was worn away in everyone as by the steps of multitudinous images flooding back and forth, language only seemed itself where sound and image, image and sound interpenetrated with such felicity that no chink was left for the penny-in-the-slot called "meaning"'. Benjamin's allusions in this passage are, not just to the dominance of the figural and the devaluation of meaning in surrealism, not just to its characteristic patterning by eruptions of the primary process into consciousnes, but also and especially to surrealism's unconditional refusal to consider art as of a different order than life. Perhaps the exemplar of this surrealist categorical imperative, was Antonin Artaud. Artaud's initial public appearance before literary France came in the form of 'life' and not art, in the publication of his personal correspondence with *Nouvelle revue française* editor Jacques Rivière, after the latter had refused his poems due to their failure to live up to certain formal canons. As Derrida (1978: 234) noted, Artaudian theatre was not to refer to life or represent life but instead to be life. Theatre was to be a 'genuine reality', an 'event' like, Artaud proposed, a police raid on a brothel. He wrote in a theoretical essay published in the collection *The Theatre and Its Doubles*, 'For if theatre is a double of life, life is a double of true theatre ... The double of theatre is *reality* which today's mankind leaves unused' (Esslin, 1976).

Artaudian theatre is profoundly figural theatre. Key here was the influence of non-western cultural forms on Artaud — first the foregrounding of actors' movements and the absence of props in Japanese theatre; then his exposure to Cambodian dance in 1922; but most importantly the Balinese Dance Theatre which Artaud witnessed at the Colonial Exhibition in Paris in 1931, after which he wrote a succession of now canonical theoretical essays on theatre. In Balinese dance, as Esslin (1976: 35, passim) notes, all of Artaud's 'ideas of a non-verbal, magical theatre of light, colour and costume seemed realized'. Several aspects of Balinese dance as interpreted by Artaud have important implications for the understanding of postmodern culture in that they illustrate cultural de-differentiation. First such theatre, in a sense reminiscent of pre-modern art, takes on important ritualistic functions; the implication is that, in contradistinction to autonomous, modernist theatre, (postmodern) theatre itself should double as cultural ritual. Second, the absence of clarity as to whether Balinese dance, on the one hand, art, or on the other, life, underscored for Artaud the importance of cancelling the separation of the two realms. Third, the centrality of body movements in such theatre helped Artaud to develop his own aesthetics 'of the body'. Fourth, the cries in Balinese dance seemed to Artaud to have a cosmic power and communicated not through the differentiated and 'shadow' realm of meaning, but, directly, through impact.

What struck Artaud perhaps most of all about Balinese dance was the centrality of actors' bodily movements. He wanted actors, through for example exaggerated breathing, to establish an identity between their bodies and the bodies of spectators. Artaud had in some ways a curiously desexualized view of the body and spoke of a 'body without organs', which was for him a body deprived mainly of functions of reproduction and defecation, that was mainly a locus of feeling and sensation. Yet his idea of theatre was, unlike poetry or the novel, intended 'to reach the organism directly, and in the period of neurosis and low sensation into which we are about to plunge, to attack that low sensuality by physical means which it will not resist' (Esslin, 1976: 70; Deleuze and Guattari, 1984: 9–15).

Theatre then in Artaud's sense is not about life, but is a *supplement* to life. Theatre's task is 'to smash language in order to touch life'; it is to show that the force of the aural lies in sound (reduplicating for Artaud the significance that dreams give to the sounds in speech) and not words (Sellin, 1968: 49–52). Speech on this account functions primarily not as a conveyor of meanings, but as incantation — in which voices have, so to speak, a magical effect independent of the meanings of words. Incantatory speech is paradigmatic in contemporary Artaudian theatre and in surrealism and postmodernism more generally, are I think a sort of bodily aesthetics. This would contrast with both a 'realist' aesthetics of meaning and modernist formalism. Walter Benjamin (1979: 239), in a rather similar context, called for a politics in which 'technology, body and image so interpenetrate that all revolutionary tension becomes bodily collective innervation, and all the bodily innervations of the collective become revolutionary discharge'. Artaud, the least political of the surrealists, promulgated an aesthetics in which 'the bodily' applies both to means of production and conditions of reception. He understood literature not to be a formal craft, but instead viewed writing as a bodily process, a process which he experienced as wreaking pain, suffering and destruction on his own body (Sellin, 1968: 83).

In its usage of the real or referent as signifier, surrealism eminently illustrates de-differentiated signification. The surrealist aesthetic advocates signification, not through meaning, but through impact. And this impact is to be achieved in a particular way, i.e. through a 'profane illumination' brought about through the juxtaposition of two or more seemingly incongruous figures. The surrealist innovation thus is a problematization not just of the nature of high modernist painting and of the signifier, but also a problematization of what constitutes the real. It is thus similar to Warhol's silk screens, which problematizes, not just high art, but also the real in that it reveals reality itself to be composed of images. The source of the surrealist and pop art's problematization of both signifier and referent are different however. For Pop Art the source is the Baudrillardian society of the image. For surrealism it is the Freudian unconscious. Surrealist allegory, which attains its 'point sublime' and impact through the juxtaposition of 'two more or less distant realities', proceeds on three levels. First as signification in the unconscious through displacement and condensation. Second, in the work of art. And third, in everyday reality. In each case the result is not only a problematization of the real, but a problematization of the positioning of the subject. The eruption of the primary process and its analogues in art and reality foster an ambivalent positioning of the subject. They foster the development of, in contradistinction to any type of fixed positioning, what Deleuze and Guattari (1984) have called the 'nomadic subject'. This mobile positioning of subjectivity is in itself political in that it leaves space for alternative forms of identity construction as well as the toleration of 'difference' in identity construction.

The second major aspect of cultural de-differentiation addressed by surrealism is the issue of avant-gardes. Although surrealism (unlike contemporary postmodernism) was rather self-consciously an avant-garde, the logic of the surrealist ethic involved a dispute of the very nature of avant-gardes. The Artaudian break with the 'double' and embrace instead of the 'supplement' entails the rejection of avant-gardism in aesthetics, politics and theory. If art is no longer to be considered as of a different order than life, then the idea of aesthetic avant-gardes is questioned. If theory itself is to be no longer the 'double' of art or life then Nietzschean affirmation, and not critical theory, would be on the intellectual agenda. It is in this context that Benjamin's work qualitatively differs from Adorno's and Habermas's. Benjaminian allegory functions perhaps as crucially as supplement as it does as 'criticism'. Finally, the challenge to political avant-gardism, exemplified in Benjamin's effective call for a politics of the supplement, quoted just above, is a shift towards de-differentiation in political culture. It is a condemnation of the strong state as well as of the centralized Marxist vanguard party, and move towards the implicit embrace of anarchist doctrines. Such a rejection of state and vanguard party with its accompanied space opened up for pluralism and difference is of potential significance for left political culture today.

Cinema: From the Representation to the Reality

Cinema, taken generically, signifies in a de-differentiated manner. No other form of cultural representation — not painting, nor literature nor music nor even television — can signify quite as figurally as can cinema. That is, cinematic signification, especially in the age of high technology and the 30 million dollar film, comes closer than other forms of signification to resemblance of reality.

Cinematic signification again taken generically is further de-differentiated in that it portrays the primary process and sexuality, not as a deep alterity, but as erupting on the very surface of representations. This is true on four counts:

1) The experience of cinematic viewing — the dark, the succession of images ('perceptual memories'), the wonder, the wish fulfilment — has, as Metz (1982: 106–9) observed, a very great deal in common with the experience of dreaming and of unconscious processes.

2) As Benjamin (1973) noted, cinematic reception, unlike reception of the painting or the novel, takes place, not in a state of 'contemplation', but of 'distraction'. Cinema consists of a set of mechanically reproduced images which can be *presented* along the lines of the temporal causality of narrative realism. But as a literal succession of images they come closer to the disconnected temporality of the succession of perceptual memories in the unconscious.

3) Film, itself, is, as De Lauretis (1984: 85–6) observes, a discourse (in the Foucauldian sense) of sexuality. Cinema was born virtually contemporaneously with the other great discourse of sexuality, psychoanalysis. Cinema, further, more than any other cultural product, has been structured around sexuality, or rather around the objectification of male desire in screen images of women — that is, film narratives themselves have been structured by such a patriarchal economy of desire. These origins continue characteristically to put their imprint even on contemporary cinematic productions.

4) Cinema has always given primacy of place to *images*. Cinema is always an 'imaging machine'. This is a point not to be neglected in the context of the film criticism which has become dominant in

Anglo-American culture studies. Grounded in the work of Barthes and Lacan, such criticism has looked instead at how cinema operates like a *language*. In doing so it has often tended to neglect crucial distinctions between the nature of language and the nature of images. In contrast to such 'an increasing grammatization of discursive and textual operations' analysts such as De Lauretis (1984: 45) want instead to examine how cinema produces its specific effects on spectators through what is specific to *images*. Images, she notes, are signifiers of a different order than language. The elements of language are relatively arbitrary in regard to their referents in the real world, whereas images signify through their 'iconicity', through their resemblance to referents in the real world (Eco, 1976: 191ff). Moreover, 'images articulate meaning *and* desire' in a way that words or 'utterances' do not. That is, more than to words, 'not only semantic and social values but affect and fantasy as well, are bound to images' (De Lauretis, 1984: 8, 38).

Given this figural 'bias' built into the cinematic apparatus, it still makes sense to speak in terms of realist, modernist and postmodernist films. One way to make sense of these different paradigms in cinematic signification is through Laura Mulvey's (1981) distinction between 'narrative' and 'spectacle'. Mulvey argued that mass-market cinema has been structured around the 'spectacle' of women's images. Here she identified film 'narrative' with Freud's ego and spectacle with the sexual instincts of the id. In her account of realist cinema, the beginning of a film would centre around the spectacle of the free, desirable, perhaps somehow dangerous female lead. As the film progressed, however, and as the male star tamed, captured and finally possessed his female counterpart, the place of spectacle would be increasingly subordinated to that of narrative. My point in this context is that in films of recent years 'spectacle' — especially if we expand the definition of spectacle to include also images marked by the aggressive instinct — does *not* any longer become subordinated to narrative. That is, there has been a shift from realist to postmodernist cinema, in which spectacle comes heavily to dominate narrative.

A number of analysts have noted this. Coates (1985: 27, 77), for example, argues that in recent decades narrative has broken down to be replaced by a cinema of 'isolated heterogeneous events held together by the ramshackle constructions of Victorian melodrama', and that from the mid-1960s we have seen the dissolution of the distinction between realist and non-realist film. Heath has noted a new presence of the body in contemporary films; in, for example, films like *Jaws* which feature mutilations of the body. He (1981: 185–8) points to the pervasion of pornographic films in popular cinema in which 'the compulsive repetition of sexuality' takes the place of narrative. He (1981: 190) observes the 'suppression of voice' in pornographic cinema, a phenomenon which has extended to commercial cinema in general, in which voice is increasingly 'a support for a certain visible presence of the body'. This shift from a narrative cinema to a postmodern cinema of spectacle can be detected in some of the biggest moneyspinning films from the mid-1960s, such as Spaghetti Westerns (Frayling, 1981: 39f), in which realist narrative structure is violated by the presence of events which are interchangeable or gratuitous, by films like Scorsese's *Mean Streets* which resolutely refuse to end. This tendency was reinforced in the mid and late 1980s in which the blockbuster box office hits have been, for example, the Indiana Jones films and *Ghostbusters* and the Stallone and Schwarznegger films which have catered especially to an audience in their early teens, and use plot as an excuse for a succession of spectacular events.

This shift to figural and postmodern films has also taken place in art cinema. Only whereas in mass-market films postmodernism has partly displaced narrative realist films, in specialist cinema it has come to challenge 'high modernism'. Modernist cinema is cast in a Brechtian mould of distantiation and bears formalist characteristics. Pivotal to such a 'discursive' is Jean-Luc Godard. He has pursued this goal via techniques which lay bare the cinematic conventions. In this context MacCabe (1980: 44) comments on the use of 'montage', which Godard counterposes to 'image'. Montage is a 'juxtaposition of images and sounds' without 'a unity imposed by the director'. Montage always 'places the spectator's look in question, (it) poses the question of its constitution, and makes the institution of cinema the question of every film'. Distancing, and the critique of spontaneity and freedom motivate such practices as the use of tableaux to break narrative continuity and let the spectator stand back, and characteristically Godardian elucidation of the relations of production in the film production process (Cook, 1985: 137, 166).

There are several techniques that Godard uses to produce distancing and consequently the disinvestment of desire in images. First is his extraordinary valuation of words themselves. Godard has used the voice-over in a documentary type style, adopted for the

Soviet director Vertov. This is true particularly in his political films, in which the relationship of language and image is questioned through the juxtaposition of political discussion, on the one hand, with prima facie unrelated images, on the other. Films such as *British Sounds* were conceived in order to 'portray the struggle between images and sounds', and were especially concerned with 'how sounds can be used against the image'. Similarly in *Deux ou trois choses*, released in 1966, the voice-over misdescribes the hair colour and actions of a part-time prostitute. Likewise, *Le Gai Savoir*, made in 1968, was a gloss on Rousseau's *Emile ou l'éducation* and propounded that 'the central problem of education is to provide some understanding of the sounds and images that bombard us in our everyday lives' (MacCabe, 1980: 20).

If Godard's post-1968 films deliberately gave primacy to sounds over images, his earlier, less didactic films were themselves critiques of an image-centred politics, and in particular of the very political use of images in advertising. Thus in *Une Femme mariée* (1964) he, conscious that 'the image is a cultural product', was 'interested in advertising, the body, the commodities produced for women and the image which sells the commodities' (Mulvey and MacCabe, 1980: 92). In the film the protagonist, Charlotte works in an ad agency; she has an affair and lies to both husband and lover. Her gaze is constantly directed at advertising images which then become *her* image. In *Deux ou trois choses*, the prostitute-protagonist's 'position is also determined by the advertisements which constantly produce images for her'. Godard has revealingly said that cinema is dependent on capitalism in two senses: first in the making of the film and second that 'in film the money comes back in the image' (MacCabe, 1980: 27). Thus the Godardian question — 'who speaks in the image?' — is given answer in Adornian tones: it is the 'system which decrees that the order of money determines the order of the image' (MacCabe, 1980: 45). Godard had instead proposed a critical cinema which gives an activist role to the spectator. By posing a challenge to the spectator's libidinal investment in the image, he returns the question of desire to the eye of the spectator him- or herself. In questioning both narrative and pictorial realism and creating an effect of distancing, he poses for the spectator the issue of actively transforming reality (Heath, 1981: 63).

Despite the sharply effective critique of patriarchal and capitalist economies of desire, Godardian modernist 'counter-cinema' does have certain limits (Wollen, 1982). The substitution of a regime of 'intellectualist displeasure' for one of visual pleasure, limits accessibility even for the art cinema audience. By contrast, as De Lauretis has noted, a different and more recent set of developments seems to be taking shape. She (1984: 46) writes,

> what matters is once again the spectacle, as in the earliest days of cinema. Contradiction, paradox, ambiguity in the image as well as the textualized overlay of sound, language and image no longer produce distancing effects by baring the device of cinema and thus inducing rationality and consciousness. *They are the spectacle*, the no longer simple but excessive, 'perverse' pleasure of current cinema.

Surely this contemporary trend towards a figural cinema of spectacle in today's avant-garde often results in a repetition for the highly educated middle classes of patriarchal and capitalist economies of desire. Yet, De Lauretis argues, this new figural cinema at least poses the question of 'how to reconstruct and organize vision from the impossible place of female desire'. She (1984: 69, 87) calls for the production of films structured by an alternative economy of desire, for a 'microanalytics' of cinema with 'effects of resistance and counterinvestment'.

It is possible then to speak of four ideal-types of cinematic signification.

1) *Realist or narrative cinema*, whose roots are a) pictorially, in Quattrocento perspective, and b) in the non-teleological causal temporality, with beginning, middle and end, of the nineteenth-century novel (Heath, 1981: 28–37).

2) *Mainstream postmodern cinema*. Here we find basically 'figural' films, which foreground spectacle over narrative, for example, several of the Spielberg films and many of the late 1980s horror and gothic films, and the Rambo and Schwarzenegger films. Like mainstream narrative cinema, these postmodernist films position the spectator in a fixed and rigid space. Analysts like Mulvey and De Lauretis assume that all forms of cinema position the spectator through his/her investment of psychic energy in films. In narrative or realist cinema this mainly takes place through the identification of the spectator's ego with the hero of the narrative who serves as a sort of model or 'ego-ideal'. In mainstream figural cinema, which foregrounds spectacle, the investment of psychic energy and hence positioning of the subject would be, not via ego and secondary process, but via primary process. The point is, in cases both of realist and mainstream postmodernist cinema that the subject is placed in a fixed, rigid and stereotyped position.

3) *Modernist or 'discursive' cinema*. In this there is a much more ambiguous and open positioning of the subject. This takes place through the problematization of cinematic representation. This is integral to cultural differentiation because it separates the process of signification from reality. It is 'discursive' in Foucault's sense of 'discourse' (in *The Archaeologty of Knowledge*) in that it draws attention to the rules, the norms and conventions of cinematic signification itself. It is further discursive in the Foucauldian sense (and exemplifies cultural differentiation) in that primacy in modernist cinema is given to this separate cultural and discursive level.

4) *'Transgressive' postmodernist cinema*. This, like mainstream postmodernist cinema, is figural and privileges spectacle. The difference is that it, like modernist cinema, positions the spectator in a 'nomadic', rather than a sedentary, manner. It does so, however, not like modernist cinema, through the problematization of the representation, but instead through the problematization of the real. The parallels with painting are immediately apparent. Modernist painting, as theorists as diverse as Adorno, Greenberg (1983), and Wollheim (1980) have observed, draws the attention away from reality and to the picture surface itself, to the systematic development of possibilities in the aesthetic material. In brief, to the signifying process. Much the opposite with postmodernist, surrealism and pop art. Here not the signifying process but the fixed nature of *reality* is questioned. Consider, say, a recent cult modernist film Jim Jarmusch's *Stranger than Paradise*. In this Jarmusch does not follow the cinematic norm of letting a sequence develop to a climax and then cutting to another sequence. Instead he lets the sequence continue until long past its climax, after which the camera unduly lingers on the characters sitting around, being bored. Jarmusch here is experimenting with and calling the spectator's attention to cinematic conventions. He thus calls the audience's attention to the signifying practice.

In comparison a postmodernist film like Beneix's *Diva* or David Lynch's *Blue Velvet* will not distance the spectator or call his/her attention to the 'picture surface'. These films instead bring the viewer right into the film with a rather startling immediacy, but having done so, the 'real' that the spectator has been drawn into is revealed as artifice. Thus at the end of *Blue Velvet* the camera focuses on a flower, which then turns out to be made of papier mache. It shows a return to 'normalcy' in its ending which is in fact a send-up and suggests an integral flimsiness and instability to reality itself. In *Diva* much of the shooting highlights the interiors of the domiciles of the two main protagonists, Jules and Borodin. But the reality of Jules' living quarters turns out already to be a set of images. It is a disused garage, in which pop art rubs shoulders with wrecked 1950s autos on the model of those in Nicholas Ray's *Rebel Without a Cause*.

The contrast of such transgressive, figural films with their mainstream counterparts should also be clear. All figural cinema, or cinema which privileges spectacle over narrative or discourse, operates — as Mulvey suggests, largely on the model of and through the primary process. Consider, for example, a mainstream figural film, like the politically objectionable *Fatal Attraction*. This — which several British critics have seen as a post-AIDS film — is postmodernist in its mixture of genres: it starts out as a straightforward melodrama and shifts into a horror or 'stalk and slash' genre. Equally, instead of the narrative coming progressively to dominate the spectacle (as in realist cinema), the spectacle instead comes to dominate the narrative. But its treatment of sexuality and violence, its treatment of the single working woman as if she were a virus (which is then set as polar opposite against the 'healthy' family unit) tends to position rigidly the spectator (Williamson, 1988). Compare, on the other hand, some of David Cronenberg's work. Cronenberg himself has commented that *The Fly* and others of his films are about how viruses deform bodies, and that his originality lies in that he is 'on the side of the virus'. In this sense *The Fly* is also a post-AIDS movie. Yet the director contrives to evoke sympathy in the spectator towards the half-human protagonist played by Jeff Goldblum, and, by implication, ambiguity towards the virus and death itself. Here the spectator is much more ambiguously positioned as he/she is by the problematization of representation and reality in Cronenberg's *Videodrome*. The same might be said for the mix of sexuality and violence in *Blue Velvet*. Some feminist critics have condemned this film for itself not roundly condemning violence towards women. Yet is not David Lynch pushing back boundaries and underlining the instability of subjectivity when he shows, not just the villain played by Dennis Hopper, but the hero, engaging in sadistic behaviour? Is not the whole notion of hero (or even anti-hero) of a narrative thus problematized? Is not the problem of sadistic behaviour towards women made deeper and more urgent through this sort of portrayal than through, say, the simple moral condemnation of a villain who beats a woman?

Conclusions

I hope that my enthusiasm for the subject material in the above discussion will not be mistaken for any wholehearted support of some sort of postmodern aesthetics or politics. In the visual arts for example I believe that the work of Barnet Newman is of immeasurably more value than that of Andy Warhol. In politics, it is true that the work of such postmodernist critics as Susan Sontag and Rosalind Krauss is marked by a notable absence of a vision of a better world. Such a vision was present in the preceding generation of modernists; in Lionel Trilling, Irving Howe, Greenberg and Daniel Bell and others, many of whose political origins were Marxist.[2] It is, however, likely we do live in a culture that is in important ways undergoing a process of de-differentiation and hence 'postmodernization'.[3] It would then be folly for the political and cultural left to ignore this process because they find it unpleasant. A lot of future conflicts are going to be fought out on this new cultural terrain and the left needs a better understanding of it. Such conflicts can be fought out with a vision of a better world as I hope some of the above discussion has suggested.

What I have tried to do in the body of this paper is to further the understanding of postmodern culture in consideration of the latter as a figural and de-differentiated mode of signification. I have no pretensions to the type of expert knowledge of semiotics that students of linguistics will have. I do not want to claim however that the sociological analysis above shows that postmodern cultural objects signify differently, than do modernist cultural objects. I have suggested then that postmodern signification is a de-differentiated 'regime of signification' on a number of counts:

1) It is a figural, as distinct from discursive, regime of signification. To signify via figures rather than words is to signify iconically. Images or other figures which signify iconically do so through their resemblance to the referent. And signifiers (figures) which resemble referents are less fully differentiated from them than signifiers (words, discourse) which do not.

2) The devaluation of meaning in postmodern signification is simultaneously the de-differentiation of signifier and signified. In this sense the recent popularity of pragmatics in academic linguistics is a postmodern phenomenon, as is the importance of speech act theory in the social sciences in the past decade or two. The study in these of the use or effectiveness of language devalues the signified and meaning. Further, in speech act theory the representation

(speech) is collapsed into the real (action). Such a de-differentiation of signifier and referent has also been present in the claims of the followers of Althusser in the 1970s that ideological practices were material practices and of the followers of Derrida in the 1980s about the 'materiality' of language. In all of these renderings, signifiers function as referents or *les mots* as *les choses*.

3) If in contemporary pragmatics, the signified begins to wither away and the signifier to function as a referent, in surrealism (and to this extent surrealism is postmodern) the referent functions as a signifier. If for Althusserians and poststructuralists the signifier has become material (a referent), then for the surrealists and for Walter Benjamin the material (referent) became signifier. In both cases there is a de-differentiation, arguably a confusion and surely the problematization, of the relationship between signifier and referent. Thus the surrealists suggested that we experience everyday life as if its materiality were a network of signifiers. In this sense the claims of poststructuralists about the materiality of language is only the flipside of their claims about life being a 'text'.

4) This de-differentiation of signifier and referent is not just a matter of everyday life being experienced as a spatio-temporal configuration of signifiers, it is also a matter of the content of properly cultural objects themselves. Thus photorealism is unlike realist renderings of the referent and unlike modernist devaluation of the referent. Photorealism indeed attributes substantial value to the referent, but understands the referent to be itself a signifier. Much the same can be said for Lichtenstein's comic-strip pop art or Alex Cox's use of Lichtenstein type devices in his film *Repo Man*. In neither case, as in modernism is attention to be drawn to the aesthetic material itself, or to Greenberg's 'surface of the canvas'; the spectator's attention is drawn instead to the referent, to the real world. But the referent again becomes signifer to the extent that the viewer is reminded how like a comic strip the real world has become, or to what extent the real world is now comprised of comic strips. This is patent as well in cult films of the 1980s such as Luc Besson's *Metro* (*Subway*) as well as others mentioned above. Like realist cinema and unlike modernist cinema, these films do not 'lay bare the device' or call the viewer's attention to cinematic conventions. Attention in these films like in realist films is called to the referent, only the referent turns out to be, like the ear or the flowers in *Blue Velvet* and the imaged and real automobiles in Jules' living quarters in *Diva*, a set of false, glossy or monstrous signifiers.

Let me finally end, both theoretically and politically, on a speculative note. To say, following Habermas, that cultural modernization is a process of differentiation and autonomization and that postmodernization is a process of de-differentiation and implosion is to be content with a purely descriptive analysis of cultural change. What, one wonders, is the 'motor' of all this? Even if one were to, as I do, empathize with sophisticated functional Marxism of say G.A. Cohen and speak of the compatibility or incompatibility of certain sets of cultural forms with certain other sets of production relations, one would still be looking for an explanation of the specific properties of those cultural forms. Perhaps the key to this lies in the realm of culture itself. Suppose we were to begin with a crude distinction of 'social nature' and 'social culture', in which the latter were conceived in its narrow sense as representation rather than in the broad sense as symbol. Given this, the cultural history of the West (and not only the West) could be captured by a process in which the totality of 'social facts' comes to be comprised of an increasingly greater proportion of 'cultural' facts and an increasingly smaller proportion of 'natural' facts. At a certain juncture (the onset of modernism?) in such a chronology, cultural facts would accumulate to a point at which they could no longer be considered solely as representations, and the whole problem of their proper materiality and hence character as representations would have to be taken seriously. This would be the time also of the fullest differentiation and autonomization of cultural facts. At some later point in time in this scenario (especially with the mechanical and then electronic production and reproduction of representations), cultural facts would become so pervasive that they would come to challenge 'natural facts' for hegemony, and would even to some extent constitute the norm. What would now be problematized is, not as in modernism, the character of representations, but the character of reality itself.

What then are some political implications of postmodernism conceived per se as cultural de-differentiation? The answer may be that some sorts of postmodernist de-differentiation are implicitly 'reactionary', and other sorts potentially integral to a reconstructed left political culture; and still other sorts can politically cut either way. I suggested above that the postmodernist rejection of avant-gardes and criticism, and embrace instead of 'affirmation' and the supplement, is not at all necessarily conservative. Its consequences are hostility to the strong state and vanguard party and sympathy with pluralism and perhaps forms of anarchism. The postmodernist reaction to commodification is of a different colour. Modernist differentiation, whether in Adornian, Brechtian or Godardian guise has provided the distance for the unambiguous critique (the 'disinvestment of desire') of the commodity form and the commodification of culture. The unhappy prophets of the mid-1960s, Venturi and Warhol, on the other hand rejoiced at the interpenetration of culture and commodity. The process of de-differentiation that they celebrated has arguably increased exponentially in the past two decades. Only its mechanism seems to have changed. Recently there has been, not so much the colonization of representations by the commodity form (though this has happened too), but the colonization of the commodity by culture. Hence advertisements began as bits of information to help market commodities. Then, with the advent of ad agencies, the adverts themselves became commodities. Not long after, images rather than information became the content of these new commodities (Leiss, 1983). The final step in very recent years is that already existent cultural representations, in pop music, have come to accompany the images. Finally the new adverts themselves were partly responsible for the revival of early 1960s soul music in the late 1980s. A similar story of the colonization of the commodity by culture could surely be told about pop videos (Frith and Horne, 1987). Thus postmodernist cultural de-differentiation of representations and commodities seems unambiguously to have reactionary political-cultural consequences.

The main argument of postmodernists who have sympathies with the political left seems to have been that postmodernism can be supportive of a left politics rooted in principles of pluralism and 'difference'. This seems a contradiction on the face of it. How can a cultural paradigm whose main principle is *de*-differentiation contribute to a political culture grounded in the apparently opposite principle of difference? Perhaps the example of 'gender bending' in contemporary adverts and popular culture in general can provide a clue here. The deliberate ambiguity in gender and sexual preference built into images problematizes reality and the normative in a sense not dissimilar to the way that surrealism and pop art (discussed above) operate. The effect is a much more ambivalent and less fixed positioning of subjectivity. If subjectivity is less fixed, then space is left for the construction of identities, and collective identities, which deviate from the norm (Lury, 1987). That is, space is left for difference. The other precondition of difference and left pluralism is tolerance. And it would seem to follow that political-cultural tolerance is also furthered by the 'relatively autonomous' subject positioning fostered by de-differentiated representation.

Notes

1. I am grateful to Celia Lury, Nick Abercrombie, Norman Fairclough, Doug Kellner, John Urry, Brian Longhurst and Mark Poster for comments on previous drafts of this paper.

2. I am indebted on this point to a conversation with Richard Rorty, Berlin, July 1987.

3. The idea that, if I was going to understand the modern in terms of differentiation (*Ausdifferienzierung*), I should understand postmodernity in terms of de-differentiation (*Entdifferenzierung*) was driven home to me in a conversation with Prof. Jürgen Kocka, Bielefeld, December 1986.

References

Anderson, P. (1984) 'Modernity and Revolution', *New Left Review* 144: 96–113.

Benjamin, W. (1973) 'The Work of Art in the Age of Mechanical Reproduction', pp. 219–54 in *Illuminations*. London: Fontana.

Benjamin, W. (1979) 'Surrealism — The Last Snapshot of the European Intelligentsia', pp. 225–39 in *One Way Street*. London: Verso.

Callinicos, A. (1985) 'Poststructuralism, Postmodernism, Postmarxism?', *Theory, Culture & Society* 2 (3): 85–102.

Coates, P. (1985) *The Story of the Lost Reflection*. London: Verso.

Cook, P. (1985) 'Authorship and Cinema', in P. Cook (ed.) *The Cinema Book*. London: British Film Institute.

De Lauretis, T. (1984) *Alice Doesn't*. London: Macmillan.

Deleuze, G. (1981) *Francis Bacon*. Paris. Eds. de la Différence.

Deleuze, G. and Guattari, F. (1984) *Anti-Oedipus*. London: Athlone.

Dell'Arco, M. (1984) 'De Chirico in America', *Artforum* Sept.: 78–83.

Derrida, J. (1978) 'The Theatre of Cruelty and the Closure of Representation', in *Writing and Difference*. London: Routledge.

Dews, P. (1984) 'The Letter and the Line', *Diacritics* 14 (3): 40–9.

Eco, U. (1976) *A Theory of Semiotics*. Bloomington: University of Indiana.

Esslin, M. (1976) *Artaud*. London: Fontana.

Frayling, C. (1981) *Spaghetti Westerns*. London: Routledge.

Frisby, D. (1985) *Fragments of Modernity*. Cambridge: Polity.

Frith, S. and Horne, H. (1987) *Art into Pop*. London: Methuen.

Greenberg, C. (1983) 'Master Leger', pp. 109–14 in F. Frascina and C. Harrison (eds) *Modern Art and Modernism*. London: Harper and Row.

Heath, S. (1981) *Questions of Cinema*. London: Macmillan.

Kätz, B. (1982) *Herbert Marcuse and the Art of Liberation*. London: Verso.

Krauss, R. (1985) *Originality of the Avant-Garde*. Cambridge, Mass.: MIT Press.

Kuspit, D. (1983) 'Dispensable Friends, Indispensable Ideologies: Breton's Surrealism', *Artforum* Dec.: 56–63.

Lash, S. (1985) 'Postmodernity and Desire', *Theory and Society* 14 (1): 1–33.

Leiss, W. (1983) 'The Icons of the Marketplace', *Theory, Culture & Society* 1 (3): 10–21.

Lury, C. (1987) 'Women's Writings Groups: An Aesthetics of Experience'. Unpublished paper, University of Lancaster: Sociology Department.

Lyotard, J.-F. (1971) *Discours, figure*. Paris: Klincksieck.

Lyotard, J.-F. (1973) *Dérive à partir de Marx et Freud*. Paris: UGE.

Lyotard, J.-F. (1979) *La Condition postmoderne*. Paris: Minuit.

Lyotard, J.-F. (1984) *Driftworks*. NY: Semiotext(e).

MacCabe, C. (1980) *Godard*. London: BFI/Macmillan.

MacIntyre, A. (1981) *After Virtue*. London: Duckworth.

Metz, C. (1982) *Psychoanalysis and Cinema*. London: Macmillan.

Mulvey, L. (1981) 'Visual Pleasure and Narrative Cinema', pp. 206–15 in T. Bennett et al. (eds) *Popular Television and Film*. London: BFI/OU.

Mulvey, L. and MacCabe, C. (1980) 'Images of Woman, Images of Sexuality', in C. MacCabe, *Godard*. London: BFI/Macmillan.

Sellin, E. (1968) *The Dramatic Concepts of Antonin Artaud*. Chicago: University of Chicago Press.

Sontag, S. (1967) *Against Interpretation*. London: Eyre and Spottiswoode.

Sontag, S. (1979) Introduction to W. Benjamin, *One Way Street*. London: Verso.

Whimster, S. and Lash, S. (1987) Introduction to S. Whimster and S. Lash (eds) *Max Weber, Rationality and Modernity*. London: Allen and Unwin.

Williamson, J. (1988) 'Nightmare on Madison Avenue', *New Statesman* 15 January: 28–9.

Wollen, P. (1982) 'The Two Avant-Gardes', in *Readings and Writings*. London: Verso.

Wollheim, R. (1980) *Art and its Objects*. Cambridge: Cambridge University Press, second edn.

Scott Lash teaches Sociology at the University of Lancaster. He has recently co-authored *The End of Organized Capitalism* (Polity) and co-edited *Max Weber, Rationality and Modernity* (Allen and Unwin).

Postmodernist Aestheticism:
A New Moral Philosophy?

Richard Shusterman

I

In this paper I shall examine an intriguing and increasingly salient current in contemporary Anglo-American moral philosophy (and culture) towards the aestheticization of the ethical. The idea here, to adumbrate its more salient aspects in a phrase, is that aesthetic considerations are or should be crucial and ultimately perhaps paramount in determining how we choose to lead or shape our lives and how we assess what a good life is. It fleshes out Wittgenstein's (1963: 146–7) cryptic dictum that 'ethics and aesthetics are one'[1] by erecting the aesthetic as the proper ethical ideal, the preferred model and criterion of assessment for the good life. Such aestheticization is understandably directed primarily to what might be called the private ethical realm, the question of how the individual should shape his life to fulfil himself as a person.[2] But it can be very naturally extended to the public realm, to questions of what a good society should be like, at the very least so as to insure the possibility, if not the productive fostering, of the good life for its constituent individuals. Moreover, it has been quite common and still remains tempting to characterize good societies themselves by aesthetic standards, conceiving them as organic unities with an optimal balance of unity in variety — that classic and still potent definition of the beautiful. Though my focus will be on Anglo-American moral philosophy, I shall make clear how this current often converges with and is swelled by Lyotard's theorizing of the postmodern.

If the aestheticization of the ethical is a dominant (though hardly unprecedented[3]) current in our postmodernist age, it is perhaps more evident in our everyday lives and the popular imagination of our culture than in academic philosophy. It is demonstrated by our culture's preoccupation with glamour and gratification, with per-

Theory, Culture & Society (SAGE, London, Newbury Park, Beverly Hills and New Delhi), Vol. 5 (1988), 337–55

sonal appearance and enrichment. The celebrated figures of our time are not men of valour or women of virtue but those significantly called the 'beautiful people'. We are less inclined to the imitation of Christ than to imitating the cosmetics and fashion of Princess Diana; no one today reads the lives of the saints for edification and example, but the biographies of film stars and the success stories of corporate millionaires are perennial best sellers. However, the postmodernist ethics of taste is not without philosophical apologists. Several philosophers seem to support the position by implication, perhaps unknowingly or even unwillingly. But, as usual, the most outspoken and outrageous philosophical exponent of America's popular imagination is Richard Rorty, who explicitly advocates 'the aesthetic life' as the ethically good life. For Rorty, 'this aesthetic life' is a life motivated by the 'desire to enlarge oneself', 'the desire to embrace more and more possibilities' (Rorty, 1986: 25), which is expressed in 'the aesthetic search for novel experiences and novel language' (Rorty, 1986: 35). In other words, aesthetic self-enrichment and gratification is sought not only through actual experiments in living but through the more timid option of employing 'new vocabularies of moral reflection' so as to characterize our actions and self-image in a more freshly appealing and richer way. Rorty's case for the aesthetic life will occupy much of this paper, as his avid advocacy of postmodernism makes such concentration appropriate. But there are other visions of and arguments for the aesthetic life which deserve and will claim our attention.

II

How can we explain or justify postmodernism's aestheticization of the ethical? The rise of the ethics of taste can be largely explained through the fall of more traditional models of the ethical. Just as once born we have to live our lives in some fashion, once we start reflecting ethically on how to live we must reflect in some fashion. Erosion of faith in traditional ethical theories left an ethical *horror vacui* which the ethics of taste naturally rushes to fill. Rorty (1980: 180) seems close to saying this when he argues that after Galileo, Darwin and Freud 'neither the religious nor the secular and liberal morality seems possible, and no third alternative has emerged', except for the aesthetic one he subsequently advocates. The most powerful reasons impelling contemporary philosophers to reject traditional ethics would seem to derive from two general philosophical attitudes. The first is an historicist and contingently pluralist anti-essentialism as to human nature, while the second expresses a perception of severe limitations in morality which make it clearly inadequate for a full-blown satisfying ethic. We might describe this second view as the underdetermination of ethics by morality. Each of these attitudes involves a number of aspects or levels which merit attention.

1. Traditionally, ethical theories have sought to justify not only themselves but the whole ethical enterprise from what Bernard Williams (1985: 29) has recently called 'an Archimedean point', 'something to which even the amoralist or skeptic is committed but which, properly thought through, will show us that he is irrational, or unreasonable, or at any rate mistaken'. Typically, such foundationalist theories base themselves on general theories of human nature, trying to derive what life is essentially good for man from what is essential to or essential in human kind, and recognizing that any ethical 'ought' depends on some non-ethical 'can'. The desire for pleasure or happiness and the capacity for an exercise of rational thought and action have been the most familiar and compelling candidates for such essential features. In synthesizing them both, as well as in giving a much more concrete and substantial picture of what constitutes the good life for man (though not for women and slaves), Aristotelian ethics seems superior to Kant's, which despite his epistemological recognition of man as both sensuous and rational, rests on a very purified and eviscerally abstract concept of man as a rational agent who therefore requires some freedom of choice of action.

The particular problems with the Aristotelian and Kantian enterprises, many of which Williams neatly outlines, need not concern us here. The more basic problem which pervades these and similar attempts to ground ethics in an account of man's intrinsic or essential nature is our strong postmodernist suspicion that there really is no such thing. We have an even stronger suspicion that there is no ahistorical essence that is both universally found and timelessly (metaphysically or biologically) fixed in human kind and yet is also determinate and substantial enough to generate or justify, by mere logical derivation or elaboration, a definite ethical theory. We have come to see that even our best candidates for essential status, like rationality and happiness, seem promising only as long as we don't probe too deeply into the culturally and historically divergent accounts of what in fact really constitutes these things.

The lack of an ahistorical ontologically given human essence does not, however, foreclose all possibility of foundationally deriving from human nature an ethical theory for historical man. For that project could perhaps get by with some non-ontological but still transhistorical, cross-cultural human essence; some sort of amalgam of linguistic, cultural and biological universals found to be universally present in and necessary to human life whenever and wherever it has flourished, and one from which could be projected a definite and coherent picture of what constitutes the good life. But scepticism here is no less potent in the face of obvious historical and cultural divergence. Even in what we conceive as the same cultural tradition — say, that which Eliot once personified as 'the mind of Europe' — we find very different answers to what is essential to or desirable for a properly human life. Moreover, given what Lyotard (1984) diagnosed as our postmodernist suspicion of grand legitimating narratives, we cannot try to explain away such divergence by appeal to the variant but progressive manifestation of the human spirit in search of liberation and/or perfection (*Bildung*).

Yet though we may reject both ahistorical human essence and the idea of some human essence shared by all ages and cultures of historical man, there still remains the more modest but still very significant project of generating an ethical theory for our own specific age and culture. This 'limited' aim is surely what we most want, since what we want to know is how to live our own lives rather than those of our ancestors or descendants which are obviously not ours to live. But even drastically narrowing the focus to our contemporary American society, we find there is just too much significant variety to talk confidently of any formative essence which could tell us what and how to seek in seeking the good life. We are perhaps unified in a commitment to freedom and the opportunity for the pursuit of happiness. But such notions, as communitarian critics of liberalism frequently complain, are helplessly vague and abstract; and the unity they apparently provide quickly disintegrates into variant rival visions of what freedom, happiness and opportunity really mean.

There are at least two good reasons why not even such localized human essences can be found. First, not only in a mammoth country like America but in any advanced civilization, there is a very high order of division of labour, a division of occupational roles. The notion of a general functional essence of man that Aristotle and other ethical theorists assumed and built upon seems no longer viable when men *and women* have so many different functional occupations which are so difficult to reconcile. How do we reconcile the functional essence of the farmer and the stockbroker, the creative artist and the factory hand, the priest and the cosmetician, the scientist and the casino operator? Much more disturbing is the fact that we not only collectively experience a conflict of divergent (occupational) functional essences, but we feel it just as powerfully on the individual personal level. The conflict between a woman's functional essence as defined by her profession and that defined by her role as mother is perhaps the most familiar and acute of such contemporary problems of identity. But there are countless other examples of how our professional roles or self-definitions sharply conflict or simply do not coherently mesh with our self-definition as friends, family or political agents, thus making it seem impossible to find man a functional essence in some coherent amalgam of his social roles.

To say that a postmodernist cannot generate a general or even personal ethic from his or her specific functional role because we all inhabit collectively and individually a plurality of inadequately integrated roles is to say with Wittgenstein and Lyotard that we inhabit such a motley variety of language-games and are shaped by so many forms of discourse that we no longer can say definitively who we are. We cannot tell what is the good life for us, because the nature of us is so questionable and unsteady with our changing roles and self-representations. It is questionable, Rorty would argue, because it is not definitively there to be discovered but instead open to be made and shaped, and should therefore be shaped aesthetically. Moreover, according to Rorty not only is there no point in trying to penetrate our social roles to find a common human essence which is not there, but even the idea of an underlying coherent individual essence of particular personhood (one's own true self) is a myth which Freud effectively exploded. One's own self or personality seems to be revealed as an uneasy combination of a number of conflicting (conscious and unconscious) 'quasi persons' composed of 'incompatible systems of belief and desire', which discredits the whole idea of a person's one 'true self' (Rorty, 1986: 5, 11, 19). Rather than something unified and consistent emerging from an autonomous, stable and rational core, the self is seen as 'centerless', a collection of 'quasi selves', the product of 'random assemblages of contingent and idiosyncratic needs', shaped and modified by 'a host of idiosyncratic, accidental episodes' transformed by distorted memories (Rorty, 1986: 4, 12, 14). For Rorty, this Freudian decentring, multiplication and randomization of the self 'opened up new possibilities for the aesthetic life' as an ethic, since with no true self to discover and conform to the most promising models of 'moral reflection and sophistication' become 'self–creation' and 'self–enlargement' rather than 'self–knowledge' and 'purification' (Rorty, 1986: 11–12).

Anti-essentialism as to human nature thus leads to an ethics of taste. It would be wrong, however, to see this as a logical derivation. If human nature's absence of essence means it implies no determinate ethic, it therefore cannot imply an aesthetic one. Yet, it still may be said to lead to an ethics of taste, since in the absence of any intrinsic foundation to justify an ethic we may reasonably be encouraged to choose one that most appeals to us; and it is plausible to think that such appeal is ultimately an aesthetic question, a question of what strikes us as most attractive or most perfect.

2. It is time to turn from anti-essentialism to the second general attitude which has worked to undermine traditional ethical theories and thereby help recommend an aestheticized ethics of taste. I have called this attitude the underdetermination of ethics by morality and it has two aspects which respectively concern the extension and dominance of moral considerations in ethical thought. The first aspect finds its most general expression in contemporary moral philosophy's increasing recognition that morality as traditionally conceived does not really cover the full gamut of ethical concern. For the ethical involves a wide range of considerations of value and goodness in respect to how one should live, many of them clearly personal and egoistic or at least not universalized (e.g. special concern for one's own interests or one's family's) and many of them non-obligational (e.g. munificence and uncalled for acts of kindness or heroism). But traditional moral thinking, as Williams and Wollheim have most recently maintained, constitutes a much narrower special 'subsystem' of the ethical, governed by obligation and universalizability. For Williams (1985: 6–7, 14), the narrower 'special system' of morality 'peculiarly emphasized certain ethical notions rather than others, developing in particular a special notion of obligation'. Wollheim (1984: 215–16) concurs in taking 'morality in the narrow sense ... to be that which has obligation as its core', and he contrasts it very sharply with the realm of value and goodness in terms of their differing psychological genealogy and consequent potential for human satisfaction. 'One (morality) derives from introjection [of a menacing figure], the other (value) derives from

projection ['of archaic bliss, of love satisfied']. One is in its origins largely defensive and largely coercive, the other is neither. One tries to guard against fear, the other to perpetuate love.' And if Wollheim's account of morality emphasizes its menacing beginnings and baneful aspects, Williams (1985: 175) is still more explicit (and perhaps more extreme) in asserting with insouciant bluntness 'that we would be better off without it'.

Williams' rejection of 'morality, the peculiar institution' or 'special system', is not so much theoretically motivated by its distressing psychological sources and effects, as by its logical peculiarities and insufficiency in accounting for our ethical thinking. What makes this mere insufficiency so vitiating is that while morality clearly underdetermines ethics, it constitutes and sees itself as a system which is globally exhaustive in its determinations. It presents itself as a consistent system of obligations (and consequent rights) which can tell us what we should do in any instance. That we should or ought to do something implies that we *can* do it, and therefore these obligations will be hierarchically ordered so as to prevent their conflicting in any final or irresolvable sense, since they cannot be allowed to issue in contradictory actions, which as incompatible cannot be performed. 'Moral obligation is inescapable' and whether you want to subscribe to the system or not, it includes you in its categorical universalizing logic and imputes to you moral blame if you do not act according to its comprehensive system of obligations (Williams, 1985: 177–78).

Williams is chiefly occupied with successfully challenging two of morality's globally categorical presumptions: its claim to exhaustive extension of application, and its supreme or all-overriding potency wherever applied. He shows how morality cannot defend the first claim against obvious cases of kindness and generosity that are non-obligatory or even in conflict with some prior definite obligation; and he exposes the failures of philosophical efforts to salvage the claim through the unconvincing positing of an elaborate hypothetical system of differently ordered obligations (particular obligations, general obligations, negative obligations, prima facie obligations, obligations to self, to others, etc.) so that any action we might look upon with favour or distaste will be seen as deriving or deviating from some relevant (or ordered complex of) obligation.

Closely connected with morality's assumption that it exhausts all ethical action and choice, that any worthy act can ultimately only be justified in terms of some obligation, is the presumption that in any ethical question moral considerations should always override all others and determine how one should act or live. Thus, if the performance of a noble unobliged act of kindness prevents me from meeting a trivial obligation, say arriving to work on time, a vague general obligation relating to kindness must be posited to justify my act's obvious worth. The idea that certain things can be good regardless of obligation and can even outweigh obligation in ethical deliberation is utterly foreign and intolerable to the system of morality. Williams (1985: 187) calls this morality's maxim 'that only an obligation can beat an obligation' and its transparent falsity constitutes the second part of postmodernism's case for the underdetermination of ethics by morality. Ethics, as distinguished from morality, recognizes that there is more to the good life than the fulfilment of obligations, and indeed 'can see that things other than itself are important . . . [to life] as part of what make it worth living' (Williams, 1985: 184). This does not mean that ethics need reject moral considerations entirely, but simply their claim to entirety and overridingness. What is denied (and this time in Wollheim's (1984: 225) words) is 'the view that morality is ultimate or overruling'.

The result of this demotion of the moral to merely one significant factor in ethical deliberation on how to live the good life is to make such deliberation much more like aesthetic judgment and justification than syllogistic or legalistic discourse. Finding what is right becomes an affair of finding the most fitting and appealing gestalt, of perceiving the most attractive and harmonious constellation of various and variously weighted, changing and changingly weighted, features in a given situation or life. It is no longer the deduction of one obligation from another more general obligation or group of obligations, nor the outcome of a logical calculation based on a clear hierarchical order of obligations. Similarly, ethical justification must come to resemble the aesthetic in appealing to perceptually persuasive argument in its attempt to convince, an attempt which relies on and aims to sustain and extend some basic consensus, and yet also recognizes and serves to promote a tolerance of difference of perception or taste emerging from it. In the manner of aesthetic interpretation and evaluation, it is crucial to us that our fellows understand our ethical perspectives and choices and see them as reasonable, but no longer so crucial that they accept them as universally right and valid for all. Ethical judgments can no more be demonstratively proven categorically true through unexceptionable principles than can aesthetic ones. Ethics and aesthetics become one in this meaningful and sensible sense; and the project of an ethical life becomes an exercise in living aesthetically. Perhaps this is what Wollheim (1984: 198) has in mind when for one brief moment he very vaguely and tentatively suggests that ethics be viewed 'like art'.[4]

III

This, however, is not (or at least not all of) what Rorty recommends as the aesthetic life, which he depicts in more radical and substantive tones. Basing his rejection of morality on the perhaps more clearly Sartrian than Freudian themes that man has no essence and that a person is the product of random and idiosyncratic contingencies, Rorty does not react with Sartrian nausea but rather upbeat radiance in embracing the (again Sartrian) conclusion that we must create ourselves. Such creation could, of course, be achieved by the acceptance of even the most traditional or ascetic of moralities, so the necessity of self-creation in no way entails or recommends what Rorty advocates as 'the aesthetic life'. Moreover, the life painted by Rorty seems to represent only one of at least three basic genres of aesthetic life which have found ardent and influential philosophical evangelists over the ages, and indeed even in this century alone.

What then is Rorty's vision of the aesthetic life and how does it compare to others? It would be fairer to cite Rorty's own account before supplying any critical caricature or comparison of our own. His aesthetic life rejects 'an ethics of purity' and self-knowledge for 'one of self-enrichment' and 'self-enlargement'. 'The desire to enlarge oneself', says Rorty (1986: 11), 'is the desire to embrace more and more possibilities, to be constantly learning, to give oneself over entirely to curiosity'. This quest for self-enlargement involves a dual 'aesthetic search for novel experiences and [for] novel language' to redescribe and thereby enrich those experiences and their experiencer (Rorty, 1986: 15). Similarly, 'the development of richer, fuller ways of formulating one's desires and hopes' makes 'those desires and hopes themselves — and thereby oneself — richer and fuller' (Rorty, 1986: 11). The aesthetic aim is not to 'see things steadily and see them whole' but to see them and ourselves through ever new 'alternative narratives and alternative vocabularies' designed 'to produce radical change' (Rorty, 1986: 10–11). Those 'exceptional individuals' who can take the breathless pace and confusion of compulsively proliferating and inhabiting a Babel of vocabularies bent on protean radical change will be able 'to make their lives works of art' (Rorty, 1986: 11).

If our postmodernist culture has been aptly characterized as narcissistic, we should not be surprised that Rorty sees the ethical 'search for perfection in oneself' as having already found it in himself. Rorty (1986: 11–12) himself turns out to be the hero of his postmodernist narrative of 'this aesthetic life, the life of unending curiosity', a narrative which works to identify 'the aesthetic life' with 'the life of the curious intellectual'. This intellectual hero is 'increasingly, ironic, playful, free, and inventive' (Rorty, 1986: 12), and displays both Lyotardian scepticism of all grand narratives (except his own Bildungsroman of self-enlargement) and Lyotardian restless greed to take the most tricks in as many new language games as he can learn to play. This curious and ironic intellectual, to fill in the character of the Rortian postmodernist hero perhaps more fully than he would like, is as bold and iconoclastic in thought as he is timid and docile in life and the transformation of social and political realities. Rorty (1986: 10–11) makes clear that his ethics of taste is a 'private morality'; his aesthetic life is not a social project but a powerfully individualistic one for private gratification rather than group welfare.[5]

We have seen enough of Rorty's portrayal of the aesthetic life to recognize the genre as essentially Romantic picaresque, a tireless insatiable Faustian quest for enriching titillation through curiosity and novelty, a quest that is as wide-ranging as it is unstructured through the lack of centre it so celebrates. However, this absence of structuring centre prevents it from being the sort of Bildungsroman it seems to want to be. For the maximized spawning of alternative and often inconsistent vocabularies and narratives of the self, an aim which explicitly seeks to undermine the idea of the true self and replace it with an open, changing, growing, multiplicity of selves or self-descriptions, makes the whole idea of an integral enduring self seem completely empty and suspect. But without such a self that is capable of identity through change or changing description, there can be no self capable of self-enrichment or enlargement, and this would nullify the Rortian aesthetic life of self-enrichment by rendering it meaningless. Further analysis and critique of this version of the aesthetic life should, however, require at least brief notice that there are others.

One different and perhaps more familiar version of the aesthetic life is a life devoted to the enjoyment of beauty: beautiful objects of nature and art, as well as those hybrid products of nature and art we are loath to regard as objects of either — beautiful people. This aesthetic life was very influential in the early part of our century through the fashionable Bloomsbury coterie who confess to having imbibed it from G. E. Moore's account of the ideal in human life. For Moore (1959: 188–9) (who, like Rorty, repudiates any ethics based on the idea of 'the true self') this ideal consisted of 'certain states of consciousness, which may be roughly described as the pleasures of human intercourse and the enjoyment of beautiful objects'; because 'personal affections and aesthetic enjoyments include *all* the greatest, and *by far* the greatest, goods we can imagine' in life. Both these components of the aesthetic life are constituted by very complex and rewarding organic unities. However, the pleasures of personal affection require 'that the object must be not only truly beautiful, but also truly good in a high degree', where a proper appreciation of human beauty must include appreciation of its 'purely material' form and the 'corporeal expression' of its mental qualities (Moore, 1959: 203–4).

If this Moorean-Bloomsbury aesthetic life strikes us as distinctively modern and even chicly contemporary in engaging with our hedonistic penchant for beautiful things and beautiful people, we should remember that it too represents a romantic genre, more particularly a late romantic ideal of aestheticism. Unwilling to accept the universal dominance of the mechanized world picture, unable to accept the traditional religious and moral claims to spirituality, and unready to be sullied by philistine politics, the aesthetes sought individual and collective salvation through the satisfying gemlike flame of art and sensation instead of through God or state. Their ideal of the aesthetic life differs from Rorty's not only in being less preoccupied with 'the curious intellect' but in being more appreciative of beauty, pleasurable sensation, and the leisurely luxury of satisfaction. It is essentially the ethic of Pater and Wilde, an exquisite flower of aestheticist decadence, which remains undeniably and captivatingly sweet, and may be the only flower capable of growing in our postmodern wasteland. However, as versions of the aesthetic life tend to overlap and be compounded, we find in Wilde's (1948) maxim that 'life itself is an art' a clear suggestion of a third notion of the aesthetic life, which I shall call, for contrast and commendation, the classical.[6] The idea is not so much a life of aesthetic consumption, but a life which is itself a product worthy of aesthetic appreciation for its structure and design as an organic unity.

The Greeks, as Williams and Wollheim both note in discussing ethical reflection, were strongly inclined to conceive and assess the good life holistically, as a unified whole. The idea that an individual's life needs to be seen, organized and evaluated in terms of such an organic rather than simply mechanical or aggregative unity gave Solon's famous injunction to 'call no man happy until he is dead' its special force. For a disastrously inappropriate end could distort beyond repair the satisfying unity of the life led thus far. One of the basic projects of Greek ethics is to try to find such a unitary life that is maximally free of the threat of disunifying misfortune; and one general strategy to achieve such unity is to establish a centre and contours for life by a kind of overarching aim or interlocking set of aims, a limiting concentration on a narrower range of goods (naturally those less susceptible to misfortune).

This kind of slimmed down, centred, limit-respecting life of unity is labelled by Rorty (1986: 11) 'the ascetic life' in unfavourable contrast to 'the aesthetic life' he advocates. But such characterization is misleading and unfair. It is simply wrong to assume that a life emphasizing strong unity and thus adopting the limits this requires cannot be an aesthetic life, that it cannot be enjoyed and praised as aesthetically satisfying or even recommended for its aesthetic appeal. One could well choose the life of an earth-rooted family-bound farmer over an air-hopping, spouse-swopping academic simply in terms of its aesthetic joys of order, coherence and harmony, which stem from a centrally structured and limited project of development, whose unity is both enhanced and largely constituted by cyclical and developmental variations on its central theme or narrative. To live life aesthetically or even to adopt as an ethic 'the aesthetic life' is not necessarily to adopt the Faustian aesthetic life of Rorty with its aim of maximizing alternative narratives and 'tinkering' changes of the self, its relentless search for 'novel experiences and novel language', and its repudiation of a centre (which can be made rather than discovered). Among the multiplicity of genres of the aesthetic life which Rorty fails to recognize there are surely some which prefer order, grace and harmony to opulence, radical change and novelty.

This non-Rortian perspective on the aesthetic life can be linked directly to the classical definition of beauty as unity in variety, a definition reaffirmed by Coleridge and other romantics and still the best definition we have. Rorty's one-sided insistence on enlargement and variety makes him insufficiently appreciative of the aesthetic claim of unity and of the threat to it posed by the decentred, unbounded variety he champions. Moreover, this threat to unity of life is not something Rorty can breezily brush aside as merely a matter of genre preference. For, as I earlier suggested, the loss of such unity would seem to render his entire project of self-enrichment incoherent and unworkable by denying any reasonably stable and coherent self to enrich.

Once we abandon a foundationalist essentialism about the self, we can only constitute the self, as Rorty himself admits, in terms of narrative about it. It follows that the unity and coherence of the self will depend on the unity and coherence of its narratives. It is largely for this reason that Alisdair MacIntyre (1982: 191), who similarly rejects any foundationalist account of personal identity, insists on 'a concept of self whose unity resides in the unity of a narrative'. Not only is this unity essential to the classical ideal (affirmed by MacIntyre 1982: 190) of seeing 'each life as a whole, as a unity', but without such unity and coherence of narrative there is no intelligible self to speak of for Rorty's aesthetic life to enrich, enlarge or perfect. If we abandon the aim of a unified or consistent self-narrative for Rorty's (1986: 8) discordant chorus of inconsistent 'quasi selves' constituted by alternative, constantly changing, and often incommensurable narratives and vocabularies, with no complex narrative 'able to make them all hang together', then the project of self-enrichment becomes mythical and incoherent with the myth and incoherence of a single self collecting these riches together. The self-unity needed to speak meaningfully of self-enrichment or perfection (if not to speak of the self at all)[7] is, however, something pragmatically and often painfully forged or constructed rather than foundationally given, and it surely involves developmental change and multiplicity, as all narrative unity must. A unified self is not a uniform self, but nor can it be an unordered collection of egalitarian quasi selves inhabiting the same corporeal machine. Rorty's confederacy (rather than centralist union) of quasi selves thus seems less the formula for a Freudian ideal of self-perfection than the recipe for a Freudian pathology of schizophrenia.

Rorty almost seems to recognize the necessity for self-unity when he asserts that the only post-Freudian version of human dignity is 'a coherent self-image' and when he tries to appropriate MacIntyre's unifying virtue of 'integrity or constancy' as part of his aesthetic life's 'search for perfection' (Rorty, 1986: 17, 19). But he implicitly denies coherence in advocating a self composed of 'a plurality of persons ... [with] incompatible systems of belief and desire' (Rorty, 1986: 19); and the only constancy that he in fact prescribes is the constancy of change, of novel alternative self-descriptions and narrations, the constancy of inconstancy which essentially nullifies the unity and integrity of the self.[8]

In learning so much from Freud, Rorty might have probed why Freud seemed much less eager to dispense with a unified, integrated self. Why, for example, did he first opt for the positing of the unconscious rather than simply multiple consciousnesses or perso-nalities residing in the same body, and why did he never portray our psychological constituents as ideally 'egalitarian' and all 'sweetly reasonable' as Rorty (1986: 7–9, 22) does, as rational quasi-persons engaging in free conversation, unordered by repression and cen-sorship which, of course, imply some organizational hierarchy gov-erning discourse? One reason may be that Freud implicitly realized what a pricelessly important and yet perhaps fragile achievement the unity of self was, how difficult and painful such a unified self or self-narration was to construct, and yet how necessary it was to lead any plausible version of a good or satisfying life in human society. It is certainly presupposed in Rorty's ideal of the Faustian aesthetic life, no matter how much he wants to reject it. In fact, what makes his portrayal of this life not only coherent but possibly attractive to us is that it centres around one kind of self-vocabulary and narra-tive, the intellectual and his quest.

The apparent incoherence of Rorty's project of self-enrichment through multiplying congeries of inconsistent alternative self-narratives should be enough to dissuade us from adopting his ver-sion of the aesthetic life as the postmodernist ethical ideal. But his advocacy of this 'private morality' of self-perfection seems still more problematic when he appeals to social and historical solidarity as somehow enhancing 'the aesthetic life', giving an individual's life more meaning and 'a Romantic sense of grandeur' by seeing that personal narrative as bound up with the life-narratives of other individuals and embedded into the larger narrative of some com-munity or tradition (Rorty, 1986: 19–20). Here we must ask with puzzlement, where is the coherent integrated individual narrative (among the myriad inconsistent narratives of quasi persons) which we wish to bind with others in a project of solidarity? Where is there a self that is unified and firm enough not only to allow a momentary self-satisfied glimpse of convergence with others but to guide the narrative enactment of continued and deepening bonds of solidarity? The Rortian self needs to get its own act together, attain its own narrative solidarity and coherence, before it can hope to cohere with others in more than a fleeting cohabitation of the same geography or language-game.

Moreover, given the familiar dialectic of self/other, the coherently unified selves which we are and which are necessary for larger projects of solidarity are themselves largely the product of such communal solidarity. The private self which Rorty wants to enlarge and perfect is thus 'always already' social and must be so as soon as it has a language for its private thoughts; and Rorty (1986: 10–11) is therefore unwise to maintain that his 'private morality' of the aesthetic life is basically independent of the 'public morality' of society and 'culture'. Indeed not only his particular private morality but his privatization of morality are obviously reflective of the society which shapes his thinking — the consumerist world of late-capitalist liberalism.

One does not need a very penetrating or subversive eye to see in Rorty's glorification and quest of the new, in his 'aesthetic search for novel experience and novel language', precisely that old worship of the new which sustains and fuels the rapid and relentless pace of commodity consumption in our late-capitalist consumer society. As critics of commodity aesthetics have clearly demonstrated, the demand for constant aesthetic innovation, urged in the noble names of creativity and progress, is really a cunningly systematic programme to increase exchange value by masking or distorting use-value, namely by making the already purchased and still very much usable item seem outdated and in need of a change, thus stimulating new purchasing (Haug, 1986). This superficial, profit-motivated aesthetic innovation is most evident in the rapidly changing fashion of the clothing and popular music industries, but its power (through the ultimate power of its profit motive) pervades our whole consumer society and thus, inevitably, its ethical thinking. Rorty's quest to acquire more and more new experiences and vocabularies is the philosophical counterpart of the consumer's quest to maximize consumption; both are narcotic dreams of happiness induced by capitalism's master dream (a grimly real one) of greater sales and greater profits.

Moreover, Rorty's very privatization of morality into a matter of mere personal fulfilment can be seen to reflect that cherished autonomy of the private individual (property owner or consumer) which was so central to the collective rise of capitalism, liberalism and the bourgeoisie. Yet, in apparent paradox or perhaps as its own immanent critique, this autonomy of self is precisely what is stricken and undermined by the administered society of late capitalism, which does all it can do to stymie any substantive manifestations of individual autonomy and self-sufficiency, or indeed any really individualistic thinking that departs from the standard and pretty narrow options of contemporary liberal pluralism. Reactionaries like Eliot and radicals like Adorno would unite in condemning our so-called individualistic society as a herd of conformists, uniformly and uncritically bent on well-advertised concepts of self-fulfilment and gratification while lacking an independent self of any integrity to fulfil. The idea that everyone can be a unique individual simply by fashioning oneself through the free and personal choice of lifestyles cannot hide the fact that not only the range of viable life-style options but the individual's very awareness and choice are severely constrained and relentlessly programmed by societal forces or sanctions far beyond his power to resist, let alone control. This late-capitalist paradox of the privatized quest for self-fulfilment issuing in the loss of real autonomy and integrity of self is perfectly reflected in Rorty's deep contradiction of exhorting self-enrichment while denying the very existence of a self that could be enriched. The Rortian non-self is indeed the ideal self for the powers governing a consumer society, a fragmented, confused self, hungrily acquiring as many new commodities as it can but lacking the unity, integrity and agency to challenge either its habits of consumption or the system which manipulates and profits from them.

Unfortunately, the theme of the decentring or dissolution of the self is not restricted to moralists like Rorty, who consciously endorse the American establishment. It has become a dominant dogma in anti-establishment literary and cultural theorists, who appropriate thinkers like Derrida, Foucault and Lacan to dissolve the self into discursive structures and thereby deny it agency. This dogma's dangerous appeal and popularity are not hard to explain. Like the privatization of the ethical and the debunking or deconstruction of the tradition and canon of high art, theory's dissolution of the self is both a product and a reinforcing cause of the intellectual's increasing self-alienation, marginalization and sense of impotence. American (and perhaps other) academics in the human sciences feel themselves declassed, marginalized and politically powerless in a society so enormous and complex that it defies intelligibility (inducing what Jameson (1984: 77) dubs the postmodern 'hysterical sublime'). By denying the self's very existence and agency we intellectuals seek to legitimate our own political and social inaction, our unjustifiable and unhappy complacency, even our own responsibility for our own lives.

Notes

1. Proposition 6.421. The English translation in this dual language edition, 'Ethics and aesthetics are one and the same' makes the assertion of identity much stronger than the German original which says only 'Ethik und Ästhetik sind Eins'.

2. This distinction between 'private morality' and 'public morality' is a fairly common one, and has recently been employed by Rorty in arguing for his own aestheticized ethic which will be critically scrutinized in what follows. Though I employ the distinction here for its pragmatic value, I doubt, for reasons that will later emerge, that the project of private morality is as clearly separable and independent from public morality as Rorty (1986) would have us believe. The private/public morality distinction is made on pages 11–12.

3. Postmodernism is surely not unprecedented in pointing to the intermingling importance of the aesthetic for the ethical. For Plato and generally for the Greeks, the ideas of the good and the beautiful were not so clearly differentiated, as can be seen from the fact that they were frequently referred to collectively in the composite term *kalon-kai-agathon* ('beautiful and good'), and that '*kalos*', the specific term for the beautiful, was used perhaps as much as '*agathos*' to denote moral goodness. Once the Greek ethical world governed by the goal of eudemonia gave way to ethics dominated by the ideas of divine commandment and duty or obligation, it was much easier to separate the ethical from the aesthetic and even to regard them as conflicting principles. The famous post-classical connections made between aesthetics and ethics express a salient awareness of their perceived divide. Kant saw beauty as a symbol of morality; Schiller saw an aesthetic education as a means to morality; and Kierkegaard saw an aesthetic attitude to life as an inferior alternative to the ethical life. Postmodernism's ethics of taste thus seems distinctive in its attempt at really merging the two principles in defiant awareness of a long tradition of philosophical bifurcation (which would distinguish it from the Greek overlap) so that the aesthetic is neither a symbol of, means to, or surrogate for an ethic, but rather the constitutive substance of one. Yet though distinctive, it hardly appears unique. Indeed, it seems to be (at least as we shall see in Rorty's version) largely a rehash of fin-de-siècle aestheticism, which shares the same feverishly anxious lust for pleasurable novelty and the same weary and faithless scepticism we postmoderns claim as our own.

4. Wollheim (1984: 221) does not in fact use the term 'ethics' but makes the same essential distinction as Williams by speaking of 'morality broadly conceived' to include also value apart from obligation as opposed to 'morality narrowly conceived' which is dominated by obligation and founded on introjection.

It is worth noting that Williams (1985: 112–17) portrays the desirable form of ethical reflection in the very manner in which aesthetic reflection is usually presented. Ethical thinking, for Williams, should eschew both the extremes of abstract systematic theorizing from unexceptionable general principles and of smug unreflective adherence to ethical intuitions or prejudices, in seeking 'for as much shared understanding as it can find'. This is the classical model of aesthetic reasoning which cannot demonstrate its verdicts by general principles but does not therefore concede they are whims of taste or prejudice which cannot be adequately justified.

5. See also Rorty's paper 'The Priority of Democracy Over Philosophy', as yet unpublished. Here he emphatically advocates the 'privatization of questions about the meaning of life' or ethical preference, where the role of society is only to give individuals 'the space necessary to work out their own salvation' and 'try out their private visions of perfection in peace' (pp. 36–8 of manuscript). Rorty, however, recognizes that private projects of self-fulfilment can find a most satisfactory form through involvement in larger social projects, but he still sees the domains of public and private morality as essentially separate and independent. The difficulty in so viewing them, even for Rorty's own project, will be discussed below.

6 Wilde's advocacy of the aesthetic life seems to combine aspects of all the three genres I have distinguished. He variously urges 1) a life of the pleasures of aesthetic consumption and the inspired momentary states of stasis and inactivity they afford, 2) the need for a life to form an aesthetically pleasing whole, and sometimes 3) something approaching the Rortian-Faustian aesthetic life when he recommends that such unity be found in constant change. Indeed, Wilde (1948: 987) already expounded Rorty's postmodernist ethic in the 1890s when he stated that the ideal aesthete 'will realize himself in many forms, and by a thousand different ways, and will be curious of new sensations and fresh points of view. Through constant change, and through constant change alone, he will find his true unity'. The coherence of such a recipe for unity is, however, dubious, and (as Wilde later sadly discovered) its results could prove disastrous for life.

It should be noted that Pater (1910: vii–xv, 233–9) also anticipated Rorty's Freudian-Faustian aesthetic life in advocating a 'quickened, multiplied conscious-ness', the thirst for the intense excitement of novelty, and the pragmatic experiential value of knowledge, not as providing any permanent truth (which is unattainable) but simply as 'ideas', 'points of view' or 'instruments of criticism' (in Rorty's terms 'vocabularies') for enriching our experience and quickening its appreciation.

7. I do not wish to maintain that all selves, by definition, are or must be adequately unified. For certainly we can and do speak sensibly of divided selves that are ridden with conflict or even split into multiple personalities. To have logical individuation of selves in the most basic sense all we need is some primitive notion of a unitary rather than unified self, having some sort of unicity and admitting of varying degrees of unity, where such unity is largely a product of social- and self-construction.

8. He also seems to recognize the need for stability of character when he praises Freud for enabling us to maintain greater stability in unstable times by acknowledg-ing the unconscious sources of many of our instabilities and thereby promoting a stabilizing 'tolerance of ambiguities' (Rorty, 1986: 9). Rorty's central mistake is to construe the need for 'tolerance' of ambiguities and alternative narratives as the need for 'celebration and maximization' of such things. He makes the same sort of mistake with respect to the need for new vocabularies, as I have argued elsewhere (Shuster-man, 1986).

References

Haug, W.F. (1986) *Critique of Commodity Aesthetics: Appearance, Sexuality and Advertising in Capitalist Society*. Minneapolis: Minnesota University Press.

Jameson, Fredric (1984) 'Postmodernism or the Cultural Logic of Late Capitalism', *New Left Review* 146.

Lyotard, Jean-François (1984) *The Postmodern Condition*. Minneapolis: Minnesota University Press.

MacIntyre, A. (1982) *After Virtue*. London: Duckworth.

Moore, G.E. (1959) *Principia Ethica*. Cambridge: Cambridge University Press.

Pater, W. (1910) *The Renaissance*. London: Macmillan.

Rorty, R. (1980) 'Freud, Morality and Hermeneutics', *New Literary History* 12.

Rorty, R. (1986) 'Freud and Moral Reflection', in J.H. Smith and W. Kerrigan (eds) *Pragmatism's Freud: The Moral Disposition of Psychoanalysis*. Baltimore: Johns Hopkins University Press.

Shusterman, R. (1986) 'Deconstruction and Analysis: Confrontation and Convergence', *British Journal of Aesthetics* 26.

Wilde, O. (1948) *The Works of Oscar Wilde*. London: Collins.

Williams, B. (1985) *Ethics and the Limits of Philosophy*. London: Fontana.

Wittgenstein, L. (1963) *Tractatus Logico-Philosophicus*. London: Routledge and Kegan Paul.

Wollheim, R. (1984) *The Thread of Life*. Cambridge, Mass: Harvard University Press.

Richard Shusterman teaches Philosophy at Temple University, Philadelphia.

Architecture to Philosophy —
The Postmodern Complicity[*]

Gillian Rose

Why is it that so many academic disciplines — literature, philosophy, sociology, anthropology — are posing the question concerning rationality in terms of 'postmodernism,' terms taken from architectural history — from the periodization of movements in style — and, yet, at least one school of exponents claim that they herald an 'anti-aesthetic' (Foster, 1985)? In this paper I shall attempt to clarify issues and evasions of the debate over postmodernism by re-examining this conflation of architecture and theory, taking as my recurring *point d'appui* the Biblical story of the Tower of Babel and asking why God punishes humankind's invention of architecture with the confusion of tongues (Steiner, 1975).[1]

> Once upon a time all the world spoke a single language and used the same words. As men journeyed in the East they came upon a plain in the land of Shinar and settled there. They said to one another, 'Come, let us make bricks and bake them hard;' they used bricks for stone and bitumen for mortar. 'Come,' they said, 'let us build ourselves a city and a tower with its top in the heavens and make a name for ourselves, or we shall be dispersed all over the earth.' Then the Lord came down to see the city and the tower which mortal men had built and he said, 'Here they are, one people with a single language, and now they have started to do this; henceforth nothing they have a mind to do will be beyond their reach. Come let us go down there and confuse their speech so that they will not understand what they say to one another.' So the Lord dispersed them from there all over the earth and they left off building the city — that is why it is called Babel, because the Lord there made a babble of the language of all the world; from that place the Lord scattered men all over the face of the earth.

That version was taken from *The Cambridge Bible Commentary* on the *New English Bible* (Davidson, 1980: *Genesis* 11: 1–9, 104). To the Christian tradition the Hebrew story tells of punishment for the

---

[*] This paper is dedicated to the memory of Mary Bottomore, who died on 30 December 1986.

Theory, Culture & Society (SAGE, London, Newbury Park, Beverly Hills and New Delhi), Vol. 5 (1988), 357–71

crime of *hubris*. For the Jewish tradition one may turn to the great commentaries: the *Talmud*, the Babylonian codification of Jewish law; the *Midrash Rabbah*, the main body of post-Biblical commentary; the *Zohar*, the major work of Jewish mysticism; Rashi, the great medieval Rabbi or scholar; and the Herz *Pentateuch*, a modern compendium of ancient commentaries.

These commentaries seem to agree that the key to the meaning of the story is the rallying cry — 'Let us ... make a name for ourselves'. For this implies making and naming a God of their own invention — an 'idol' of brick and bitumen — usurping the name of God because these people desire to become invulnerable and apart from God. The image of the Tower derives from the Assyrian or Babylonian Ziggurat, the Mesopotamian Temple Tower, atop a mound itself erected on a flat plain and surmounted by a shrine of the Deity. To the Babylonians they were a gate of God, but to the Hebrews, in exile by the waters of Babylon, they were symbols of impiety, for they appeared to scale or wage war against the heavens.

It is, however, important not to forget that the ambition was to build a city as well as a tower. If the act of building a tower is synonymous with inventing, erecting and worshipping a named idol and rejecting the Holy Name then the connection between an impious religious architecture and language seems to become clearer. In this light the confusion of tongues may be understood as the way humankind are taught a lesson about the relation between divine and human power.

According to the *Zohar* (Sperling and Simon, trs, 1984: 256) humankind had not understood that speaking the holy tongue is the source of their own power. Once the tongue is confounded, the rebels are not able to express their desires so that the angels, God's messengers, can understand what they want; nor, it may be added, as a consequence, can they express their desires to each other, and as a result communal labour becomes impossible.[2] The attempt to exercise power independently of God seems to end with loss of power, for they are not able to continue building. This may explain what happens to the tower, but it does not explain the fate of the city. The culture of cities is founded on the need for unity and defence which arises out of the mix of customs, languages and buildings. Is the confusion of tongues a punishment — as both Rabbinical and Christian sources seem to concur? Is it a loss or might it be some kind of gain in power or is it perhaps both?[3]

According to the *Talmud* (Epstein, 1935: Seder Nezikim, vol 111,

Tractate Sanhedrin 109a 748) the rebels who built the tower split up into three parties: one said, 'Let us ascend and dwell there;' the second said, 'Let us ascend and serve idols;' the third said, 'Let us ascend and wage war against God'. The first was scattered; the third was turned into apes, spirits, devils and night demons. The second, however, the Lord did confound the language. But, this account continues, 'A third of the tower was burnt, a third sank into the earth, and a third is still standing'. Rab concludes, 'The atmosphere of the tower causes forgetfulness'. In this retelling the confusion of tongues is only one — and the better one — of a number of less desirable fates. It reminds us that many worst ones are conceivable. Perhaps the atmosphere of that third still standing has made us forget. This *Talmud* discussion suggests that the story is trying to account for a determining and perennial feature of the destiny of humankind. It is aetiological.[4]

I propose, initially, to think of a tower in relation to a wall, as a special or limiting case of a wall: as a wall that has been made continuous, completed as a circle and then elevated. This idea of the perfected and elevated wall by contrast to the initial linearity of a wall which stands as a barrier, implies that the centre has been appropriated and become radial — the former barrier or limit transgressed by being denied as a limit. Perhaps the rebels have taken control — taken into their own hands what would otherwise be a limit to their own activity. This is surely dangerous. The word 'dangerous' comes from the Latin *dominus*, master, and means to be subject to the domination of another. The idea that human powers and their successful execution are dangerous to their perpetrators is common to many ancient cultures. Pindar's cosmopolitan odes, commemorating and expiating the victors of the Panhellenic games are another striking instance of this. And this is surely why in Kafka's story (1976: 71), 'The Great Wall of China,' the first person narrative voice explicitly states that the issue is how to rebuild the Tower of Babel on 'a secure foundation'. Yet the secure foundation turns out to consist of building a wall and not a tower, and building it 'piecemeal,' so that it never joins up into a continuity.[5] And within the story itself this system of construction is interpreted in terms of what relation to take to an absolute yet absent authority which will best preserve and develop human powers and potentialities.

In *Genesis*, 10: 5 (Davidson, 1980: 98–9) just before the account of the Tower of Babel a complex genealogy of the 'peoples of the coasts and islands each with their own languages, family by family, nation by nation', is given. This genealogy is resumed — after the Tower of Babel — in *Genesis*, 11: 10 (108–9). It terminates with Abraham — one nomad among nomads — who receives a special call. From this perspective the story of the Tower of Babel clearly presupposes that the plurality of language has already come about. The purported transgression punished by the multiplicity of languages captures or pinpoints the change in self-awareness that occurs when one people encounter another people when, previously, they had only known their own WAY (Strauss, 1953: 81–119). Many of the ancient words now translated as 'law' originally meant 'the way': the Hebrew word for law, *Halachah*, means, literally, 'the going' — the way one should go; the Arabic word for law, *Shari'a*, means, literally, 'the road to the watering place'; the Greek name for the Goddess of Vengeance, *Dike*, means, 'the way things happen'.

As a result of the encounter of one people with another people, 'the' way becomes distinguishable from other 'ways' in terms of law, language and labour; and the relation between law, language and labour becomes problematic. One community has become aware of itself as different from other communities — as having its 'own' ways. These distinct ways of law, language and labour become the third term — or mean or middle — by which the community understands, represents or relates to itself and others.

It would, therefore, be just as wrong to see the confusion of tongues as a punishment or degeneration as it is to see the eating of the fruit of the Tree of Knowledge in the Garden of Eden story as a fall. Instead, both of these stories are the *mise en scène* of a paradox: the semi-elevation of a humanity which understands itself to possess one half of an absolute or divine power — from the Garden of Eden gaining knowledge but not immortal life; from the Tower of Babel deploying that knowledge and the curse of labour inherited from the expulsion from Eden to try to win back immortality and the Adamic gift of naming. The labour and the knowledge how to construct bricks and mortar and plan a city and tower are projected into an architecture designed to defy death by usurping the realm of God who decreed labour and death for humankind in the first place.

In the Garden of Eden story (Davidson, 1980; *Genesis* 3: 22, 46) God comments, after the eating of the forbidden fruit, 'The man has become like one of us, knowing good and evil, what if he now reaches out his hand and takes the fruit from the tree of life also eats it and lives for ever?' In the Tower of Babel story God says, 'henceforth nothing they have a mind to do will be beyond their reach'. The paradox acknowledged in the first story is that of beings with a mind (knowledge) but without the reach — immortality. In the second story the paradox acknowledged is that of beings with the reach to build a city and tower, but without the mind — the confused tongue. In both cases the prodigious combination of power and impotence together with its changing negotiation is being recognized as the narrative unfolds. In the earlier story the scenario consists of individuals in a 'natural,' albeit paradisical and walled, setting. In the subsequent story after the Flood, the scenario consists of an ethical community in a social setting, self-aware because of the necessity of labour, and because of the existence of other communities without which there would be no need to build a city, an organization for collective external and internal defence.

'The Lord made a babble.' The confusion of tongues does not simply mean the origin of different languages in the empirical sense: it does not simply imply the plurality of languages, but that language itself is plural. Because 'the way' is now divided into law, language and labour, archetypical speech in which words were deeds — the Hebrew *da'bar* means act, event, deed, thing, word — and in which there is no distinction between thought, word, thing, is replaced by the notion of language itself as a signifying system distinct from law and labour, in which word, thought, thing may not coincide. Architecture, whether the wall around Paradise or the Tower of Babel, exhibits the limit at which human and divine agency encounter each other. It registers in the visible world outcomes of that encounter which would otherwise remain intangible.[6]

The reading thus far developed sees the story as a stage in the development of the potentiality for freedom. In opposition to this reading it might be argued, however, that the Tower of Babel story is a fiction which deals with the metaphysics of discourse in the setting of omniabsent (*sic*) yet contested powers. The Tower of Babel story may therefore illustrate some of the key oppositions characteristic of the 'postmodern' debate, and hence help to explain why the distinction between 'modern' and 'postmodern' has been adopted in recent theoretical discussion outside the field of architecture. First, the story concludes with 'plurality' defining 'discourse' as opposed to unity of meaning; secondly, it reveals itself as an aetiological fiction and does not claim universal validity; thirdly, it may imply that history consists of ineluctable paradox and is not the progressive resolution of dynamic contradiction.

Architecture has come to provide a paradigm for this new atheoretical nominalism by means of three analogies between philosophy or social theory and architecture — analogies which are themselves based on dubious characterizations and accounts of architecture to begin with. In the first place, it is argued that the history of architecture has been simply periodized into nineteenth-century historicism, twentieth-century early modernist movement, post-World War II failure of modernism, and, nowadays, 'post-modernism'. The conclusion is then drawn that a plural account and a plural alternative will remedy this; an example is Charles Jencks' *Modern Movements in Architecture* (1973) — the 's' is the crux. Secondly, it is argued that the meaning of rationality in architecture is simple, that it may be identified with slogans of the modern movement, such as 'buildings are machines for living in', or 'form follows function', misinterpreted, respectively, from Le Corbusier, *Towards a New Architecture* (1927), and Hitchcock and Johnson, *The International Style* (1932). By extension it appears that the failure of that rationality — its dialectic of enlightenment: the instrumental rationalism which suppresses the totality and the individual — may be easily analysed. Thirdly, it is argued that the theoretical and practical solutions in architecture are simple. An example of the practical is Robert Venturi's infamous proposition in *Learning from Las Vegas* (1972), 'Main Street is almost alright,' which aims to restore signs and symbols to overly functionalized building. The theoretical solution is a 'plural' theory of architectural signs, yet generalized and dehistoricized under the protection of an overarching typological historicism — similar to Comte's 'Law of the Three Stages'. An example of this is provided by Jencks' use of Umberto Eco's (1980: 11–69) architectural semiotics in the former's *The Language of Post-Modern Architecture* (1984).

Instead of developing sociological analysis to cover architecture, such as Max Weber's sociology of domination, a 'postmodern' thesis resting on strained analogies with these dubious accounts of the development of architecture is exploited to obscure the way in which *an unexamined opposition of positions within the 'modern' is thereby recreated and perpetuated in both architecture and philosophy*. For the 'modern' has always involved such internal contestations.

In social theory the notions of the 'modern' and the 'postmodern' are, in the first place, fundamentally the same, and, in the second place, are not 'modern' or 'new' — for want of a neutral term. The debate between Jürgen Habermas (1985: 11–29) and Jean-François Lyotard (1986), which has taken over Jencks' terminology into social theory and philosophy, is defined in a way that returns to Hegel's exposition of Kant. This Kantianism is taken from two works by Theodor W. Adorno: Habermas takes his terms from Horkheimer and Adorno, *Dialectic of Enlightenment* (1944); Lyotard takes his terms from Adorno's posthumous *Aesthetic Theory* (1970). Both Habermas (1981: 3–14), who defends modernist rationality, and Lyotard (1986), who defends postmodernist plurality, understand themselves to be reviving Kant against Hegel. In spite of Lyotard's emphasis on 'games,' this revival arises from *misunderstanding Adorno's speculative play of Kant against Hegel/ Kant against Hegel as a refutation of Hegel*. Habermas defends the notion of 'communicative rationality' which depends on Kant's distinction in the three critiques between three realms of experience — theoretical, practical and aesthetic. Lyotard defends Kant's notion of the 'sublime' from the third critique as a kind of non-determinate judgment which offers the possibility for an aesthetic education which would remain open. Habermas appears to defend discursive critical rationality, Lyotard the sublime beyond formal rationality. Yet it may be argued that both are engaging in an enterprise which has characterized both humanism and anti-humanism in architecture and in philosophy — they seek to enlarge the idea of reason beyond the instrumental so that it may acknowledge the uncontainable, the aporia.

As Reyner Banham (1986: 56) argues in an article on the Lloyd's building, whether the new architecture understands itself as 'realizing modernism' for the first time, or as 'postmodern', it shares 'the compulsion to try and make sense of . . . human dilemmas' — even when the dilemma is perceived as aporia and not as ideal. It is this celebration of aporia which makes Lyotard's aesthetic of the 'sublime' comparable to self-styled 'anti-aesthetic' versions of postmodernism (Foster, 1985). At the 1986 exhibition of New Architecture at the Royal Academy, the first architecture exhibition at that venue for forty years, half of the display was devoted to unbuilt, rejected or still undecided projects for restoring whole areas of London to pedestrians in the wake of the perceived destruction of social life by the values of modern architecture. Yet the only sociological concept used in the exhibition itself and in the scholarly catalogue (Sudjic, 1986) is 'the creation of a public realm' — a phrase and concept which Habermas (1962) has taken over and developed from the work of Hannah Arendt (1958). Architecture, social theory and philosophy seem to be complicit in exchanging each other's most undifferentiated and general concepts and theses.

In the scholarly symposium which accompanied an exhibition held in Berlin in 1984, 'The Adventure of Ideas — Architecture and Philosophy since the Industrial Revolution,' may be found a German translation of a discussion between Jacques Derrida (1984: 96–106) and Eva Meyer, 'Labyrinth und Archi/Textur,' in which they discuss the Tower of Babel, postmodernism, architecture and philosophy.[7] This discussion exemplifies how the three analogies between architecture and philosophy are employed.

Derrida interprets the Tower of Babel story as a 'defeat' for God. He argues that the attempt to give themselves a name on the part of a tribe, the Semites, is the main event. The name 'Semite' means 'name' already, but the Semites want to 'make themselves a name' in order to colonize and dominate the other tribes and their languages from the place they intend to usurp in Heaven. God devastates this undertaking by uttering one word — 'Babel' meaning confusion. The Semites plan of domination is nullified by the bestowal of a proper name and by the deconstructing of their architectural construction. Accordingly, universal language is terminated; henceforth the plurality of languages cannot be mastered, and there can be no universal translation: language becomes labyrinthine. It also means that there is no single architecture: architecture is also henceforth plural and labyrinthine in spite of its axonometric grids of plan and elevation. The Tower of Babel story thus opposes architectural as well as linguistic difference to the unificatory ambition which has been vanquished. Derrida argues that reading the story in terms of this plurality is neither anthropocentric nor theocentric. The almightiness of God is undermined when He is forced to intervene and speak the word 'Babel:' for 'Babel' means 'confusion' — but it only means that because of the confusion according to which the word 'Babel' sounds like the word for 'confusion' in Hebrew. God is equivocal: he commands and forbids translation of His Name and lapses into the same situation as those he opposes. He cannot dominate this situation which gives rise to the plenitude of architecture as well as the plenitude of language. Postmodernity, Derrida infers, takes off from this 'defeat and beginning'.

Derrida's thesis is here couched in the form of a classic Kantian transcendental argument (Rose, 1981: 1f): 'It is the impossibility of the Tower of Babel which makes it possible for architecture like language to have a history.' This history is *always* to be understood (he claims and I emphasize) in relation to a *divinity which is finite*. Modernity, he continues, is the striving for absolute mastery or domination; postmodernity is the establishment or experience of the end of this plan and elevation for mastery and domination. Postmodernity, he concludes, is a new relation to the divine — not Greek, nor Christian, but *the conditions*(sic) for architectural thinking. This strange phraseology is another transcendental deduction with a metacritical twist. The 'conditions' for architectural thinking are the 'dwelling', the event of place — an idea which comes from Heidegger's (1951: 143–61) famous essay 'Building, Dwelling, Thinking'. The 'event' of place is the precondition of architectural form: a communal relating of human beings to concrete, unmeasurable dwelling not to abstract, measured, architectural planning. It is this delineation of the absolute event which Derrida offers as a new idea of our relation to God — and surely it amounts to a new humanism.

How is the account of the Tower of Babel developed above different from Derrida's? There are four main points: history, humanity, God, language and architecture. According to Derrida, the Tower of Babel story narrates the origin of the history of architecture and language. I argue that this reading opens and closes history at the same time: for its notion of history does not imply development. Derrida argues the dichotomy of humanity as rebellious/God as sovereign and infinite is dissolved; all dichotomies — human/divine, nature/culture — are replaced by the idea of labyrinthine plurality. I argue that the dissolution of this opposition between human and divine, absolute and relative power, dissolves potentiality too, and cancels the negotiating of the relation between potentiality and actuality through history. Similarly, Derrida's argument that God is defeated and becomes finite apparently offers instant release from the master/slave dichotomy and from humanity's desire for domination and mastery. I would argue, on the contrary, that it robs humanity of any experience whereby that trying of power may be acknowledged and cultured through a third. Derrida's position that history is 'always in relation to a finite divinity' is dogmatic in the precritical sense; it implies no dialectic of dependence and independence, no political or spiritual life. Derrida's argument that the plurality of language and of architecture is at stake legislates a current perception into a universal — employing and undermining universal explanation at the same time. The reading developed above expands architecture as the means, the third term, by which a community negotiates its relation to itself and to other communities. Where Derrida deals with dichotomies and their abolition, I propose the changing configuration of two in a third. Then the current experience is not frozen: it is seen as transitory but not as relative.

A return to the notion of the Tower may concretize this argument. The problem of its meaning may also be encountered in Rodin's 'Tower of Labour' and Tatlin's 'Tower', the Monument to the Third International. The importance of the Tower to the postmodern argument is that it is an exemplar of what Hegel in the *Aesthetics* (1975) calls 'symbolic' architecture so as to distinguish it from 'classical' and 'romantic' architecture (Payot, 1982). Norbert Linton (1986) captures Hegel's meaning when he explains Tatlin's Tower as an image of the forerunner, St John the Baptist, who cannot deliver salvation but proclaims it is 'at hand,' and calls us to repent. Symbolic architecture is monumental, the dwelling place of the god not of human beings, an external not an interior space; and it arises when meaning (absolute power) and configuration (form) remain ununified. The symbolic form of art or architecture does not present (classical) nor re-present (romantic) the absolute, but refers or points to it ambiguously, employing symbols which always also imply things other than the meaning for which they furnish the image. The Tower is analogous to the pointing finger of the Baptist in the Grünewald alterpiece, occupying a different kind of space from the crucified body of Christ.

According to Hegel (1975: vol 1, 363) the sublime is a special instance of the symbolic, 'an attempt to express the infinite without finding in the sphere of finite phenomena an object which proves adequate for this representation'. In this particular passage Hegel is himself citing with approval Kant's distinction of the sublime from the beautiful. However, unlike the postmodern aesthetics for which this very proposition of Kant's cited by Hegel is also the key text, Hegel (1975: vol 2, 1051) develops the proposition into a question: 'First the question arises about what character the world situation must have if it is to provide a ground on which a [sublime] event can be adequately presented.' Hegel compares the 'unconscious' symbolism of Oriental and Jewish architecture with later 'conscious' literary symbolism, such as fable, parable, riddle and allegory. It is the unconscious obliquity of meaning and configuration which links the postmodern 'conscious' symbolism with the story and image of the Tower, and with monumental symbolic architecture and with the sublime in art generally.

Yet this is to take a development — a changing relation between form and configuration — and to freeze it. For in Hegel the symbolic may overlap with and change into the classical and the romantic and back again. Hegel criticizes (1975: vol 1: 312) — and his warning is peculiarly apposite —

> the extension of symbolism to *every* sphere which is by no means what we have in mind here in considering the symbolic form of art. For our endeavour does not rise to finding out how far artistic configuration could be interpreted symbolically or allegorically in this sense of the word 'symbol'; instead we have to ask, conversely, how far the symbolic itself is to be reckoned an *art-form*. We want to establish the artistic relation between meaning and configuration insofar as that relation is symbolic in distinction from other modes of presentation, especially the classical and romantic.

The romantic form of art also consists of a lack of unity between meaning and configuration, between the absolute or whole and its representation as form, its appearance in the sensuous medium or means, but the lack of unity is represented not referred to as in the symbolic. It is illusion (*Schein*) and this illusion is derived from a specific socio-historical experience in which spheres of life — religious and political, or law, language and labour — have become separated from each other.

To conclude this reference to Hegel and the paper in general five points may be drawn out. First, there may be more than one kind of divorce between meaning and configuration, whereas the postmodernism considered here with its focus on the 'sublime' or the abolition of recurrent dichotomy is only able to conceive of one. Therefore a dialectical approach is more open and plural than the modernism or postmodernism arguments themselves. Secondly, it is the form of that divorce or *form* itself *in its specificity* which can be seen to have historical presuppositions, not the divorce *in its generality* as in most versions of postmodernism. In this sense the means of law, language and labour have a changing fate. Thirdly, these changes may be related chronologically and systematically without producing a metanarrative or a progressive, teleological philosophy of history; it is not a question of employing discredited metanarratives but of seeing narratives themselves as different kinds of form. In this sense genealogy may be found — in Hegel and Marx as well as in Nietzsche — within aporetic philosophy of history. Fourthly, in Hegel and the dialectical tradition, the 'ending' of art has a different history from the 'ending' of religion and politics, and the end of art characterizes modernity. It is the modernist defence of an aesthetic realm and postmodernism's aesthetics of the sublime or anti-aesthetics which produce a uniform philosophy of history over all disciplines, not the dialectical approach.

Finally, on the view developed here, configuration is related to confrontation with absolute power and becomes an indicator of human potentiality which is constantly renegotiated. In the Tower of Babel story humanity achieves an *initial* measure or idea of its own potentialities by encountering its limit. That encounter does not arrest it in an endless 'labyrinth', but sets it off on further encounters where what has been learnt or not learnt is tried out again and again, constantly changing both the idea of the potential and the idea of the limit; these encounters cannot be assimilated to the meanings or 'signs' of the first one. This reading is different from pluralism, vernacularism, nominalism: it is not rationalistic nor is it the 'compulsion to make sense of human dilemmas'; it is the human dilemma being represented or referred to.

Paradoxically, the claim advanced formerly by modern and now by postmodern architecture and philosophy, that each alone offers a genuine 'opening' disowns previous openings — attempts to re-negotiate potentiality and actuality[8] — by characterizing the other position without differentiation as 'total', 'closed', 'functionalist', 'rationalistic', 'dominatory', instead of drawing on the experience of those openings and their subsequent subversion, instead of comprehending illusion: the relation between the limit of the meaning at stake and its configuration or form. I conclude that the use of architecture in philosophy bolsters a tendency to replace the concept by the sublimity of the sign, which is, equally, to employ an unexamined conceptuality without the labour of the concept.

Notes

1. Steiner (1975: 48, 57f, 235, 473) only considers the tower as a metaphor for the mutual opacity of languages and does not raise the question of the connection between architecture, language, society and God.

2. Compare Kant's opening to 'The Transcendental Doctrine of Method' of the *Critique of Pure Reason* (1965: A707, B745, 573): 'If we look upon the sum of all knowledge of pure speculative reason as an edifice for which we have at least the idea within ourselves, it can be said that in the Transcendental Doctrine of Pure Elements we have made an estimate of the materials, and have determined for what sort of edifice and for what height and strength of building they suffice. We have found,

indeed, that although we had contemplated building a tower which should reach to the heavens, the supply of materials suffices only for a dwelling house, just sufficiently commodious for our business on the level of experience, and just sufficiently high to allow of our overlooking it. The bold undertaking that we had designed is thus bound to fail through lack of material — not to mention the babble of tongues, which inevitably gives rise to disputes among the workers in regard to the plan to be followed, and which must end by scattering them all over the world, leaving each to erect a separate building for himself, according to his own design.'

3. Compare the commentary of Samson Raphael Hirsch (1986: 53–8) (1808–1888), the arguably Hegelian founder of Jewish neo-orthodoxy: 'If the united community so misuses its authority that, instead of employing it to serve the treasure entrusted to it ... it will seek to make the individual subservient not to God but only to itself, then the individual must rise up and say, "I do not recognize this community; I recognize only myself". In making this declaration, of course, he pours out the child with the bath water; he cuts himself off from the root through which he was to have absorbed all human wisdom from its Divine source, and flings himself into a vague uncharted subjectivity ... This subjectiveness, this self-awareness on the part of the individual which defines things not in terms of the coercion exercised by the community but in terms of the way in which he, the individual, sees them, was the new element ... which God awakened in the minds of men when He caused their language to disintegrate ... From that time on it was such factors as obstinacy, wilfulness, mood and even passion that devised names for things — of course no longer in the uniform manner in which God had formerly defined them. And so it came to pass that men no longer understood each other.'

4. Compare the American Indian version (Thompson, 1966: 263): 'Many generations ago Aba, the good spirit above, created many men, all Choctaw, who spoke the language of the Choctaw and understood one another. These came from the bosom of the earth, being formed of yellow clay, and no men had ever lived before them. One day all came together and, looking upward, wondered what the clouds and the blue expanse above might be. They continued to wonder and talk among themselves and at last determined to endeavour to reach the sky. So they brought many rocks and began building a mound that was to have touched the heavens. That night, however, the wind blew strong from above and the rocks fell from the mound. The second morning they again began work on the mound, but as the men slept that night the rocks were again scattered by the winds. Once more, on the third morning, the builders set to their task. But once more, as the men lay near the mound that night, wrapped in slumber, the winds came with so great force that the rocks were hurled down on them. The men were not killed, but when daylight came and they made their way from beneath the rocks and began to speak to one another, all were astounded as well as alarmed — they spoke various languages and could not understand one another. Some continued henceforth to speak the oriental tongue, the language of the Choctaw, and from these sprung the Choctaw tribe. The others who could not understand this language, began to fight among themselves. Finally they separated. The Choctaw remained the original people; the others scattered, some going north, some east, and others west, and formed various tribes. This explains why there are so many tribes throughout the country at the present time.' Thanks to Jacob Murray for this reference.

5 'How could the wall which did not form even a circle, but only a sort of quarter or half-circle, provide the foundation for a tower? That could obviously be meant

only in a spiritual sense. But in that case why build the actual wall, which after all was something concrete, the result of lifelong labour of multitudes of people?' (Kafka, 1976: 71). Compare Steiner's (1975: 65–7) discussion of Kafka's 'uses of Babel'.

6. I say 'law', 'language' and 'labour' not for their alliteration, but as part of a developing argument that it is their inseparability which gives rise to the philosophical illusion now current that the 'realm of discourse' is our exclusive mode of actuality — which replaces the contrary illusion that representations give us access to a reality independent of them. My argument would stress that all categories or social institutions are *conceptual*: equally ideal and real they can only be articulated and recognised in legal/linguistic form. Since architecture illustrates these paradoxes *par excellence* this approach might suggest why architecture has become the cipher for the postmodern debate.

7. Derrida (1984: 101) also discusses his 'architectural metaphor' of 'deconstruction' which is not to be understood as retracing the construction of a building or philosophical system, but as 'a questioning of technique,' of the 'authority of architectural metaphor,' and as a deconstruction of architectural rhetoric itself. 'Deconstruction' is thus not a technique of reversed construction but 'a thinking of the idea of construction itself'.

8. By 'possibility' as employed throughout this paper I do not mean to imply a romantic yearning (*Sehnsucht*), but a severe category: 'possibility' is a translation of Aristotle's *dynamis*. It might be argued that post-Kantian thought is characterized by its transforming of Kantian a priori possibility which debases actuality to a mere empirical instance into 'real possibility' (Hegel), 'will to power' (Nietzsche — a reversal of power to will or faculty), 'scientific' versus 'utopian' possibility (Marx). Lyotard (1988: 292–93) not only overlooks the fate of this category in post-Kantian thought but even in Kant he ignores the connection between 'faculty' as power or possibility and transcendental a priori possibility.

References

Adorno, T.W. (1970) *Aesthetic Theory*. Translated by C. Lenhardt. London: Routledge, 1984.

Arendt, H. (1958) *The Human Condition*. Chicago: The University of Chicago Press, 1973.

Banham, R. (1986) 'The Quality of Modernism', *The Architectural Review* CLXX, 1076 (October).

Davidson, R. (1980) *Genesis 1–11 The Cambridge Bible Commentary on the New English Bible*. Cambridge: Cambridge University Press.

Derrida, J. and Meyer, E. (1984), 'Labyrinth and Archi/Textur', in *Das Abenteuer der Ideen Architektur und Philosophie seit der industriellen Revolution*. Berlin: Frolich und Kaufmann.

Eco, U. (1980) 'Function and Sign: The Semiotics of Architecture', in G. Broadbent, R. Bunt and C. Jencks (eds.) *Signs, Symbols and Architecture*. Chichester: John Wiley.

Epstein, I. (tr.) (1935) *The Babylonian Talmud*. London: The Soncino Press.

Foster, H. (ed.) (1985) *Postmodern Culture*. London: Pluto.

Habermas, J. (1962) *Strukturwandel der Öffentlichkeit*. Neuwied: Luchterhand, 1969.

Habermas, J. (1981) 'Modernity versus Postmodernity', *New German Critique* 22.

Habermas, J. (1985) 'Moderne und postmoderne Architektur', in *Die neue Unübersichtlichkeit*. Frankfurt am Main: Suhrkamp.

Hegel, G.W.F. (1975) *Aesthetics* vols. I & II. Translated by T.M. Knox. Oxford: Clarendon Press.

Heidegger, M. (1951) 'Building, Dwelling, Thinking', in A. Hofstadter (tr.), *Poetry, Language, Thought*. New York: Harper, 1971.

Hirsch, S.R. (1986) *The Pentateuch*. Translated by G. Hirschler. New York: The Judaica Press.

Hitchcock, H.-R. and Johnson, P. (1932) *The International Style*. New York: Norton, 1966.

Horkheimer, M. and Adorno, T.W. (1944) *Dialectic of Enlightenment*. Translated by J. Cumming. New York: Herder and Herder, 1972.

Jencks, C. (1973) *Modern Movements in Architecture*. Harmondsworth: Penguin.

Jencks, C. (1977) *The Language of Post-Modern Architecture*. London: Academy Editions, 1984.

Kafka, F. (1976) 'The Great Wall of China', in *Metamorphosis and Other Stories*, W. & E. Muir (trs). Harmondsworth: Penguin.

Kant, I. (1965) *Critique of Pure Reason*. Translated by N. Kemp Smith. New York: St Martin's Press.

Le Corbusier (1927) *Towards a New Architecture*. Translated by F. Etchells. London: The Architectural Press, 1982.

Linton, N. (1986) 'Icon of the Revolution', in *The Times Higher Educational Supplement* 4.4.

Lyotard, J.-F. (1979) *The Postmodern Condition: A Report on Knowledge*. Translated by G. Bennington and B. Massumi. Manchester: Manchester University Press, 1984.

Lyotard, J.-F. (1986) *Le Postmoderne expliqué aux enfants*. Paris: Galilée.

Lyotard, J.-F. (1988) 'An Interview with Jean-François Lyotard', *Theory, Culture & Society* 5 (2–3): 292–93.

Payot, D. (1982) *Le Philosophe et l'architecte sur quelques determinations philosophiques de l'idée d'architecture*. Paris: Aubier Montaigne.

Rose, G. (1981) *Hegel contra Sociology*. London: Athlone.

Sperling, H. and Simon, M. (trs.) (1984) *The Zohar*. London: The Soncino Press.

Steiner, G. (1975) *After Babel Aspects of Language and Translation*. Oxford: Oxford University Press.

Strauss, L. (1953) *Natural Right and History*. Chicago: The University of Chicago Press, 1971.

Sudjic, D. (1986) *New Architecture: Foster, Rogers, Stirling*. London: Royal Academy of Arts.

Thompson, S. (1966) *Tales of the North American Indians*. Bloomington: Indiana University.

Venturi, R., Scott-Brown, D. and Izenour, S. (1972) *Learning from Las Vegas: The Forgotten Symbolism of Architectural Form*. Cambridge: MIT, 1982.

Gillian Rose teaches Sociology and Philosophy at the University of Sussex. She is author of *Dialectic of Nihilism: Poststructuralism and Law* (Blackwell).

Cultural Critique

Cultural Critique examines and critiques received values, institutions, practices, and discourses in terms of their economic, political, social, cultural, and aesthetic genealogies, constitutions, and effects. The journal encourages and solicits analyses utilizing various methodologies and combining different fields.

Number 8 (Winter 1987-88)

Jonathan Elmer
The Exciting Conflict: The Rhetoric of Pornography and Anti-Pornography

Hans Robert Jauss
The Question of Modernism from Rousseau to Adorno

Gregory S. Jay
Values and Deconstructions: Derrida, Saussure, Marx

Susan Jeffords
"Things Worth Dying For": Gender and the Ideology of Collectivity in Vietnam Representation

Richard Kostelanetz
The Literature Program at the National Endowment for the Arts

Vincent P. Pecora
Adversarial Culture and the Fate of Dialectics

Mark Poster
Foucault, the Present and History

Leslie R. Rabine
A History of Ecriture Feminine as Metaphor: Reading Clare Demar with Hélène Cixous

Jochen Schulte-Sasse
The Neo-Conservative Joust with the Windmills of Postmodernity

Allon White
The Struggle Over Bakhtin: Fraternal Reply to Robert Young

UPCOMING SPECIAL ISSUES
Popular Narratives
The Construction of Gender and Modes of Social Division

Subscriptions: Check or money order (in U.S. dollars) should be made payable to *Cultural Critique* and sent to English Department, University of Minnesota, 207 Church St. S.E., Minneapolis, MN 55455

Individuals: $17.50 per year (three issues) Institutions: $35 per year (Subscriptions outside the U.S. add $3 postage per year).

Submissions: Three copies of article to *Cultural Critique*, English Dept., 207 Church St. S.E., University of Minnesota, Minneapolis, MN 55455

Social Criticism without Philosophy: An Encounter between Feminism and Postmodernism

Nancy Fraser and Linda Nicholson

Feminism and postmodernism have emerged as two of the most important political-cultural currents of the last decade. So far, however, they have kept an uneasy distance from one another. Indeed, so great has been their mutual wariness that there have been remarkably few extended discussions of the relations between them (exceptions are: Flax, 1986; Harding, 1986a, 1986b; Haraway, 1983; Jardine, 1985; Lyotard, 1978; Owens, 1983).

Initial reticences aside, there are good reasons for exploring the relations between feminism and postmodernism. Both have offered deep and far-reaching criticisms of the 'institution of philosophy'. Both have elaborated critical perspectives on the relation of philosophy to the larger culture. And, most central to the concerns of this essay, both have sought to develop new paradigms of social criticism which do not rely on traditional philosophical underpinnings. Other differences notwithstanding, one could say that, during the last decade, feminists and postmodernists have worked independently on a common nexus of problems: they have tried to rethink the relation between philosophy and social criticism so as to develop paradigms of 'criticism without philosophy'.

On the other hand, the two tendencies have proceeded, so to speak, from opposite directions. Postmodernists have focused primarily on the philosophy side of the problem. They have begun by elaborating antifoundational metaphilosophical perspectives and from there have gone on to draw conclusions about the shape and character of social criticism. For feminists, on the other hand, the question of philosophy has always been subordinate to an interest in social criticism. So they have begun by developing critical political perspectives and from there have gone on to draw conclusions about the status of philosophy. As a result of this difference in

Theory, Culture & Society (SAGE, London, Newbury Park, Beverly Hills and New Delhi), Vol. 5 (1988), 373–94

emphasis and direction, the two tendencies have ended up with complementary strengths and weaknesses. Postmodernists offer sophisticated and persuasive criticisms of foundationalism and essentialism, but their conceptions of social criticism tend to be anaemic. Feminists offer robust conceptions of social criticism, but they tend, at times, to lapse into foundationalism and essentialism.

Thus, each of the two perspectives suggests some important criticisms of the other. A postmodernist reflection on feminist theory reveals disabling vestiges of essentialism while a feminist reflection on postmodernism reveals androcentrism and political naivete.

It follows that an encounter between feminism and postmodernism will initially be a trading of criticisms. But there is no reason to suppose that this is where matters must end. In fact, each of these tendencies has much to learn from the other; each is in possession of valuable resources which can help remedy the deficiencies of the other. Thus, the ultimate stake of an encounter between feminism and postmodernism is the prospect of a perspective which integrates their respective strengths while eliminating their respective weaknesses. It is the prospect of a postmodernist feminism.

In what follows, we aim to contribute to the development of such a perspective by staging the initial, critical phase of the encounter. In section I, we examine the ways in which one exemplary postmodernist, Jean-François Lyotard, has sought to derive new paradigms of social criticism from a critique of the institution of philosophy. We argue that the conception of social criticism so derived is too restricted to permit an adequate critical grasp of gender dominance and subordination. We identify some internal tensions in Lyotard's arguments; and we suggest some alternative formulations which could allow for more robust forms of criticism without sacrificing the commitment to anti-foundationalism. In section II, we examine some representative genres of feminist social criticism. We argue that, in many cases, feminist critics continue tacitly to rely on the sorts of philosophical underpinnings which their own commitments, like those of postmodernists, ought, in principle, to rule out. And we identify some points at which such underpinnings could be abandoned without any sacrifice of social-critical force. Finally, in a brief conclusion, we consider the prospects for a postmodernist feminism. We discuss some requirements which constrain the development of such a perspective and we identify some pertinent conceptual resources and critical strategies.

I. Postmodernism

Postmodernists seek, inter alia, to develop conceptions of social criticism which do not rely on traditional philosophical underpinnings. The typical starting point for their efforts is a reflection on the condition of philosophy today. Writers like Richard Rorty and Jean-François Lyotard begin by arguing that Philosophy with a capital 'P' is no longer a viable or credible enterprise. From here, they go on to claim that philosophy, and, by extension, theory more generally, can no longer function to *ground* politics and social criticism. With the demise of foundationalism comes the demise of the view that casts philosophy in the role of *founding* discourse vis-à-vis social criticism. That 'modern' conception must give way to a new 'postmodern' one in which criticism floats free of any universalist theoretical ground. No longer anchored philosophically, the very shape or character of social criticism changes; it becomes more pragmatic, ad hoc, contextual and local. And with this change comes a corresponding change in the social role and political function of intellectuals.

Thus, in the postmodern reflection on the relationship between philosophy and social criticism, the term 'philosophy' undergoes an explicit devaluation; it is cut down to size, if not eliminated altogether. Yet, even as this devaluation is argued explicitly, the term 'philosophy' retains an implicit structural privilege. It is the changed condition of philosophy which determines the changed characters of social criticism and of engaged intellectual practice. In the new postmodern equation, then, philosophy is the independent variable while social criticism and political practice are dependent variables. The view of theory which emerges is not determined by considering the needs of contemporary criticism and engagement. It is determined, rather, by considering the contemporary status of philosophy. As we hope to show, this way of proceeding has important consequences, not all of which are positive. Among the results is a certain underdescription and premature foreclosing of possibilities for social criticism and engaged intellectual practice. This limitation of postmodern thought will be apparent when we consider its results in the light of the needs of contemporary feminist theory and practice.

Let us consider as an example the postmodernism of Jean-François Lyotard, since it is genuinely exemplary of the larger tendency. Lyotard is one of the few social thinkers widely considered postmodern who actually uses the term; indeed, it was he himself who introduced it into current discussions of philosophy, politics, society and social theory. His book, *The Postmodern Condition*, has become the *locus classicus* for contemporary debates, and it reflects in an especially acute form the characteristic concerns and tensions of the movement (Lyotard, 1984a).

For Lyotard, postmodernism designates a general condition of contemporary western civilization. The postmodern condition is one in which 'grand narratives of legitimation' are no longer credible. By 'grand narratives' he means, in the first instance, overarching philosophies of history like the Enlightenment story of the gradual but steady progress of reason and freedom, Hegel's dialectic of Spirit coming to know itself, and, most importantly, Marx's drama of the forward march of human productive capacities via class conflict culminating in proletarian revolution. For Lyotard, these 'metanarratives' instantiate a specifically modern approach to the problem of legitimation. Each situates first-order discursive practices of inquiry and politics within a broader totalizing metadiscourse which legitimates them. The metadiscourse narrates a story about the whole of human history which purports to guarantee that the 'pragmatics' of the modern sciences and of modern political processes, that is, the norms and rules which govern these practices, determining what counts as a warranted move within them, are themselves legitimate. The story guarantees that some sciences and some politics have the *right* pragmatics and, so, are the *right* practices.

We should not be misled by Lyotard's focus on narrative philosophies of history. In his conception of legitimating metanarrative, the stress properly belongs on the 'meta' and not the 'narrative'. For what most interests him about the Enlightenment, Hegelian and Marxist stories is what they share with other, non-narrative forms of philosophy. Like ahistorical epistemologies and moral theories, they aim to show that specific first-order discursive practices are well-formed and capable of yielding true and just results. 'True' and 'just' here mean something more than results reached by adhering scrupulously to the constitutive rules of some given scientific and political games. They mean, rather, results which correspond to Truth and Justice as they really are in themselves independently of contingent, historical, social practices. Thus, in Lyotard's view, a metanarrative is meta in a very strong sense. It purports to be a privileged discourse capable of situating, characterizing and evaluating all other discourses, but not itself infected by the historicity and contingency which render first-order discourses potentially distorted and in need of legitimation.

In *The Postmodern Condition*, Lyotard argues that metanarratives, whether philosophies of history or non-narrative foundational philosophies, are merely modern and dépassé. We can no longer believe, he claims, in the availability of a privileged metadiscourse capable of capturing once and for all the truth of every first-order discourse. The claim to meta status does not stand up. A so-called metadiscourse is in fact simply one more discourse among others. It follows for Lyotard that legitimation, both epistemic and political, can no longer reside in philosophical metanarratives. Where, then, he asks, does legitimation reside in the postmodern era?

Much of *The Postmodern Condition* is devoted to sketching an answer to this question. The answer, in brief, is that in the postmodern era legitimation becomes plural, local and immanent. In this era, there will necessarily be many discourses of legitimation dispersed among the plurality of first-order discursive practices. For example, scientists no longer look to prescriptive philosophies of science to warrant their procedures of inquiry. Rather, they themselves problematize, modify and warrant the constitutive norms of their own practice even as they engage in it. Instead of hovering above, legitimation descends to the level of practice and becomes immanent in it. There are no special tribunals set apart from the sites where inquiry is practiced. Rather, practitioners assume responsibility for legitimizing their own practice.

Lyotard intimates that something similar is or should be happening with respect to political legitimation. We cannot have and do not need a single, overarching theory of justice. What is required, rather, is a 'justice of multiplicities' (Lyotard, 1984a; see also: Lyotard and Thébaud, 1987; Lyotard, 1984b). What Lyotard means by this is not wholly clear. On one level, he can be read as offering a normative vision in which the good society consists in a decentralized plurality of democratic, self-managing groups and institutions whose members problematize the norms of their practice and take responsibility for modifying them as situations require. But paradoxically, on another level, he can be read as ruling out the sort of larger scale, normative political theorizing which, from a 'modern' perspective at least, would be required to legitimate such a vision. In any case, his justice of multiplicities conception precludes one familiar, and arguably essential, genre of political theory: identification and critique of macrostructures of inequality and injustice which cut across the boundaries separating relatively discrete practices and institutions. There is no place in Lyotard's universe for critique of pervasive axes of stratification, for critique of broadbased relations of dominance and subordination along lines like gender, race and class.

Lyotard's suspicion of the large extends to historical narrative and social theory as well. Here, his chief target is Marxism, the one metanarrative in France with enough lingering credibility to be worth arguing against. The problem with Marxism, in his view, is twofold. On the one hand, the Marxian story is too big, since it spans virtually the whole of human history. On the other hand, the Marxian story is too theoretical, since it relies on a *theory* of social practice and social relations which claims to *explain* historical change. At one level, Lyotard simply rejects the specifics of this theory. He claims that the Marxian conception of practice as production occludes the diversity and plurality of human practices. And the Marxian conception of capitalist society as a totality traversed by one major division and contradiction occludes the diversity and plurality of contemporary societal differences and oppositions. But Lyotard does not conclude that such deficiencies can and should be remedied by a better social theory. Rather, he rejects the project of social theory *tout court*.

Once again, Lyotard's position is ambiguous, since his rejection of social theory depends on a theoretical perspective of sorts of its own. He offers a 'postmodern' conception of sociality and social identity, a conception of what he calls 'the social bond'. What holds a society together, he claims, is not a common consciousness or institutional substructure. Rather, the social bond is a weave of criss-crossing threads of discursive practices, no single one of which runs continuously throughout the whole. Individuals are the nodes or 'posts' where such practices intersect and, so, they participate in many simultaneously. It follows that social identities are complex and heterogeneous. They cannot be mapped onto one another nor onto the social totality. Indeed, strictly speaking, there is no social totality and a fortiori no possibility of a totalizing social theory.

Thus, Lyotard insists that the field of the social is heterogeneous and nontotalizable. As a result, he rules out the sort of critical social theory which employs general categories like gender, race and class. From his perspective, such categories are too reductive of the complexity of social identities to be useful. And there is apparently nothing to be gained, in his view, by situating an account of the fluidity and diversity of discursive practices in the context of a critical analysis of large-scale institutions and social structures.

Thus, Lyotard's postmodern conception of criticism without philosophy rules out several recognizable genres of social criticism. From the premise that criticism cannot be grounded by a foundationalist philosophical metanarrative, he infers the illegitimacy of large historical stories, normative theories of justice and social-theoretical accounts of macrostructures which institutionalize inequality. What, then, *does* postmodern social criticism look like?

Lyotard tries to fashion some new genres of social criticism from the discursive resources that remain. Chief among these is smallish, localized narrative. He seeks to vindicate such narrative against both modern totalizing metanarrative and the scientism that is hostile to all narrative. One genre of postmodern social criticism, then, consists in relatively discrete, local stories about the emergence, transformation and disappearance of various discursive practices treated in isolation from one another. Such stories might resemble those told by Michel Foucault, though without the attempts to discern larger synchronic patterns and connections that Foucault (1979) sometimes made. And like Michael Walzer (1983), Lyotard seems to assume that practitioners would narrate such stories when seeking to persuade one another to modify the pragmatics or constitutive norms of their practice.

This genre of social criticism is not the whole postmodern story, however. For it casts critique as strictly local, ad hoc and ameliorative, thus supposing a political diagnosis according to which there are no large scale, systemic problems which resist local, ad hoc, ameliorative initiatives. Yet Lyotard recognizes that postmodern society does contain at least one unfavourable structural tendency which requires a more coordinated response. This is the tendency to universalize instrumental reason, to subject *all* discursive practices indiscriminately to the single criterion of efficiency or 'performativity'. In Lyotard's view, this threatens the autonomy and integrity of science and politics, since these practices are not properly subordinated to performative standards. It would pervert and distort them, thereby destroying the diversity of discursive forms.

Thus, even as he argues explicitly against it, Lyotard posits the need for a genre of social criticism which transcends local mininarrative. And despite his strictures against large, totalizing stories, he narrates a fairly tall tale about a large-scale social trend. Moreover, the logic of this story, and of the genre of criticism to which it belongs, calls for judgments which are not strictly practice-immanent. Lyotard's story presupposes the legitimacy and integrity of the scientific and political practices allegedly threatened by 'performativity'. It supposes that one can distinguish changes or developments which are *internal* to these practices from externally induced distortions. But this drives Lyotard to make normative judgments about the value and character of the threatened practices. These judgments are not strictly immanent in the practices judged. Rather, they are 'metapractical'.

Thus, Lyotard's view of postmodern social criticism is neither entirely self-consistent nor entirely persuasive. He goes too quickly from the premise that Philosophy cannot ground social criticism to the conclusion that criticism itself must be local, ad hoc and non-theoretical. As a result, he throws out the baby of large historical narrative with the bathwater of philosophical metanarrative and the baby of social-theoretical analysis of large scale inequalities with the bathwater of reductive Marxian class theory. Moreover, these allegedly illegitimate babies do not in fact remain excluded. They return like the repressed within the very genres of postmodern social criticism with which Lyotard intends to replace them.

We began this discussion by noting that postmodernists orient their reflections on the character of postmodern social criticism by the falling star of foundationalist philosophy. They posit that, with philosophy no longer able credibly to ground social criticism, criticism itself must be local, ad hoc and untheoretical. Thus, from the critique of foundationalism, they infer the illegitimacy of several genres of social criticism. For Lyotard, the illegitimate genres include large-scale historical narrative and social-theoretical analyses of pervasive relations of dominance and subordination.[1]

Suppose, however, one were to choose another starting point for reflecting on postfoundational social criticism. Suppose one began, not with the condition of Philosophy, but with the nature of the social object one wished to criticize. Suppose, further, that one defined that object as the subordination of women to and by men. Then, we submit, it would be apparent that many of the genres rejected by postmodernists are necessary for social criticism. For a phenomenon as pervasive and multi-faceted as male dominance simply cannot be adequately grasped with the meagre critical resources to which they would limit us. On the contrary, effective criticism of this phenomenon requires an array of different methods and genres. It requires at minimum large narratives about changes in social organization and ideology, empirical and social-theoretical analyses of macrostructures and institutions, interactionist analyses of the micro-politics of everyday life, critical-hermeneutical and institutional analyses of cultural production, historically and culturally specific sociologies of gender.... The list could go on.

Clearly, not all of these approaches are local and 'untheoretical'. But all are nonetheless essential to feminist social criticism. Moreover, all can, in principle, be conceived in ways that do not take us back to foundationalism even though, as we argue in the next section, many feminists have so far not wholly succeeded in avoiding that trap.

II. Feminism
Feminists, like postmodernists, have sought to develop new paradigms of social criticism which do not rely on traditional philosophical underpinnings. They have criticized modern foundationalist epistemologies and moral and political theories, exposing the contingent, partial and historically situated character of what have passed in the mainstream for necessary, universal and ahistorical truths. And they have called into question the dominant philosophical project of seeking objectivity in the guise of a 'God's eye view' which transcends any situation or perspective (see for example Harding and Hintikka, 1983).

However, if postmodernists have been drawn to such views by a concern with the status of philosophy, feminists have been led to them by the demands of political practice. This practical interest has saved feminist theory from many of the mistakes of postmodernism: women whose theorizing was to serve the struggle against sexism were not about to abandon powerful political tools merely as a result of intramural debates in professional philosophy.

Yet even as the imperatives of political practice have saved feminist theory from one set of difficulties, they have tended at times to incline it toward another. Practical imperatives have led some feminists to adopt modes of theorizing which resemble the sorts of philosophical metanarrative rightly criticized by postmodernists. To be sure, the feminist theories we have in mind here are not 'pure' metanarratives; they are not ahistorical normative theories about the transcultural nature of rationality or justice. Rather, they are very large social theories, theories of history, society, culture and psychology which claim, for example, to identify causes and/or constitutive features of sexism that operate cross-culturally. Thus, these social theories purport to be empirical rather than philosophical. But, as we hope to show, they are actually 'quasi-metanarratives'. They tacitly presuppose some commonly held but unwarranted and essentialist assumptions about the nature of human beings and the conditions for social life. In addition, they assume methods and/or concepts which are uninflected by temporality or historicity and which therefore function de facto as permanent, neutral matrices for inquiry. Such theories, then, share some of the essentialist and ahistorical features of metanarratives: they are insufficiently attentive to historical and cultural diversity; and they falsely universalize features of the theorist's own era, society, culture, class, sexual orientation, and/or ethnic or racial group.

On the other hand, the practical exigencies inclining feminists to produce quasi-metanarratives have by no means held undisputed sway. Rather, they have had to co-exist, often uneasily, with counterexigencies which have worked to opposite effect, for example, political pressures to acknowledge differences among women. In general, then, the recent history of feminist social theory reflects a tug of war between forces which have encouraged and forces which have discouraged metanarrative-like modes of theorizing. We can illustrate this dynamic by looking at a few important turning points in this history.

When, in the 1960s, women in the new left began to extend prior talk about 'women's rights' into the more encompassing discussion of 'women's liberation', they encountered the fear and hostility of their male comrades and the use of Marxist political theory as a support for these reactions. Many men of the new left argued that gender issues were secondary because subsumable under more basic modes of oppression, namely, class and race.

In response to this practical-political problem, radical feminists such as Shulamith Firestone (1970) resorted to an ingenious tactical manoeuvre: Firestone invoked biological differences between women and men to explain sexism. This enabled her to turn the tables on her Marxist comrades by claiming that gender conflict was the most basic form of human conflict and the source of all other forms, including class conflict. Here, Firestone drew on the pervasive tendency within modern culture to locate the roots of gender differences in biology. Her coup was to use biologism to establish the primacy of the struggle against male domination rather than to justify acquiescence to it.

The trick, of course, is problematic from a postmodernist perspective in that appeals to biology to explain social phenomena are essentialist and monocausal. They are essentialist insofar as they project onto all women and men qualities which develop under historically specific social conditions. They are monocausal insofar as they look to one set of characteristics, such as women's physiology or men's hormones, to explain women's oppression in all cultures. These problems are only compounded when appeals to biology are used in conjunction with the dubious claim that women's oppression is the cause of all other forms of oppression.

Moreover, as Marxists and feminist anthropologists began insisting in the early 1970s, appeals to biology do not allow us to understand the enormous diversity of forms which both gender and sexism assume in different cultures. And in fact, it was not long before most feminist social theorists came to appreciate that accounting for the diversity of the forms of sexism was as important as accounting for its depth and autonomy. Gayle Rubin (1975: 160) aptly described this dual requirement as the need to formulate theory which could account for the oppression of women in its 'endless variety and monotonous similarity'. How were feminists to develop a social theory adequate to both demands?

One approach which seemed promising was suggested by Michelle Zimbalist Rosaldo and other contributors to the influential 1974 anthropology collection, *Woman, Culture and Society*. They argued that common to all known societies was some type of separation between a 'domestic sphere' and a 'public sphere', the former associated with women and the latter with men. Because in most societies to date women have spent a good part of their lives bearing and raising children, their lives have been more bound to 'the domestic sphere'. Men, on the other hand, have had both the time and mobility to engage in those out of the home activities which generate political structures. Thus, as Rosaldo (1974) argued, while in many societies women possess some or even a great deal of power, women's power is always viewed as illegitimate, disruptive and without authority.

This approach seemed to allow for both diversity and ubiquity in the manifestations of sexism. A very general identification of women with the domestic and of men with the extra-domestic could accommodate a great deal of cultural variation both in social structures and in gender roles. At the same time, it could make comprehensible the apparent ubiquity of the assumption of women's inferiority above and beyond such variation. This hypothesis was also compatible with the idea that the extent of women's oppression differed in different societies. It could explain such differences by correlating the extent of gender inequality in a society with the extent and rigidity of the separation between its domestic and public spheres. In short, the domestic/public theorists seemed to have generated an explanation capable of satisfying a variety of conflicting demands.

However, this explanation turned out to be problematic in ways reminiscent of Firestone's account. Although the theory focused on differences between men's and women's spheres of activity rather than on differences between men's and women's biology, it was essentialist and monocausal nonetheless. It posited the existence of a 'domestic sphere' in all societies and thereby assumed that women's activities were basically similar in content and significance across cultures. (An analogous assumption about men's activities lay behind the postulation of a universal 'public sphere'.) In effect, the theory falsely generalized to all societies an historically specific conjunction of properties: women's responsibility for early child-rearing, women's tendency to spend more time in the geographical space of the home, women's lesser participation in the affairs of the community, a cultural ascription of triviality to domestic work, and a cultural ascription of inferiority to women. The theory thus failed to appreciate that, while each individual property may be true of many societies, the conjunction is not true of most.[2]

One source of difficulty in these early feminist social theories was the presumption of an overly grandiose and totalizing conception of theory. Theory was understood as the search for the one key factor which would explain sexism cross-culturally and illuminate all of social life. In this sense, to theorize was by definition to produce a quasi-metanarrative.

Since the late 1970s, feminist social theorists have largely ceased speaking of biological determinants or a cross-cultural domestic/public separation. Many, moreover, have given up the assumption of monocausality. Nevertheless, some feminist social theorists have continued implicitly to suppose a quasi-metanarrative conception of theory. They have continued to theorize in terms of a putatively unitary, primary, culturally universal type of activity associated with women, generally an activity conceived as 'domestic' and located in 'the family'.

One influential example is the analysis of 'mothering' developed by Nancy Chodorow (1978). Setting herself to explain the internal, psychological, dynamics which have led many women willingly to reproduce social divisions associated with female inferiority, Chodorow posited a cross-cultural activity, mothering, as the relevant object of investigation. Her question thus became: how is mothering as a female-associated activity reproduced over time? How does mothering produce a new generation of women with the psychological inclination to mother and a new generation of men not so inclined? The answer she offered was in terms of 'gender identity': female mothering produces women whose deep sense of self is 'relational' and men whose deep sense of self is not.

Chodorow's theory has struck many feminists as a persuasive account of some apparently observable psychic differences between men and women. Yet the theory has clear metanarrative overtones. It posits the existence of a single activity, 'mothering', which, while differing in specifics in different societies, nevertheless constitutes enough of a natural kind to warrant one label. It stipulates that this basically unitary activity gives rise to two distinct sorts of deep selves, one relatively common across cultures to women, the other relatively common across cultures to men. And it claims that the difference thus generated between 'feminine and masculine gender identity' causes a variety of supposedly cross-cultural social phenomena, including the continuation of female mothering, male contempt for women and problems in heterosexual relationships.

From a postmodern perspective, all of these assumptions are problematic because essentialist. But the second one, concerning 'gender identity', warrants special scrutiny, given its political implications. Consider that Chodorow's use of the notion of gender identity presupposes three major premises. One is the psychoanalytic premise that everyone has a deep sense of self which is constituted in early childhood through one's interactions with one's primary parent and which remains relatively constant thereafter. Another is the premise that this 'deep self' differs significantly for men and for women but is roughly similar among women, on the one hand, and among men, on the other hand, both across cultures and within cultures across lines of class, race and ethnicity. The third premise is that this deep self colours everything one does; there are no actions, however trivial, which do not bear traces of one's masculine or feminine gender identity.

One can appreciate the political exigencies which made this conjunction of premises attractive. It gave scholarly substance to the idea of the pervasiveness of sexism. If masculinity and femininity constitute our basic and ever-present sense of self, then it is not surprising that the manifestations of sexism are systemic. Moreover, many feminists had already sensed that the concept of 'sex-role socialization', an idea Chodorow explicitly criticized, ignored the depth and intractability of male dominance. By implying that measures such as changing images in school textbooks or allowing boys to play with dolls would be sufficient to bring about equality between the sexes, this concept seemed to trivialize and co-opt the message of feminism. Finally, Chodorow's depth-psychological approach gave a scholarly sanction to the idea of sisterhood. It seemed to legitimate the claim that the ties which bind women are deep and substantively based.

Needless to say, we have no wish to quarrel with the claim of the depth and pervasiveness of sexism, nor with the idea of sisterhood. But we do wish to challenge Chodorow's way of legitimating them. The idea of a cross-cultural, deep sense of self, specified differently for women and men, becomes problematic when given any specific content. Chodorow states that women everywhere differ from men in their greater concern with 'relational interaction'. But what does she mean by this term? Certainly not any and every kind of human interaction, since men have often been more concerned than women with some kinds of interactions, for example, those which have to do with the aggrandizement of power and wealth. Of course, it is true that many women in modern western societies have been expected to exhibit strong concern with those types of interactions associated with intimacy, friendship and love, interactions which dominate one meaning of the late twentieth-century concept of 'relationship'. But surely this meaning presupposes a notion of private life specific to modern western societies of the last two centuries. Is it possible that Chodorow's theory rests on an equivocation on the term 'relationship'?[3]

Equally troubling are the aporias this theory generates for political practice. While 'gender identity' gives substance to the idea of sisterhood, it does so at the cost of repressing differences among sisters. Although the theory allows for some differences among women of different classes, races, sexual orientations and ethnic groups, it construes these as subsidiary to more basic similarities. But it is precisely as a consequence of the request to understand such differences as secondary that many women have denied an allegiance to feminism.

We have dwelt at length on Chodorow because of the great

influence her work has enjoyed. But she is not the only recent feminist social theorist who has constructed a quasi-metanarrative around a putatively cross-cultural female-associated activity. On the contrary, theorists like Ann Ferguson and Nancy Folbre (1981), Nancy Hartsock (1983) and Catharine MacKinnon (1982) have done something analogous with 'sex-affective production', 'reproduction' and 'sexuality' respectively. Each claims to have identified a basic kind of human practice found in all societies which has cross-cultural explanatory power. In each case, the practice in question is associated with a biological or quasi-biological need and is construed as functionally necessary to the reproduction of society. It is not the sort of thing, then, whose historical origins need be investigated.

The difficulty here is that categories like sexuality, mothering, reproduction and sex-affective production group together phenomena which are not necessarily conjoined in all societies, while separating off from one another phenomena which are not necessarily separated. As a matter of fact, it is doubtful whether these categories have any determinate cross-cultural content. Thus, for a theorist to use such categories to construct a universalistic social theory is to risk projecting the socially dominant conjunctions and dispersions of her own society onto others, thereby distorting important features of both. Social theorists would do better first to construct genealogies of the *categories* of sexuality, reproduction and mothering before assuming their universal significance.

Since around 1980, many feminist scholars have come to abandon the project of grand social theory. They have stopped looking for *the* causes of sexism and have turned to more concrete inquiry with more limited aims. One reason for this shift is the growing legitimacy of feminist scholarship. The institutionalization of Women's Studies in the US has meant a dramatic increase in the size of the community of feminist inquirers, a much greater division of scholarly labour and a large and growing fund of concrete information. As a result, feminist scholars have come to regard their enterprise more collectively, more like a puzzle whose various pieces are being filled in by many different people than a construction to be completed by a single grand theoretical stroke. In short, feminist scholarship has attained its maturity.

Even in this phase, however, traces of youthful quasi-metanarratives remain. Some theorists who have ceased looking for *the* causes of sexism still rely on essentialist categories like 'gender identity'. This is especially true of those scholars who have sought to develop 'gynocentric' alternatives to mainstream androcentric perspectives, but who have not fully abandoned the universalist pretensions of the latter.

Consider, as an example, the work of Carol Gilligan (1982). Unlike most of the theorists we have considered so far, Gilligan has not sought to explain the origins or nature of cross-cultural sexism. Rather, she set herself the more limited task of exposing and redressing androcentric bias in the model of moral development of psychologist Lawrence Kohlberg. Thus, she argued that it is illegitimate to evaluate the moral development of women and girls by reference to a standard drawn exclusively from the experience of men and boys. And she proposed to examine women's moral discourse on its own terms in order to uncover its immanent standards of adequacy.

Gilligan's work has been rightly regarded as important and innovative. It challenged mainstream psychology's persistent occlusion of women's lives and experiences and its insistent but false claims to universality. Yet insofar as Gilligan's challenge involved the construction of an alternative 'feminine' model of moral development, her position was ambiguous. On the one hand, by providing a counter-example to Kohlberg's model, she cast doubt on the possibility of any single universalist developmental schema. On the other hand, by constructing a female countermodel, she invited the same charge of false generalization she had herself raised against Kohlberg, though now from other perspectives such as class, sexual orientation, race and ethnicity. Gilligan's (1982: 2) disclaimers notwithstanding, to the extent that she described women's moral development in terms of *a* different voice; to the extent that she did not specify which women, under which specific historical circumstances have spoken with the voice in question; and to the extent that she grounded her analysis in the explicitly cross-cultural framework of Nancy Chodorow, her model remained essentialist. It perpetuated in a newer, more localized fashion traces of previous, more grandiose quasi-metanarratives.

Thus, vestiges of essentialism have continued to plague feminist scholarship even despite the decline of grand theorizing. In many cases, including Gilligan's, this represents the continuing subterranean influence of those very mainstream modes of thought and inquiry with which feminists have wished to break.

On the other hand, the practice of feminist politics in the 1980s has generated a new set of pressures which have worked against metanarratives. In recent years, poor and working class women, women of colour and lesbians have finally won a wider hearing for their objections to feminist theories which fail to illuminate their lives and address their problems. They have exposed the earlier quasi-metanarratives, with their assumptions of universal female dependence and confinement to 'the domestic sphere', as false extrapolations from the experience of the white, middle-class, heterosexual women who dominated the beginnings of the second wave. For example, writers like Bell Hooks (1984), Gloria Joseph (1981), Audre Lord (1981), Maria Lugones and Elizabeth Spelman (1983; 1980–1) have unmasked the implicit reference to white Anglo women in many classic feminist texts; likewise, Adrienne Rich (1980) and Marilyn Frye (1983) have exposed the heterosexist bias of much mainstream feminist theory. Thus, as the class, sexual, racial and ethnic awareness of the movement has altered, so has the preferred conception of theory. It has become clear that quasi-metanarratives hamper rather than promote sisterhood, since they elide differences among women and among the forms of sexism to which different women are differentially subject. Likewise, it is increasingly apparent that such theories hinder alliances with other progressive movements, since they tend to occlude axes of domination other than gender. In sum, there is growing interest among feminists in modes of theorizing which are attentive to differences and to cultural and historical specificity.

In general, then, feminist scholarship of the 1980s evinces some conflicting tendencies. On the one hand, there is decreasing interest in grand social theories as scholarship has become more localized, issue-oriented and explicitly fallibilistic. On the other hand, essentialist vestiges persist in the continued use of ahistorical categories like 'gender identity' without reflection as to how, when and why such categories originated and were modified over time. This tension is symptomatically expressed in the current fascination, on the part of US feminists, with French psychoanalytic feminisms: the latter propositionally decry essentialism even as they performatively enact it (Cixous, 1981; Cixous and Clément, 1986; Irigaray, 1985a, 1985b; Kristeva, 1980, 1981; see also critical discussions by Jones, 1985; Moi, 1985). More generally, feminist scholarship has remained insufficiently attentive to the *theoretical* prerequisites of dealing with diversity, despite widespread commitment to accepting it politically.

By criticizing lingering essentialism in contemporary feminist theory, we hope to encourage such theory to become more consistently postmodern. This is not, however, to recommend merely *any* form of postmodernism. On the contrary, as we have shown, the version developed by Jean-François Lyotard offers a weak and inadequate conception of social criticism without philosophy. It rules out genres of criticism, such as large historical narrative and historically situated social theory, which feminists rightly regard as indispensable. But it does not follow from Lyotard's shortcomings that criticism without philosophy is in principle incompatible with criticism with social force. Rather, as we argue next, a robust, postmodern-feminist paradigm of social criticism without philosophy is possible.

III. Towards a Postmodern Feminism   •

How can we combine a postmodernist incredulity towards metanarratives with the social-critical power of feminism? How can we conceive a version of criticism without philosophy which is robust enough to handle the tough job of analysing sexism in all its 'endless variety and monotonous similarity'?

A first step is to recognize, *contra* Lyotard, that postmodern critique need foreswear neither large historical narratives nor analyses of societal macrostructures. This point is important for feminists, since sexism has a long history and is deeply and pervasively embedded in contemporary societies. Thus, postmodern feminists need not abandon the large theoretical tools needed to address large political problems. There is nothing inconsistent in the idea of postmodern theory.

However, if postmodern-feminist critique must remain 'theoretical', not just any kind of theory will do. Rather, theory here would be explicitly historical, attuned to the cultural specificity of different societies and periods, and to that of different groups within societies and periods. Thus, the categories of postmodern-feminist theory would be inflected by temporality, with historically specific institutional categories like 'the modern, restricted, male-headed, nuclear family' taking precedence over ahistorical, functionalist categories like 'reproduction' and 'mothering'. Where categories of the latter sort were not eschewed altogether, they would be genealogized, that is, framed by a historical narrative and rendered temporally and culturally specific.

Moreover,   postmodern-feminist   theory   would   be   non-universalist. When its focus became cross-cultural or transepochal, its mode of attention would be comparativist rather than universalizing, attuned to changes and contrasts instead of to 'covering laws'. Finally, postmodern-feminist theory would dispense with the idea of a subject of history. It would replace unitary notions of 'woman' and 'feminine gender identity' with plural and complexly constructed conceptions of social identity, treating gender as one relevant strand among others, attending also to class, race, ethnicity, age and sexual orientation.

In general, postmodern-feminist theory would be pragmatic and fallibilistic. It would tailor its methods and categories to the specific task at hand, using multiple categories when appropriate and foreswearing the metaphysical comfort of a single 'feminist method' or 'feminist epistemology'. In short, this theory would look more like a tapestry composed of threads of many different hues than one woven in a single colour.

The most important advantage of this sort of theory would be its usefulness for contemporary feminist political practice. Such practice is increasingly a matter of alliances rather than one of unity around a universally shared interest or identity. It recognizes that the diversity of women's needs and experiences means that no single solution, on issues like child care, social security and housing, can be adequate for all. Thus, the underlying premise of this practice is that, while some women share some common interests and face some common enemies, such commonalities are by no means universal; rather, they are interlaced with differences, even with conflicts. This, then, is a practice made up of a patchwork of overlapping alliances, not one circumscribable by an essential definition. One might best speak of it in the plural as the practice of 'feminisms'. In a sense, this practice is in advance of much contemporary feminist theory. It is already implicitly postmodern. It would find its most appropriate and useful theoretical expression in a postmodern-feminist form of critical inquiry. Such inquiry would be the theoretical counterpart of a broader, richer, more complex and multi-layered feminist solidarity, the sort of solidarity which is essential for overcoming the oppression of women in its 'endless variety and monotonous similarity'.

Notes

We are grateful for the helpful suggestions of many people, especially Jonathan Arac, Ann Ferguson, Marilyn Frye, Nancy Hartsock, Alison Jaggar, Berel Lang,

Thomas McCarthy, Karsten Struhl, Iris Young, Thomas Wartenburg and the members of SOFPHIA. We are also grateful for word-processing help from Marina Rosiene.

1. It should be noted that, for Lyotard, the choice of Philosophy as a starting point is itself determined by a metapolitical commitment, namely, to anti-totalitarianism. He assumes, erroneously, in our view, that totalizing social and political theory necessarily eventuates in totalitarian societies. Thus, the 'practical intent' which subtends Lyotard's privileging of philosophy (and which is in turn attenuated by the latter) is anti-Marxism. Whether it should also be characterized as 'neo-liberalism' is a question too complicated to be explored here.

2. These and related problems were soon apparent to many of the domestic/public theorists themselves. See Rosaldo's (1980) self criticism. A more recent discussion, which points out the circularity of the theory, appears in Sylvia J. Yanagisako and Jane F. Collier (1988) .

3. A similar ambiguity attends Chodorow's discussion of 'the family'. In response to critics who object that her psychoanalytic emphasis ignores social structures, Chodorow has rightly insisted that the family is itself a social structure, one frequently slighted in social explanations. Yet she generally does not discuss families as historically specific social institutions whose specific relations with other institutions can be analysed. Rather, she tends to invoke 'the family' in a very abstract and general sense defined only as the locus of female mothering.

References

Chodorow, Nancy (1978) *The Reproduction of Mothering: Psychoanalysis and the Sociology of Gender.* Berkeley: University of California Press.

Cixous, Hélène (1981) 'The Laugh of the Medusa'. Translated by K. Cohen and P. Cohen in E. Marks and I. de Courtivron (eds) *New French Feminisms.* New York: Schocken Books.

Cixous, Hélène and Clément, Catherine (1986) *The Newly Born Woman.* Minneapolis: University of Minnesota Press.

Ferguson, Ann and Folbre, Nancy (1981) 'The Unhappy Marriage of Patriarchy and Capitalism', in L. Sargent (ed.) *Women and Revolution.* Boston: South End Press.

Firestone, Shulamith (1970) *The Dialectic of Sex.* New York: Bantam.

Flax, Jane (1986) 'Gender as a Social Problem: In and For Feminist Theory', *American Studies/Amerika Studien* June.

Foucault, Michel (1979) *Discipline and Punish: The Birth of the Prison.* Translated by Alan Sheridan. New York: Vintage Books.

Frye, Marilyn (1983) *The Politics of Reality: Essays in Feminist Theory.* Trumansburg, NY: The Crossing Press.

Gilligan, Carol (1982) *In a Different Voice: Psychological Theory and Women's Development.* Cambridge, Mass.: Harvard University Press.

Haraway, Donna (1983) 'A Manifesto for Cyborgs: Science, Technology and Socialist Feminism in the 1980s', *Socialist Review* 80: 65–107.

Harding, Sandra (1986a) *The Science Question in Feminism.* Ithaca, NY: Cornell University Press.

Harding, Sandra (1986b) 'The Instability of the Analytical Categories of Feminist Theory', *Signs: Journal of Women in Culture and Society* 11(4): 645–64.

Harding, Sandra and Hintikka, Merrill B. (eds) (1983) *Discovering Reality: Feminist Perspectives on Epistemology, Metaphysics, Methodology and Philosophy of Science*. Dordrecht: D. Reidel.

Hartsock, Nancy (1983) *Money, Sex and Power: Toward a Feminist Historical Materialism*. New York: Longman.

Hooks, Bell (1984) *Feminist Theory: From Margin to Center*. Boston: South End Press.

Irigaray, Luce (1985a) *Speculum of the Other Woman*. Ithaca, NY: Cornell University Press.

Irigaray, Luce (1985b) *This Sex Which is Not One*. Ithaca, NY: Cornell University Press.

Jardine, Alice A. (1985) *Gynesis: Configurations of Women and Modernity*. Ithaca, NY: Cornell University Press.

Jones, Ann Rosalind (1985) 'Writing the Body: Toward an Understanding of l'Ecriture féminine', in E. Showalter (ed.) *The New Feminist Criticism: Essays on Women, Literature and Theory*. New York: Pantheon Books.

Joseph, Gloria (1981) 'The Incompatible Menage à Trois: Marxism, Feminism and Racism', in L. Sargent (ed.) *Women and Revolution*. Boston: South End Press.

Kristeva, Julia (1980) *Desire in Language: A Semiotic Approach to Literature and Art*, in L. S. Roudiez (ed.). New York: Columbia University Press.

Kristeva, Julia (1981) 'Women's Time'. Translated by A. Jardine and H. Blake, *Signs: Journal of Women in Culture and Society* 7(1): 13–35.

Lord, Audre (1981) 'An Open Letter to Mary Daly', in C. Moraga and G. Anzaldua (eds) *This Bridge Called My Back: Writings by Radical Women of Color*. Watertown, MA: Persephone Press.

Lugones, Maria C. and Spelman, Elizabeth V. (1983) 'Have We Got a Theory for You! Feminist Theory, Cultural Imperialism and the Demand for the Women's Voice', *Hypatia, Women's Studies International Forum* 6(6): 578–81.

Lyotard, Jean-François (1978) 'Some of the Things at Stake in Women's Struggles'. Translated by D.J. Clarke, W. Woodhull and J. Mowitt, *Sub-Stance* 20.

Lyotard, Jean-François (1984a) *The Postmodern Condition: A Report on Knowledge*. Translated by G. Bennington and B. Massumi. Minneapolis: Minnesota University Press.

Lyotard, Jean-François (1984b) 'The Differend'. Translated by G. Van Den Abbeele, *Diacritics* Fall: 4–14.

Lyotard, Jean-François and Thebaud, Jean-Loup (1987) *Just Gaming*. Minneapolis: Minnesota University Press.

MacKinnon, Catharine A. (1982) 'Feminism, Marxism, Method, and the State: An Agenda for Theory', *Signs: Journal of Women in Culture and Society* 7(3): 515–44.

Moi, Toril (1985) *Sexual/Textual Politics: Feminist Literary Theory*. London: Methuen.

Owens, Craig (1983) 'The Discourse of Others: Feminists and Postmodernism', in H. Foster (ed.) *The Anti-Aesthetic: Essays on Postmodern Culture*. Port Townsend, WA: Bay Press.

Rich, Adrienne (1980) 'Compulsory Heterosexuality and Lesbian Existence', *Signs: Journal of Women in Culture and Society* 5(4): 631–60.

Rosaldo, Michelle Zimbalist (1974) 'Woman, Culture and Society: A Theoretical Overview', in M.Z. Rosaldo and L. Lamphere (eds) *Woman, Culture and Society*. Stanford: Stanford University Press.

Rosaldo, Michelle Zimbalist (1980) 'The Use and Abuse of Anthropology: Reflections on Feminism and Cross-cultural Understanding', *Signs: Journal of Women in Culture and Society* 5(3): 389–417.

Rubin, Gayle (1975) 'The Traffic in Women', in R.R. Reiter (ed.) *Toward an Anthropology of Women*. New York: Monthly Review Press.

Spelman, Elizabeth (1980–1) 'Theories of Race and Gender: The Erasure of Black Women', *Quest* 5(4): 36–62.

Walzer, Michael (1983) *Spheres of Justice: A Defense of Pluralism and Equality*. NY: Basic Books.

Yanagisako, Sylvia J. and Collier, Jane F. (1988) 'Toward a Unified Analysis of Gender and Kinship', in J.F. Collier and S.J. Yanagisako (eds) *Gender and Kinship: Toward a Unified Analysis*. Stanford: Stanford University Press.

Nancy Fraser teaches Philosophy at NorthWestern University. She is the author of *Unruly Practices: Power, Discourse and Gender in Late-Capitalist Social Theory* (University of Minnesota Press and Polity Press).

Linda Nicholson teaches Philosophy of Education at State University of New York at Albany. She is the author of *Gender and History: The Limits of Social Theory in the Age of the Family* (Columbia University Press).

On Gianni Vattimo's Postmodern Hermeneutics

Peter Carravetta

Gianni Vattimo is presently regarded as one of Italy's leading philosophers and cultural critics, and foremost exponent of hermeneutics. Through several important and timely books he has, during the last quarter of a century, given hermeneutics unquestionable currency among the long established Faculties of Aesthetics. Author of exegetical works on Schleiermacher, Nietzsche and Heidegger, and translator of Gadamer's *Truth and Method*, he has brought hermeneutic discourse into critical contact with the leading currents of the twentieth century, from historicism to existentialism, from Marxism to deconstruction, from German sociology to American pragmatism. In the midst of this he has developed his own ontological hermeneutics, followed immediately by the hypothesis of a 'weak ontology' which is presently taking on the shape of 'the play of interpretations', a general theory of being and interpretation in which the following tenets are explored and serve as reference points:

a) The History of Being as the Westering of the Greek Logos, and according to which our age would be witnessing 'the Decline of Ontology'; this is corroborated by studies into the essence and configuration of technology (in the Heideggerian canon);

b) Modern society is witness to the decline and eventual disappearance of the notion of subject and subjectivity: beginning with Nietzsche and through Heidegger the metaphysical Subjectum (Aristotle, Descartes, Hegel) has revealed itself to be no more than a mask, a role, a fiction, at worst an ideological construct, at best a nostalgic effigy;

c) A 'weakening' of Being means that the human person should now be able to articulate discourse without adhering to the grammar and demands of a 'strong' metaphysical tradition, that is, a metaphysic which insists on believing in 'foundations', in 'the

Theory, Culture & Society (SAGE, London, Newbury Park, Beverly Hills and New Delhi), Vol. 5 (1988), 395–97

identity principle', or the absent Eternal Unity. Weak thought is more like a *Gelassenheit* which has not relinquished the actual struggles of historical man, perhaps because a greater amount of concern and thinking is directed toward bodily presence, its 'external' history and therefore the experience of living *against* finitude (or death). In this view, problems relating to the abstracting, alienating epistemologies and technologies of our age are read as an interplay of strong, consensus (power) seeking discourses, each parading the idea of supreme being, 'true' knowledge, and the way to salvation.

Vattimo holds that this state of affairs is not to be critiqued by relying upon the authority of some sociological or political philosophy (which would entail adopting yet another strong, centring metaphysic), rather, the strong technological enframing of the world could and would more effectively be explored by means of an idea of existence which recovers the dimension of the aesthetic and of the existential (in Heidegger's sense), accepting the risk of constant distortion and misreading. Moreover, this favours the reappropriation of Modernist thought as instances of being which are no more privileged than the discourse of myth, fable, local interpretations, limited artistic involvement, day-to-day non-linguistic experience. From the perspective of interpretation theory, this could mean the possibility of introducing generally unaccepted — or untimely, or 'disturbing' — views, like nihilism, as well as freeing the critical-imaginative project by recounting interpretations new and old endlessly. Though this would seem to 'flatten' history somewhat, Vattimo's 'gamble' appears to be headed toward a sort of molecular, temporally 'compressed' *ethical* awareness, a perspective which in the age of absolute simultaneity and media-oriented social intercourse is not only 'new' but would offset the 'anything goes' attitude which in some circles is considered 'postmodern'. By bringing the aesthetic both back and forward in time in order to recover its hermeneutic dimension, Vattimo appears to be disclosing alternative spaces not only for interpretation, but for a general conception of being and existence.

Major Published Works by Gianni Vattimo

Il concetto di fare in Aristotele Torino, 1961.
Essere, storia e linguaggio in Heidegger Torino, 1963.
Poesia e ontologia Milano, 1967 (2nd edn 1985).
Schleiermacher filosofo dell'interpretazione Milano, 1968.

Introduzione a Heidegger Bari, 1971 (2nd edn 1985).

Il soggetto e la maschera; Nietzsche e il problema della liberazione Milano, 1974 (2nd edn 1979).

Le avventure della differenza; che cosa significa pensare dopo Nietzsche e Heidegger Milano, 1979.

Al di là del soggetto Milano, 1981 (2nd edn 1984; Engl. trans. forthcoming).

La fine della modernità; nichilismo ed ermeneutica nella cultura post-moderna Milano, 1985 (Engl. trans. forthcoming).

Translated into Italian Gadamer's *Warheit und Methode* Milano, 1972 (2nd edn 1983).

Co-edited, with Pier Aldo Rovatti, *Il pensiero debole* Milano, 1983 (Engl. trans. forthcoming).

Edited *Filosofia '86* Bari, 1987.

Forthcoming: *Il gioco dell'interpretazione*

Peter Carravetta teaches in the Department of Romance Languages at Queens College/CUNY. He is editor of *Differentia: Review of Italian Thought*.

The Oxford Literary Review

COLONIALISM
& other essays

Vol.9 £6.95 Overseas £8 or $13.95
Institutions £15 Overseas £17.50 or $30
Make cheques payable to OLR

ISBN 0 9511080 1 8 ISSN 0305 1498
OLR, Dept. English, The University, Southampton S09 5NH, UK

Hermeneutics as Koine

Gianni Vattimo

What is the meaning of the thesis according to which hermeneutics is the 'koine' of philosophy and, more generally, of culture in the 1980s? The claim, which can be reasonably argued, is that in much the same way in which we witnessed in the past decades a marxist hegemony (in the 1950s and the 1960s) and a structuralist hegemony (in the 1970s, generalizing somewhat), today the common idiom of both philosophy and culture is hermeneutics. Obviously we do not intend to 'prove' that in the decades just referred to 'there was' a marxist and then a structuralist hegemony, nor that today 'there exists' a hermeneutic hegemony. The claim concerning hermeneutics as 'koine' holds that, from the viewpoint of factual description, the way in which in the past the great majority of literary and philosophical discussions had to rise to the challenge of marxism and structuralism, often without necessarily accepting any of their tenets, today this central role belongs to hermeneutics. At the time when Gadamer first published *Truth and Method* (1960), hermeneutics was no more than a technical term indicating, for culture at large, a very specialized discipline that dealt with the interpretation of literary, juridical and theological texts. As has often happened with other expressions, like 'philosophy of language', which for a while stood to signify Analytic Philosophy *tout court*, today the term hermeneutics has acquired a more broad philosophical meaning which denotes both a specific philosophical discipline and a theoretical orientation, a 'current'. With reference to either or both these meanings (and with a certain, inevitable, ambiguity) the centrality of hermeneutics and its connected thematics and texts is attested by the presence of the term in cultural discussions, education, university courses and even in those areas such as medicine, sociology, architecture, to name just a few, which are presently seeking new links with philosophy.

Vague as it may sound, all this adds up to ascertaining the in-

Theory, Culture & Society (SAGE, London, Newbury Park, Beverly Hills and New Delhi), Vol. 5 (1988), 399–408

creased popularity of hermeneutics in today's culture. Yet the claim becomes less generic the moment we start looking for the plausible reasons behind this relevance [*attualità*] of hermeneutics. The search for these reasons constitutes a first step toward a clearer understanding of the initial thesis: we shall ask ourselves what does it mean, and what needs and transformations are articulated by the fact — if that's what it is — that hermeneutics is enjoying such popularity. This first question — what is articulated in the relevance of hermeneutics? — spurs a second one: in what direction and toward what ends is the interest in hermeneutics pointing? Both questions and their respective answers are theoretically relevant to the contents and development of hermeneutics itself: the fact that it has become if not altogether hegemonic at least a common idiom means that hermeneutics today is faced with problems and tasks which are new and different with respect to those that were pertinent to the Gadamerian project of 1960. Confronted with new questions and tasks it is likely that hermeneutics must redefine itself, and attempt to circumscribe the indefiniteness which characterizes it precisely insofar as it is a 'koine'. For example, in the last few years in America hermeneutics has come to represent more or less all of Continental European philosophy, that is to say what not too long ago, in the same cultural environment, was called phenomenology or existentialism: today in fact hermeneuticists are not only Gadamer and Ricoeur, but Derrida, Foucault, Apel and Habermas as well.

The question then remains: if hermeneutics has become the cultural 'koine' of the past few years, to what do we owe this state of affairs? A preliminary answer to the question might be formulated as follows: hermeneutics is the form in which, with the waning of the structuralist hegemony, an historicist exigency is once again demanding to be heard. It is in fact unlikely that the crisis and dissolution of structuralism is to be imputed solely to the exhaustion of a critical fad, that is to say, that at a given point in time structural method was reduced to a caricature of itself for having imposed on all the human sciences rigid patterns of description and cataloguing. Grounded upon binary oppositions, these critical grids favoured above any concern with content the pure and simple possibility of discovering ordering principles, and even certain exaggerated claims made by microhistory reflect this extremely formalistic cultural climate in which everything appeared to be worthy of investigation as long as it exhibited some structuring principle. But if the runaway proliferation of descriptive schemes more or less an end in themselves contributed in no uncertain way to the dissolution of the structuralist hegemony (owing precisely to its excessive radicalization), the crisis of structuralism has even deeper roots. Brought to its ultimate consequences structural method reduced content to its inessentiality because it placed in a position of abstract and never thematized neutrality the 'deploying' subject of the method itself. The contents to which the method was applied — the comic strip, the *feuilleton*, the history of smell and so on — were considered irrelevant to the degree in which the interest of the observer was considered purely cognitive. But it was precisely this purity and cognitivity that needed to be questioned. It is true that the structuralists rightly appealed to the 'political' significance of wanting to study people as if they were ants (following Lévi-Strauss in polemic with Sartre the 'humanist') against a historicist and evolutionistic tradition that made of the West the centre of the world and easily justified the ideology of imperialism. Indeed structuralism has been also, around 1968, one of the theoretical weapons of the left, the theory of decolonization, partaking in the effort to give 'other' cultures the right to speak. Yet all of this came about, as we perceive today, at the cost of a 'positivistic' restoration of the presupposed neutrality of the observer: perhaps that was, ultimately, the sense of Althusser's oxymoron 'theoretical practice'. Within the scope of these broad generalizations concerning the sociology of culture, it is likely that the exhaustion of the structuralist fad corresponds moreover to a new phase in the relation between western culture and 'other' cultures. Today, when for better or for worse these 'other' cultures have gained the right to speak — above all the Islamic culture, with its pressure political and otherwise on the West — we can no longer ignore the problem of the relation between the 'observer' and the 'observed'. The dialogue with different cultures is finally become a true dialogue, and it is pointless to liquidate the Eurocentric perspectives which structuralism in years past rightfully meant to defuse: the question today is rather to truly exercise this dialogue beyond a purely descriptive position.

Without meaning to overstate these rather approximative observations, we can call to mind, among the signs of this passage from a structuralist 'koine' to a hermeneutic 'koine', certain representative vicissitudes of the semiotic work of Umberto Eco. During the past few years Eco has in fact shown an increased interest in the pragmatic aspects of semiotics, shifting in the meantime the emphasis from Saussure to Peirce, with all that this entails. On the same scale we can perceive the itinerary of a thinker who, though he never identified himself as a structuralist, has greatly influenced the definition of structuralist thematics and their mode of interaction in culture, namely Jacques Derrida. As Maurizio Ferraris (1984) pointed out, Derrida's more recent works are marked by a growing interest in the institutional collocation of the philosopher and in general by the 'conflict of faculties', in other words by the pragmatic and historical-concrete aspects of metaphysics and of its deconstruction. These facts seem to indicate that the crisis of the structuralist 'koine' is motivated by demands which are by and large historicist. It is these exigencies that explain the shift, the 'passage' to hermeneutics, its coming onto the scene as the most likely candidate to represent the cultural 'koine' of the 1980s.

But how does hermeneutics perceive, more than structuralism ever did, this exigency to reconfer an essential aspect to contents and to thematize the historical position of the observer? We are now faced with the second question concerning the timeliness [*attualità*] of hermeneutics. At this juncture I wish to discuss not only if and to what extent hermeneutics can validate its claim to the essentiality of historical collocation, but also to try to demonstrate that, in order to understand these exigencies, hermeneutics must redefine itself in a more rigorous and coherent manner by recovering its original inspiration, that is, the Heideggerian meditation on metaphysics and its destiny.

In general, the fact that thinking turns to hermeneutics in order to retrieve the historicity and essentiality of contents which structuralism had forgotten is legitimated by the determining importance which interpretation theory, in Gadamer's classic formulation, attributes to the *Wirkungsgeschichte* and the *wirkungsgeschichtliches Bewusstsein*: interpretation is not description on the part of a 'neutral' observer, rather, it is a dialogic event in which the interlocutors are equally played out and from which their result changed in some way. They understand one another in measure of their being situated within a third horizon, a horizon they do not have any control over but within which and by which they are placed [*entro un orizzonte terzo, di cui non dispongono, ma nel quale e dal quale sono disposti*]. Whereas structural thinking had as its *telos* the evidencing and taking possession of, on the part of the observing consciousness, orders linked according to rules, hermeneutic thinking emphasizes the fact that both observer and observed belong together within a common horizon, underscoring truth as an event which, in the dialogue between the two interlocutors, 'realizes' or 'sets into play' (*mette in opera*) and modifies at the same time this horizon. In the context of play, which in *Truth and Method* Gadamer takes as the model for the disclosure of hermeneutic truth, the players are also and always being played; thus consciousness, insofar as it is historically determined, cannot ever reach total self-transparency. Formulated in this fashion, hermeneutics retrieves and develops the heritage of existentialism's critique of Hegelian metaphysical rationalism, as well as existentialism's critique of that positivistic scientism which in some ways is still echoed by structuralism. If the above hypotheses are valid, the political-concrete-historical distress experienced by thinking when the effective historical collocation of the observer is not accounted for is really not too different from the existentialist critique of idealism and positivism. Phenomenologically ascertained lived experience of thought refuses to accept philosophical schemes which presuppose an observing subject as a neutral point of view, or, which amounts to the same thing, as an opacity that clarifies itself until it reaches the absolute self-transparency of the Hegelian spirit. Against the alleged (at times implicitly) positivistic and structural neutrality, hermeneutics vindicates the fact that the 'subject' belongs to the play necessary to comprehension and to the event of truth; however, instead of seeing this play as process motivated by the *telos* of self-transparency (Hegel), hermeneutics considers the belonging, the playing while being played, as a definitive phase which cannot be overcome in a final moment of appropriation and fruition of the subject's presuppositions.

In what sense is the 'fusion of horizons', the reciprocal understanding of the two interlocutors in the 'objective spirit', an event of truth for Gadamer? In an essay which is important to understand the significance Gadamer (1973) himself attributes to his thought within contemporary philosophy — 'The Philosophical Foundations of the Twentieth Century' — he states that today philosophy should seek for its guide the Hegelian notions of objective spirit. The total mediation which Hegel conceived as the task and supreme *telos* of thought does not take place in the self-consciousness of absolute spirit — a 'monologic' self-consciousness which is still understood as the consciousness of a Cartesian ego — but rather in objective spirit, that is to say, in culture, institutions, the 'symbolic forms' that make up the substance of our lived humanness. Here we can take almost literally Lacan's reading of Freud: not 'wo Es war, soll *ich* werden', but 'wo *Es* war, soll ich werden'. Truth is experienced solely by advancing to where the concreteness of objective spirit is given, not by dissolving this concreteness in a fully displayed self-consciousness. The ethical-political perspective Gadamer has worked in recent writings on the basis of premises already in *Truth and Method* (1960), for instance, in *Reason in the Age of Science* (1976), illustrate the meaning he attributes to this choice for a Hegelian objective spirit: the task of thinking consists in bringing everything — for example, and above all, the results of specialistic approaches to reality, as well as the formalized languages of science and their technological applications — to the *logos* that dwells in the tradition of language, to what Habermas in his more recent writings calls 'lifeworld' (with a term that, though Husserlian in the letter, is substantially hermeneutic). But why, one might still ask, does the hermeneutic experience of truth take the shape of a 'moving toward the objective spirit?' Are we dealing with that abdication to the overpowering object for which Adorno (1966) reproached Heidegger in the chapter on 'Ontological Need' in *Negative Dialectics*? Gadamer however is not so much a 'traditionalist' (for whom truth is what 'adapts' to common sense, the cultural patrimony actually inherited by a society, that which is handed down), as he is a 'classicist': the experience of truth is for him an experience of 'integration', of non-conflictual belonging. Crucial to this are the pages he devotes to the notion of the beautiful — the *kalón* of the Greeks — both in *Truth and Method* (1960) and in the already cited *Reason in the Age of Science* (1976). It is legitimate to call such a position 'classicist' to the degree in which it recovers the seventeenth- and eighteenth-century dream of a Greek experience understood as the full correspondence between internal and external, between man and citizen: the same which is perceived in Hegel's notion of 'beautiful ethicalness' and his conception of classical art.

But this conception of truth as a classicistically modelled belonging, does it really respond to that need for historicalness which hermeneutics as a posthistoricist, poststructuralist 'koine' is called upon to satisfy? Isn't there perhaps a danger that experience of truth as *kalón* (non-conflictual belonging of the interlocutors between themselves and with respect to the horizon of language, of objective spirit, and of living tradition that mediates them) is just another way in which the transparent, ahistorical, neutralized subject manifests itself? It is a legitimate doubt if we think for a moment of the apparent inconclusiveness which hermeneutics seems to manifest, though not so much in Gadamer's own work as in its current public image. For the Gadamer (1960) of *Truth and Method* it was a question of vindicating the legitimacy of an 'extramethodic' experience of truth: the truth of art, the truth of history, the truth of tradition living in language, as well as the constitutive linguisticalness of experience. Gadamer successfully achieved these goals, but as a result of this, and with the present pre-eminence of hermeneutics as a 'koine', it becomes clear that hermeneutics cannot stop here. It is a question neither of vindicating a 'classicistic' model of truth against the objectivism of scientific method erected as sole arbiter of the true, nor of acknowledging that there exists an 'extramethodic' truth side by side with scientific truth. Ultimately, it is not a question of substituting an hermeneutic 'description' of experience with one which is 'realistic' or objectivistic. Perhaps it is true that a philosophy cannot become a 'koine' without realizing itself as an emancipatory programme. From this point of view, Habermas' objections to Gadamer were right on target (though its results were unacceptable because tied to a revival of Kantianism and therefore in favour of a 'ahistorical' subjectivity (see Vattimo, 1981). However it is also true that to require an emancipatory perspective is theoretically outside the scope of hermeneutics. Yet, by the same token one cannot demand of philosophical hermeneutics that it limit itself to yet another 'description' of the structures of experience. By holding that truth is not exclusively the proposition that describes faithfully from the outside a state of affairs, but rather it is events, responses and messages that hail from a tradition and, moreover, the interpretation of these messages as well as the coming into being of new messages communicated to other interlocutors, hermeneutics cannot but engage concretely in responding to its own tradition and in opening up the dialogue to 'other' traditions with which it comes into contact. Hermeneutics cannot be only a theory of dialogue; as a matter of fact, perhaps it cannot think of itself as a *theory* of dialogue at all (understood as the true structure of any human experience, which in its universal essence would still have to be described 'metaphysically'). Rather, if it intends to be coherent with its own premises, hermeneutics must articulate itself *as* dialogue, thus committing itself concretely vis-à-vis the contents of tradition.

Here the 'external' exigency that demands of hermeneutics an emancipatory perspective meets up with the internal exigency of 'coherence' and consequence of the discipline itself. In the end, is a 'theory of dialogue' enough? Will a description of experience as 'continuity', an appeal to bring experience to bear on the stratified wealth of our tradition, therefore a certain classicism in the most literal and historical sense of the term, suffice? Will an emphasis — which is what in the last analysis we find in Habermas' (1984) theory of communicative action — on tolerance, on argumentative exchange, on reason as reasonableness and persuasion exercised in social dialogue be enough? But, in a dialogue, we do have — insofar as we are hermeneuticists who do not wish to be solely transcendental philosophers — something to say: and what is it that we want to say besides the fact that we talk about dialogue as the only possible place for the event of truth?

Confronted with questions that surface the moment it becomes a 'koine', hermeneutics ought to reconsider its foundations, and more pointedly its Heideggerian heritage. In the wake of Gadamer's 'urbanization' (Habermas' observation) of Heidegger, what has been partially lost (or at least pushed in the background) is the Heideggerian conception of metaphysics as the history of being. As is well known, Gadamer does not endorse Heidegger's verdict against Greek metaphysics. In the light of a 'phenomenology' of lived experience which is, by the way, highly problematical from the hermeneutic perspective (insofar as it is guided by the idea that we can reach the things in themselves and not only the transmitted 'words' . . .) Gadamer holds that what needs to be critiqued is the consignment of truth to the ambit of scientific-positive method, a reduction which took place between the eighteenth and nineteenth centuries (and in which Kantianism played a crucial role). On the basis of these premises, *Truth and Method* does not appear to be radical enough to grasp the situation of modern techno-scientific civilization. It is true that, on the ethic-political level, Gadamer appeals to the necessity of bringing specializations and sectorial finalities in contact with common awareness and its continuity with the tradition embodied in language, but this tradition runs the risk of appearing a bit overly humanistically stylized, as a (though respectable) 'supplement of the soul'.

If, on the other hand, and in line with Heidegger, we think of metaphysics as the history of being — which means above all that we grant an underlying unity between the 'two cultures', the humanistic and the scientific, as expressions of the same 'epoch' of being —

it is possible that hermeneutic thought succeeds in formulating a more radical emancipatory programme, the consequence of a more explicit commitment to its proper historical collocation. The living continuity of tradition to which we must appeal in order to give a norm to science and technics and, more generally, to find the bearings for the problem of ethics, is precisely what Heidegger calls history of metaphysics or history of being. In this history what comes to the fore is not only the problem of recognizing, beyond (and more fundamentally than) the truth of science, the truth of art, history, and so on; this is certainly important, of course, but only as a moment in a more vast process which Heidegger places under the sign of the constitutive 'tendency' of being to withdraw while revealing itself, that is to say, being as the ongoing happening of metaphysics until the moment in which, culminating in the *Ge-stell* (the universal techno-scientific organization of the world), metaphysics comes to an end and its overcoming becomes possible. It is with reference to this notion of history — and not, therefore, to a historicity which runs the constant risk of being broadly understood as belonging and dialogicalness — that hermeneutics historically commits itself and thinks its proper task in terms which are radically nontranscendental. If hermeneutics is not the 'discovery' of the constitutive and *objective* dialogic-finite structure of *each* human experience, but rather a moment in the history of metaphysics as the history of being, both the problem of thinking oneself coherently as the interlocutor of a dialogue, as well as the related problem of defining oneself in terms of an emancipatory task (or: a historical task) take on different configurations. To say that hermeneutics is a decisive stage in the course through which being withdraws (even by literally dissolving) from the dominion of the metaphysical categories of fully displayed presence, is tantamount to saying that hermeneutic thought situates itself in a non-contemplative position, being rather engaged with respect to this course, supplying moreover guidance and criteria in order to make content choices.

To respond to the questions elicited by its new position as 'koine' hermeneutics seems compelled to rediscover, paradoxically, the philosophy of history; I say paradoxically because the sense of this philosophy of history is nothing more than the (protracted) end of the philosophy of history. After all, even the modern philosophies of history are essential moments of that metaphysics which, according to Heidegger, can be overcome only in the form of the *Verwindung*, that is to say, in recovery-acceptance-distortion. Ricoeur too, by concentrating on 'time and narrative', has perhaps captured this need to rethink historicalness, though once again he appears to have resolved it on the plane of a structural description instead of a radical conception of hermeneutics as a moment in the history of being. Outside of such a radicalization I cannot see other means by which hermeneutics can respond to the questions posed not only by philosophy but also by ever different and numerous fields of culture today.

Translated by Peter Carravetta.

Note

The Italian text originally appeared in *AUT AUT*, No. 217–218, 1987, pp. 3–11.

References

Adorno, T.W. (1966) *Negative Dialektik*. Frankfurt: Suhrkamp; English translation *Negative Dialectics*. London: Routledge and Kegan Paul.

Ferraris, Maurizio.(1984) 'Derrida 1975–1985. Sviluppi teoretici e fortuna filosofica', *Nuova Corrente* 3: 351–78.

Gadamer, H.G. (1960) *Wahrheit und Methode*. Tübingen: J.C.B. Mohr; translated as *Truth and Method*. London: Sheed and Ward.

Gadamer, H.G. (1973) *Ermeneutica e metodica universale*. A cura di U. Margiotta, Marietti: Casale Monferrato; a new translation is forthcoming in the volume *Filosofia 86*, translated by G. Vattimo, Bari: Laterza; English translation in H.G. Gadamer *Philosophical Hermeneutics*. Translated and edited by D.E. Linge. Los Angeles: University of California Press, 1976.

Gadamer, H.G. (1976) *La ragione nell'età della scienza*. Translated by A. Fabris with an Introduction by G. Vattimo. Genoa: Il Melangolo, 1982; English translation *Reason in the Age of Science*. Cambridge, Mass.: MIT Press, 1986.

Habermas, J. (1984) *Theory of Communicative Action, Volume I*. London: Heinemann.

Vattimo, G. (1981) *Al di là del soggetto*. Milan: Feltrinelli.

Gianni Vattimo is Professor of Philosophy at the University of Turin. His latest book is *La fine della modernità: nihilismo ed ermeneutica nella cultura post-moderna* (1985). An English translation of the volume he co-edited with Pier Aldo Rovatti, *Il pensiero debole* (1983) is forthcoming.

The *Dialectic of Enlightenment* Read as Allegory

Willem van Reijen

Measures such as those taken on Odysseus' ship in regard to the Sirens form presentient allegory of the dialectic of enlightenment. (Horkheimer and Adorno, 1972: 34)

Jürgen Habermas (1983), with characteristic commitment to the realization of the ideals of Enlightenment and democracy, analyses Horkheimer and Adorno's (1972) *Dialectic of Enlightenment* in his essay 'The Entwinement of Myth and Enlightenment'. Habermas (1983: 412) is critical of the *Dialectic of Enlightenment* for failing to provide a fair evaluation of the rational content of cultural modernity. In developing this criticism Habermas makes three points: (1) against Horkheimer and Adorno's assumption that the theoretical momentum of science and its inherent self-reflection constantly pushes beyond the production of technically useful knowledge; (2) the book neglects the fact that in contemporary democratic states — while recognizing their incompleteness — universal foundations for law and morality have been established; and (3) it does not take into account, that in modern art, which is liberated from conventions and aspects of utility, spheres of freedom for the unfolding of decentred individuality have been created. These are the three points, cited by Habermas, in which the *Dialectic of Enlightenment* does not do justice to modernity. In concealing the possibility of differentiating between power and validity, it also forces our interest, to take a stance in terms of 'Yes' and 'No' propositions, into a state of insignificance. A central point of discussion in the debate over modernity and postmodernity is identified here. In order to clarify this point, in one respect at least, I wish to point out in this essay that with the questioning of the meaningfulness of the totality, a transition occurs from metaphorical to allegorical representation and patterns of thought. Modernity becomes catastrophic. I want to

Theory, Culture & Society (SAGE, London, Newbury Park, Beverly Hills and New Delhi), Vol. 5 (1988), 409–29

further argue that Benjamin's studies of tragedy (*Das Trauerspiel*) forms an important source of inspiration for these perspectives and that one can establish via allegory a connection between Baroque and postmodernity. I will firstly refer to the *Dialectic of Enlightenment* as the central topos of my thesis and engage with Habermas' interpretation of the *Dialectic of Enlightenment*; and secondly discuss in detail the connection between allegory, melancholy and postmodernity; and finally present the Odysseus section to further illuminate these themes.

(1) Modernization as Self-Destruction

In the *Dialectic of Enlightenment* Horkheimer and Adorno state that 'in the present collapse of bourgeois civilization not only the process but the meaning of science has become problematical' (Horkheimer and Adorno, 1947: XI). With their attack on a science that has become affirmative, and with the critique of one-dimensional culture and society, the authors analyse, according to Habermas, the process of modernization as a process of the self-destruction of enlightenment. While in 1944, when these fragments were written and put together as a book, they must have had concrete reasons for developing such a dark perspective, today one has to assume, as Habermas does following Dubiel, that their perspective can no longer be maintained. None the less, as Habermas remarks, today, through the influence of a poststructuralist restoration of Nietzsche, attitudes and positions are produced which are so similar as to appear interchangeable (Habermas, 1983: 405). Habermas wants to prevent this interchangeability. The grounds for this confusion are to be found in the entwinement of myth and enlightenment, which is already indicated in the title of Habermas's article. From the perspective of the Enlightenment, thought is here able to be understood as the opposition and the counter-force to myth. As opposition, because argument now proves to be stronger than any dogmatic tradition; as counter-force, because it aims to break the spell of collective powers through individually acquired understanding which becomes transformed into motives for action (Habermas, 1983: 406).

The change in orientation from dogma to argument, from collective power to individual understanding, irrevocably separates the complex of myth from the complex of Enlightenment. For Habermas, then, Horkheimer and Adorno necessarily recourse to scientific, philosophical and political-cultural achievements, when they suspect myth and enlightenment of being clandestine accomplices (Habermas, 1983: 406). That they nevertheless do not want to abandon the now 'paradoxical' 'labour of the concept' forces them into a self-contradiction; their position evidently does not stand up to argumentative examination. Whoever claims that thought has been corrupted cannot any longer legitimize this judgment by reference to thought. This situation, described by Habermas as a paradox, is a serious consequence of the neglect of the processes of differentiation which are characteristic of modernity: the spheres of law (and morality), the sphere of science (and its application) and the sphere of art. It is true that along with differentiation there is instrumentalization, that is to say the autonomization and over-valuation of means-end rationality, but these are not accepted without opposition. For Habermas, modernity can draw on its own power-potential to break the spell of instrumental thought. It is precisely this differentiation of the spheres that allows us to take 'Yes-No' positions. One can, in other words, discuss whether de facto power relations are legitimate and whether dominant opinions can be justified. The entwinement between myth and enlightenment in the *Dialectic of Enlightenment* therefore undermines the already effective transition in perspective from de facto power, from dogma and the collective on the one hand, to argumentation and the individual on the other.

The topic of sacrifice provides Horkheimer and Adorno with an example of how myth and enlightenment are mutually entwined. There is the gift for the gods — at a long way off to be a true sacrifice — in their eyes rather a symbolic overestimation, and de facto more or less worthless. Into the mythical relation between mankind and their gods, according to Horkheimer and Adorno, there entered from the very beginning cunning — a rational calculation. On the other hand, they state that orientations and legitimations directed towards efficiency and profitability range first in our contemporary ways of thought and action — and meanwhile one could even say that they became principles of constitutional significance. We could consider this more concretely by looking at the example of self-preservation. In our prehistory, cunning was affiliated with the action of sacrifice, and aimed at securing the preservation of the self. This infiltration of rational reflection into mythical thought and action had the consequence that the self which was to be preserved underwent a change. Here the means of action, both in form and content, dominate the end. It is thus directed against that self which was to be preserved. Self-affirmation is not only self-denial but also self-destruction (Horkheimer and Adorno, 1947: 71; 73; 86).[1] The self which reconstitutes itself by means of this self-destruction has now to be understood as that antithetical moment which allegory stands for. The self stood in a mimetical relationship to nature, fellow men and God, but has now come to assume a more distant, even self-distancing, attitude. Here it has ceased to identify with any value which makes life worth living and which attributes dignity and grace to humankind. Such values are replaced by calculation.

But, while domination and rationality persist as contradictory mechanisms, the domination of means also implies the critique of domination (Horkheimer and Adorno, 1947: 51). After having completed these steps, we can see that the enlightenment has become self-reflexive. As Habermas puts it, it criticizes the lopsided development which arises together with a growing and finally total domination of an ends-means rationality over all value orientations. But, for Habermas, it is the potentiality of enlightenment to develop the motives and methods of its critique from within itself. The levelling of power and truth can only be revoked by a form of thought which takes an enlightenment attitude towards itself.

Horkheimer and Adorno, however, take a step further and for Habermas this is a step too far: they create a second instance of reflexivity in enlightenment. The critique of ideology, now, is itself to be suspected by being unable to produce truth (Habermas, 1983: 415, 418). Nevertheless — as Habermas admits — Horkheimer and Adorno sustain an intention of continuing enlightenment: their intention is to show humankind that we live in a situation in which power and validity can no longer be distinguished from each other. And here Habermas redirects the critique which Horkheimer and Adorno constructed earlier against the separation of means from ends, against their own argument. In Horkheimer and Adorno, he concludes, the self-criticism of reason separates itself and alienates itself from reason; it is thus ungrounded and falls into its own self-destruction (Habermas, 1983: 415; 418). For Habermas it is a paradox to identify reason with power and nevertheless to insist — explicitly with reference to this statement — on a continuation of a claim as to the possibility and justifiability of critique. The identification of domination and explanation, for Habermas, would imply that it is not possible to break out of the hermetic constellation of dogma and domination. This applies to the concept of total ideology just as much as to the totalizing suspicion of ideology.

Habermas reads the *Dialectic of Enlightenment* against the background of the traditional critique of ideology. Alienation and false appearance can be exposed by means of Hegel's speculative dialectic of the motion of thought and reality in one by means of the concept. The propositional, that is verbally expressed judgment, according to Habermas, allows for the adoption of 'Yes' or 'No' positions, that is, an evaluation of the legitimacy of arguments.

With his *Theory of Communicative Action* Habermas has proposed an overall reconstruction of the development of the social sciences and of Western-European political systems in the light of a positive evaluation of argumentative solution to conflict. He has defended this evaluation, being never afraid of polemics, in various articles. Common to all these articles and to the *Theory of Communicative Action* is the reference to language as a medium and as the substance of understanding. Here, however, Habermas engages in a dispute with those philosophers who, like Nietzsche and his neo-structuralist followers, assume that language itself — and not only perception, experience and thought — is corrupted.

For convenience we could call these philosophers postmodern. For them the recourse to hermeneutic, transcendental and dialectical methodology as a means of exposition of truth is no longer immediately possible; (however, this does not necessarily mean: absolutely impossible). They distrust any discursive and linguistic deduction and formation of consensus, because it takes place within language itself. Structural linguistics which had dissolved any inherent logic within the relation between sign and meaning has also philosophically dissolved entities into differences.

If it is no longer possible to form a substantive determination of mankind and its judgment of things and human relations, if everything only becomes comprehensible in relational terms, then the problem that language suggests an unreal consistency arises no longer only on the level of conflictual dispute, but also as a result of conceptual analysis. Habermas assumes wrongly that conceptual analysis would thus move into a self-contradiction which would be destructive for any judgment. It cannot claim to achieve more, nor less, than discursive analysis: i.e. a self-reflexive metaphoric description of mankind in its relation to its natural and social surrounding.

In the final instance any description, the scientific no less than the one based on everyday observation, remains metaphoric. The fact that any scientific language is based on the selection of specific metaphors can, as a result of the recent philosophical and epistemological debates, not be doubted. Within the framework of this paradigm, we would only like to refer to Mary Hesse who has given an epistemological reassertion to Nietzsche's insight, that there are no pure facts. Facts, Hesse says, are always 'theory laden'. Theories should be understood, therefore, as certain, well-defined perspectives on reality — a reality which would be described differently if one chose another perspective. In the natural sciences there exists an agreement or concerted convention to call that description 'true', which can be best, that is by the shortest way, modelled in the form of a mathematical calculus.

The 'humanities' as we know follow other criteria of selection of a specific description. Just to name the two extremes: one could follow a (neo-)Aristotelian, politically conservative, philosophy of nature, or one could vote for a discursive, politically democratic, philosophy of enlightenment. I would like to consider those reflections which we might characterize as postmodern as a meta-critique of both options. They clarify the metaphoric character of all our descriptions. However, we have to keep in mind that here, as well as in both the criticized options, the systematic epistemological perspective relates to a substantive content, to a diagnosis of pathological phenomena of our society and culture, which Habermas also points towards. This diagnosis, as Habermas clearly elaborates, is of a more radical character than all the other extremes mentioned before. It includes the idea — to formulate this in rather global terms — that the separation of reality and fiction cannot be maintained any longer with the surety generally assumed. This, we should note, is meant as a diagnosis, not as a statement of positive valuation. However, Habermas calls for the theoretical and practical acceptance of the fact that our social relations have evaporated into abstractions and that these abstractions became reality. The scepticism with respect to the possibility of deducing reliable criteria for the truth of statements from metaphysical evidence or from consensus coincides with his refusal of any argumentative or consensual foundation of norms.

The postmodern perspective on the other side does not, or rather not so easily, allow for any recourse to the nature-bound determination of humankind or discursive dispositions and thus stands across both of the above mentioned extremes. This, however, seems not to exclude — in the words of Rorty — a 'social democratic conversation (or rather conversion) of mankind', which Lyotard also seems to suggest. Anyhow it no longer seems feasible to argue for the monopolistic claims of rationality. It can be easily shown that the sensitivity to the metaphorical character of our statements and models of thought increases in times when such a radical self-scepticism, like the one articulated by postmodernity, is brought about. This increasing uncertainty leads to a reflection on a past which seems to have become increasingly remote. (Perhaps the reverse speculation is also valid, that this loss of the past has contributed a great deal to the uncertainty in contemporary thinking and art.)

To summarize my argument: on the basis of the current growing sensibility for the metaphoric content of our knowledge, a qualitative shift in our evaluation of the status of knowledge is taking place. For Habermas, and if we share his global estimation of modernity, it is true that, while doubts about the correctness of this or that judgment are possible or even necessary, the correction of misjudgments within the whole framework of occidental rationality is also imperative. The *Theory of Communicative Action* (Habermas, 1981, 1984) offers a theoretical foundation for such corrections from both theoretical and practical perspectives, without putting into question the general framework of modernity. Antagonisms and contradictions could then be localized within an all embracing whole on the grounds of transcendental, dialectical or communicative-theoretical reasoning. The metaphorical content of singular cognitions is not out of harmony with the metaphorical status of knowledge itself. The radicalization of doubt — not only towards the correctness of this or that judgment, but more precisely towards the solidity of the foundations — could lead to the realization that our judgments are not to be seen as metaphors which could, within a context of meaning, be related to one another and to an overarching meaning. The loss of the latter can only be understood in the form of an allegory. As we will see, the allegory is the form in which contradictions can be described as being unbridgeable and unreconcilable. There is no symbolic order which could dissolve them. For the postmodern thinkers, our knowledge as much as reality can only be understood in terms of allegory.

(2) The Link between Allegory, Melancholy and Postmodernity

In the remainder of the essay I will attempt to show that there is an internal affiliation between the Baroque and postmodernity.[2] A key figure in this process of transition from modernity to postmodernity is Walter Benjamin. He has traced the allegoric content in the poetry of Baudelaire, and has shown that modernity, when driven to the height of its own development, turns into allegory. Benjamin's (1977) interest in allegory, developed in his *Das Trauerspiel* (*The Origin of German Tragedy*) shows this quite clearly. But Horkheimer and Adorno, too, detected this relationship between allegory and modernity and explicitly covered this theme in the *Dialectic of Enlightenment*.

Although there are great differences between the epochal uncertainty of the sixteenth century which found its artistic expression in the Baroque and the postmodern confusion of today, there also exists something in common: the interest in allegory and the assumption that our world is allegorically constituted. Walter Benjamin's interpretation of the concept of allegory and the 'melancholy' of Dürer in the *Ursprung des deutschen Trauerspiels* can provide an example.

Benjamin moves into the centre of his reflections the contradiction between the mourning figure and the *vita activa* which is represented in Dürer's painting by unused instruments which are dispersed over the space. Quite in opposition to Warburg he interprets 'melancholy' not as a pause within a creative process but rather as the embodiment of the vanity of all human action. Similarly he interprets the ruin and the fragment — they are like other symbols of history, the *facies hippocratica* of history, a history, in which everything relates to salvation and consolation but which also consolidates the impossibility of salvation and the lack of consolation. This is the background to Benjamin's insight: 'Only for those who have no hope is hope given.' It is a futile attempt to save history. To quote a figure of antiquity (or antiquity as a whole) within the allegory as Benjamin does confirms the unbridgeable gap between antiquity and today. The past is irrevocably past; and it becomes clear that even today it is no longer, as naively assumed, part of the present. Both dimensions of time are gone and there is no synopsis of an illustrative or conceptual type that could be offered instead. Benjamin refers to Christian tradition in which melancholy is defined as a mortal sin. Here melancholy stands for a forgetting of God and it refers further to mourning, sorrow, brooding and acedia, the lazy heart (see Steinhagen, 1979: 666–85). There are two types of melancholics and allegorics: the one who knows appears in the figure of the scholar, the ponderer, the artist and the genius; and the one who acts appears in the figure of the ruler, the tyrant and the courtier.

Steinhagen (1979) assumes that it is characteristic of the early work of Benjamin that both the one who knows and the one who rules are seen as sharing the precedence of subjectivity over objectivity. In his later work on Baudelaire and in his theses on the philosophy of history, this priority to subjectivity has been replaced by the domination of the objectively given, through the abstraction of exchange and the commodity.

I will return to this point later. First, however, allegory should first be explained as a figure of thought. Allegory expresses first of all secret, privileged knowledge and tyranny over dead objects (to which humankind, being mortal, also belongs) (Steinhagen, 1979: 671). The allegorical person has lost sight of revelation, he can only see the transient world, the world of the profane. For him, nature turns into history and history into nature, in a way which does not, however, allow their contradictions to be solved (cf. van Reijen, 1986).

The allegorical person as Steinhagen rightly remarks is a materialist who remains faithful to things; he does not revolt and work towards a new order, rather he merely rebels. In a sovereign way he negates all transcendence, he makes the sphere of transience absolute and hollows out his own sovereignity and the 'order' established on the strength of it. What remains to him are those contradictions which symbolize the missing order: fragments, ruins, corpses. (From the viewpoint of death — says Benjamin — the production of the corpse is the meaning of life.) This perspective draws not unexpected parallels to the central theme of postmodern philosophy. Here, in the form of the assertion of the death of the subject the diagnosis is made that mankind believes itself to be attributing meaning to things, but at a closer look this is unmasked as an error. Just as the sphere of divinity, of revelation, for the allegoric/melancholic character of the sixteenth and seventeenth century had lost its meaning, so the postmodern actor is led to doubt the possibility of a stable, profane attribution of meaning. Rational thought implies a tyranny in the sphere of meaning no less so than in the sphere of politics and culture. A critique which refers back to Nietzsche and Heidegger destroys this tyranny and the respective ideology. What traditionally appeared as meaning and order, whether on the level of social reality or on the level of text or as text itself, now shows itself as an illegitimate projection of a subject setting itself up as absolute. The destruction of meaning implies the destruction of the subject as a sovereign meaning-giving individual. Insofar as there is meaning, then it is a product of structure — as Derrida believes — or more correctly of 'Differance', that is of a delay, of the difference between the signs.[3]

The figure of allegory expresses that it is the subjects who give meaning to the fragments, the ruins, in short to the transient world, but this meaning is one of decline and decay. In the turmoil of decay everything that is considered meaningful, as much as everything that attributes meaning is swept away. The act of a sovereign attribution of meaning appears as self-destructive. And even the hope for salvation suffers from this destruction. Allegory is synonymous with critique, a mortification of the product and its own procedure.

Steinhagen detects a development in Benjamin's conception of allegory. Whereas in the *Trauerspiel* book (Benjamin, 1977) allegory was placed within the history of ideas, it is now located on the level of material production, that is to say, in capitalism (Benjamin, 1985). In other words, allegory is now to be seen as a socially mediated product. The devaluation of things is not traced back to nature, nor to the subject, but to a commodity-producing society; or more precisely, to the commodity itself (Steinhagen, 1979: 675). The commodity, one could say, devalues things more thoroughly than any other object. Following Marx, Benjamin asserts that in a market-based society it is no longer use-value (the qualitative determination of goods) that matters, but exchange-value. That products of labour are offered as commodities coincides with their devaluation — they are turned into fetishes. This analysis has been radicalized recently by Baudrillard (1982). Where commodities are turned into signs, there — as Horkheimer and Adorno (1947: 5) put it — thoughts have already been turned into commodities and language into their eulogy. This devaluation has however its price: sign and reality are separated from each other by an unbridgeable gulf. Reality and fiction become indistinguishable. It is in Baudelaire's poetry that Benjamin discovered the artistic articulation of this state of affairs.

Craig Owens (1980) in his essay 'The Allegorical Impulse' has usefully outlined some characteristics of allegory with special reference to painting. Following Benjamin he, too, places the relationship of past and present at the centre of his account. Allegorical art liquidates what is already ruined. On the other hand, this liquidation saves that which is in danger of disappearing into historical oblivion. Allegory is consequently situated in the gulf between past and present. Past and present are moved into an unimaginable distance and leave vacant, to speak metaphorically, the 'centre' where we are placed. Allegory does not invent images and representations but confiscates them. Thereby these images are permanently transformed into different ones. Allegory permanently states something different. Allegorical procedures should therefore not be seen as a hermeneutic or as restoration but as an act of replacement and completion of meaning. Benjamin (1977) showed in his *The Origin of German Tragedy* that under the gaze of the melancholic the object turns into allegory, it is saved as something that is defunct. Objects have no meaning in themselves but an inferred one.

The *facies hippocratica* of history, as we find it in a ruin or a fragment, makes present the temporality of (human) nature and also the moment of rescue from oblivion. This salvation, this 'saving critique' as Benjamin calls it, is not of a psychological but of an ontological kind.

It confirms and denies in one that *promesse de bonheur* that is art. Allegory completes as *supplement* (Derrida) the uncompleted work of art, but drives it at the same time into a new state of incompleteness, thereby confirming the ontological absence of presence. The work of art, as uncompleted, is a fragment or a rune that has to be deciphered without it being possible to arrive at a definitive meaning (presence). This points as much towards the permanent, repetitive change of meaning as to the ritualistic aspects of meaning in allegories. Allegory places itself and us beyond narrative form and content, it relativizes the classical requirement of the unity of form and content, it imbues the concept of structure with a dynamic element, and it leads the sequence to freeze.

This procedure is most manifest in what Benjamin calls 'citing the past'. The image of antiquity gets superimposed by a contemporary one, and in this procedure an allegory is formed. It always appears when an image or text is doubled. We are then forced to perceive one through the other, to read a text through another. The painted allegories of the Baroque, the Old and New Testament, the tragedy, and the *Trauerspiel* are examples of such duplications, as are all palimpsests. If we restrict ourselves here to texts, then we can conceive of this duplication also as the relationship of text and commentary. One text is a commentary on the other, and vice versa, without it being possible to assign primacy to one over the other, to regard one demonstrably as text, the other indisputably as commentary. In the same way each text is its own commentary, its own critique. (An example has been provided by Jorge Luis Borges in his story 'Pierre Menard . . .', in which the text of *Don Quixote* is doubled.)

In this way, each text contributes something to itself, provides over and above the story it recounts its own commentary critique — its supplement. This supplement leads the text — understood as discursive, directed at the transmission of information — to over-flow; it drives it into excess, just as the Baroque is excessive. In the demonstrative surplus, apparent in the Baroque still life, this sur-plus becomes evident as emptiness.

This means that allegory is not about restoration, as the *Anciens* recommend in the famous *Querelle des anciens et des modernes*, nor is it a hermeneutic procedure in which a meaning is 'saved'. Alleg-ory is a continuing restlessness, pendulating between contrary, irreconcilable readings that are contained in the text itself. This is not due to the arbitrary understanding of different readers but to the text, more exactly its 'surplus'. This is to say that there *cannot* be one definitive reading. And since it is further the case that no text can be fixated as either text or commentary, it follows that texts and commentaries remain fragments pointing towards an Other that cannot be reached and a wholeness that does not exist as a symbolic unity.

The perpetual reference of one to the other and vice versa deter-mines the repetitive moment contained within an allegory. The continuous to-and-fro of the pendulum can be understood as a representation of the restless, yet aimless, movement of life and within life. It materializes that being-rooted-on-the-spot, that powerlessness which, according to Benjamin's analysis of sovereignity, overcomes the prince just at the moment of decision. This moment of indecisiveness, that brings together in one image powerlessness and concomitant melancholy, is penetratingly de-scribed by Benjamin (1930) in a text which Kurz interprets as an allegory (Kurz, 1982: 27). It concerns the text *Moewen* (seagulls) in his *Denkbilder*.

This text tells of a passenger who observes two groups of seagulls to the left and right of the boat he is travelling on. The reader is called upon, as in the reading of so many travelogues, to penetrate from the surface through to another layer of meaning. There is talk of a 'readable pinion mesh' that is woven — like a text. The seagulls give off 'signs' and 'winks', are apostrophized as 'messengers' — all hints at 'another' world from the one actually described.

The story of the seagulls allegorizes a world that is split politically into East and West, Left and Right. The seagulls follow the swinging movement of the ship's mast (the swaying of the intellectual). Indecisive swaying has for a long, long time been the accepted image of the mood of loneliness and melancholy characteristic of the intellectual or the pensive person (Hamlet), inhibiting him in his movements.

The theme of the self-destruction of rationality (Horkheimer and Adorno, 1947: 11) permeates the whole *Dialectic of Enlightenment*. Habermas is right to state that the 'dark writers', Nietzsche and de Sade, have influenced Horkheimer who had always been attracted to their 'dark predecessors', Hobbes and Schopenhauer. The last sentence of the penultimate section of the *Dialectic of Enlightenment* reads:

> If there is anyone today to whom we can pass the responsibilities for the message, we bequeath it not to the 'masses', and not to the individual (who is powerless), but to an imaginary witness — lest it perish with us. (Horkheimer and Adorno, 1972: 256)

It may not be an exaggeration to consider a sea voyage as the classic topic for allegories, as did Blumenburg in his *Schiffbruch mit Zuschauer* (1979). Leaving home, submitting oneself to unknown dangers, going down with the harbour in sight, the return. They are just so many themes for life, the transition from one stage in life to another, failure or the accomplishing of a set goal. Homer's *Odyssey* stands at the beginning of a number of famous examples which Frank (1979) and Drux (1979) cited independently of each other. From Quintilian, past Ovid, Alkaios, Dante, Angelus Silesius, Opitz, the legend of the Flying Dutchman, to Kafka and James Joyce we find sea voyage as an allegory of a successful or unsuccessful, in any case endangered, life. Frank, in his treatment, moves the theme of the violation of the sacred and the resulting danger into the foreground. He interprets the legend of the Flying Dutchman as the story of the disaster that afflicts people when *curiositas* drives them into violating the sacred. From there he draws a line to the treatment of this legend by Wagner who connects the theme of sacrilege with the ruthless pursuit of economic interests that disregards accepted values — with all the effect that has on human relationships. People become insecure, are deceased while alive, as Kafka describes Gracchus the Hunter.

(3) The Section on the *Odyssey* in the *Dialectic of Enlightenment*

I shall now go on to account in more detail for the view that the *Odyssey*-section has to be seen as the key to the whole of the *Dialectic of Enlightenment*, but also as an allegorization of the actual historical processes of the dialectic of enlightenment. We remember that Odysseus after his stay with Circe had to resist the alluring song of the Sirens in order to reach Ithaca. If he succumbs, his bones too will soon be bleaching on the shore. The song of the Sirens leads Odysseus, as Homer says, back into the past — in psychological terms a regression — while he is, at the same time, the prototype of modern man who has to orient himself fixedly on the future. Odysseus is still partially tied to a mythical standpoint that does not require him to differentiate between internal and external, past and future, but at the same time he is no longer harmoniously integrated into the symbolic unity of time. If he gives in to the temptation of the Sirens, the seduction of regression (the past), he has forfeited the future. If he decides in favour of the future, and escapes the Sirens, he will come to recognize the future as empty progress and as the unstoppable increase in power. Odysseus does overcome the Sirens through tying himself to the mast and plugging the ears of his oarsmen with wax, but the consequences of this ploy are catastrophic, for the Sirens (art) as well as for Odysseus and his workers. For the former, because, like the Sphinx whose riddles have been solved, they have to throw themselves into the sea; for the latter, because they appear now no longer as individuals but as prototypes, as capitalist and proletarian. Odysseus' companions have to work for their master without being able to enjoy the pleasures of art, without even knowing of its beauty.

In accordance with the eternal law of fate, the Sirens inflict upon themselves what they have previously inflicted upon others; and in the same way Odysseus inflicts upon himself what he demands of his companions; whatever form it takes it is never anything else than self-destruction. After art, in the shape of the Sirens has come to an end, that which takes its place is merely the eternal repetition of the same.

Odysseus is now forever subject to this empty compulsive repetition. He does not really overcome the Sirens. It is difficult to imagine that their alluring song does not remain present in him to the end of his days as a longing for fulfilment. In this way he is forced to repeat the passage time and time again. Permanent repetition, thought of as a lack of movement, is the hallmark of the melancholic attitude presented most often in Baroque allegories.

The *Odyssey* section brings into focus the central themes of our culture and the theme of its decline: the relationship of past, present and future; of domination and myth; the work and pleasure of art, of life and death; of regression and progress; of ploys and victims; of autonomous identity and self-denial. Lastly, this section addresses the place and meaning of the book itself, in fact that of philosophy in general.

There are parallels between the figure of Odysseus in the *Dialectic of Enlightenment* and that of the 'flâneur' in Benjamin's (1982, 1973) work. The double meaning of 'the passage' in Horkheimer and Adorno's *Dialectic of Enlightenment* corresponds to the 'twilight' of the passages (arcades) in Paris noted by Benjamin. This is to be understood not only literally but also allegorically. The passage is for Benjamin not only throughfare and transition but also interior. The passage invites the passerby to remain. Following E.R. Curtis, Benjamin notes that people are driven into the streets as their living accommodation gets smaller; there they face the temptation to be enveloped again. Benjamin draws a parallel here with the increasing use of lining material and covers for the keeping of utility objects. In this way, the passage also functions as a lining, it maintains one just as a collector looks after his objects. The collector removes his pieces from circulation, divests them of their property as commodities; they are taken out of the living context of circulation (Marx) and are, so to speak, killed, turned into *nature morte*, into a still-life. For this reason, the passage is also a place of boredom, even of melancholy. Time comes to a standstill — as does the dialectic. The passerby freezes on the threshold of the passage — the passage as such turns into a threshold. All movement ceases without the goal having been reached, repeats itself permanently, aimlessly. For the allegoric, the passages are, as caves were previously, 'soul spaces of the psyche' (Faber, 1986; Frank, 1979).

The melancholy brought about by being in the passage stresses the connection between the Baroque and modern times. The passage as a 'world without windows' (Benjamin) offers no prospect of salvation, of a true destiny being realized. The story of the Flying Dutchman — which Manfred Frank has already interpreted as

Wagner's critique of capitalism — now becomes a comprehensive allegory in the form of a critique of culture.

Just as Odysseus shows his true nature in passing the Sirens, so does the 'flâneur' in the passages. Benjamin owes his interest in the phenomenon of the passage to Aragon's *Le Paysan de Paris* but does not wish to leave it just at the level of a cultural critique. He aims to resolve a central problem in Historical Materialism, i.e. to visualize its abstract concepts, as it is done in an allegory. To this end he develops a novel, his 'micrological' approach: from a concrete phenomenon he extrapolates general characteristics of its social and cultural context. Benjamin proceeds accordingly with the concept of 'commodity' (for exchange), i.e. its fetish character (Tiedemann, 1982: 13). He considers the passages as a temple in which goods are worshipped as a fetish. In that commodities are regarded as a fetish it becomes apparent that the awareness that they are a product of social relations has been lost and that social relations have been turned into relations between things.

The reification of social processes is due to the paradoxical character of the commodity, i.e. to be both exchange — and use — value. But in contrast to Marx, and after the events of the Second International, Stalin and fascism, Benjamin can no longer hope for a real revolution. As a consequence, he moves from the sphere of production to the domination of 'phantasmagory', already mentioned by Marx, in order to explain the persistence of capitalism. (Marx [1976: 165]: 'A definite social relation between men ... assumes ... the phantasmagorical form of a relation between things.')

Paris, as the capital of consumption, the department store and particularly the arcades are materializations of this phantasmagory; they give expression to, as Benjamin says, the sex appeal of the inorganic in the fetish character of commodities. People have lost the consciousness they would need to direct their society. That is to say, they regress to the magical or mythical stage. Under capitalism they themselves have been turned into objects, commodities; they have relinquished their independence.

The prime example of this self-created dependence is provided by the 'flâneur'. He prefers to spend his time in the arcades, the 'lascivious street of commerce, existing only to waken desires' (Benjamin, 1982: 93). Here fashion stages the eternal return of the new and prescribes the ritual according to which the fetish wants to be worshipped. The 'flâneur' is exposed to a surfeit of goods no less than to the illusion of being able to avail himself of them. He is not aware that he is turning himself into a commodity among many. He does not go to the market to see, as he might think, but to let himself be looked at. He offers himself for sale, takes, as Benjamin puts it, the concept of being 'for sale' awalking (Benjamin, 1982: 93).

The 'flâneur' is thus the male, intellectual mirror-image of the whore who, for Benjamin, not only sells objects but is also an object herself. She is the embodiment of the allegory of the commodity as exchange- and use-value in one. The 'flâneur' and the whore are marginals, they subject themselves time and time again to the *rite de passage* that leads them into hell. 'To determine the totality of the traits in which the "modern" comes to be expressed is to represent Hell' (Benjamin, 1982: 1011).

The arcades as the 'heaven of consumption' are at the same time hell. As heaven, they attract people; they radiate like fairy grottoes. Whoever dares, like a contemporary Odysseus, to enter the passages is attracted on one side by the song of the Sirens of the gas lighting, on the other side by the oil flames carried by odalisques (Benjamin, 1982: 700). Odysseus' classic passage is devalued into a shopping precinct, the fairy into a whore. Just like any other commodity subject to the dictates of fashion, so the arcades too become obsolete. Like these, they carry the cause of their devaluation within themselves because in capitalism nothing devalues commodities to such a degree as commodities themselves. Fashion as permanent repetition of the new is the permanent devaluation.

The Figure of Odysseus

Odysseus is introduced to us in the first Excursus of the *Dialectic of Enlightenment*, 'Odysseus or Myth and Enlightenment', as a living contradiction. On the one hand, Odysseus embodies a quite modern kind of rationality, cunning, which is needed in order to survive in a hostile environment (and self-preservation is the main priority in 'modernity'). Already, the cunning employed by Odysseus makes it clear how enlightenment and myth are entwined. Odysseus does not think of that ploy himself, it is Circe, a mythical figure, who suggests it to him; on the other hand, it is clear that the price he has to pay for self-preservation is self-destruction. The question again arises, what Self is it that is maintained with the help of cunning. It certainly is not the Self that is formed mimetically — and that, for Horkheimer and Adorno, stands paradigmatically for the Self formed through the experience of art. To 'rescue the past moment as something living' would only be possible in art and through art. In present conditions, after the fall of the Sirens, art can no longer maintain its position as happiness, as knowledge in the emphatic sense. It relinquishes its *promesse de bonheur* and remains content, as Adorno says, to be tolerated as something pleasurable.

Odysseus could only partake in the present if he listens to the song of the Sirens to experience a unity of art and knowledge. But we know that he denies himself just that, this mimesis, in order to survive. He hears the song of the Sirens but does not listen to it. Because he does not risk himself he can't hear what he otherwise would. Odysseus makes up his mind not only to avoid the consequences of hearing, but to stop listening altogether. In this way he looses the very self that was to be saved. He thereby prepares himself for obedience, work and domination, in a way as a subject and object. As it is said, 'he becomes an enemy to his own death as well as his own happiness'.

It is however not just the Sirens who led Odysseus to commit self-destruction under the guise of self-preservation. Like them, adventures are in general temptations 'removing the self from its logical course'. Odysseus is like a 'novice still impervious to good advice'; 'the knowledge which comprises his identity and which enables him to survive, draws its content from experience of the multitudinous, from digression and salvation; and the knowing survivor is also the man who takes the greatest risks when death threatens, thus becoming strong and unyielding when life continues'. The self is 'an entity only in the diversity of that which denies all unity' (Horkheimer and Adorno, 1947: 62; 1972: 47). 'Odysseus loses himself in order to find himself.' '. . . the identity of the self is so much a function of the unidentical' (Horkheimer and Adorno, 1947: 63; 1972: 48). Odysseus is at the same time landowner and nomad; priest and victim.

Concluding Remarks

Just as much as Odysseus is an allegory of modern man, so the *Dialectic of Enlightenment* is an allegory of the philosophical work, and no less so is our modern development of the allegory of history. With the image of Odysseus whose impotence is documented in the fact that, being tied to the mast, he is only able to nod his head, Horkheimer and Adorno demonstrate the impotence of the intellectual, of their work in their own period, their position. Did they hear the song of the Sirens, the call to revolution, when they were on their way in the 1930s. In any case, at the time of writing the *Dialectic of Enlightenment* they had to experience their return politically as well as philosophically as the story of a refusal, as allegory. All they could do was to send off a message with the receiver unknown.

Translated by Josef Bleicher, Georg Stauth and Bryan S. Turner

Notes

1. Here they state that the dominated and suppressed substance which is dissolved through self-preservation is nothing else but the vital force of life, exactly that which is to be preserved.

2. The literature and the range of definitions of Baroque is vast. In this text, however, I am not concerned with a controversy in the history of art: I use 'Baroque' to refer to an epoch, but also to a notion of style which, even if imprecise, has a systematic and a cultural-philosophic connotation. Heinrich Wölfflin's (1965) study of Roman Baroque architecture gives us the background for such an interpretation. With his open sympathy for the Renaissance, Wölfflin elaborates the characteristics of Baroque which are not only in contradiction to the Renaissance but also in accordance with the orientations of our time. Wölfflin describes the Renaissance as an epoch and a style or form (1965: 1) of a rigid drawing of lines, of calmness, of being, of harmony, of completeness (1965: 75), of intuition (1965: 70). Against this, however, the art of Baroque represents the formless and free (1965: 1), the becoming and the moving without any measure of regulation, the tension, the delight and the incomplete (1965: 75), instead of intuition: mood (1965: 70). It is not difficult to find in all those characteristics the features of what could be called the postmodern or the poststructuralist philosophical definitions of the reality of our time. Wölfflin thus refers to the well-known etymology of the word Baroque. Baroque signifies accordingly the unregulated form of a natural pearl, but also a logically contradictory deduction. Adverbs of similar meaning are: capriccioso, bizarro, stravagante (1965: 9). Wölfflin rather assumes that the epoch of Baroque in contrast to the Renaissance was not accompanied by a theory. Through this protest against the Baroque it becomes quite clear what was the intention of the Baroque: it is essentially the representation of unbridgeable contradictions which keeps and signifies everything in movement. Baroque represents unrest, which results from the contradiction between earth and heaven. It also results from the dissonances and emotions which derive from the fact of transitoriness of the natural life (*nature morte*) and the immortality of the soul. Body and will separate from each other. The human being dominates his body no longer. Every movement is to be characterized by a familiar saying: constrained movement. Thus there is no limit to space in the famous paintings of the domes, but there is a tendency to pass through the clouds and to catch a glimpse of the eternal light of the sky. But also the recoiled pillar shows movement; the still-life contrasts incomprehensible abundance with the *tristesse* of mortality; the bodies appear to be heavy and if this heaviness is not enough plaited gowns add to a massive effect. The parts of the body do not refer to each other in harmony (*contraposto*), (Wölfflin, 1965: 67). Wölfflin gives specific attention to the allegories

in graveyards figures in the chapel of the Medicis. From the point of view of composition it is remarkable that the middle of all pictures and buildings remains empty. If we summarize these characteristics of the Baroque by Wölfflin, we can draw a picture which in many points is similar to the one which some contemporary philosophers have drawn. In short, there is no foundation, there is no centre, no midst, which could embrace the whole. Everything is in movement, but there are many contradictory movements. There are no clear lines which a clear reason could follow. Both in architecture as well as in the cultural industry we are faced with the voluminous, the impressive, the destructive. The whole appears to be without rule, to be incomplete, to be chaotic; it leads both view and thought into the realm of the incomprehensible, the unimaginable, the eternal unembraceable, the graceful (1965: 71). What Winckelmann once called 'noble simplicity and calm greatness' has been dismissed. Wölfflin refers to the room of the giants in the palace del Te (Mantua) where there are unformed pieces of rocks on the place of the moulding shelf. 'Chaos dominates the room' (1965:32). Fantasy is demanded, not rigid ratio. Perhaps, what Wölfflin regards as the foundation of the Baroque as having wider relevance than art: 'Art attempts to provide what human beings want to be' (1965: 62).

For Goethe, too, the discussion on the inadequacies of the Baroque, with its allegoric method in opposition to the symbolic method is of importance. In his maxim 279 Goethe formulates the distinction between a symbolizing and an allegorizing method for poetry which has become crucial for later discussions. Goethe formulates here in opposition to Schiller what he calls a continuous 'zarte Differenz' (tender difference). 'There is a great difference whether a poet only searches for the general in the particular or searches for the particular within the general' (cf. for this discussion Sørensen, 1979; Hübscher, 1922). Sørensen shows that the symbolizing poet, Goethe terms the real poet, has to search for the general in the framework of the particular. In the real appearance he has to visualize the idea. The allegorizing poet, however, searches in addition to the general also searches for the particular. The general — says Sørensen — is only a product of his subjective consciousness.

3. Manfred Frank (1987) has pointed out that signs and 'differance' can in no way produce meaning by themselves since that requires individuals.

References

Baudrillard, Jean (1982) *Der symbolische Tausch und der Tod*. München.

Benjamin, W. (1930) *Frankfurter Zeitung* (18 September). Reprinted in Benjamin, W. (1972) *Gesammelte Schriften*, vol. 4. Frankfurt.

Benjamin, W. (1973) *Charles Baudelaire: A Lyric Poet in the Era of High Capitalism*. London.

Benjamin, W. (1977) *The Origin of German Tragedy*. London: New Left Books.

Benjamin, W. (1982) *Das Passagen-Werk*, in *Gesammelte Schriften*, vol. 5. Frankfurt.

Benjamin, W. (1985) 'Central Park', *New German Critique* 34.

Blumenberg, H. (1979) *Schiffbruch mit Zuschauer*. Frankfurt.

Drux, R. (1979) 'Des Dichters Schiffahrt', in Haug (1979).

Faber, R. (1986) 'Paris, das Rom des 19. Jahrhunderts', in N. Bolz and R. Faber (eds) *Antike und Moderne. Zu W. Benjamins 'Passagen*. Würzburg.

Frank, M. (1979) *Die unendliche Fahrt*. Frankfurt/M.

Frank, M. (1988) 'Subjekt, Person, Individuum', in M. Frank, G. Raulet and W. van Reijen (eds) *Die Frage nach dem Subjekt*. Frankfurt.

Frank, M., Raulet, G. and v. Reijen, W. (eds) (1988) *Die Frage nach dem Subjekt*. Frankfurt.

Habermas, J. (1981) *Theorie des Kommunikativen Handelns*. Frankfurt: Suhrkamp; volume one has been translated as *The Theory of Communicative Action*. London: Heinemann, 1984.

Habermas, J. (1983) 'Die Verschlingung von Mythos und Moderne', in K.-H. Bohrer (ed.) *Mythos und Moderne*. Frankfurt; translated as 'The Entwinement of Myth and Enlightenment', *New German Critique*, 26, 1982.

Haug, W. (ed.) (1979) *Formen und Funktionen der Allegorie*. Stuttgart.

Horkheimer, M. and Adorno, Th. (1947) *Dialektik der Aufklaerung*. Amsterdam; translated as *Dialectic of Enlightenment*. New York: Herder and Herder, 1972.

Hübscher, A. (1922) 'Barock als Gestaltung des antithetischen Lebensgefuehls', *Euphorion* 24: 517–62.

Kamper, D. and van Reijen, W. (eds) (1987) *Die unvollendete Vernunft. Moderne versus Postmoderne*. Frankfurt/M.

Kurz, G. (1982) *Metapher, Allegorie, Symbol*. Goettingen.

Maravall, J.A. (1986) *Culture of the Baroque*. Manchester.

Marx, K. (1976) *Capital*, Volume I. Harmondsworth: Penguin.

Owens, C. (1980) 'The Allegorical Impulse: Toward a Theory of Postmodernism', *October* 12 (spring): 67–80.

Reiss, G. (1979) 'Allegorisierung als Rezeptionsplanung', in W. Haug (ed.) (1979).

Schlaffer, H. (1981) *Faust Zweiter Teil. Die Allegorie des 19. Jahrhunderts*. Stuttgart.

Sørensen, B. (1979) 'Die zarte Differenz', in W. Haug (1979).

Steinhagen, H. (1979) 'Zu Walter Benjamins Begriff der Allegorie', in W. Haug (1979).

Tiedemann, R. (1982) 'Einleitung', in W. Benjamin (1982).

van Reijen, W. (1986) *Philosophie als Kritik*. Kronberg.

van Reijen, W. (1987) 'Die Dialektik der Aufklaerung gelesen als Allegorie', in W. van Reijen and Schmid Nörr (1987).

van Reijen, W. and Schmid Nörr, G. (eds) (1987) *Vierzig Jahre Flaschenpost. Die Dialektik der Aufklaerung 1947–1987*. Frankfurt/M.

Welsch, W. (1987) *Unsere postmoderne Moderne*. Weinheim.

Wölfflin, H. (1888, 1965) *Renaissance und Barock*. Stuttgart.

Willem van Reijen teaches Philosophy at the University of Utrecht.

The Postmodern Debate over Urban Form

Sharon Zukin

During the 1980s scholarship in a number of fields has been permeated by the terms of 'postmodern' debate. To some extent this reflects a broadening of intellectual horizons, with a transdisciplinary migration of concepts infusing new life into inquiries and arguments that had become predictable. The postmodern influence also reflects a long-term disintegration of hegemonic discipline in most of the social sciences and the seductiveness — in the twilight of marxist political parties — of literary, as opposed to political, models. But the shared attraction to postmodernism responds at a deeper level to something 'out there' in the world beyond academic crisis. Many social scientists identify with the multiplicity and pervasiveness of new cultural forms, and they yearn to explain, though so far inconclusively, the 'fragmented' social structure from which these forms derive.

There is no coherent definition of postmodernism to guide its appropriation by those social scientists who are so inclined. Fredric Jameson (1984) distinguishes between postmodernism as a cultural product and a cultural period; in either case it arises in the late twentieth century from the ashes of a discredited modern movement. While in architectural theory postmodernism refers to a style, in literary theory it refers to a method; both buildings and books are 'read' for the primacy of an internally consistent 'language' (cf. Jencks, 1984) or 'text' (cf. Hassan, 1987). It could be argued, further, from the many references to music videos, ornamentation, and pastiche that postmodernism in general is inherently a visual — as opposed to verbal — apprehension of the world; yet there is no consensus that films and paintings are more postmodern than other cultural forms. Even as a rallying point for a political agenda, there is both 'a postmodernism of resistance and a postmodernism of reaction' (Foster, 1983: xii). When aesthetic and political agenda meet, moreover, as in the state-run art museum, postmodernism

Theory, Culture & Society (SAGE, London, Newbury Park, Beverly Hills and New Delhi), Vol. 5 (1988), 431–46

becomes a programme for reviewing the history of art in both more populist and more elitist ways (cf. Mainardi, 1987).

The fungibility of the concept may account for some of its appeal. Yet it also speaks to the zeitgeist in which those who merely study society play a part: postmodernism is 'the sum of self-awareness, of a shared culture, of a niche in time [and] space' (Dear, 1986: 373).

When Jameson's article 'Postmodernism, or the Cultural Logic of Late Capitalism' was published in *New Left Review* (1984), it was widely read by sociologists and political economists in the United States. People who had barely marked the passage of authority from Althusser to Foucault and Derrida, who couldn't tell 'complexity' from 'contradiction' in architecture, who still thought of Philip Marlowe as the direct descendant of Sherlock Holmes (Poster, 1984; Venturi, 1977 [1966]; Tani, 1984) — these people were both stimulated and provoked by Jameson's approach.

Many criticized Jameson for his facile elision of capital and culture and the superficial sense in which he called for a postmodern 'mapping' of the cognitive world. Some objected to the polymorphous postmodernism that Jameson found in equal measure in art and architecture, cinema and writing. Still others rebuked him (Davis, 1985) on the problematic identification of postmodernism with an expanding rather than a crisis-ridden capitalism. Yet largely by means of Jameson's essay, the issues he identified and the examples he described gained currency in social analysis.

In urban research the postmodern debate struck a common chord. First, the rhetoric of Jameson's statement — especially the call for mapping and the impressive though flawed example of John Portman's atrium-hotels — spoke to geographers, sociologists and political economists who studied urban space. Second, urban researchers were already attuned to an interdisciplinary reading of the 'built environment'; by necessity, they had to take into account architecture, art markets, urban planning, and capital investment in order to make sense of contemporary urban developments (Zukin, 1982). Marxist urban studies, moreover, had recently undergone a traumatic self-examination, in which economic determinism receded before a more open materialist analysis that embraced culture and politics as well as economic structures (Berman, 1982; Castells, 1983; Harvey, 1985; Gottdiener, 1985).

Jameson's linking postmodernism to a current stage of capitalism complemented the tendency to connect urban and regional developments to the global reorganization of capital (cf. Massey,

1984). Often the analysis of local 'restructuring' was accompanied by an effort to visualize the changing power relations between capitalists, or between capitalists and other social groups, in spatial terms (see the vastly different approaches of Fainstein and Fainstein, 1982; Smith, 1984; and Soja, 1986). Perhaps the postmodern debate has had its greatest impact on urban studies by framing issues of uneven economic development in terms of the mutual relation between a more socially conceptualized space and a more spatially conceived society (Soja, 1987).

While this contribution has been called 'the postmodernization of geography' (Soja, 1987), the acknowledgment seems to outweigh the actual intellectual debt. Urban researchers have had a great deal of trouble in moving postmodernism from an aesthetic category into the debate over urban forms.

Certainly the postmodern notion of pluralism in the visual arts has influenced an appreciation of plural or 'flexible' strategies of capital accumulation, especially in cities (Harvey, 1987; Cooke, 1988). Further, the postmodern concept of narrative fragmentation seems relevant to the fracturing of social relations based on geographical or other traditional ties, a process that is evident in older industrial cities and regions (Friedmann, 1983; Scott and Storper, 1986). Finally, the language of postmodern architecture and post-structuralist criticism is apt for describing a material environment that 'decontextualizes' and recreates historical forms of city building for purposes of distraction, entertainment and 'spectacle' (Debord, 1983 [1967]). These urban spaces include the atrium-hotel as Jameson describes it, Disneyland and various reconstructed downtown shopping centres (Faneuil Hall, South Street Seaport, Inner Harbor) and more generally, the 'non-place' spaces that standardize or ignore regional traditions (cf. Relph, 1976; Frampton, 1983).

Using the term postmodernism in the debate over urban form offers certain advantages. Intuitively it 'sounds right' because it resonates with the fragmentation of geographic loyalties in contemporary economic restructuring and its expression in new urban polarities. It also solidifies a commitment among urban political economists and geographers to bring culture out of the superstructure and study it, along with politics and economics, as a basic determinant of material forms. And using postmodernism aligns urbanists in an interdisciplinary enterprise with a more or less common vocabulary and a common subject, the city.

Yet if social scientists don't move beyond the sensual evocation of the city that postmodernism now represents, they risk being overwhelmed by another of the 'chaotic concepts' that have plagued recent urban studies (Sayer, 1982; Zukin, 1987). To use postmodernism reasonably, we must conceptualize it as a social process and periodize it in terms of production as well as consumption of urban space. The historical continuities that come to light challenge the identification of postmodernism with a new stage in the social organization of capital (cf. Fainstein and Fainstein, forthcoming).

'Postmodernization' as a Social Process

The awkward term postmodernization signals our interest in a dynamic process whose scale and complexity are comparable to the great structuring forces of modernization. Like modernization, postmodernization presents the problem of analysing discontinuous or dissonant social processes on different geographic scales. On the global level postmodernization refers to the restructuring of socio-spatial relations by new patterns of investment and production in industry and services, labour migration and telecommunications (cf. Portes and Walton, 1981; Urry, 1987). On the level of the metropolitan region, postmodernization refers to socio-spatial relocation based on opposing claims of affordability and legitimacy (cf. Smith and Williams, 1986; Smith, 1987). Both global and metropolitan processes are represented by some degree of decentralization. On the urban level, however, postmodernization is represented by some sort of recentralization in core cities of global markets (e.g. Soja, 1986).

If aesthetically postmodernism suggests new neo-classical buildings and historical recreations, it covers only part of the changes in major US and European cities since the early 1970s. This description works best when it is limited to the high-class rebuilding of downtowns and waterfronts for highly competitive business services, high-rent residences, and high-volume or high-style cultural consumption. The conjunction of historic preservation and the arts as a method of real estate investment and a means of perception does reflect real changes in culture and society (Zukin, 1982, 1988; Wright, 1985; Hewison, 1987). Yet limiting postmodernism to this usage doesn't deal with the relation between visualization and social reconstruction, a dual effort 'to map one form of social control upon another' (Clark, 1985: 49; cf. Harvey, 1985; Boyer, 1987).

In looking at postmodernism we should be guided by older

notions of polarities in architectural patronage and perception (Sarfatti Larson, 1982, following Walter Benjamin). Adapting these categories, on the one hand, postmodernization refers to the structural polarity between markets and places, between the forces that detach people from or anchor them to specific spaces. On the other hand, postmodernization refers to the institutional polarity between the public and private use of urban space. The analysis of postmodern urban forms emphasizes markets over places and denies the separation of private and public space. It therefore requires attention to both *structural* forces and political, economic, and cultural *institutions*.[1]

Architectural Production

The constant rebuilding of cities in core capitalist societies suggests that the major condition of architectural production is to create shifting material landscapes. These landscapes bridge space and time; they also directly mediate economic power by both conforming to and structuring norms of market-driven investment, production and consumption.

While architects today work mainly under corporate patronage, they also work — along with urban planners, real estate developers, and city officials — in a matrix of state institutions and local preferences. They are neither free nor unfree from market forces and the attachments of place. Although architects usually work to specifications set by individual clients, their largest commissions come from businesses and real estate developers who build 'on speculation', that is, with the intention of selling or renting space after construction has begun. These clients impose market criteria on architects by demanding more rentable or saleable space in less construction time. More and more, such clients are national and international investors rather than local developers. For this reason, Jameson and others see urban architecture as a direct expression of 'multinational capitalism' (Jameson, 1984; Davis, 1985; Logan and Molotch, 1987).

Architects, moreover, pursue these clients under conditions of increasing competition. Major architectural firms have recently experienced the same kind of growth and international expansion of activity as corporate law, accounting and advertising firms — although professional corporations are legally prohibited from selling ownership shares to the public and typically grow by opening branches rather than making mergers and acquisitions. Consequently, new architecture and urban forms are produced under nearly the same social organization as consumer products and business services.

We see, therefore, in urban forms market-driven patterns of standardization and differentiation. Despite local variations, as well as variations that are imposed for aesthetic, ideological or 'sentimental' reasons (Jager, 1986; Logan and Molotch, 1987: ch. 4; Harvey, 1987), the major influence on urban form derives from the internationalization of investment, production and consumption. In socio-spatial terms, however, internationalization is associated with the concentration of investment, the decentralization of production, and the standardization of consumption.

After 1945, the process of suburbanization in the United States demanded centralized control over finance and construction even while it rapidly decentralized housing and shopping malls, with their anchor stores, controlled environment, and inner streets of shops, and destroyed the commercial viability of many central business districts (Checkoway, 1986; Kowinski, 1985; Mintz and Schwartz, 1985: 43). From the early 1970s, however, centralized, multinational investment supported both continued decentralization and a reconcentration, with greater stratification, of urban shopping districts. The same products and ambiance came from multinational corporations in New York, France, Japan and Italy. Increasingly, they could just as well be found in shops on upper Madison Avenue as on Rodeo Drive, the Rue du Faubourg St. Honoré, or the via Montenapoleone. When local merchants were displaced by the higher rents these tenants paid, they correctly blamed showplace boutiques whose rents were subsidized by their parent multinational corporations. In a subtle recapitulation of earlier transformations, more international investment shifted shopping districts from craft (quiche) to mass (McDonald's or Benetton) production and consumption (Giovannini, 1986; Meislin, 1987).

McDonald's and Benetton epitomize the connections between international urban form and internationalized production and consumption. Their shops are ubiquitous in cities around the world, giving strength to the parent firms' strategy of international expansion (Lee, 1986; *Business Week*, October 13, 1986). The two companies differ in the way they run their worldwide operations: while McDonald's sells traditional franchises to local operators, Benetton neither invests in nor collects franchise fees from Benetton stores.

McDonald's managers, moreover, buy their food supplies locally, but Benetton managers buy all their inventory from Benetton. The uniform standards of both chains are maintained by other corporate policies: rigorous training of store managers; adherence to company standards for quality, service, and at Benetton, decor and window display; and frequent on-site inspections by visitors from company headquarters.

Despite differences in the types of products that they sell, both Benetton and McDonald's owe their growth in part to organizational innovation. Much of this advance centres on production and distribution. McDonald's honed to a fine point the 'robotized' operations of fast-food cuisine; Benetton developed cheaper methods for softening wool and dying coloured garments as well as investing in computerized manufacturing and design and real robots for warehouse operations. In the process, both chains developed a total 'look' that merges product, production methods, a specialized consumption experience, and an advertising style. Just as their 'classic' mass-produced sweaters and burgers link consumers around the world, so do these multinational corporations become more significant players in each domestic economy. McDonald's voracious demand for beef inflicts potential damage up and down the food chain in cattle-raising countries of Latin America (Skinner, 1985); by contrast, Benetton's new US factory in North Carolina provides (automated) employment to textile workers.

Unlike mass-produced consumer goods, architecture maintains a high profile. While individual buildings become more standardized, their designers claim more distinction for their clients. Professional architects continue to theorize an underlying aesthetic or social programme, especially the faux populism that adheres to many postmodern styles. The demotic urge facilitates architects' acceptability to corporate patrons, who want to gain public acceptance as well as to distinguish their companies from those that inhabit the glass boxes commercially adapted from modernism from the 1950s through the 1970s (see Venturi, 1977 [1966]; Venturi et al., 1977; cf. Kieran, 1987).

Developers are less constrained in talking about the conditions of architectural production. 'My buildings are a product,' a developer says (*Architectural Record*, June 1987: 9). 'They are products like Scotch Tape is a product, or Saran Wrap. The packaging of that product is the first thing that people see. I am selling space and renting space and it has to be in a package that is attractive enough to be financially successful.' He emphasizes, 'I can't afford to build monuments because I am not an institution'.

The distinguished architectural critic Ada Louise Huxtable (1987) turns this comment around in her criticism of the monumentally sized, egregiously individualized new skyscrapers that are especially common in New York City. 'In the last five years,' she says, 'a new kind of developer has been remaking the city with something called "the signature building", a postmodernist phenomenon that combines marketing and consumerism in a way that would have baffled Bernini but is thoroughly understood by the modern entrepreneur.'

An emphasis on individualized products that can be identified with individual cultural producers is inseparable from intensified market competition in an age of mass consumption (Forty, 1987). The 'Egyptoid' character of postmodern skyscraper design was paralleled, in the 1920s, by the 'Mayan' pyramids of speculative office buildings competing in a real estate boom (Stern et al., 1987: 511–13). Similar competition among Hollywood film studios from the 1930s through the 1950s for audience loyalty to their products encouraged individual directors to make the 'signature film'. In architecture, as labour costs have increased and craft skills have atrophied, the burden of social differentiation has passed to the use of expensive materials and the ingenuity of the design itself. Not surprisingly, like Hollywood directors, architects assume and even become commercial properties.

To some extent, the commercialization of architects reflects the market competition of architectural products. But it also reflects the increasing commercialization of the social category of design. This occurs both under market and nonmarket competition. Indeed, it occurs so typically in a fluid social space that joins market and nonmarket institutions (and their patrons) that it draws our attention to a public-private 'liminal space' in new urban forms.

Liminal Spaces

The liminal space of postmodern urban forms is socially constructed in the erosion of autonomy of cultural producers from cultural consumers. Autonomy from patrons has always been especially problematic for architects and designers because of the material resources required to realize their designs. In theory, professionalization, with its special educational requirements and licensing procedures, should enhance the distance between architectural producers and their patrons. In practice, however, the activities of these producers and 'cultivated' cultural consumers increasingly converge.[2]

Convergence is structured by new and revived institutional forms, such as trade fairs, department store promotions, and museum events, that have become major urban attractions. While New York City and Los Angeles can no longer claim to be world centres of garment and furniture production, for example, they do expand their design and cultural centres and merchandise marts for the concentration of business activities connected with conception, display and sales. It is important for these cities to claim to be world centres of design. That role both symbolizes and provides material resources for the specialization in high-level business services to which core cities aspire. And it attracts the heterogeneous new elites of business, politics and fashion that comprise a visible part of an international upper class (cf. Silverman, 1986).

The common socio-spatial element shared by department stores and museums is that they create a new linkage between designers, mass consumers and wealthy patrons of high culture. Regional genres and individual artists' *oeuvres* provide motifs that are invoked as a consumption package for both cultural and mass consumption. Annual sales promotions at Bloomingdale's parallel new exhibitions at the costume wing of the Metropolitan Museum of Art, and both are used to enhance the competitive status of their respective institutions (Silverman, 1986).

Much as it did in the late nineteenth century, the department store frames 'the democratization of luxury' (Williams, 1982: 11) so that it encourages consumption by both affluent and lower classes. Similarly, the heightened competition among museums for such nonmarket resources as government patronage encourages them to frame a democratized connoisseurship that appeals to segments of a cultivated upper and middle class.

Department stores and museums thus form liminal spaces that frame the perception of cultural products as straddling pure art and art for markets. In both institutions public gatherings for display and sales merge with private functions (market and nonmarket competition for resources, charity 'events').

While postmodern art critics have noted the outcome of these social processes, they generally limit themselves to observing that cultural producers no longer preserve a critical distance from the market (Jameson, 1984; Solomon-Godeau, forthcoming). On the contrary, it is the very essence of postmodern cultural institutions to blur distinctions between high and low culture, especially by plying cultural meanings to an enlarged public of 'connoisseurs'. Similarly, it is the very essence of postmodern urban forms to provide the liminal spaces for such meanings to be played out, blurring distinctions between privacy and publicity and market and nonmarket norms.

Periodizing Postmodern Urban Form

The institutional symbiosis between department stores and museums dates back to the 1920s (DiMaggio, 1986; Stern et al., 1987: 336–8). Similarly, the production of highly individualized buildings and public-private liminal spaces derives from the speculative building booms of modern architecture between 1870 and 1930. History thus complicates an attempt to define postmodernism as a distinct period in architectural production. On the contrary, in modernism begins the marketing of design as both a spatial and a cultural commodity.

'Superstar architecture' is taken to be a hallmark of postmodern urban form. Like superstars in rock music or on Wall Street, production of superstar architects reflects the desire by major corporations in the services to recoup value from long-term, large-scale investments in product development. Investments on this scale in urban redevelopment generate market demand for highly individualized yet increasingly standardized architectural designs. Many of the important commissions that are involved are awarded to internationally active architects with superstar reputations.

Just as these projects are often out of scale with the histories of specific places, so the architects who are recruited to design them have reputations that are out of scale with those of local cultural producers. 'Suddenly,' a local architect complains about Fan Pier, a major new project on the Boston waterfront, 'the demand for the "name" architect, often overcommitted elsewhere, has placed these architects and their products side by side.' This threatens 'the identity of Boston, Back Bay, and Newbury Street' with being submerged in that of any other place (*Architectural Record*, May 1987: 4).[3]

Yet the production òf superstar architecture derives from the same speculative building activity that generated high modernism. As early as the 1870s in Chicago, constant cycles of rebuilding initiated by business cycles and fires resulted in an aggressive construction industry and a commercially-oriented architecture. 'Chicago architects', said a French observer undoubtedly immured by Haussmann and the Napoleonic *corps*, 'brazenly accepted the conditions imposed by the speculator' (Saint, 1983: 84).

When Henry James returned to New York in 1905 after 20 years of living in Europe, he found the mid-nineteenth-century Trinity Church threatened with sale by its own wardens and imminent demise (James, 1968 [1907]: 83–4). The architectural monotony with which it would be replaced confirmed, for James, 'the universal will to move — to move, move, move, as an end in itself, an appetite at any price'.

For the next generation in the two American capitals of big business and modern architecture — New York and Chicago — rising land values, growing corporations and real estate speculation made a constantly changing landscape. The average longevity of an office building in New York shrank to only 20 years. Modern replacement buildings, moreover, as James had suspected, were less distinguished — and cheaper to build or maintain — than their classical predecessors. By the 1920s, production of commercial buildings depended on a nexus of speculators whose financing got a project underway, architects who could 'draw ... an imposing picture of a skyscraper; if it is several stories higher than the Woolworth Tower, so much the better,' and newspapers that eagerly published 'pictures of high buildings, real or imagined, because ... readers have a weakness for them' (builder William A. Starrett [1928] quoted in Stern et al., 1987: 513–14).

The historic nexus of superstar architecture, commercialization and speculation is paralleled by a hybrid public-private mode in the appropriation and production of urban forms.

Current observers tend to suggest that this institutional hybrid is historically new. Consequently, the postmodern period of urban redevelopment refers to the public-private partnerships which thrive even under 'progressive' municipal administrations (Hartman, 1984; Bennett, 1986; Judd, 1986) as well as to the 'privatization' that occurs with the transformation of public spaces along the waterfront into emporia of mass consumption and the encroachment of private institutions into public space (e.g. the expansion of the Metropolitan Museum into Central Park).

But again the postmodern perception derives from processes inherent in high modernism. From the 1880s, increasing use of new mechanical inventions for transportation and telecommunications forged hybrid public-private cultural forms (Kern, 1983: 187–91). Telephones provided men and women with both accessibility and distraction. Newspapers achieved mass circulation as means of both intimacy and information. Railroads, moreover, bridged the private scale of the journey and public arrival in the city with the liminal transparent tunnel of the great railroad station, built of iron and glass (Schievelbusch, 1979: 161–9). Similarly, social life in modern cities has often been generated by new means of market consumption — coffee houses, tearooms, restaurants, department stores — that are diffused from an essentially private group to a broader public (Thorne, 1980; Barth, 1980; Williams, 1982; Benson, 1986; cf. Wolff, 1985).

In contrast, moreover, to the 'postmodern' Portman-built hotel that Fredric Jameson describes, the private use of public space was first noted by that earlier intrepid consumer, Henry James, when he visited New York's Waldorf-Astoria Hotel (1968 [1907]: 104–5; cf. Agnew, 1983).

For James, the tearooms and shops of the American grand hotel created 'a world whose relation to its form and medium was practically imperturbable; ... a conception of publicity *as* the vital medium organized with the authority with which the American genius for organization, put on its mettle, alone could organize it'. In the cavernous lobby of 'the universal Waldorf-Astoria' James saw entrapped 'the great collective, plastic public' by 'the great glittering, costly caravansery'. No less than Jameson in the atrium does James in the Waldorf see 'the whole housed populace move as in mild and consenting suspicion of its captured and governed state, its having to consent in inordinate fusion as the price of what it seemed pleased to regard as inordinate luxury' (James, 1968 [1907]: 440–1).

Conclusion

The postmodern debate over urban form suggests a more subtle 'cultural logic of capitalism' (Jameson, 1984) than has so far been entertained. Conveying a sense of rupture and discontinuity, and taking for granted that progress is fragile, the postmodern landscape represents the same destruction of longevity, of cultural layers, and of vested interests that opposes markets to place. For this reason there is both similarity and continuity with the modernism that represents (and opposes) the 'high' capitalism of an advancing industrial age.

By contrast, postmodernization occurs in a social context when markets are more volatile and places — even the occupational category of cultural producers — less autonomous. The part played by postmodern urban form is to appropriate or restore designated meaning through processes of social and spatial redifferentiation. Just as economic internationalization has very different spatial and social consequences in the spheres of investment, production and consumption, so postmodernization should be carefully analysed for the social production of its aesthetic effects.

Notes

1. The following material is drawn from chapter 2 of my book-in-progress, *American Market/Place* (Berkeley and Los Angeles: University of California Press), and represents a greatly condensed version of the argument.

2. These terms bring up the usual modern distinctions between clients who directly commission architectural products and patrons who by their connoisseurship and command of institutionalized cultural resources support the general process of architectural production. As we shall see, the marketing of connoisseurship calls in turn for new terms of distinction.

3. The same submersion of locality (and local capital) by superstar architecture is illustrated by 1 Liberty Place, Helmut Jahn's new office building in Philadelphia. The design by Jahn, a well-known postmodern architect based in Chicago, had to receive special authorization from the city government because it rose above the symbolic limit set by the statue of William Penn atop City Hall. Penn, founder of the commonwealth of Pennsylvania, laid out Philadelphia's initial city plan in the seventeenth century.

References

Agnew, Jean-Christophe (1983) 'The Consuming Vision of Henry James', in Richard Wightman Fox and T.J. Jackson Lears (eds) *The Culture of Consumption*. New York: Pantheon.

Barth, Gunther (1980) *City People: The Rise of Modern Culture in Nineteenth-Century America*. New York: Oxford University Press.

Bennett, Larry (1986) 'Beyond Urban Renewal: Chicago's North Loop Redevelopment Project', *Urban Affairs Quarterly* 22: 242–60.

Benson, Susan Porter (1986) *Counter Culture: Saleswomen, Managers and Customers in American Department Stores, 1890–1940*. Urbana: University of Illinois Press.

Berman, Marshall (1982) *All That Is Solid Melts Into Air*. New York: Simon and Schuster.

Boyer, M. Christine (1987) 'The City of Collective Memory'. Unpublished paper.

Castells, Manuel (1983) *The City and the Grassroots*. Berkeley and Los Angeles: University of California Press.

Checkoway, Barry (1986) 'Large Builders, Federal Housing Programs, and Postwar Suburbanization', in Rachel G. Bratt et al. (eds) *Critical Perspectives on Housing*. Philadelphia: Temple University Press.

Clark, Timothy (1985) *The Painting of Modern Life*. New York: Viking.

Cooke, Philip (1988) 'The Postmodern Condition and the City', *Comparative Urban and Community Research*.

Davis, Mike (1985) 'Urban Renaissance and the Spirit of Postmodernism', *New Left Review* 151 (May-June): 106–13.

Dear, M.J. (1986) 'Postmodernism and Planning', *Environment and Planning D: Society and Space* 4: 367–84.

Debord, Guy (1967, 1983) *Society of the Spectacle*. Detroit: Black and Red.

DiMaggio, Paul J. (1986) 'Why Are Art Museums Not Decentralized After the Fashion of Public Libraries'. Paper presented to Workshop on Law, Economy and Organizations, Yale Law School (December).

Fainstein, Norman I. and Fainstein, Susan S. (1982) 'Restructuring the American City: A Comparative Perspective,' in Fainstein and Fainstein (eds) *Urban Policy Under Capitalism*, *Urban Affairs Annual Review* 22.

Fainstein, Susan S. and Fainstein, Norman I. (forthcoming) 'Technology, The New International Division of Labor, and Location: Continuities and Disjunctures', in Robert Beauregard (ed.) *Industrial Restructuring and Spatial Variation*, *Urban Affairs Annual Review*.

Forty, Adrian (1987) *Objects of Desire: Design and Society From Wedgwood to IBM*. New York: Pantheon.

Foster, Hal (ed.) (1983) *The Anti-Aesthetic: Essays on Postmodern Culture*. Port Townsend, Wash.: Bay Press.

Frampton, Kenneth (1983) 'Towards a Critical Regionalism: Six Points For an Architecture of Resistance', in Hal Foster (ed.) *The Anti-Aesthetic*. Port Townsend, Wash.: Bay Press.

Friedmann, John (1983) 'Life Space and Economic Space: Contradictions in Regional Development', in Dudley Seers and Kjell Ostrom (eds) *The Crises of the European Regions*. London: Macmillan.

Giovannini, Joseph (1986) 'The "New" Madison Avenue: A European Street of Fashion', *New York Times* (June 26).

Gottdiener, Mark (1985) *The Social Production of Urban Space*. Austin: University of Texas Press.

Hartman, Chester (1984) *The Transformation of San Francisco*. Totowa, New Jersey: Rowman and Allenheld.

Harvey, David (1985) 'Paris, 1850–1870', in *Consciousness and the Urban Experience*. Baltimore: Johns Hopkins University Press.

Harvey, David (1987) 'Flexible Accumulation Through Urbanization: Reflections on "Post-Modernism" in the American City'. Paper presented to Symposium on Developing the American City: Society and Architecture in the Regional City, Yale School of Architecture (February).

Hassan, Ihab (1987) *The Postmodern Turn: Essays in Postmodern Theory and Culture*. Columbus, Ohio: Ohio State University Press.

Hewison, Robert (1987) *The Heritage Industry*. London.

Huxtable, Ada Louise (1987) 'Creeping Gigantism in Manhattan', *New York Times*, (March 22).

Jager, Michael (1986) 'Class Definition and the Aesthetics of Gentrification: Victoriana in Melbourne', in Neil Smith and Peter Williams (eds) *Gentrification of the City*, Winchester, Mass.: Allen and Unwin.

James, Henry (1907, 1968) *The American Scene*. Bloomington, Ind.: Indiana University Press.

Jameson, Fredric (1984) 'Postmodernism, or the Cultural Logic of Late Capitalism', *New Left Review* 146 (July-August): 53–93.

Jencks, Charles (1984) *The Language of Postmodern Architecture*. 4th edn, New York: Rizzoli.

Judd, Dennis R. (1986) 'Electoral Coalitions, Minority Mayors, and the Contradictions in the Municipal Policy Agenda', in M. Gottdiener (ed.) *Cities in Stress, Urban Affairs Annual Review* 30.

Kern, Stephen (1983) *The Culture of Time and Space, 1880–1918*. Cambridge, Mass.: Harvard University Press.

Kieran, Stephen (1987) 'The Architecture of Plenty: Theory and Design in the Marketing Age', *Harvard Architecture Review* 6: 103–13.

Kowinski, William Severini (1985) *The Malling of America*. New York: William Morrow.

Lee, Andrea (1986) 'Profiles: Being Everywhere' (Luciano Benetton), *The New Yorker* (November 10).

Logan, John and Molotch, Harvey (1987) *Urban Fortunes*. Berkeley and Los Angeles: University of California Press.

Mainardi, Patricia (1987) 'Postmodern History at the Musée D'Orsay', *October* 41 (summer): 30–52.

Massey, Doreen (1984) *Spatial Divisions of Labor*. New York: Methuen.

Meislin, Richard J. (1987) 'Quiche Gets the Boot on Columbus Avenue', *New York Times* (July 25).

Mintz, Beth and Schwartz, Michael (1985) *The Power Structure of American Business*. Chicago: University of Chicago Press.

Portes, Alejandro and Walton, John (1981) *Labor, Class and the International System*. New York: Academic.

Poster, Mark (1984) *Foucault, Marxism and History*. Cambridge: Polity Press.

Relph, E. (1976) *Place and Placelessness*. London: Plon.

Saint, Andrew (1983) *The Image of the Architect*. New Haven: Yale University Press.

Sarfatti Larson, Magali (1982) 'An Ideological Response to Industrialism: European Architectural Modernism'. Unpublished paper.

Sayer, Andrew (1982) 'Explanation in Economic Geography: Abstraction versus Generalization', *Progress in Human Geography* 6 (March): 68–88.

Schievelbusch, Wolfgang (1979) *The Railway Journey*. Translated by Anselm Hollo. New York: Urizen.

Scott, A.J. and Storper, M. (eds) (1986) *Production, Work, Territory*. Winchester, Mass.: Allen and Unwin.

Silverman, Debora (1986) *Selling Culture: Bloomingdale's, Diana Vreeland, and the New Aristocracy of Taste in Reagan's America*. New York: Pantheon.

Skinner, Joseph K. (1985) 'Big Mac and the Tropical Forests', *Monthly Review* (December): 25–32.

Smith, Neil (1984) *Uneven Development*, Oxford: Basil Blackwell.

Smith, Neil (1987) 'Of Yuppies and Housing: Gentrification, Social Restructuring, and the Urban Dream', *Environment and Planning D: Society and Space* 5: 151–72.

Smith, Neil and Williams, Peter (eds) (1986) *Gentrification of the City*. Winchester, Mass.: Allen and Unwin.

Soja, E.W. (1986) 'Taking Los Angeles Apart: Some Fragments of a Critical Human Geography', *Environment and Planning D: Society and Space* 4: 255–72.

Soja, E.W. (1987) 'The Postmodernization of Geography: A Review', *Annals of the Association of American Geographers* 77 (2): 289–323.

Solomon-Godeau, Abigail (forthcoming) 'Living With Contradictions: Critical Practices in the Age of Supply-Side Aesthetics', in *The Politics of Postmodernism*, Andrew Ross (ed.). Minneapolis: University of Minnesota Press.

Stern, Robert A.M. et al. (1987) *New York 1930: Architecture and Urbanism Between the Two World Wars*. New York: Rizzoli.

Tani, Stefano (1984) *The Doomed Detective: The Contribution of the Detective Novel to Postmodern American and Italian Fiction*. Carbondale, Ill.: Southern Illinois University Press.

Thorne, Robert (1980) 'Places of Refreshment in the Nineteenth-Century City', in Anthony D. King (ed.) *Buildings and Society*. London: Routledge and Kegan Paul.

Urry, John (1987) 'Some Social and Spatial Aspects of Services', *Environment and Planning: Society and Space* 5: 5–26.

Venturi, Robert (1966, 1977) *Complexity and Contradiction in Architecture*, rev. edn. New York: Museum of Modern Art.

Venturi, Robert et al. (1977) *Learning From Las Vegas*, rev. edn. Cambridge, Mass.: MIT Press.

Williams, Rosalind H. (1982) *Dream Worlds: Mass Consumption in Late Nineteenth-Century France*. Berkeley and Los Angeles: University of California Press.

Wolff, Janet (1985) 'The Invisible Flaneuse: Women and the Literature of Modernity', *Theory, Culture & Society* 2 (3): 37–48.

Wright, Patrick (1985) *On Living in an Old Country*. London: Verso.

Zukin, Sharon (1982) *Loft Living: Culture and Capital in Urban Change*. Baltimore: Johns Hopkins University Press.

Zukin, Sharon (1987) 'Gentrification: Culture and Capital in the Urban Core', *Annual Review of Sociology* 13: 129–47.

Zukin, Sharon (1988) 'Postscript: More Market Forces', *Loft Living*. 2nd edn. London: Radius/Hutchinson.

Sharon Zukin teaches Sociology at Brooklyn College and the Graduate Center of the City University of New York. The second edition of her *Loft Living* has just been published by Hutchinson.

Cultural Logics of the Global System: A Sketch

Jonathan Friedman

The aim of the following discussion is to shift the current view from within capitalist culture on the question of modernity and post-modernity to an external perspective on the transformations of the identity structure of our kind of civilization and its effects on the production of culture. I shall present an argument in the form of a series of propositions, beginning first with the kind of legitimating remarks that make the ensuing discourse possible.

  1. Seeing how postmodern fragmentation often takes the form of a critique of the implicit monopolistically authoritarian content of rational discourse I think it necessary to state that there is no reason to defend the 'rational' style of the following argument. There is no such thing as a pluralistic means of expression in the kind of communication to be made here. The reference to the collapse of the authority of language must be made in terms of that very authority for its significance to be unambiguously communicated. If this is not necessarily the case, it has certainly never been tried — i.e. no one has seriously considered playing the piano to make the point. The fact is, that the very content of the critique of rationalism is itself rational and makes a point that is unfailingly expressed in the language of rational argument. No more need be said on this matter.

  2. Modernity, postmodernity and tradition are expressions of the poles of the cultural space of capitalist identity. They can be understood as a system of oppositions defined by the dominance of modern identity (Friedman, 1987).

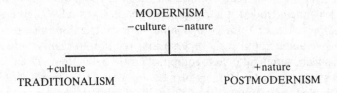

MODERNISM
−culture −nature

+culture +nature
TRADITIONALISM POSTMODERNISM

Theory, Culture & Society (SAGE, London, Newbury Park, Beverly Hills and New Delhi), Vol. 5 (1988), 447–60

3. The above structure of oppositions is meant to represent, in structuralist fashion the three poles of capitalist identity space. I say 'capitalist' guardedly for the following reason. The identity space represented here is tendentially present in all commercial civilizations to the extent that the social world is atomized into individuals who can neither conceive of nor experience them*selves* as parts of a larger cosmological realm without the aid of drugs or oppositional movements of a religious character.

4. In order to grasp the logic of this structure we briefly summarize the content of its three terms with respect to one another. First, it is necessary to concede that we are defining these terms as greatly reduced in their content since they are used in relation to a very broad range of phenomena.

a. *Modernism* can be defined in Goethian terms as a continuous process of accumulation of self, in the form of wealth, knowledge, experience. It is a dangerous state where in order to survive the person must be in constant movement. It is an identity without fixed content other than the capacity to develop itself, movement and growth as a principle of selfhood. This self is epitomized in the definition of the ego in Freudian and especially Marcusian terms, a sublimation of the libido, the transfer of primitive desire into civilization (culture) building, the driving force of social evolution. Thus the realm of control and of the formation of the self merge into the sphere of self-control. And beyond the self there is no universe of meaning into which one can be inserted. There is only discovery, growth, increasing control over nature, i.e. development — but then the cosmological prerequisite of infinite accumulation is an infinite field of accumulation, an infinite universe, both temporally and spatially. The universe is thus the arena of expansion where the self-controlled ego can realize itself just as capital. The space of growth is the space of control. This space is opposed to the realm of the primitive, the realm of infantile desire. The latter harbours all that is uncontrolled: the confusion of eating, sexuality, aggression and pleasure, epitomized in cannibalistic fantasy, but also the impulsive and compulsively superstitious relation to reality; religious fetishism, fanatical belief, compulsive rule behaviour, the need to construct totalistic systems of meaning etc. These aspects of the repressed correspond to the specificity of modernism as negative to both tradition and nature, to both filthy desire and neurotic superstition, i.e. to both nature and culture. The culture of Freud is not anthropological culture but civilization, i.e. modernity.

b. *Traditionalism*, neo-traditionalism, neo-conservatism express a specific reaction to the modernist pole from within the same universe of meaning. Tradition is one aspect of modern existence that must be repressed or even dissolved if the civilizing process is to proceed. It is that aspect that is represented by culture, defined as a system of rules and etiquette pegged to a totalistic cosmology that provides an ultimate meaning to existence, defining man's place in the universe as well as the significance of all his activities. It embodies a structure of legitimate authority, of belief, a system of concrete values pertaining to a world of personal relations. It opposes itself to modernity which is defined from this perspective as a universe emptied of meaning, peopled by alienated individuals dominated by the structures of *Gesellschaft*, a system of abstract roles and functions. Postmodernism is opposed in this as the ultimate outcome of the modernist onslaught on culture, the total dissipation of value and meaning.

c. The *postmodern* pole is only one of two possibilities, here accentuating the opposition of nature, natural force, libido, unchained human creativity, to the fetters of modernity, seen as a structure of power and control, the ego writ large. It defines the primitive as all that freedom from civilized control is meant to be, the confusion of the sexes, the liberation of infantile desire and its capacity for merging with the other, the expression of immediate feeling, a social existence based on communion rather than social distance. The conception of the modern here is that of culture as a set of imprisoning constraints, culture as opposed to nature, and repressive of nature. As such this position is also opposed to traditionalism which is conceived as an expression of increased control, a reaction to the false freedom generated by modernity.

5. A more complete picture of the postmodern configuration is one that is more symmetrically opposed to modernism, one that is both +culture and +nature, dedicated to both libido and 'sagesse', to the polymorphous perverse as well as the deeper wisdom of the primitive. It emphatically challenges the obliterating effect of modernity on culture while, via its absolute relativism praises the value of all culture and all nature. From this position, modernism is

denatured as well as decultured. Postmodernity represents a return to both, a return to the concrete. This provides us with a more complete set of oppositions:

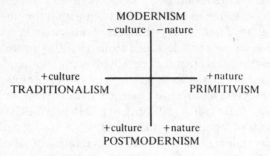

MODERNISM
−culture   −nature

+culture ———————————— +nature
TRADITIONALISM   PRIMITIVISM

+culture   +nature
POSTMODERNISM

6. Postmodernity must not be confused with cynicism, an attitude born of the dissolution of any form of identity. While often associated with the postmodern disenchantment with modernity, and expressed in a kind of combinatorial blasé-faire it is a product of the self-contradictory nature of postmodernism as a form of social identity. Since the latter does away with the nature/culture opposition, not by denying both of them but by fusing them it obliterates any form of determinate identification, thus paving the way for 'anything goes'.[1] Total relativism, 'mutual edification' militates against any form of engagement in a particular identity and thus harbours a potentially deep cynicism.

7. Our argument here is that these polarities mark the extrema of a field of cultural strategies in capitalist civilization. They do not correspond to particular strategies as such but to the tendencies that they exhibit. Individuals, of course, can combine various aspects of the different poles to some extent; one can be a modernist about education and a traditionalist about one's teenage daughter. The problem is merely one of consistency. And the strain toward consistency is a function of the existence of crisis situations that effect identity. It is important to emphasize that the four poles define a single space defined by modernist identity so that traditionalism, primitivism and postmodernism are included as logical markers of modernism which is the dominant or 'normal' identity of capitalist civilization.

8. Logical consistency is provoked by identity crisis. It leads to polarization. Modernist identity depends on expanding horizons, the possibility of individual and social development, mobility and liberation from the fixed and concrete structures of surviving non-

capitalist forms: family, community, religion. This in its turn depends on an expanding modern sector of a global system, i.e. an expanding hegemonic centre. Where such expansion ends or turns to decline, modern identity becomes increasingly difficult to maintain. It is in such circumstances that we expect bi- and trifurcation in the space, polarized by the non-modernist sectors in what for better terms we might call capitalist identity space.[2] And, of course, modernism where it is maintained, tends to become more extreme, even hysterical, in face of the onslaught by the 'uncivilized'. There is, then, a link up between cycles of hegemony, cycles of shifting centres of accumulation in the world system and cycles of cultural identity.

9. Elsewhere we have discussed the oscillation between poles in capitalist identity space (Friedman, 1983, 1987). There have been previous declines of modernist identity, as in the dissolution of progressive evolutionism at the end of the last century and the emergence of culturalism, of relativism and even of primitivism. This is clear in much of the intellectual and academic debate. From the birth of cultural anthropology, of the shift from evolutionism to functionalism and relativism, and the Gemeinschaft/Gesellschaft discussions. The present decline of modernism is perhaps more definitive than previous crises, but its contours are very much the same.

10. While we might seem to be arguing that the dissolution of modernist identity trifurcates toward traditionalism, primitivism and true postmodernism, there is a certain amount of 'snapping' in the constitution of social identities that skew the space that we have outlined in such a way that it takes on the qualities of a moebius strip. Thus certain versions of marxist prophecy would connect modernism with traditionalism insofar as communism is understood as a dialectical return to the primitive community on a higher level. And in a certain sense, as has been argued by Bell (1976), the modernist project itself dissolves the social and cultural fabric to such an extent that it generates postmodernity. It is in such terms that the postmodern strategy can be seen as a continuation of the modernist project of liberation. Finally, the so-called 'reactionary modernism' (Herf, 1984) of Weimar and Nazi Germany, but also present in most of Northern Europe in the 1920s and 1930s, connects modernism and postmodernism in a singular phenomenon in which the modern project is subsumed by a racialized *Gemeinschaft* in which development is driven by a primitive will to power.

11. In other words, the four poles that define the identity space do not define the particular identities that may tend to emerge within it.

12. We have argued that, while the space is a constant defining characteristic of capitalist civilization, movement within the space depends very much upon political economic processes in the world system. Specifically we have argued that modernist identity dominates in periods of hegemonic expansion and trifurcates in periods of contraction or crisis. It might also be suggested here that the trifurcation is heavily weighted in favour of traditionalism, since the latter provides the roots and values that are necessary to maintain identity in the absence of modernism without requiring an outright rejection of the world.

Configurations of Modern Identity in the World System

13. There are certain critical prerequisites for the establishment of a modernist identity. Society must be individualized in such a way that subjects can envisage their lives in terms of a developmental scheme. There must, then, be a modern individual, not just in terms described by Dumont (1983), but a person that experiences his self as an autonomous bounded totality. This is a person who is not bound or integrated into a larger network that ascribes to him a personal identity. We expect to find such persons in regions of the world system in which community, kin and family networks have been largely dissolved by the penetration of the capitalist sector.

14. The very heterogeneous and incomplete nature of the capitalization, commodification and/or commercialization process in the world provides many a situation where the above identity space is inapplicable. But as such regions are integrated into the world system it is necessary to understand the way in which they participate in it.

15. Let us briefly delineate the essential capital flows in a world system in hegemonic crisis. The structural plight of the West and increasingly of Japan is expressive of the decentralization of capital accumulation in the world. For even if an increasing portion of total capital accumulation is in the hands of multinationals, the cycle of production and reinvestment of capital is increasingly fragmented. This can be seen in the increasing ratio of export of capital to export of manufactured goods for all of the central nations. It is a situation that leads a combined de-industrialization of the centre and a complex configuration of accumulation in the rest of the world; where

there are a number of points of intensive capital import and economic growth, such as India, Brazil, much of Southeast Asia and Southeast China, with the concomitant emergence of new patterns of peripheralization at specific and regional levels. At the same time there are areas that have become increasingly entrenched in their peripheral status, such as much of Africa. This implies that while long cycles of the world economy affect everyone, they do so in different ways. While some sectors and regions decline others ascend. And while the stock markets are all linked and crash together, their local economies are shifting positions with respect to one another.

This configuration of change provides the material logic within which the world's cultural logics find their variable expressions. While modernism declines in the West giving rise to a myriad expression of ethnicities, religious cults, and various traditionalisms, there is an apparent rise of an Eastern variant of modernism in Southeast Asia, one of its forms being neo-Confucianism. The most recent decline of the Austrian economy, the fiscal crisis of the state, increasing unemployment etc. is dissolving the social democratic modernity of that society where the return to roots has revived a traditionalism tinged with racism. Austria, as such, joins the pattern that has already emerged so strongly in France and Germany. If there is a renaissance of ethnicity in Europe as a subnational phenomenon, there is also, following the same logic, an increasing ethnification of national identities.

17. One's position in capitalist identity space is not a function of wealth, nor even of position in the world system, but rather of the direction of change in position. Brazil with its extremes of slumification is strongly modernist in outlook, while wealthy Japan in the midst of a major crisis of accumulation is already rife with antimodern cultural movements.

18. All of these remarks pertain to the modern sectors of the world system. These sectors are not identical as social spaces or even as identity spaces, even if we might argue that they are constituted of the same kinds of polarities. While the atomic self-developing individual is specific to the West unlike the more kin and group orientation of Asia, the latter too has a public sphere of abstract roles and a competitive strategy of accumulation of wealth and power, as well as a largely future and development-oriented perspective that organizes the world into a hierarchy of ranks (Nakane, 1970; Smith, 1983; DeVos, 1985; Wei-ming, 1985; Chu, 1985).

Non-modern Sectors and the Crisis of Modernity

19. We shall tentatively define the non-modern sectors of the world systems in terms of the following criteria:

a. Those populations that are not fully, nor in some cases even partially integrated into world systemic reproductive processes. By fully is meant integrated in such a way that prior kinship and community forms of reproduction have been dissolved. Integration thus implies disintegration.

b. As a concomitant to this we can suggest that such populations, even where they reproduce themselves via the world economy and are integrated into larger political units, maintain distinctly local structures of reproduction that are subsumed but not eliminated by the larger system.

c. This implies, finally, the existence of distinct models of identity and specific cultural strategies, external to and different from the capitalist space described above.

20. These criteria define an open continuum rather than a closed set. But a continuum forms an axis of variation, some of the properties of which we shall explore here.

21. For the purpose of simplification we can suggest several ideal typical populations or critical positions in the above continuum:

a. Groups that are integrated as political regions and whose resources or territory may be in demand by the larger polity, but whose processes of local reproduction are not directly articulated to a larger social network. Such are some very few Amazonian Indian societies, some of the so-called tribal minorities of Assam, Burma and other Southeast Asian states and even China.

b. Groups whose processes of local reproduction are subsumed by the larger politico-economic process, via cash cropping or specialization, systematic trade in vital socially valuable goods, labour etc., but where local social strategies of reproduction are still quite intact. This is the situation in large parts of Africa, Melanesia, West Polynesia and Asia.

c. Groups whose internal social reproduction has been dissolved by a stronger integration of the region into the larger system. Such populations live in the modern sector and reproduce themselves entirely via its relationship set. But insofar as the capitalization or integration of such populations is incomplete, they maintain numerous, if highly transformed, elements of a non-modern culture. Socialization, ghettoization and stigma combine to reinforce a network structure of interpersonal relations creating subjects that are unlike the modernist ego in their dependency on the local group, but without a viable or even conceivable strategy of local reproduction.

22. The kinds of cultural strategies characteristic of peripheral populations are closely related to their positions or the nature and degree of their integration in the global system.

a. In the first example above we are confronted by a situation where there is no real social integration but a relationship of control, conquest and potential integration. In world systemic terms, many such populations are located in areas to which capital has been exported and accumulated and which are at present expanding rapidly — Brazil, India. These are populations in danger of becoming absorbed. Their cultural identity is the outcome of identification by greater powers. This is achieved by the internalization of the identification by others. Their leaders may have been partially assimilated into the modern sector or they may quite simply be represented by western organizations. Their struggles are usually characterized as fourth world insofar as their interests are represented by such organizations. Their strategy with respect to the larger system is essentially to maintain their resource base and to continue to practise their way of life in ways that are to be self-determined.

b. The strategy implied in the second example is what might be called classically third world in the most 'negative' sense. It has been disparagingly referred to by some as the 'economy of affection' (Hyden, 1983). It is focused on the modern sector yet dominated by 'traditional' goals. It is exemplified by a strategy in which the objects of modernity are symbols of power, a power defined in traditional terms as always coming from an external source, *mana* from the world beyond, 'cargo', a sign of the fertility of the possessor of the 'exotic' wares, the very definition of social well-being. Here, modernity is subsumed by the traditional strategy itself expressive of a clan or kinship network. The cultural logic is one that appropriates modernity in terms of 'traditional' premises. The big-man stands in front of his modern western style house. His household goods and furniture are still outside since it is here that people live. Behind the house is a garage packed with refrigerators and parts, airplane motors, electrical equipment, televisions, radios, etc., all of which define his power, his capacity to fuel the network of kinship and alliance, his social fecundity and, of course, the source of his authority and control over his 'clients'. Modernity is transformed into prestige-goods and bridewealth.

c. The third kind of strategy is another more transformative version of the fourth-world model. It is practised by people on the margins of their own culture, by those who have lost their cultural identity to such an extent that they can represent it to themselves. Areas that have been integrated into the world political economy, where local social reproductive schemes have been destroyed and populations marginalized and stigmatized, such as North American Indians or Hawaiians, are populations that may maintain elements of a previous culture in the form of knowledge or in the values that are imparted in socialization. But the individuals of such populations are very much integrated as individuals into the larger system. Their marginalized status, however, itself a result of the incompleteness of the capitalization process, places them in a position in which the values of family and community loyalty, 'the crab principle', appears to prevent individual mobility in a situation where precisely those qualities of the local 'culture' are singled out for low rank.

This alternate fourth-world strategy consists in the concerted effort to re-establish a culturally unified way of life on the part of people that have lost it; the reconstruction of a socio-cultural totality as well as the reconstitution of a people (such 'ethnic' groups often show a dramatic increase in numbers). But as such culture exists in the form of text and objectified representation for such people, we might describe the strategy as one that appropriates 'tradition' in terms of modern premises. As an ideal type such a strategy would be equivalent to traditionalism. But there is a big difference here. Because such populations are not fully integrated into the world system, their identities and cultural strategies are not completely 'modern'. I would argue that due to their partial integration, there are enough elements in their socialization and local community forms to place them somewhere in the middle, able or forced to participate as individuals in the capitalist sector, yet psychologically bound by the strategy of 'kinship' affection whose goal is the maintenance of 'equality' and solidarity in the local group.

This fourth-world strategy dovetails with the earlier one in the following way. The first strategy is a defence against encroachment by the larger system, on the part of populations that maintain distinctive forms of life and social reproduction. The second strategy is an attempt to recreate such a distinctive form of life by populations that have lost it. In formal terms, the first strategy occurs in the expansive phases of hegemonic growth, while the second occurs in periods of contraction. But since the decline of the hegemony of a central power logically entails the expansion of new smaller centres, the two kinds of fourth-world strategy are bound to co-exist in time if not in space. And since the world systemic arena includes both processes, the two strategies can come together in a single political identity, however problematic, such as the World Council of Indigenous Peoples.

Discussion

23. There have been several years of debate on the questions of modernity and postmodernity, on the transformation or perhaps disintegration of modern identity. Much of the discussion has been couched in moral and political terms, often polarizing itself along the left–right axis. We have argued here for a more objectivist understanding of the crisis of modernity that places current transformations of world cultures and identities in the context of transformations of the world system, understood, not as an evolutionary totality on its way to a socialist or post-industrial world, but as a more cyclically sinister history of civilizational systems.

24. We have argued that the crisis of modernity is a phenomenon specific to the declining centres of the world system, whether this decline is reversible or not. It has been triggered as a threshold effect of the decentralization of the global accumulation of capital. The latter process generates contradictory conditions in different parts of the world. In areas of new capital concentration we expect to find centres of modernism, new expansions into previous hinterlands provoking resistance or accommodation of 'tribal' peoples and their ultimate integration as peripheries into new hegemonic spheres. In areas where peripheralization has remained the stable course of things, entailing the absence of capital accumulation and the continued existence of a matrix of non-capitalist (modern)

relations, the third world strategies discussed above have remained dominant even where they have become exceedingly involuted, as in cases like Uganda or the Central African Republic. It is not unusual that crisis in such societies still takes the form of witchcraft epidemics and millenarian reactions. In areas that have been more thoroughly capitalized, the decline of modern identity has given rise to the elaboration and restoration of former cultural identities. Where such identities contain models of total social existence including material reproduction they can be identified as fourth-world strategies to either maintain or establish a separate existence. Where such social models do not exist the strategies in question are 'ethnic', establishing cultural identities as social boundaries, and rights of access to goods and services in the larger system.

25. It is, of course, true, that from a certain perspective, we are witnessing a cultural pluralization of the world as well as what some have referred to as the globalization of culture, i.e. the formation of a single world culture. It is true that coke, tourist t-shirts and transistors have become universal, i.e. that the things and symbols of western culture have diffused into the daily lives of much of the world's peoples, even if they are made in Hong Kong. Yet, still their mode of appropriating these things is vastly different from our own. And this kind of cultural mix is not a product of the current state of the world system. It is indeed, much older than spaghetti, much older than the creole hodgepodge that we call the English language! The older use of the notions of creole and pluralism were related to situations of colonially induced ethnic differentiation maintained by exclusionary politics, so that European-imposed identities become local social realities. While virtually all cultures are plural and creole in terms of the origins of their constituents, they neither appear nor are experienced as such unless they identify themselves as such. In fact it might well be argued that the pluralist conception of the world is a distinctly western mode of apprehending the current fragmentation of the system, a confusion of our own identity space. When hegemony is strong or increasing, cultural space is similarly homogenized, spaghetti becomes Italian, a plural set of dialects becomes a national language in which cultural differences are translated into a continuum of correct to incorrect or standard to non-standard. This is the cultural content of emergent power that on a world scale, turns western cheap cloth and glass beads, then tin cans and transistors into focal points of power in the periphery. This power has gone to such extremes that certain key symbols of local

identity in the periphery have been produced in the centre. African cloth was, virtually in its entirety, made in certain European countries like Holland, a distinct pattern for every group and none of it for sale in Europe — enough indeed to fool any unsuspecting tourist. All that has, of course, changed today. Western clothing is in large part imported from the newly industrializing zones of the periphery, to say nothing of our transistors. Cultural pluralism is the western experience of the real postmodernization of the world, the ethnicization and cultural pluralization of a dehegemonizing, de-homogenizing world incapable of a formerly enforced politics of assimilation or cultural hierarchy.

26. Contrary to the purely culturalist view of world objects, we have suggested that the way to understanding the production and reproduction of culture depends on an understanding of the changing constitution of identity spaces and their concomitant strategies. And the construction of identity is, as we have tried to argue very much part of the historical dynamics of the global system.

Notes

1. Identity in western civilization consists in opposing ego to id, culture to nature. Without this opposition cultural specification becomes impossible. A specific mode of being opposed to other modes of being, a specific lifestyle, etiquette, morality cannot be constituted. The non-cultural or uncultured or uncivilized ceases to exist as an identifiable category.

2. While I use the word capitalist quite often to characterize a particular universe of identities, I would agree with Simmel (1978) that a large part of modernity as an organization of experience is dependent on the process of monetization, commodification, i.e. the penetration of abstract wealth into the network of personal relations. This is a more general phenomenon than capitalist reproduction, but the two are closely linked especially since it is only the capitalist economy that provides the possibilities of the total commodification of social life.

References

Bell, D. (1976) *The Cultural Contradictions of Capitalism*. London: Heinemann.

Chu, G. (1985) 'The Changing Concept of the Self in Contemporary China', in A.J. Marsella, G. De Vos and F. Hsu (eds) *Culture and Self: Asian and Western Perspectives*. New York: Tavistock.

De Vos, G. (1985) 'Dimensions of the Self in Japanese Culture', in A.J. Marsella, G. De Vos and F. Hsu (eds) *Culture and Self: Asian and Western Perspectives*. New York: Tavistock.

Dumont, Louis (1983) *Essais sur l'individualisme*. Paris: Seuil.

Friedman, J. (1983) 'Civilizational Cycles and the History of Primitivism', *Social Analysis* 14.

Friedman, J. (1987) 'Cultural Identity and World Process', in N. Rowlands (ed.) *Dominance and Resistance*. London: Allen & Unwin.

Herf, J. (1984) *Reactionary Modernism*. Cambridge: Cambridge University Press.

Hyden, G. (1983) *No Shortcuts to Progress: African Development Management in Perspective*. London: Heinemann.

Nakane, C. (1970) *Japanese Society*. Berkeley: California University Press.

Simmel, G. (1978) *The Philosophy of Money*. London: Routledge & Kegan Paul.

Smith, R.J. (1983) *Japanese Society: Tradition, Self and the Social Order*. Cambridge: Cambridge University Press.

Wei-Ming, T. (1985) 'Selfhood and Otherness in Confucian Thought', in A.J. Marsella, G. De Vos and F. Hsu (eds) *Culture and Self: Asian and Western Perspectives*. New York: Tavistock.

Jonathan Friedman is Professor of Anthropology at the University of Copenhagen.

Blue Velvet:
Postmodern Contradictions

Norman K. Denzin

It is a strange world, isn't it? (Sandy, in *Blue Velvet*, 1986)

There is no more fiction that life could possibly confront. (Baudrillard, 1983: 148)

The Postmodern would be that ... which searches for new presentations ... in order to impart a stronger sense of the unpresentable. (Lyotard, 1984: 81)

Introduction

The following thesis organizes my argument: contemporary films like David Lynch's *Blue Velvet* (1986) may be read as cultural statements which locate within small-town America (Lumberton, USA), all the terrors and simulated realities that Lyotard (1984) and Baudrillard (1983) see operating in the late postmodern period.[1] A reading of such films should provide a deeper under-standing of the kinds of men, women and biographical experiences the late-postmodern period makes available to its members (see Mills, 1959: 166 on this question; and Corliss, 1986, for a discussion of this film as well as *True Stories* (1986), and *Peggy Sue Got Married* (1986); *Something Wild* (1986) could also be added to this list). Such readings should serve to further clarify the various cul-tural, aesthetic and sociological meanings of the term postmodern in the late 1980s. They should also contribute to further conceptual and interpretive refinements within postmodern cultural theory (see Denzin, 1987a; Lyotard, 1984; Jameson, 1983; Featherstone, 1987a, 1987b; Elias, 1987: 223; Games, 1987). I shall, accordingly, first discuss the narrative structure of this film, and then turn to a reading of it which builds on the interpretive points to be developed below.[2] (This reading will build upon the reviews of the film in the popular culture press.) I will argue, after Grossberg (1986: 86) that 'the meaning of a text is always the site of a struggle'. And so it is

Theory, Culture & Society (SAGE, London, Newbury Park, Beverly Hills and New Delhi), Vol. 5 (1988), 461–73

with this film. Reviewers have been divided over its meanings. Robertson (1986: 11), writing in *The New York Times*, observed:

> The movie — one of the most talked about of the year, seeming to divide audiences into those who love it and find it brilliant and bizarre, and those who hate it and find it sick and disgusting — has been drawing around-the-block lines in New York for the last three weeks.

Interpretive Framework
First, films like *Blue Velvet* simultaneously display the two features of postmodernism texts that Jameson (1983: 111–113, 125) has identified. Namely an effacement of the boundaries between the past and the present (typically given in the forms of pastiche and parody), and a treatment of time which locates the viewing subject in a perpetual present. Second, these films, which I shall call late-postmodern nostalgia, bring the unpresentable (rotting, cut off ears, sexual violence, brutality, insanity, homosexuality, the degradation of women, sado-masochistic rituals, drug and alcohol abuse) in front of the viewer in ways that challenge the boundaries that ordinarily separate private and public life (Baudrillard, 1983: 130). Third, the wild sexuality and violence that these films represent signify, in the Bataille (1928) sense, modes of freedom and self-expression that the late-postmodern period is both fearful of, and drawn to at the same time.

Fourth, *Blue Velvet*, and the other films in this emerging genre, have been read as denigrating women (see McGuigan and Huck, 1986: 67). These are not pro-feminist social texts. Women are treated as traditional sexual objects, and in *Blue Velvet* the recipients of sexual and physical violence. Women are contained within one of two categories: respectable, middle-class marriage, or disrespectable, occupational and sexual categories (see Gledhill, 1978). These cultural texts maintain images of the gender stratification system that are decidedly pre-postmodern.

Fifth, these films do not just return to the past in a nostalgic sense, and bring the past into the present, as Jameson suggests. They make the past the present, but they locate terror in nostalgia for the past. The signifiers of the past (i.e. 1950s and 1960s rock and roll music) are signs of destruction. In Lyotard's sense, (1984: 81), these films wage a war on nostalgia.

Sixth, in so doing they identify two forms of nostalgia: the safe and the unsafe. By creating the comfortable illusion that adult middle-class life is connected to the past in an unbroken chain, these films argue that the rock and roll music of youth, if carried into adulthood, will lead to self-destruction and violence.

Seventh, by moving two versions of the past (the sacred and the profane) into the present, *Blue Velvet* pushes the boundaries of the present farther and farther into the future where the unreal and the hyperreal (Baudrillard, 1983) are always real, and not just possibilities.

Eighth, in the process, films like *Blue Velvet* expose and bring to the centre of safe society, the margins of the social (see Hall, 1986). These violent margins (dope fiends, sexual perverts), are now placed in small towns, next door to middle- and lower-class Americans who are attempting to live safe, respectable lives. These late postmodern films locate violence and the simulacrum, not just in Disneyland (Baudrillard, 1983), MTV or in television commercials. They locate these phenomenon within the everyday (see Featherstone, 1987b: 209) and give to the simulacram a violent turn that it never had before. It is these arguments that I shall explore in this paper. I turn now to the narrative of the film.

The Narrative
Blue Velvet's narrative is straightforward (see Ansen, 1986). It is set in Lumberton, USA. The hero, Jeffrey Beaumont, is the son of a middle-class hardware store owner who suffers a stroke as the film opens. Jeffrey, home from college for the summer, works in the store. Walking across a vacant lot he discovers a severed ear. He takes the ear to a detective and becomes involved in a mystery to discover who the ear belongs to, and how it got in the field. He is aided by the detective's sweet blond daughter, Sandy. Jeffrey and Sandy stake out a disturbed nightclub singer, Dorothy Vallens, who lives on the seventh floor of an apartment building. Jeffrey sneaks into Dorothy's apartment and hides in her closet. He is discovered by Dorothy, who commands him at knife point to strip. She begins to seduce him, but is interrupted by Frank, an obscenity-spouting, drug-inhaling, constantly drinking, local drug dealer. Jeffrey witnesses a bizarre sexual ritual between Frank and Dorothy. Dorothy is the sexual slave of Frank who has kidnapped her son and husband Don. Frank cut off Don's ear. Jeffrey is subsequently drawn into Dorothy's world of wild, sado-masochistic sexuality, and is seduced by her. At her request he beats her. Discovered by Frank, Dorothy and Jeffrey are taken to one of Frank's clubs where Frank's cronies hang out. There they confront Dean Stockwell, a 'suave',

mannequin-like nightclub singer who sings 'Sand Man' to Frank and his friends. They leave the club, and go to the edge of town where Jeffrey is beaten up and left. Jeffrey makes his way back to town to Sandy's. They go to a high school party, dance, cheek-to-cheek, like lovers. Driving home they are confronted, on the steps of Sandy's house, by a naked Dorothy, who proclaims her love to Jeffrey ('Your seed is in me'). Sandy's mother covers up Dorothy, and offers solace to a shocked Sandy. They send Dorothy off to the hospital. Jeffrey leaves for Dorothy's apartment and there he finds two dead men: Don and a corrupt policeman. Sandy's father, the detective comes, takes Jeffrey home. The film closes with Sandy and Jeffrey married, having a barbecue dinner with both sets of family relatives.

The Hegemonic/Realist Reading

How has this film been read at the hegemonic, realist level? In the following section I will examine the hegemonic readings that have been given in the 'mainline' American popular culture texts.[3] *Blue Velvet*'s morality story is simple. A young man takes on evil in the world. He succumbs to this evil, but is ultimately redeemed, and finds his place back within the safe, sexual confines of married middle-class life, with a beautiful young bride. This simple rite of passage story, however, locates all of the unpresentables in everyday life (cut off ears, murders, wild sexuality, alcohol and drug-related violence, sado-masochistic rituals) within a nostalgia for the past that includes a soundtrack full of 1950s and 1960s rock and roll songs ('Mysteries of Love', 'In Dreams', 'Blue Velvet'). These unpresentables are seen as existing next door to and just below the surface of smalltown, homespun American life.

Blue Velvet *as Parable of Sin and Redemption*

Nearly every review read the film as a coming of age parable. The following statements are representative. David Ansen, of *Newsweek* wrote: '*Blue Velvet* is a guilty parable of sin and redemption and true love in which Betty and Archie and Veronica archetypes are set loose in the hallucinatory world of the id' (Ansen, 1986: 69). Ansen continues: '*Blue Velvet* ... unfolds like a boys' adventure tale of the '40s and '50s, but it's as if a Hardy boy has wandered into a scenario devised by the Marquis de Sade.' Pauline Kael (1986: 99) of the *New Yorker* wrote:

A viewer knows intuitively that this is a coming-of-age picture — that Jeffrey's discovery of this criminal sadomasochistic network has everything to do with his father's becoming an invalid and his own new status as an adult. It's as if David Lynch were saying, 'It's a frightening world out there, and — tapping his head — in here'.

Blue Velvet *as Religious Art Portraying Evil*

The coming of age parable, connected with sin and redemption, is further elaborated by those readings which combine the sin elements within a religious text that deals with evil. James M. Wall, writing in the *Christian Century*, called it the best film of 1986 because of its sensitive probing of evil as an ugly reality in life. Wall (1987: 7) calls the film a contemporary metaphor of one of Paul's letters to the church at Rome. In his letter Paul described sinfulness as a condition of all creatures (Wall, 1987: 7). The film, Wall argues clearly communicates Paul's point that all of God's creatures are inventors of evil, disobedient to parents, foolish, faithless, heartless, and ruthless' (Romans, 1: 29–30). Still, he states that he can't recommend the film as must-seeing for everyone, because its scenes of brutality and violent sex are so realistic and ugly. Nonetheless, he compares the film to the work of the fifteenth-century artist Hieronymus Bosch (Wall, 1987: 9). Lynch's film, like Bosch's paintings, goes to the heart of a work of art: it realistically portrays the unpresentable, so as to make its point about ultimate human values. Wall's realist reading is to be contrasted to John Simon's which sees the film as pornography.

Blue Velvet *as Pornographic Cult*

Here is Simon (1986: 54):

> How long has it been since an American movie has garnered a harvest of laurels like the one being heaped on a piece of mindless junk called *Blue Velvet*? . . . True pornography, which does not pretend to be anything else, has at least a shred of honesty to recommend it; *Blue Velvet*, which pretends to be art, and is taken for it by most critics, has dishonesty and stupidity as well as grossness on its conscience.

Simon, contrary to Wall, sees the film's treatment of sadomasochism, voyeurism, latent homosexuality and fetishism as attempt to shock, titillate and sexually arouse the viewer. He sees Lynch's efforts to comment on small-town American mores as pretentious, and suggests that 'this trash' has been raved about because of a decline of intelligence on the part of those critics who write for sophisticated magazines and family newspapers (Simon, 1986: 56).

Simon goes on to criticize the film's cinematography and acting (poster colours and amateurish).

Playboy (Williamson, 1986: 25) reads the film, not so much as pornography, but as a text that continues Lynch's reputation as a builder of cult films. Focusing on the film's surreal, bizarre, hypnotic and sex-charged scenes, Williamson (1986: 25) suggests that the film 'lapses into gratuitous violence and vulgarity' and that Lynch has gone overboard 'while testing how far a maverick moviemaker can go'.

Locating Blue Velvet *within a Film Genre*
In their attempts to give the film meaning, critics have sought to locate it within a genre. As the foregoing reactions indicate, it has been called both pornographic, and a cult film. Those who call it a cult film, speak of Lynch as a director who has produced earlier cult classics: *The Elephant Man* and *Erasehead*.

Other critics (Kael, 1986: 102) have called it 'gothic', a 'comedy', 'a coming-of-age' film, and 'surrealistic'. Rabkin (1986: 53) suggests that it is 1980s *film noir* with its having 'a person getting involved with something over which he has no control'. Corliss (1986: 10) locates *Blue Velvet* within the 'small-town' films genre-tradition, and reads it as an extension of the Frank Capra movies of the 1940s.

The inability of critics to agree on what genre the film belongs to, speaks, in part, to its contradictory text and to its arresting sexual and erotic images. By locating a film within a genre, pre-established meanings can be brought to it, and it can be judged by the canons of the genre. Clearly Lynch's film resists classification. Hence it is read in multiple ways. But it is clear that at least some critics lean toward the negative (pornography) in their interpretations.

Lynch on Blue Velvet
What does Lynch say about his film?

> In a way this is still a fantasy film. It's like a dream of strange desires wrapped inside a mystery story. It's what could happen if you ran out of fantasy. (Lynch in Chute, 1986: 35)

> *Blue Velvet* is a trip beneath the surface of a small American town, but it's also a probe into the subconscious or a place where you face things that you don't normally face. (Lynch in Chute, 1986: 32)

> *Blue Velvet* a very American movie. The look of it was inspired by my childhood in Spokane, Washington. Lumberton is a real name. (Lynch in Chute, 1986: 32)

> It's like saying that once you've discovered there are heroin addicts in the world

and they're murdering people to get money, can you be happy? . . . It's a tricky question. Real ignorance is bliss. That's what *Blue Velvet* is about. (Lynch in Rabkin, 1986: 55)

Asked to locate his film with a genre, Lynch comments: 'It's not a genre film in my mind. It's *Blue Velvet* . . . .' On genre, he states, in response to the inverviewer (Rabkin, 1986: 55), who pushes him to locate the film within a category: 'You're saying it like you find a genre to fit every film into. But you don't have to obey the rules of a genre. There are many things in *Blue Velvet* that are against some sort of rules or this normal setup'. (Lynch in Rabkin, 1986: 56) Asked to discuss the meaning of his film, Lynch remarks:

> . . . it doesn't make any difference what I say. It's like digging some guy up after he has been dead for 400 years and asking him about his book. His book is what's there, and what he's going to say about it isn't going to change it . . . I think if you're really allowed to be honest . . . then it could be understood little by little at different levels and still hold true. I think that life is like that, that you can work it down lower and lower and it will always make some kind of fantastic sense. (Lynch in Rabkin, 1986: 56)

Lynch, like a reader-response theorist, locates the meaning of his film in the viewer's experiences with its text. For him the film is fantasy, a dream, an exploration of the subconscious, a study of what goes on just below the surface in American small towns.

Viewer Reactions

Viewers, as would be expected, have been divided in their reactions to the film. McGuigan and Huck (1986: 66–7) provide a sampling of these reactions.

— in Chicago two men fainted during the film.
— Outside a Los Angeles movie house, a woman who hated it got into a fight with a stranger who loved it. They settled the dispute by going back in to see it again.
— Elsewhere people have demanded their money back.
— Viewers are shocked by certain images: a severed ear, a scene of sadomichistic fetishism, a naked woman who's been beaten. Or they're repelled by the outrageously evil bad guy (Dennis Hopper) who violently inhales helium through a face mask.
— I felt like a pervert watching it.
— I wanted to wash as soon as I got out of the movie.
— I was thrilled. I was completely absorbed.
— When people hear I've seen it six times, they say I'm a sick person.
— Wow, I think I might have hated it.
— I don't know what was weirder — the movie or the people watching it.
— Its like Norman Rockwell meets Hieronymus Bosch.

A local film critic (Champaign-Urbana, Illinois) stated: 'I love it. I watched again last night. Its got everything, mystery, film noir, Hitchcock, horror, outstanding soundtrack, lighting, atmosphere, the way they changed the melodic structure of the song, "Blue Velvet," how it builds tension.'

These interpretations reflect the same contradictory reactions of the film's critics. As one viewer stated, 'You either love this film or you hate it'. Viewers connect the film's meanings back to the feelings they experienced while viewing it: perverted, dirty, sick person. I will argue below that these opposing, conflictual positions speak to contradictions and tensions in late postmodern American life. *Blue Velvet* awakens desires and fears that expose the limits of the real and the unreal in contemporary, everyday life.

Interpreting the Hegemonic Realist Readings
The following meanings of *Blue Velvet* can now be enumerated: pornography, parable of sin and redemption, like religious art, a cult film, gothic, coming-of-age film, trash, mindless junk, *film noir*, murder-mystery, small-town film, dream film, comedy, surrealism, the most important film of 1986. The many interpretations of the film speak to and support Grossberg's position that 'the meaning of a text is always the site of a struggle'.

At the hegemonic, realist (and negotiated) levels, two clusters of consensual meanings and interpretations emerge: The film is either high cinematic art or it is trash. It is a coming-of-age film and in its portrayal of evil, violence and wild sexuality it leans toward an expansion of classic 1940's small-town films, or it is perversion and pornography, if not trash.

These two clusters of hegemonic meaning speak, of course, to tensions within the film; but more importantly, they speak to the postmodern desire to see evil, while being repulsed by it. The morally conservative readings thus reify the culture's desire to repress the sexual and violent themes of postmodern life. The morally liberal readings valorize the film's aesthetic qualities, and locate it within the classic film tradition of the 1940s, and earlier religious, symbolic art. As the film evokes these contradictory readings its cult status is elevated. Viewers continue to be drawn to it. This is so because of the opposing emotional meanings that are evoked by its symbolism and by these earlier cultural interpretations. With few exceptions (McGuigan and Huck, 1986) the dominant cultural readings did not dwell on the violent treatment of women in the film's text.

Reading *Blue Velvet* as a Contradictory Postmodern Text
I return now to the eight interpretive points developed above: I will show how this film is pastiche, and parody, an effacement of the boundaries between the past and the present, a presentation of the unpresentable, derogatory of women, an assault on nostalgia, and a threat to safe, middle-class life. The negative and contradictory readings that postmodern texts receive can be explained, in part, by these features.

Pastiche and Parody, Past and Present
From its opening scenes, which begin with a clear blue sky, and bright, blooming red roses waving in front of a white picket fence, to a classic 1940's fire truck with a dalmation dog on the fender, slowly gliding down a tree-lined street, and the sound track of Bobby Vinton singing 'She wore Blue Velvet' the movie's hyperrealism signals to the reader that this film is going to be a parody of small-town, 1940s movies. Within four scenes the film shows cars from the 1950s, 1960s and 1980s moving along Lumberton's streets. Sophisticated 1980's computerized medical equipment is shown in a late 1940's hospital room, and a scene from a 1950's movie flashes across a black and white TV screen. High school students are shown in dress which spans three decades. This is a film which evokes, mocks, yet lends quasi-reverence for the icons of the past, while it places them in the present. The film has effaced the boundaries between the past and the present. Jeffrey, Sandy, Dorothy and Frank move through the film, as if they were dreaming.

The Unpresentable
Within three minutes Jeffrey has discovered the rotting ear in a vacant lot. The viewer is taken inside the ear. It fills the screen. Strange, roaring sounds are heard. In an even earlier scene Lynch takes the viewer into a front lawn where blades of grass 'as tall as redwood trees' (Kael, 1986: 99) are teeming with big black insects. The film quickly moves from this violence in nature, to the sado-masochistic rituals between Frank and Dorothy and Dorothy and Jeffrey described earlier. Violence, and the unpresentable, Lynch seems to be suggesting, are everywhere, not only in nature, but next door to the middle-class homes in Lumberton, USA.

Women

Dorothy's degradation is used as a vehicle for Jeffrey's sexual education. Sandy's pure sexuality is contrasted to Dorothy's decadence and her sick desire to be abused. By locating women within these opposing identities and by unglamorously photographing Dorothy in her nude scenes Lynch symbolically and simultaneously makes his film pro- and anti-woman. In so doing he parodies the 'playboy' women of soft pornography, yet sustains a traditional view of the 'pure' woman in American life. His treatment of women contains all the contradictions toward women that the decade of the 1980s has produced.

Nostalgia

Earlier I argued that *Blue Velvet* locates two forms of nostalgia, the safe and the unsafe and that the rock and roll music of the film signifies violence and destruction. Lynch parodies 1950's rock and roll in the character of Dean Stockwell, suggesting that persons risk becoming like Stockwell (and Frank) if they stay too long within this music. Rock and roll loses its youthful innocence in Lynch's film. But by framing the film with rock's sounds he appeals to a 1980's adult generation that still venerates the music of its adolescence. It is as if Lynch were saying this music is not as innocent as it appears to be. But more is involved. By locating the sexual sounds of rock at the centre of his film Lynch is arguing that the central illusions of rock and roll (sexuality, true love) have to be lived out before persons can find their true romantic and sexual identity in life.

Consider the lyrics from the Roy Orbison song, 'In Dreams', which is sung in the film's most violent scenes:

> A candy-colored clown they call the sandman.
> Tiptoes to my room every night
> just to sprinkle stardust and whisper
> 'Go to sleep. Everything is all right.'
> In dreams I walk with you
> In dreams I talk to you
> In dreams you're mine all of the time
> Forever in dreams.

Jeffrey lives out his wildest sexual dreams with Dorothy, only to return to Sandy at the end of the film, inside the dreams the sandman sings.

Sandy dreams too. Hers is the dream of a world that was dark 'because there weren't any robins, but then thousands of robins were set free and there was the blinding light of love'. Sandy relates this dream to Jeffrey when they are parked in front of a church, an organ plays in the background. Hearing her dream Jeffrey replies, 'You're a neat girl, Sandy'.

The film ends with a robin flying to the window sill of the family kitchen. Sandy looks up at the robin, it has a worm in its beak. Lynch closes his film, like he opened it, with nature and its violence in front of the viewer.

The Postmodern Terrain

Postmodern cultural texts, like *Blue Velvet* echo and reproduce the tensions and contradictions that define the late 1980s. These texts locate strange, eclectic, violent, timeless worlds in the present. They make fun of the past as they keep it alive. They search for new ways to present the unpresentable, so as to break down the barriers that keep the profane out of the everyday. However, they take conservative political stances, while they valorize, and exploit the radical social margins of society. Nothing escapes the postmodern eye. But this eye, its visions and its voices, is unrelenting in its unwillingness to give up the past in the name of the future. The postmodern eye looks fearfully into the future and it sees technology, uncontrolled sexual violence, universally corrupt political systems. Confronting this vision, it attempts to find safe regions of escape in the fantasies and nostalgia of the past. Dreams are the postmodern solution to life in the present.

More than the future is looked into. It is the everyday that has become the subject matter of these postmodern nostalgia films. Small-town, any-town, USA is no longer safe. The fantasies of the past have become realities in the present. These realities are now everywhere. By showing this, these films make the global village even smaller. It is now called Lumberton. 'The world that dreams are made of. Our town' (Corliss, 1986: 17). Our town is filled with good people like Jeffrey Baumount and Sandy. In Lumberton their dreams, good and bad, come true. And in this fairytale town individuals meet and confront problems that old-fashioned law and order policemen still help them resolve.

The postmodern landscape and its people are filled with hope. Schizophrenic in their visions, these people know that in the end everything will turn out all right. And it does. Villains die, or are reformed. Male heroes transgress moral boundaries but come back home to mother and father. In the end these films build their stories around individuals and their fantasies. In so doing they keep alive the middle-class myth of the individual. The postmodern person still confronts the world through the lens of a nineteenth- and early twentieth-century political ideology. Perhaps this is the chief function of the 1980's nostalgia film. As the world political system turns ever more violent and conservative, the need for cultural texts which sustain the key elements of a conservative political economy increases. It seems that postmodern individuals want films like *Blue Velvet* for in them they can have their sex, their myths, their violence and their politics, all at the same time.

Notes

1. *Blue Velvet* was, according to some critics McGuigan and Huck (1986), the most talked about American film in 1986. Lynch was nominated for an academy award as best director.

2. I will, following Gledhill (1978/1985) and Hall (1980), develop hegemonic, negotiated and oppositional readings of this text. Elsewhere (Denzin, 1987b), following Gledhill (1978) I have combined these three forms of interpretation into the realist (hegemonic and negotiated) and the subversive (oppositional) categories. I will argue against an intentionist reading of the text (Derrida, 1976), in favour of a reader-response framework (see Dolby-Stahl, 1985 for a review), and thus contrast my readings to Lynch's meanings of his movie, which are themselves open-ended and inconclusive (see Chute, 1986; Rabkin, 1986).

3. These texts include *Newsweek*, *The New Yorker*, *The New York Times*, *New York*, *Christain Century*, *Dissent*, *Fangoria*, *National Review*, *Playboy* and the more specialized cinema text, *Film Comment*.

References

Ansen, David (1986) 'Stranger Than Paradise', review of *Blue Velvet*, *Newsweek* 108 (September 15): 69.

Bataille, Georges (1928, 1982) *The Story of Eye*. New York: Berkeley Books.

Baudrillard, Jean (1983) *Simulations*. New York: Semiotext(e). Foreign Agent Press.

Chute, David (1986) 'Out to Lynch', *Film Comment* 22 (September/October): 32–5.

Corliss, Richard (1986) 'Our Town: George Bailey Meets "True, Blue and Peggy Sue"', *Film Comment* 22 (November/December): 9–17.

Denzin, Norman. K. (1986) 'Postmodern Social Theory', *Sociological Theory* 4 (Fall): 194–204.

Denzin, Norman K. (1987a) 'On Semiotics and Symbolic Interactionism', *Symbolic Interaction* 10(1): 1–19.

Denzin, Norman K. (1987b) 'Reading Tender Mercies: Two Interpretations', Presented to the 1987 Annual Spring Symposium of the Society for the Study of Symbolic Interaction, 8 May, Urbana, Illinois.

Derrida, J. (1976) *07 Grammatology*. Chicago: University of Chicago Press.

Dolby-Stahl, Sandra K. (1985) 'A Literary Folkloristic Methodology for the Study of Meaning in Personal Narrative', *Journal of Folklore Research* 22 (January): 45–69.

Elias, Norbert (1987) 'The Retreat of Sociologists into the Present', *Theory, Culture & Society* 4(4): 223–47.

Featherstone, Mike (1987a) 'Lifestyle and Consumer Culture', *Theory, Culture & Society* 4(1): 55–70.

Featherstone, Mike (1987b) 'Norbert Elias and Figurational Sociology: Some Prefatory Remarks', *Theory, Culture & Society* 4(4): 197–211.

Games, Stephen (1987) 'Post-Modern Disagreements', *The Times Literary Supplement* 4,413 (30 October-5 September): 1194.

Gledhill, Christine (1978) 'Klute: Part I: A Contemporary Film Noir and Feminist Criticism', in E. Ann Kaplan (ed.) *Women in Film Noir*. London: British Film Institute.

Gledhill, Christine (1978/1985) 'Recent Developments in Feminist Criticism', in G. Mast and M. Cohen (eds) *Film Theory and Criticism* 3/e. New York: Oxford University Press. (Originally published in *Quarterly Review of Film Studies*, 1978.)

Grossberg, Lawrence (1986) 'Reply to the Critics', *Critical Studies in Mass Communication* 3: 86–95.

Hall, Stuart (1980) 'Encoding/decoding', in S. Hall, D. Hobson, A. Lowe and P. Willis (eds) *Culture, Media, Language*. London: Hutchinson.

Hall, Stuart (1986) 'History, Politics and Postmodernism: Stuart Hall and Cultural Studies', Interview with Lawrence Grossberg, *Journal of Communication Inquiry* 10 (summer): 61–77.

Jameson, Frederic (1983) 'Postmodernism and Consumer Culture', in Hal Foster (ed.) *The Anti-Aesthetic: Essays on Postmodern Culture*. Port Townsend, WA: Bay Press.

Kael, Pauline (1986) 'Current Cinema: Out There and In Here: Review of *Blue Velvet*', *The New Yorker* 52 (22 September): 99–103.

Lyotard, Jean François (1984) *The Postmodern Condition: A Report on Knowledge*. Minneapolis: University of Minnesota Press.

McGuigan, Cathleen and Huck Janet (1986) 'Black and Blue Is Beautiful? Review of *Blue Velvet*', *Newsweek* 108 (27 October): 65–7.

Mills, C. Wright (1959) *The Sociological Imagination*. New York: Oxford University Press.

Rabkin, William (1986) 'Deciphering *Blue Velvet*: Interview with David Lynch', *Fangoria* 58 (October): 52–6.

Robertson, Nan (1986) 'The All-American Guy Behind Blue Velvet', *The New York Times* Saturday, (11 October): 11.

Romans 1: 29–30.

Simon, John (1986) 'Neat Trick', *National Review* 38 (7 November): 54–6.

Wall, John M. (1986) 'The Best Film of 1986: Probing The Depths of Evil', *Christian Century* 60 (7–14 January): 7–9.

Williamson, Bruce (1986) 'Movies: Review of *Blue Velvet*', *Playboy* 37 (December): 25.

Norman K. Denzin is Professor of Sociology at the University of Illinois, Urbana-Champaign. His latest books include *On Understanding Emotion* (Jossey-Bass) and *The Alcoholic Self* (Sage).

SOCIAL PROBLEMS

Established in 1953, SOCIAL PROBLEMS is one of the most widely read and highly regarded journals in the social sciences. As a general journal of research and theory, it features work covering a wide range of topics, methods, and theoretical approaches to the study of social problems. Recent issues include articles on political scandals, television violence and violent crime, mental illness among the homeless, the anti-nuclear power movement, abuse of the elderly, and the origins of sexual psychopath laws. Occasionally, entire issues of the journal are devoted to important themes such as feminist thought and women's problems or critical perspectives on social problems and criminological theory. Throughout its history, the journal's editors have emphasized both scholarly excellence and stylistic clarity in publishing work that will be of interest to a broad readership.

**PUBLISHED BY THE UNIVERSITY OF CALIFORNIA PRESS
FOR THE SOCIETY FOR THE STUDY OF SOCIAL PROBLEMS**

For subscription/membership information, contact:
University of California Press Journals
2120 Berkeley Way
Berkeley, California 94720

Modernity, Postmodernity and the City

Philip Cooke

Modernity and Postmodernity: a Debate

In his remarkable book, Berman (1983) seeks to rethink the culture of capitalism through the historical experience of *modernity*. Modernity is presented as a mediating concept linking two related transformative processes. The first of these is the objective process of *modernization*, a diverse unity of socioeconomic changes generated by scientific and technological discoveries and innovations, industrial upheavals, population movements, urbanization, the formation of national states and mass political movements, all driven by the expanding capitalist world market. The second is the cultural vision which attends, in contradictory form, this unleashing of change — *modernism* — the infinite variety of ideas derived from the overturning of an old order. These ideas make men and women subjects and objects of modernization but, in turn, give them powers to change the relationships that are transforming them. This transformation of individuals through a heightening of human powers and a broadening of experience links back conceptually from the subjective to the objective through the shared concept of *development*; self-development and economic development. Modernity is the experience of the economic process and the cultural vision.

When does modernity begin? This is where Berman's grand sweep approach to historiography begins to raise questions in the minds of his critics. He says it begins around 1500 with the emergence of a recognizable, proto-capitalist system of world trade and the beginnings of expansion in some European national markets. But until 1790 or so the perception of change lacked any common vocabulary in which it could be discussed. Modernism per se he dates thereafter from the emergence of literary and artistic culture in which the contradictions of the now dominant mode of production and its transformations of the material and spiritual world are both celebrated and denounced. Goethe and Baudelaire writing

Theory, Culture & Society (SAGE, London, Newbury Park, Beverly Hills and New Delhi), Vol. 5 (1988), 475–92

respectively of Faust 'unbinding the self in binding back the sea' (Berman, 1983: 24) and of the new experience both liberating and frightening, of the city technology of Paris forcing changes in older habits of bodily perception, are taken as particular symbols of modernism, the cultural expression of the experience of modernity. As modernity develops in art, music and architecture he shows how the contradictions of modernity cut across political left and right opinion, e.g. Marcuse and Leavis condemned modernity as 'an iron cage of conformity', 'a spiritual wilderness of populations bleached of organic community' (Anderson, 1984) while Marinetti, Corbusier, Buckminster Fuller and McLuhan celebrated it for its machine-built excitement and technological daring.

Modernity is, according to Berman a mode of spatial and temporal experience which promises adventure and self-transformation while threatening to destroy the familiar. It bisects geographic, ethnic, class, religious and ideological boundaries, uniting as it disunites such bases of collective identity. And this leads to the ultimate expression of the insecurity which modernity entails, the question of how, if all new social relations become redundant amid the flood of modernity before they take more permanent form, can the ideals of communal solidarity and mutual aid be kept alive? His answer is a 'back to the futureish' calling up of the tradition of nineteenth-century visions of modernism to create the renewed, communal modernisms of the twenty-first century, an approach shared, incidentally, with Raymond Williams in *Towards 2000* (Williams, 1983) though in other respects the books are very different.

Criticism of Berman's thesis tends to be sympathetic and to remain on the terrain of debate which his work has created. In the most thorough of assessments (Anderson, 1984) three important critical points are made which help to hone Berman's argument, lay the foundations for a sharper theorization of modernity and lead to the development of a concept of *postmodernism* (for an alternative theorization, see Lyotard, 1984).

The first of Anderson's criticisms is of Berman's individualistic approach, especially in its emphasis on the psychology of subjectivity under the experience of modernity. And, while accepting the validity of the discussion of modernization as a structural unity of processes, he concludes that the book lacks a concept of societal (i.e. class) order and movement, of the tension of political struggle. This he blames partly on a tendency of many writers on modernity to equate it with technology and leave out the people who produce and consume it. But he also questions Berman's interpretation of Marxian theory of capitalist development. This Berman conceives as a planar process exemplified by the ever-expanding circle of the world market. In *Grundrisse* (Marx, 1973), Anderson argues, capitalist development is seen rather as a parabola with decline following the achievement of the highest flowering of the productive forces, a point also coinciding with the richest development of the individual. Berman's planar, undifferentiated, effectively unperiodized, theory of modernization obscures crucial aspects of the trajectory of capitalism — competitive, monopoly, global — which, argues Anderson, have important implications for changes within modernism, and hence the experience of modernity. On this point, Anderson questions Berman's equation of modernism with the early nineteenth-century onset of competitive capitalism, arguing that modernism proper, especially as expressed in art, is mainly to be seen as a product of the twentieth century not before.

Anderson's second point is that once modernism is treated in this way it is striking how *geographically* uneven its distribution actually is. Even in Europe and the developed West major societies, notably England and the Scandinavian countries scarcely generated sustained modernist movements whereas Germany, Italy, France, Russia and America, even the Netherlands did. Although offering no explanation for this, and probably underestimating — for England anyway — some not insignificant later efflorescences, the undoubted unevenness of the development of modernism in countries which were otherwise quite well *modernized* undermines Berman's thesis somewhat.

Finally, Anderson criticizes Berman's conception of the homogeneousness of the modernist cultural experience. What he calls modernism is actually a congeries of movements which are quite heterogeneous — symbolism, expressionism, cubism, futurism, constructivism, surrealism and so on, are diverse and often mutually contradictory. It is Berman's generally planar thinking in respect of modernism which leads him, erroneously in Anderson's view, to look backwards to the individual production of nineteenth-century visions of the future and at modernism as a constantly renewable classical spirit.

Anderson's own alternative anatomization of modernity rests on an analysis which recognizes:

(i)   a highly formalised *academicism* in the arts in states dominated by aristocratic, landowning classes.

(ii)   the novel emergence in these countries of new technologies such as telephone, radio, automobiles and aircraft in the absence of the social conditions for mass-consumption of such technologies.

(iii) the 'imaginitive proximity' of social revolution.

So, rebellious cultural forms taking stimulus from new technologies could confront politically archaic structures and have their 'revolutions' against such cultural bases as bourgeois democracy was gradually replacing them politically. He goes on to argue that these three coordinates were snapped post-World War II by the generalized ascendancy of Fordism in Western Europe, after its rise in the USA, embodying as it did a technology which consolidated a stable, industrial capitalist civilization whose objects lacked the depth and psychic energy which, for example, surrealism had earlier found in juxtaposed commodity forms (Jameson, 1971: 96). Interesting though Anderson's analysis is, however, it too falls into the trap he earlier identified as ensnaring most writers on modernism, of equating it with new technology — in Anderson's case it is both product and process technology which are predominant in the use of 'Fordism' as a mode of discourse to theorize postwar production and consumption relations in Europe.

Nonetheless, Anderson usefully sees a cultural break setting in during the immediate postwar decades and this is taken up in a development of the debate beyond modernity to *postmodernism* (Jameson, 1984). Jameson's paper relies on an analysis of space and, in particular, of city planning and development to assist his definition of postmodernism. This echoes Berman's approach to defining modernity through accounts of early modern Paris, Petersburg and modern New York in his book. Much of Jameson's thesis derives from his interleaving of theories of the development of late capitalism and of the built form and social relations of the contemporary city. The key signifier in this debate is the Los Angeles Bonaventure Centre, an icon of postmodernist development along with the Peachtree Development in Atlanta, the Easton Centre, Toronto and Beaubourg in Paris. To these can be added some of the new architecture of central London, notably in the City as exemplified by Rogers' Lloyds Insurance building, the Broadgate complex and proposals to develop enormous towers in the eastward extension of London's financial centre into Canary Wharf and Docklands. The style is also represented in new developments in Hong Kong such as the Four Exchanges and the Hong Kong and Shanghai Bank, Canada in downtown Vancouver and the Edmonton Mall, and in American cities such as Detroit, Denver and Dallas. It takes a monumental domestic form in Ricardo Bofill's buildings in Paris and Montpellier.

So what is the style? Jameson's argument is that the core of postmodernism comes from debates within architecture and the production of the built environment, and is founded on the critique of high modernism or the International Style as represented in the work of Frank Lloyd Wright, Corbusier and Mies Van Der Rohe. This style has now been negatively associated with the destruction of traditional city forms and older, neighbourhood cultures. By contrast, postmodernism presents itself as *aesthetic populism*, symbolized in the work of one of its leading exponents, Robert Venturi and his book *Learning from Las Vegas*. Postmodernism blurs the frontier between high and mass culture and embodies many aspects of the so-called mass-production 'Culture Industry' despised by cultural gatekeepers of the right and left, from Leavis to Adorno. Postmodernism is imbued with the spirit of airport-lounge 'paraliterature', soap operas and advertising. However, though deliberately depthless, the form is not without its connections to deeper structures, argues Jameson. He rejects arguments which equate postmodernism with Daniel Bell's 'postindustrial society' or with even more superficial notions of 'information', 'electronic' or 'high technology' society, each of which seeks to show how the new social form has escaped from the constraints of classic capitalism. On the contrary, Jameson sees postmodernism as equated with Mandel's (1975) third stage in the evolution of capitalism, the 'purer' stage of Late (or Global) Capitalism, following on from its Competitive and Monopoly stages. Modernism, argues Jameson, enshrouded Monopoly Capitalism as Postmodernism envelops Global Capitalism.

Unlike Berman, though, Jameson sees postmodernism as more than just a homogeneous and homogenizing style, it is what he calls a 'cultural dominant, allowing for the presence and coexistence of a range of very different, yet subordinate features' (Jameson, 1984: 56). It is represented in the city's built form particularly clearly because architecture and city planning are tightly bound to the economic sphere of land values, on the one hand, and the patronage of multinational business, on the other.

Summarizing then, Jameson conceives the features of postmodernism to be: a new depthlessness based on the culture of the TV image; a weakening of historicity in the face of new, speeded-up forms of private temporality; a reverence towards 'new technology' as a key emblem of the new world economic system; and a change in the lived experience of built space itself, domination and disorientation being major intended effects. We do not, continues Jameson, possess the perceptual equipment, to match this new *hyperspace* in built environments having the professed aim to be total spaces, complete worlds, miniature cities supplying a new mode in which individuals congregate, *the hypercrowd*.

In such developments, the mirror-glass skins of the buildings repel the city outside just as reflector sunglasses convey a relationship of aggression/passivity between wearer and observer. In Los Angeles, Dallas, Atlanta and other hyperspace locales the complexes themselves reveal only distorted images of everything around them. Within the hyperspaces elevators and escalators conduct the subject on alarming vertical journeys, intentionally depriving the individual of the capacity freely to find his or her way about. Jameson conceives this induced disorientation as a metaphor 'for the incapacity of our minds, at present, to map the great global multinational and decentred communicational network in which we find ourselves caught as individual subjects' (Jameson, 1984: 84). He ends by calling for a new form of cognitive mapping to match these new global and local hyperspaces. He takes a lead from Kevin Lynch's (1960) approach to decoding space through a sort of 'nautical itinerary'. Lynch's spatial 'edges' and 'nodes' help link imagined and real conditions of existence in a manner Jameson sees as sensitive to the poststructuralist insight that there can be no true maps, no congruence between the fluidity of the world and the static system of concepts we lay over it (Dews, 1986).

In a critical response to this analysis of postmodernism Davis (1985) seeks, as with Anderson's response to Berman, to refine the conceptualization rather than fundamentally overturn it. He makes three critical refinements.

First, he takes Jameson to task for failing, analytically, to separate the concept of postmodernism from the experience of it, in the way that Berman did in his treatise on modernity. This leaves Jameson open to the charge of conflating subject and object. Jameson's analysis is thus held to require the Bermanesque distinction between the experience of *postmodernity* and the cultural vision of *postmodernism* to be analytically workable. However, to complete the triad, the economic process of *postmodernization* clearly should also be included, though Davis doesn't do so (for an attempt to specify it see Cooke, 1986).

Secondly, Jameson's equation of postmodernism with Mandel's conception of late capitalism is seen as unnecessarily reductionist. Moreover, the functional aesthetic of what Mandel talked and wrote of as late capitalism (circa 1968–73) was more the dying gasp of High Modernism or the International Style, as represented in New York's World Trade Centre or the Sears Building, than post-modernism. In passing, this seems an equally reductionist comment from Davis, albeit with a better chronology.

This, in a sense, undermines the force of Davis' last point which is that Jameson should have sought to establish the constitutive rela-tionships between a postmodernist ethic, a new technology of re-production rather than production and the contemporary form of multinational capitalism, since he doesn't do that satisfactorily him-self. Davis' alternative attempt to relate postmodernism to the stage of capitalist development is two-dimensional. It is to be interpreted in terms of

(i) the rise of new international rentier circuits in the current crises phase of capitalism (e.g. foreign money rushing into the US to take advantage of Reaganomic interest rates);
(ii) the abandonment of the ideal of urban reform, part of a new class polarization in the USA.

But it is not clear why, from the interaction of these two socio-political forces, a new aesthetic in the built form of the city should have emerged. In other words there is no satisfactory *cultural* underpinning to Davis' more sophisticated reading of the rise of postmodernism. And this need have no necessarily economic causa-tion. Rather, if Anderson's (1984) three-dimensional analysis is deployed in postmodernist guise, we would have to take seriously into account the existence of a hegemonic academicism around modernism itself, and the challenge to that bloc of interests mounted from within e.g. Philip Johnston's AT+T building with its Chippendale pediment, or without, e.g. Michael Graves' Portland (Oregon) Public Services Building or Venturi's celebration of Las Vegas.

Postmodernism needs to be understood as a deformed critique of the elitism of High Modernism, buttressed by the popular perception that Miesian 'stumps' and Corbusien towers have destroyed community and comfortable urbanity. It involves a certain 'decentring' (Derrida, 1978: 280) of culture away from the High Modernist aesthetes towards a more popular definition of culture 'as seen on TV'. Hence buildings as chocolate boxes (Graves), hotel lobbies as Cape Canaveral (Portman), skyscrapers as Chippendale furniture (Johnson), although the last-mentioned has obvious elite appeal, too.

Postmodernization and Social Space

If we accept that the spirit of postmodernism inhabits a socioeconomic process of postmodernization, what are some of the key characteristics of the latter and what is the nature of the experience of postmodernity?

In a previous paper (Cooke, 1986) I argued that a definite break has occurred, observably in the 1980s but prefiguratively from say 1975, in the socioeconomic dynamics of the UK, and to varying degrees in other OECD economies (Albertsen, 1986). The present can be contrasted with the 1945–75 period which I call the 'modernization' era of, specifically, UK capitalism (see also Massey, 1984). Modernization consisted in the following realities: the perceived moral superiority of state intervention over market domination in key areas of social and economic life, expressed in the widespread provision of social housing, a policy of taking work to the workers over wage-cost equalization through migration, and a widespread socialization of both the basic production industries and the necessary conditions for social reproduction. Despite the arguments of Aglietta (1978), Lipietz (1982), Andersen (1984) and Davis (1985) I do not think this modernization era equates with the triumph of Fordism *in the UK*, since neither full-blooded mass production nor mass consumption as modes of regulation on the American pattern took root in the UK to even the same extent that they did in, say, Italy (e.g. FIAT vis à vis Turin). The coupling of Keynes and Beveridge in Britain produced a model of regulation more akin to that of Scandinavia than Detroit.

I argue further that modernization entailed its own 'spatial paradigm' in both a generalized sense and in the sense that particularly representative kinds of socioeconomic space were conserved or created: the three main ones being the older Victorian industrial areas which were not simply allowed to die as market imperatives would have dictated; the New Towns and Expanded Towns which were developed as emblems of the quest for 'classless egalitarianism'; and the peripheral suburban and inner city public housing schemes. These locales express the transient ascendancy of the dynamic social strata of the time, namely the skilled and semi-skilled Labour-voting working class. In a more generalized sense the socio-spatial paradigm of modernization included:

(i)   the relatively even geographical spread to the periphery, semi-periphery and suburbs of modernization processes
(ii)   the partial convergence in income and unemployment indices between the classes and the regions
(iii) a characteristic posture towards producing standardized products for volume markets, aiming for economies of scale
(iv) economic development in close proximity to new 'collective consumption' environments
(v)   a characteristic demand for skilled and semi-skilled labour to fill secure, 'lifetime', occupations.

Postmodernization, as I term it, has been constructed as both an ideology and a series of practices, with specific spatially paradigmatic effects, out of the failure of modernization to regenerate the UK economy. The principles underlying postmodernization include: the appeal to unadorned market relations as the source of economic success, the rolling back of the 'nanny-state' with its too comforting disposition towards the 'lame ducks' of society and economy, the weakening of established solidarities in the workplace and the elevation of the private over the public sphere in matters of cultural and social provision. Its socio-spatial form consists in:

(i)   a markedly uneven spread of postmodernization characteristics (e.g. the emergence of a serious North–South division)
(ii)   the empirical divergence of income and unemployment indices between the classes and the regions
(iii) production disposed towards customized output, for niche markets aiming for economies of 'scope' (i.e. variety)
(iv) economic development occurring in areas of privatized consumption (the outer-metropolitan 'sunbelt')
(v)   labour market opportunities limited and insecure — e.g. the growth of casualization, part-time working, informal activity.

The locales in which the postmodern socio-spatial paradigm is most pronounced are mostly, though not exclusively Southern, small-to-medium tentacles of London: Guildford, Aldershot, Basingstoke, Winchester and Southampton (M3 axis); Slough, Reading, Newbury and Swindon (M4 axis); and Hertford, Harlow, Cambridge and Newmarket (M11 axis). Elsewhere, 'southern' towns in the North include successes such as Chester, York, Lincoln and Lancaster, post-Roman and postmodern. All of these localities owe their current prosperity to the possession of industries embodying the technologically most advanced social relations and methods of production, or to the fact that they have strong military and civilian high technology producing industries, or finally, that they are centres of the burgeoning producer services industries (banking, finance, insurance, business services, R & D).

As such, these are the spaces socially dominated by the most dynamic strata of the present epoch, the 'service class' (Abercrombie and Urry, 1983). This class, consisting of employers, managers and professionals grew in number by 475,000 between 1971 and 1981 (Population Census) and in 1981 constituted 13.2 percent of the workforce compared with 11.0 percent in 1971. In 1982 87 percent were owner-occupiers of housing, 85 percent had central heating, 22 percent had private medical insurance, 25 percent were smokers, 37 percent were heads of two-car households and 17 percent owned dishwashers. The equivalent percentages for semi-skilled manual workers were 35 percent, 44 percent, two percent, 41 percent, seven percent and one percent (Thrift, 1987).

To exemplify the spatial unevenness in the growth of this class between representative 'North' and 'South' localities from 1971 to 1981, in 'Northern' Tyne and Wear County the change was −2.1 percent whereas in 'Southern' Berkshire it was +3.5 percent compared with a Great Britain average of +1.4 percent (Thrift, 1987). As the service class has grown so the working class has declined. The percentage of males in skilled, semi-skilled and unskilled manual work fell from 61.7 percent in 1971 to 56.3 percent in 1981 while that of females fell from 43.4 percent to 36.5 percent during the same period. Unemployment has, of course risen everywhere but the gap in unemployment levels between South and North, which had reduced to 32 percent by 1971, had widened to 59 percent by 1984 (Cooke, 1986). Nevertheless, within that prospering South, Greater London has a concentration of over 400,000 unemployed and local concentrations of unemployment as high as those found in the North.

This, then, is the sociological profile of the postmodern era, the development of an hourglass shape to the social structure with a burgeoning service class, an attenuating working class and a burgeoning underclass of unemployed, subemployed and the 'waged poor' of part-time and/or casualized labour, classically found in fast food outlets and service stations.

The picture portrayed here for the UK echoes that presented for the USA by Davis (1984; 1985). He talks of the spirit of postmodernism revolting against the functionalist 'use-value domination' of High Modernism with a jokiness that produces 'a package of standardised space gift-wrapped to the clients' taste' (Davis, 1985: 110). It is made possible by the flood of oil rents, Third World debt, military outlays and the global flight of capital to the haven of the US. This, in turn, has produced what he calls a hypertrophic expansion of producer services employment, itself a morbid symptom of financial overaccumulation. Moreover, in combination with the restructuring of the relations of production as represented by the processes of postmodernization he concludes, against Jameson (1984) that postmodernism is not to be equated with a new stage of capitalist development but rather a return to a sort of primitive accumulation based, in part, upon the superexploitation of the urban proletariat.

The postmodernist built form becomes comprehensible in the socioeconomic context of postmodernization, class polarization, labour over-supply, capital over-accumulation and the emergence of what Davis (1984) refers to as *overconsumptionism*. This derives from the deepening and widening of the internal economic base of the USA in capitalist terms, especially through the expansion of increasingly 'qualified' high-wage jobs, and the spreading of development into the Sunbelt. The continued growth of the nouveau riche strata with the enlargement of supervisory servicing occupations in the multinational headquarters, banks, research consultancies, software houses and so on, has stimulated a massive secondary economic demand in services from private health care to fast food. And in its wake a Rightward shift in political culture based on the desire to protect highly-priced property and keep cheap labour available to service the demands of overconsumption. The postmodernist towers are, in such a context, fortresses protecting the new rich from the new poor whom they nevertheless need, but at arms' length. Thus the hyperspaces to which access by pedestrians is all but impossible become comprehensible. And the metaphor is completed in the later styles to be found in construction in Manhattan where new towers are coned and crenellated, and in one case surrounded by a moat and provided with drawbridges (Davis, 1985).

Two Brief Excursions: Los Angeles and London

Does postmodernism signify the revival of 'urbanity' as a distinctive concept, following a decade or more in which its differences from non-urbanity appeared to have become occluded (see Paris, 1983)? Perhaps only in this sense is postmodernism reviving a distinctive urbanity: the centres from which the communicative networks of global capitalism and its information systems (not excluding conferences, conventions, symposia and the like) are controlled, and those from which national and international populations are surveilled, the places where hyperincomes are earned, the areas which provide the cheap labour to service corporate overconsumption (waiters, drivers, cleaners, shop assistants, hotel staff, security guards, etc.), and especially the buildings in which these activities take place, are concentrated in relatively tightly-defined, not necessarily centralized spaces. Around these spaces may well be ethnic enclaves, dreadful enclosures (Damer, 1974) and decaying bunkers of collective consumption, the juxtaposition of opposites expressing a heightened semiology of urbanity under capitalism. Castells' (1977) analysis of the way ideology structures space through *legitimation* — the making of particular interests appear general ones — and *communication* — transmitting commonly understood meanings — is relevant here. This system of urban signs communicates the particular interests of an internationally dominant class in the practices of exchange, coercion and segregation as something commonplace and unexceptionable.

Los Angeles

Los Angeles is a version of this overconsuming, socially polarized, global-local, postmodern urbanity of which I have been trying to write. Its signs have been given an appropriate reading in the recent work of Soja (1986) building on earlier work by Soja, Morales and Wolff (1983) and Soja, Heskin and Cenzatti (1985). Soja's odyssey around Los Angeles touches many of the themes already discussed. He begins by delineating what he calls the Sixty Mile Circle centred upon City Hall. This circle, which effectively bounds Greater Los Angeles bisects a surprising number of 'ramparts': starting at five o'clock and moving anticlockwise are Camp Pendleton (US Marines), March Air Force Base, Norton Air Force Base, George Air Force Base, Edwards Air Force Base, Oxnard Air Force Base, finishing at 10 o'clock in ramparts seven and eight at the Naval Construction Battalion Center and the Naval Air Missile Center. What, asks Soja, is being protected? It is Los Angeles as the anchor of the Pacific Rim that is being secured — more manufacturing employment than Greater New York; 250,000 high technology jobs compared with Silicon Valley's 160,000; a vast recipient of Department of Defense research and procurement expenditure; and above all the new postmodern, Central City reflecting Los Angeles' growing challenge to San Francisco as banker to the Pacific Rim and beyond.

Tentacles of these functions reach out, as with the producer services corridor down Wilshire Boulevard twenty miles to Santa Monica; 'Aerospace Alley' from Santa Monica south through the vast landholdings of Hughes Aircraft, TRW and Rockwell past LAX International Airport; and Orange County, the high technology complex to the southeast of that. In between, neatly packaged, are the socially graded tracts of residential space ranging from health-conscious Mission Viejo which won more Olympic medals than 133 of the 140 competitor nations in 1984, through segregated little Tokyo, little Korea, Chinatown and (out in Orange County) little Vietnam, to still tightly enclosed Watts and the *barrio* of East Los Angeles. And at the heart of this matrix, turning its back on the mosaic it has helped to recreate, protecting its interests while reflecting the world outside is the Bonaventure:

> ... like many other ... urban citadels ... a concentrated representation of the restructured spatiality of the Late Capitalist city: fragmented and fragmenting, homogenous and homogenizing, divertingly packaged yet curiously incomprehensible, seemingly open in presenting itself to view but constantly pressing to enclose, to compartmentalize, to circumscribe. (Soja, 1986)

London

London is the prototype for postmodern Los Angeles. Its global domination of finance capital finally took on physical form when a definably high-rise, curtain-walled, City of London arose from the ashes of the blitz in the 1950s and 1960s. But those merely modernist glass boxes on London Wall are now on the verge of being torn down to make way for Manhattan-scale skyscrapers like the logoform NatWest Building, or Meccano-type constructs such as the

Lloyds Insurance Building which, like Beaubourg, and true to Derrida's (1981) inside/outside paradox where the 'pure' inside must be protected from the 'impure', surplus or excess of the outside, wears its plumbing on its skin. It is surely no coincidence that the proposal for a High Modernist Mies-inspired building (the Palumbo stump) to be built amongst the Bank of England and Mansion House classicism of the Victorian City was refused by the Minister for the Environment in 1985 on the grounds that it would introduce too ascetic an element into a 'lively' if slightly shabby Victorian townscape. Modernism has become antique.

One of the great changes that has underwritten the emergence of a postmodern social and economic landscape in London has recently been commented on in an astute series of articles by Neal Ascherson (1986a; 1986b; 1986c; 1986d). Much of his argument can be presented in his own words; his analysis begins as follows:

> ... London, if it ever was, is no longer a proletarian city. Industrial employment has drained away. Instead, millions of men and women wander and scavenge through a myriad transient jobs or none, servicing, typing, making-up clothes, delivering, cleaning, existing as semi-students on the fringes of the media. London is slipping backwards in time and becoming a plebeian city, a restless mass no longer to be regimented and organized by union or by class-party. (Ascherson, 1986a)

Into this force-field of social restructuring consequent upon de-industrialization has been inserted a further transformation:

> Under the surface of London there are strange tremors. Something is rising to the surface, and when it bursts through it will — so I begin to believe — create a new and almost unrecognisable type of urban society. . . . That something is middle-class money. . . . For cashing-in time is coming. It's a matter of time and genera-tions. James and Lavinia Yupsley, journalists in their late twenties are living in a mortgaged house in Islington worth £120,000. . . . Now the older occupiers of 'fairy money' houses and flats are beginning to die. Their heirs do not need the property left to them and will sell it . . . Even after the mortgage and tax are paid off, the possession of £500,000 spending money will be common. (Ascherson, 1986b)

As well as on conspicuous consumption, this money will be spent on private education and:

> ... among other things, the return of servants ... commuter servants, as in Johannesburg, who catch a 5 a.m. train in a distant suburb to wear maid's uniform or even butler's livery all day ... a brochure for a Bayswater apartment block (is) illustrated with the picture of 'a pretty Victorian tweeny, all white lace and black bombazine'. (Ascherson, 1986b)

And just to show that this isn't fantasy, Ascherson quotes Falklands hero Sir Raymond Lygo, now chief executive of British Aerospace:

> 'The mass employment of service industry', he said 'has got to come by people actually providing a physical service to those in productive(!) work, by working in hotels and in leisure but, equally important, there has to be a return to domestic service.' ... The new ruling classes intend to wallow in their wealth ... by living like this the rich are only doing their duty. (Ascherson, 1986c)

The inheritors are not, of course, the only overconsumers in contemporary London. Outer London, not unlike Outer Los Angeles has its Aerospace Alleys in Weybridge-Aldershot and Hertford-Stevenage. It too has its high technology tentacles along the motorways, M3, M4, M11. Above all it has the City of London, still one of the top three financial centres in the world, now having exploded with deregulation, metaphorically dubbed the 'Big Bang'. Vast salaries and gifts in the form of 'golden hellos' as well as 'golden handshakes' are being distributed as the Americanization of the City proceeds (Thrift, 1986). And London, too, has its substantial ethnic minority communities segregated away in Southall and Brixton. This may be the pattern for the postmodern city — poor people in a hyper-rich world with the beneficiaries of the latter ostentatiously, yet securely, spending on splendid residences, castellated offices and magnificent retinues. It might be argued that such behaviour will provoke rebellion, but postmodern Britain looks no more collectively rebellious a society than the USA. The urban masses of both countries have been stupefied by the invasion of their relatively secure world of employment by Thatcherism, Reaganomics and world industrial recession, they are the subjects of more proficient surveillance than ever before, and are policed in Britain, as in the USA by increasingly abrasive methods of social control. For the moment we are not only without an adequate cartography of global capitalism we lack political maps of our own backyards.

Conclusions

If modernization, modernism and the experience of modernity may be conceptualized as embodying the possibilities and practices of development and reform, then postmodernization, postmodernism and the experience of postmodernity seem to imply the opposite. Modernity means rebellion, in the sense that it consists in the consciousness of individual and collective, social and political potential. Postmodernity means, if anything, coercion, whether that of the enforced redivision of labour which deindustrialization, new technology and casualization bring, or that of the market place with its segregating and enclosing effects on social groups.

I have tried to show that there is an important debate about the conditions of existence of members of modern societies, that the analysis of these conditions links together, initially relatively crudely, but with developing critiques in considerably more refined ways, the structural processes of socioeconomic development as capitalism unfolds (modernization), the cultural consciousness and vision expressed through the arts, architecture and the built environment (modernism), and the existential experiences of liberation and insecurity which underlie processes of self-development of the individual in these circumstances (modernity). Modernity has spatial and temporal coordinates which cannot be reduced simply to the stage of development of the dominant mode of production, but which cannot entirely be divorced from it either.

As the processes characteristic of modernization, notably state intervention in social reproduction and economic production, notions of an emergent egalitarianism, and collectivist urban reform have become deformed, perhaps with a peaking in the parabola of capitalist development, so a deformation of modernism has come on to the scene. Postmodernism, as a depthless, aesthetically populist but conspicuously over-consumptionist cultural form, parallels in the built environment of cities a new stage of rentier-led over-accumulation based on third-world debt, military outlays and capitalist flight to monetarist havens. This is of a piece with a significant restructuring of the social relations of production based on casualization, informalization and super-exploitation of an increasingly flexible workforce. The experience of postmodernity is of vastly inflated incomes and inherited wealth for a privileged few capable of creating their own environments of overconsumption, and of an enforced redivision of labour, the loss of old employment securities, and a return to the social relations of the premodernist era as capital retrenches to its more dynamic redoubts in international finance, property, high technology and military production.

Finally, I sought to show with reference to the cases of Los Angeles and London just how the combinations of deindustrialization, the emergence of a sub-proletarian, ethnically divided, mass of available labour power, hypertrophic expansion of producer services, internationalization of the key financial circuits of capital, militarization of the leading sectors of industry and a massively regressive redistribution of income were leading to the production of increasingly enclosed and isolated urban spatial structures, increasingly defensive architectural forms in the core of the urban environment, and through the juxtaposition of hyperspace and overconsumption with the unemployment, sub-employment and environmental decay of the superexploited poor, a new, degraded form of urbanity itself.

Note

I wish to thank John Hassard of UWIST for providing me with unpublished material on the links between postmodernism and poststructuralism. I am grateful to Michael Dear, Allen Heskin, Rebecca Morales, Allen Scott and Ed Soja for guiding me physically and intellectually around Los Angeles, and to John Urry, Peter Dickens and Derek Gregory for exchanging their thoughts on modernity and postmodernity with me.

References

Abercrombie, N. and Urry, J. (1983) *Capital, Labour and the Middle Class*. London: George Allen and Unwin.

Aglietta, M. (1978) *A Theory of Capitalist Regulation*. London: Verso.

Albertsen, N. (1986) 'Towards Post-Fordist Localities? An Essay on the Socio-spatial Restructuring Process in Denmark'. Paper presented at XI World Congress of Sociology, New Delhi, August.

Anderson, P. (1984) 'Modernity and Revolution'. *New Left Review* 144: 96–113.

Ascherson, N. (1986a) 'Why Livingstone's GLC Has to Die', *The Observer* March 30: 11.

Ascherson, N. (1986b) 'London's New Class: the Great Cash-in', *The Observer* May 25: 9.

Ascherson, N. (1986c) 'The New Rich Spend, the Old Rich Sulk', *The Observer* July 13: 9.

Ascherson, N. (1986d) 'Stoke Newington: Settlers and Natives', *The Observer* August 3: 7.

Berman, M. (1983) *All That Is Solid Melts Into Air*. London: Verso.

Castells, M. (1977) *The Urban Question*. London: Edward Arnold.

Cooke, P. (1986) 'Britain's New Spatial Paradigm: Locality, Technology and Society in Transition', paper to XI World Congress of Sociology, New Delhi, August. Published in *Environment and Planning A* (1987), 19: 1289–1301.

Damer, S. (1974) 'Wine Alley: the Sociology of a Dreadful Enclosure', *Sociological Review* 22: 221–48.

Davis, M. (1984) 'The Political Economy of Late-Imperial America', *New Left Review* 143: 6–38.

Davis, M. (1985) 'Urban Renaissance and the Spirit of Postmodernism', *New Left Review* 151: 106–14.

Derrida, J. (1978) *Writing and Difference*. London: Routledge & Kegan Paul.

Derrida, J. (1981) *Dissemination*. London: Athlone Press.

Dews, P. (1986) 'Adorno, Post-Structuralism and the Critique of Identity', *New Left Review* 157: 28–44.

Jameson, F. (1971) *Marxism and Form*. New Jersey: Princeton University Press.

Jameson, F. (1984) 'Postmodernism, or the Cultural Logic of Late Capitalism', *New Left Review* 146: 53–94.

Lipietz, A. (1982) 'Towards Global Fordism? *New Left Review*, 132: 33–48.

Lynch, K. (1960) *The Image of the City*. Cambridge: MIT Press.

Lyotard, J.-F. (1984) *The Postmodern Condition: a Report on Knowledge*. Manchester: Manchester University Press.

Mandel, E. (1975) *Late Capitalism*. London: Verso.

Marx, K. (1973) *Grundrisse*. Harmondsworth: Penguin.

Massey, D. (1984) *Spatial Divisions of Labour*. London: Macmillan.

Paris, C. (1983) 'The Myth of Urban Politics', *Society and Space* 1: 89–108.

Soja, E. (1986) 'Taking Los Angeles Apart: Some Fragments of a Critical Human Geography', *Society and Space* 4.

Soja, E., Morales, R. and Wolff, E. (1983) 'Urban Restructuring: an Analysis of Social and Spatial Change in Los Angeles', *Economic Geography* 59: 195–230.

Soja, E., Heskin, A. and Cenzatti, M. (1985) *Los Angeles through the Kaleidoscope of Urban Restructuring*. Graduate School of Architecture and Urban Planning, UCLA.

Thrift, N. (1986) 'Localities in an International Economy: Introduction to the Workshop'. Paper presented to ESRC Workshop on Localities in an International Economy, Cardiff, September.

Thrift, N. (1987) 'An Introduction to the Geography of Class Formation', in N. Thrift and P. Williams *Class and Space*, pp. 207–253. London: Routledge and Kegan Paul.

Williams, R. (1983) *Towards 2000*. London: Chatto & Windus.

Philip Cooke is Reader in Town Planning at the University of Wales Institute of Science and Technology.

Religion and Postmodernism:
The Durkheimian Bond in Bell and Jameson

John O'Neill

In contemporary cultural criticism, whether neo-conservative or neo-Marxist, it is generally agreed that our cultural malaise is at its height in postmodernism. But whereas Daniel Bell (1976; 1980; 1987) would argue that the collapse of the modern temper is to blame for the incivility of post-industrial society,[1] Fredric Jameson (1984) would consider late capitalism itself to be the source of the postmodern fragmentation of its cultural values. However, despite this analytic difference and their opposing political values, Bell and Jameson (1981) are inclined to call for a renewal of religious symbolism to restore the social bond against postmodern values which undermine equally the conservative and Marxist tradition. Postmodernism appears, therefore, to create a neo-modern opposition from both left and right. In turn, it inspires a Durkheimian reflection on the ultimate value of the social bond which is either backward looking, as in Bell's neo-conservatism, or else resolutely utopian, as in Benjamin, Bloch, Marcuse and Jameson.

I think it is not unfair to Bell's argument to put it as follows. Capitalism has successfully changed itself and the world without destroying itself through the class and ideological conflicts predicted by Marxists. Indeed, capitalism has successfully moved into a post-industrial phase in which its information sciences continuously revise its technological future, thereby solving the problem of history and again disappointing its Marxist critics. The post-industrial phase of the capitalist economy appears, however, to be threatened more by the contradictions which derive from its postmodern culture and policy than early capitalism was endangered by the cultural tensions of modernism. In short, late capitalism may prove unable to integrate its postmodern culture with its technological base. This is because the efficiency values of the latter are difficult to reconcile with a culture of narcissism and a politics of egalitarianism. While

Theory, Culture & Society (SAGE, London, Newbury Park, Beverly Hills and New Delhi), Vol. 5 (1988), 493–508

Bell insists that previous cultural critics were naive in supposing that modern society can collapse at any single point, his own articulation of the triplex of economy, policy and culture, nevertheless envisages the possibility of the post-industrial techno-culture being sapped by postmodern hedonism and self-gratification. For, despite the contempt which modernist artists expressed towards bourgeois scientism and materialism, they nevertheless shared the same bounded individualism exemplified in the Protestant ethic and its affinity for industrialism. That is to say, there existed a tension in modernism between its religious and its secular values as well as between its attitudes towards the self and society. But this tension has collapsed in postmodernism and its disappearance threatens to bring down post-industrialism. However, Bell is quite unclear whether it is modernism, or the collapse of modernism (and thus postmodernism), which undermines late (post-industrial) capitalism. How do we choose between the two following observations?

> Today modernism is exhausted. There is no tension. The creative impulses have gone slack. It has become an empty vessel. The impulse to rebellion has become institutionalized by the 'culture mass' and its experimental forms have become the syntax and semiotics of advertising and haute couture. As a cultural style, it exists as radical chic, which allows the cultural mass the luxury of 'freer' life-styles while holding comfortable jobs within an economic system that has itself been transformed in its motivations. (Bell, 1976: 20)

Here, then, modernity is damned if it does and damned if it does not underwrite capitalism. In the next passage, however, we can hear more clearly Bell's neo-conservative lament for the moral values of a solidary bourgeois society in which the bond of religion is strong and resilient enough to bear the creative tensions of bounded Protestantism and spirited capitalism. At bottom, Bell (1976: 21–2) attributes the crisis of capitalism to a crisis of religion, to a loss of ultimate meaning which undercuts its civic will. By this he means that the obligations of collective life are reduced to subjective rights, the will to endure calamity is softened into the demand for instant gratification, and religion is replaced by the utopiates of progress, rationality and science:

> The real problem of *modernity* is the problem of belief. To use an unfashionable term, it is a spiritual crisis, since that new anchorages have proved illusory and the old ones have become submerged. . . . The effort to find excitement and meaning in literature and art as a substitute for religion led to modernism as a cultural mode. Yet modernism is exhausted and the various kinds of post-modernism (in the psychedelic efforts to expand consciousness without boundaries) are simply

the decomposition of the self in an effort to erase individual ego. (Bell, 1976: 28–9)

Bell's conception of postmodernism seems to turn upon a rejection of everything in modernism except its puritanism as the matching ethic of bourgeois culture and industry. Everything else is thrown into a catch-all of hedonism, neurosis and death which exceeds the bounds of 'traditional modernism' whose subversion, as he says, 'still ranged itself on the side of order and, implicitly, of a rationality of form, if not of content'. But the vessels of art are smashed in postmodernism and religious restraint vanishes from the civil scene. Man himself disappears as a transcendental value. Worse still, for Bell is not worried so much by philosophical extravaganzas, postmodernism ushers in a crisis of middle-class values! Here bathos is the result of Bell's attempt to combine historical, philosophical and sociological generalities to create a vision of cultural crisis which is universal and yet decidedly American. What he gains in assigning a certain grandeur to the diagnosis of American problems, Bell loses when it comes to tackling them in any specific institutional setting. For example, he claims that the road to post-industrialism involves three stages. In the first, we encounter a natural world; in the second, we deal with a fabricated world, whereas, in the third, our world is ourselves and our social interaction. Although one might have expected him to celebrate this last stage of sociability as a sociologist's (Simmel, Goffman) paradise, Bell finds instead that we have lost all sense of the social bond due to our progressive secularization:

> The primordial elements that provide men with common identification and effective reciprocity — family, synagogue, church and community — have become attenuated, and people have lost the capacity to maintain sustained relations with each other in both time and place. To say, then, that 'God is dead' is, in effect, to say that the social bonds have snapped and that society is dead. (Bell, 1976: 155)

Because he is at pains to avoid a Marxist (even a Critical Theory) analysis of the sources of 'instability' in the American social order, Bell is obliged to leave things at the level of a neo-conservative lament over neo-liberalism, hedonism and postmodernism. Thus America's legitimation crisis is blamed upon a moral crisis whose sources are found in any number of institutions (ignorance, poverty, AIDS) which exceed the social compact and the proper arbitration of public and private goods. Without naming the excesses of the corporate culture and its wilful barbarization of the masses, by keeping silent with regard to the industrial military adventures that enraged American youth, Bell falls into dismissing the critical culture of the 1960s in the same vein that Christopher Lasch dismisses the culture of narcissism. Because they both suppress relevant distinctions regarding the system of power, whose production of the culture they despise determines its mass consumption, (O'Neill, 1983) Bell and Lasch cannot avoid the voice of a genteel modernism lamenting its own lost contexts of value and the fall into postmodernism.

Overall, Bell seems worried that the project of modernity will be overwhelmed by its own antinomianism. The latter may have served a positive good in its break with patriarchal and feudal authority, but without such authorities to kick against, antinomianism soon loses all sense of its own limitations and the result is that liberty turns to liberation against which we lack any overarching principle of legitimation. The death of God and now the death of man, rather than his or her expected resurrection, leaves society without value. This is the terrible price of the anti-bourgeois assault upon modernism. The curious thing, however, is that despite Bell's vision of the erosion of authority we have not seen any expansion of social revolutions other than in the name of the very bourgeois, nationalist and religious values discounted by postmodernism. The reason may be, as the Grand Inquisitor well knew, that the masses retain that coherence of meaning and value which Bell and other intellectuals believe it is the task of their own exhausted elite to reimpose. Thus, whatever the changes in the institutions and rites of religion, its basic existential responses are perhaps less endangered because they are more necessary than ever. Bell seriously underestimates the popular resistance (if not indifference) to the elite culture of unrestrained individualism, impulsive art and moral nihilism which he defines as modernity's gift to postmodernism. Apart from remarking upon the resurgence of idolatry in the Chinese and Soviet Party, he does not make enough of the power of religious values to sustain resistance among intellectuals as well as old women. Of course, one is not appealing to the current prevalence of cults and sects of one sort and another which flourish whilst the official religions appear to wane. Yet Bell (1980) in his essay 'The Return of the Sacred? Argument on the Future of Religion' is bold enough to forecast the appearance of three new religions or types of religious practice:

(1) *Moralizing religion*: Fundamentalist, evangelical, rooted in the 'silent majority'

(2) *Redemptive religion*: Retreating from the (post) modernity, rooted in the intellectual and professional classes; and the growth of intellectual and professional classes; and the growth of 'mediating institutions' of care (family, church, neighbourhood, voluntary associations), opposed to the state;

(3) *Mystical religion*: Anti-scientist, anti-self, past oriented, rooted in the eternal cycle of existential predicaments.

If Bell's prediction were to be borne out, then we might expect (post) modernism to erase the 'beyond' of modernity, and to reimpose upon us the limits which the great civilizations have imposed upon themselves.

In the meantime, we may turn to Jameson's reflections on postmodernism and his attempt on quite different grounds to restore Marxism as what Bell would call a redemptive religion. It may be remarked nonetheless that both arguments make a residual appeal to Walter Benjamin's insistence upon the indestructibility of the aura of religion in human history. Ordinarily, social scientists and Marxists in particular are not kind to Messianism. This has made the reception of Benjamin slower on this score than his studies of commodity fetishism. In short, Benjamin's analysis and his response to modernism have been separated, in part expropriated as an analysis of postmodernism and for the rest left to those whose sympathies lie with the unhappy consciousness.

It would exceed the limits of the present argument to attempt to develop Jameson's position from anything but his own forceful restatement of it in his well-known article in *New Left Review* (1984) on the cultural logic of late capitalism (see also Eagleton, 1986a, 1986b). The similarities and differences between Bell and Jameson as diagnosticians of late capitalism should, however, emerge with sufficient clarity if we restate Jameson's formulation of the thesis of cultural contradiction or of the conflict between the forces of homogenization and heterogeneity in commodity capitalism. We shall then extract from the very rich series of interpretative studies and methodology in *The Political Unconscious* (1981) Jameson's defiant argument for the irrevocable claim of Marxism as a transcendental cultural imperative. At this point, however, it is interesting to see how Jameson makes the same Durkheimian turn towards the sacred as does Bell when on the same issue of the fundamental ground of the communicative community. Thus we find two cultural critics framed to the left and to the right of holy ground. The following comment from Jameson nicely ties together the progression from his essay on cultural capitalism to his transcendental hermeneutics developed in *The Political Unconscious* and the remainder of our own argument is concerned to explicate its sense:

> Durkheim's view of religion (which we have expanded to include cultural activity generally) as a symbolic affirmation of human relationships, along with Heidegger's conception of the work of art as a symbolic enactment of the relationship of human beings to the nonhuman, to Nature and to Being, are in this society false and ideological; but they will know their truth and come into their own at the end of what Marx calls prehistory. At that moment, then, the problem of the opposition of the ideological to the Utopian, or the functional-instrumental to the collective, will have become a false one. (Jameson, 1981: 293)[2]

We turn now to Fredric Jameson's reflections upon the place of postmodernism in the cultural logic of late-capitalism because, as an unrepentant Marxist, Jameson draws some of the necessary distinctions we found lacking in Bell's account of the role of mass culture in late capitalism. Yet we want also to show that, despite their opposing political values, Bell's neo-conservatism and Jameson's neo-Marxism both resort to a Durkheimian lament over the dissolution of the social bond. Whereas Bell's 'ancien liberalism' separates him from the Marxist vision of community, Jameson can invoke this communal vision as the ultimately emancipatory drive in the political unconscious of our culture.

Postmodernism certainly reflects the sense of an ending. The question is, what is ended? Is it industrialism — in which case both capitalism and socialism are finished? Bell would probably take this view. Yet he can find nothing to celebrate in post-industrialism because in the end he remains a high priest of modernism. But then Bell, Habermas and Jameson, despite their mutual differences, are all open to the taunts of Lyotard (1984) who finds everything to celebrate in the postmodern dissolution of right and left consensus. For Habermas (1985), too, is unwilling to abandon the modernist project to which Marxism is committed. With quite different values from those of Bell, Habermas has also set about the destruction of the French branch of postmodernism which currently infects North America and Western Europe. Between such figures, Jameson's position is a little difficult since certain aspects of postmodern cultural criticism must appeal to him inasmuch as it belongs to the received radicalism of literary studies with which he identifies himself. Overall, however, Jameson manages to extricate himself from the postmodern fascination and to oppose it with an eloquent, even if surprisingly religious appeal on behalf of Marxism as the transcendental ground of all human culture and community.

It might well be argued that such sociologies as those of Bell's (1974) post-industrialism, Lasch's (1979) 'culture of narcissism' and Toffler's (1980) 'third wave', are themselves prime examples of the postmodern exorcism of ideology and class struggle essential to the culture industry of late capitalism. Thus Jameson insists upon drawing a number of distinctions in order to avoid both cultural homogeneity and cultural heterogeneity as twin aspects of postmodern mass culture. He therefore argues that:

(i) Cultural analysis always involves a buried or repressed theory of historical periodization;

(ii) Global and American, postmodern culture is the superstructural expression of American domination;

(iii) Under late capitalism aesthetic production has been integrated into commodity production;

(iv) Postmodernism cannot be treated as part of modernism without ignoring the shift from early to late capitalism and the latter's redefinition of the culture industry.

These distinctions enable Jameson, like Habermas, to argue that Marxism must survive as the neo-modernist opposition to late-capitalism, absolutely opposed to its superficiality, its imaginary culture and its total collapse of public and private history (O'Neill, 1972). Jameson and Habermas are therefore insistent that Marxist discourse cannot flirt with contemporary fragmentation and subjectlessness. For Jameson Marxism is the transcendental story, a people's story which remains lively with human hope; it is a utopian gesture without which humanity is unthinkable.

However, incapable it has become of shocking the bourgeoisie, postmodernism certainly seems to *épater les marxistes*! Consider how Jameson (1984: 58–62) contrasts Andy Warhol's 'Diamond Dust Shoes' with Van Gogh's 'Peasant Shoes', or rather Heidegger's reflections upon them. Warhol's shoes are colourless and flat; they glitter like Hollywood stars, consumed by a light that bathes them in superficiality, denying them all interiority, making them crazy for any gesture that is rooted in a world beyond artifice. By contrast, Heidegger claims that the peasant's shoes tell a story that involves ordinary people; they are continuous with institutions whose meaningful history is the broader framework in which they figure as human artifacts. According to Jameson, all this is lost in the world of video space time, in the hyperspatiality of postmodern architecture, and in the self-consuming arts of postmodern literature and music. Like Bell, Jameson refuses the postmodern celebration of the fragment, the paralogical and paratactical arts that dissolve the modernist narrative, dancing upon the grave of identity, rationality and authority. Yet Jameson (1983: 113), insists that postmodernism should not be considered solely as a phenomenon of style:

> It (postmodernism) is also, at least in my use, a periodizing concept whose function is to correlate the emergence of new formal features in culture with the emergence of a new type of social life and a new economic order — what is euphemistically called modernization, post-industrial or consumer society, the society of the media or the spectacle, or multinational capitalism.

Here, as so often, Jameson's piling up of alternative epithets for the description of the socioeconomic system leaves it unanalysed in favour of its exploration in terms of two further cultural phenomena — pastiche and schizophrenia — to which we now turn. The fascination of these phenomena for postmodernist theorists is itself a sign of the inextricable sense and non-sense that characterizes the ahistorical and an-ecological predicament of late capitalism (Foster, 1985).

Pastiche involves the intertextuality, inter-pictoriality, the inter-modishness of codes-without-context whose inappropriateness suggests they never had even a local value and hence always prefigured the contemporary value chaos. As I see it, such codes create the illusion that Bogart experienced himself and his social institutions with the same affectation exhibited by today's *Rocky Horror Show* for kids without a society and for whom character can not mean anything else than caricature. The illusion of recycled popular culture is that bourgeois capitalism never created the institutional settings in which Bogey was taken by himself and others for real. This is appealing because in the bureaucratic contexts of late capitalism 'Bogey' could only be a pastiche/parody of lost subjectivity and individualism. Postmodern sophisticates would, of course, claim that 'Bogey' is all there was from the beginning, i.e., the essential myth of individualism. Hence all that remains is to democratize the myth — everyman his own 'Bogey', everywoman her own 'Bacall'. All we can aspire to is auto-affection through style, fashion, fad, the moment, the scene, regrouped on the collective level through nostalgia, with everyday life reduced to an open museum, a junk store, a replay.

While drawing upon the evaluative connotations of schizophrenia as a diagnostic concept, Jameson nevertheless disallows any intention to engage in cultural psychoanalysis beyond the confines of the literary community. Thus schizophrenia, as Jameson takes it from Lacan, is a linguistic pathology, the inability — through faulty oedipalization — to assign signifiers any temporal and spatial fixed points of identity and reference. Everything floats in an imploded present; action, project and orientation collapse in the literal, nauseous and real present in which teenagers are typically trapped. To keep them in this docile state is a task for our education system as a part of the larger system of mass culture to which it occasionally opposes itself, as I have argued elsewhere (O'Neill, 1986) regarding the functions of the disciplinary society and its therapeutic apparatus. What Jameson (like Bell and Habermas, but from a different interpretation of the same materials) finds at work in pastiche and literary schizophrenia is the collapse of the oppositional culture of modernism so that these two cultural elements of postmodernism now feed the cultural style of late capitalist consumerism:

> I believe that the emergence of postmodernism is closely related to the emergence of this new moment of late, consumer or multi-national capitalism. I believe also its formal features in many ways express the deeper logic of the particular social system. (Jameson, 1983: 125)

By foreshortening the production process to the production of consumerism, the more difficult analysis of the social relations of production, power, class and racism is reduced to the operation of an imaginary logic of the political economy of signifiers, where everything floats on the surface of communication. Here Jameson's reliance upon Baudrillard (1981) commits him to the company of Daniel Bell in a lament over the flood of narcissistic consumerism deprived of the mirrors that reflected the old order identities of societies which subordinated exchange value to the higher symbolisms of gift, sacrifice and community. Rather, postmodern consumers find themselves as mere switching points at video screens which miniaturize their lives in order to speed them up. The result is that their everyday lives are left devastated by the contrast between the archaic symbolic orders that consumers nevertheless inhabit and the imaginary flux in which they drift. Thus, inside those soft bodies which wander through our shopping malls and whose minds are operated upon from the outside world, desire is deprived of all intelligence:

> This is the time of miniaturization, telecommand and the microprocession of time, bodies, pleasures. There is no longer any ideal principle for these things at a higher level, on a human scale. What remains are only concentrated effects, miniaturized and immediately available. This change from human scale to a system of nuclear matrices is visible everywhere: this body, our body, often appears simply superfluous, basically useless in its extension, the multiplicity and complexity of its organs, its tissues and functions since today everything is concentrated in the brain and in genetic codes; which alone sum up the operational definition of being. (Baudrillard, 1983: 128)

Here, then, we have a curious effect. How can analysts as varied as Bell, Jameson, Lasch, Baudrillard and Habermas join common chorus against late-capitalism when their politics vary so widely from right to left? The answer seems to be that as cultural critics of late capitalist consumerism they are all *neo-modernists*. In turn, Marx's own modernism may well be the guiding influence. The centrality of Marxism to the project of modernity, as argued for by Habermas and Jameson, can also be claimed on consideration of Marx's writing, his imagery, style and narrative conventions. Thus Berman (1982) and O'Neill (1982b) have drawn attention to the modernist reading required in order to grasp Marx's polyvalent writings without reducing them either to narrow science or to mere mythology. O'Neill (1982a) has argued it is because Marx's text so obviously turns upon its modernist aesthetics that the Althusserian reading of it as a text of science must be rejected, without, however, surrendering to Lyotard's (1974) reading of it as a lunatic text, or as a pure work of art. The tension in the modernist sentiment is very well expressed by Berman in a recent effort to separate what is good from what is bad in modernity. Marx, Nietzsche and Baudelaire still represent relevant dimensions of the modern world because, as he says:

> They can illuminate the contradictory forces and needs that inspire and torment us: our desire to be rooted in a stable and coherent personal and social past, and our instable desire for growth — not merely for economic growth but for growth in experience, in pleasure, in knowledge, in sensibility — growth that destroys

both the physical and social landscapes of our past, and our emotional links with those lost worlds; our desperate allegiances to ethnic, national, class and sexual groups which we hope will give us a firm 'identity', and the internationalization of everyday life — of our clothes and household goods, our books and music, our ideas and fantasies — that spreads all our identities all over the map; our desire for clear and solid values to live by, and our desire to embrace the limitless possibilities of modern life and experience that obliterate all values. . . . Experiences like these unite us with the nineteenth century modern world: a world where, as Marx said, 'everything is pregnant with its contrary' and 'all that is solid melts into air'; a world where as Nietzsche said, 'there is danger, the mother of morality — a great danger . . . displaced onto the individual, onto the nearest and dearest, onto the street, onto one's own child, one's own heart, one's own innermost secret recesses of wish and will.' (Berman, 1982: 35–6)

What unites Bell and Jameson, despite the nuances in their response to the culture of postmodernism, is the will to order. In Bell the order is backward-looking, in Jameson it is forward looking. Both are in search of a new social bond and both believe that it cannot be discovered by severing our links with the past as the most mindless forms of postmodernism imagine. In this regard, even Lasch and Habermas share the same modernist sentiment, despite different ideas about its historical sources. Although orthodox Marxism and neo-conservatism are as opposed to postmodernism as they are to one another, with respect to the value of the past each is shot through with the contradictory impulses of modernism. Each may blame the self-consuming artifacts of postmodernism for their cultural malaise. But the fact is that it is industrialism which institutionalizes discontent and, so to speak, condemns us to modernity. Yet the neo-Marxists seem just as unwilling as the neo-conservatives to switch their gods. As Marcuse saw, both continue to cling to the old god Prometheus. Both fight to keep out the young gods Orpheus and Narcissus whose premodern and post-industrial figures still fail to seduce Habermas and Bell. This is so, even though the social forecast of post-industrialism calls for a more creative divinity:

In the light of the idea of non-repressive sublimation, Freud's definition of Eros as striving to 'form living substance into ever greater unities, so that life may be prolonged and brought to higher development' takes on added significance. The biological drive becomes a cultural drive. The pleasure principle reveals its own dialectic . . . the abolition of toil, the amelioration of the environment, the conquest of disease and decay, the creation of luxury. All these activities flow directly from the pleasure principle, and, at the same time, they constitute *work* which associates individuals to 'greater unities'; no longer confined within the mutilating dominion of the performance principle, they modify the impulse without deflecting it from its aim. There is sublimation and, consequently, culture; but this sublimation proceeds in a system of expanding and enduring libidinal relations, which are in themselves work relations. (Marcuse, 1962: 193–4)

Given the neo-Marxist and neo-conservative refusal of the new god Eros, a void is created in which Jameson can work to refurbish the Marxist vision of a productive utopia. Thus he argues that the death of the subject, the end of man, the migration of reason into madness, the collapse of social and historical narratives into schizophrenic case histories, are only acceptable visions of postmodern critique if we work for a renewal of Marxist history and hermeneutics. Jameson, still apprenticed to Marcuse and Bloch, assumes the Promethean task of binding his own myth to the utopian future of industrialism. He thereby seeks to retain the historical identity of the original Promethean myth with its utopian science of action and community bound by hope and memory:

> Now the origin of Utopian thinking becomes clear, for it is memory which serves as the fundamental mediator between the inside and outside, between the psychological and the poetical. . . . The primary energy of revolutionary activity, derives from this memory of prehistoric happiness which the individual can regain only through its externalization through its reestablishment for society as a whole. The loss or repression of the very sense of such concepts as freedom and desire takes, therefore, the form of a kind of amnesia . . . which the hermeneutic activity, the stimulation of memory as the negation of the here and now, as the projection of Utopia, has its function to dispel, restoring to us the original clarity and force of our own most vital drives and wishes. (Jameson, 1971: 113–14)

Whereas capitalism displaces its own myths with secular science, utopian Marxism keeps the bond between myth and science as a history-making institution. Utopianism, then, is not a romanticism or nostalgia that refuses to learn from history. Rather, what can be learned from history which preserves rather than represses its own genealogy is that romanticism and myth cannot be contained by secularism and that in the end they are to be joined to the sciences of action and collectivity that they prefigure:

> Thus, to insist upon this term of Breton which corresponds both to Freudian usage and to our own hermeneutic vocabulary, a genuine plot, a genuine narrative, is that which can stand as the very *figure* of desire itself: and this not only because as the Freudian sense pure physiological desire is inaccessible as such to consciousness, but also because in the socio-economic context, genuine desire risks being dissolved and lost. . . . In that sense desire is the form taken by freedom in the new commercial environment. . . . (Jameson, 1971: 100–1)

In short, Jameson argues that every genre of thought (myth, literature, science) has to be grasped as a psycho-historical master-narrative (the political unconscious) which when properly interpreted, is Marxism. Postmodernism cannot be a stage in this narrative because it abandons history as a human motive, i.e., as the motive to make ourselves human individually *and* collectively (O'Neill, 1982c). The latter conjunction is the social bond whose dissolution Bell and Lasch lament, whereas Habermas and Jameson continue to affirm its ultimate historical, normative and analytic primacy.

Jameson's particular strength, it must be said, lies in his will to carry the burden of the dialectical switching between the secularization and the re-enchantment of the life-world and its modern vocation while seeking to avoid Weberian pessimism as well as Nietzschean cynicism. He does so fully conscious that the age of religion has passed and that for this very reason we are tempted to produce an 'aestheticized' religion, an imaginary or hallucinated community, in an age that is neither religious nor social. How, then, can Marxism exempt itself from such aestheticism of sentimentalism? Jameson's reply is that Marxism and religion can be embraced as elements of a 'marital square' in which history and collectivity join individual and community action and understanding against inaction and ignorance that disposses the community and exploit it in favour of its masters. Jameson's fundamental claim is that all forms of social consciousness — both of oppressor and of oppressed — are utopian inasmuch as these groups are themselves figures for an unalienated collective life. He is at pains to deny that such an affirmation merely represents a return to a Durkheimian symbolics of social solidarity, or to a neo-Marxist marriage of aesthetics and social hygiene. Marxism needs both a positive as well as a negative hermeneutics of social solidarity if it is not to degenerate into postmodern fragmentation, or into an absurd negativity that would separate forever its scientific utopianism from its primitive myth of communism:

> Only Marxism can give us an adequate account of the essential *mystery* of the cultural past, which, like Tiresias drinking the blood, is momentarily returned to life and warmth and allowed once more to speak, and to deliver its long forgotten message in surroundings utterly alien to it. This mystery can be re-enacted only if the human adventure is one; only thus — and not through . . . antiquarianism or the projections of the modernists — can we glimpse the vital claims upon us of such long-dead issues as the seasonal alternation of the economy of a primitive

tribe, the passionate disputes about the nature of the Trinity . . . only if they are
retold within the unity of a single great collective story . . . for Marxism, the
collective struggle to arrest a realm of Freedom from a realm of Necessity. . . . It is
in detecting traces of the uninterrupted narrative, in restoring to the surface of
the text the repressed and buried reality of this fundamental history, that the
doctrine of a political unconscious finds its function and its necessity. (Jameson,
1981: 19–20)

Such passages are among the best in literary Marxism. Yet Jameson's claims are clearly exorbitant. They are so because he cannot
identify any specific social forces to carry his utopianism — and so
he throws the holy water of marxist utopianism over any group,
whether oppressor or oppressed, insofar as they are 'figures' of an
ultimately classless society! Such a vision verges upon the mystical
or, as he would say, the 'allegorical':

> . . . all class consciousness of whatever type is Utopian insofar as it expresses the
> unity of a collectivity; yet it must be added that this proposition is an allegorical
> one. The achieved collectivity or organic group of whatever kind — oppressors
> fully as much as oppressed — is Utopian not in itself, but only insofar as all such
> collectivities are themselves *figures* for the ultimate collective life of an achieved
> Utopian or classless society. (Jameson, 1981: 291)

On the right and on the left, we are still waiting for history to deliver
itself. Whether politics or religion will be the midwife remains
undecided. After a bitter lesson, Bell as a sociologist puts his money
on religion. Jameson meantime perseveres with the alchemy of a
Marxist hermeneutics that will deliver history, politics and religion.
And so the stage of history takes another turn. The Ghost of Marx
returns; there is much talk about talk in which Jameson is apparently more agile than Habermas who waits for a chance to articulate a
final economy of truth, sincerity and justice. Bell is silenced but
offstage the laughter of Lyotard still reaches us. Benjamin, Marcuse, Bloch — and perhaps ourselves — remain, saddened.

Notes

1. Bell's essays were written for the most part between 1969 and 1975. Although
unavailable to me while writing this essay, the exhaustive account in Howard Brick's
Daniel Bell and the Decline of Intellectual Radicalism (1986) requires no change in my
account.

2. The extraordinary critical liberty which Jameson allows himself in his own
writing is the subject of another essay of mine 'Baudlairizing Postmodernism' where
I carefully reconstruct his account (Jameson, 1985) 'Baudelaire as Modernist and
Postmodernist'.

References

Baudrillard, Jean (1981) *For a Critique of the Political Economy of the Sign*. St Louis: Telos Press.

Baudrillard, Jean (1983) 'The Ecstasy of Communication', in H. Foster (ed.) *The Anti-Aesthetic: Essays in Postmodern Culture*. Port Townsend: Bay Press.

Bell, Daniel (1976a) *The Coming of the Post-Industrial Society*. London: Heinemann.

Bell, Daniel (1976b) *The Cultural Contradictions of Capitalism*. New York: Basic Books.

Bell, Daniel (1980) 'Liberalism in the Postindustrial Society' and 'Beyond Modernism, Beyond Self', in *The Winding Passage: Essays and Sociological Journeys 1960–1980*. Cambridge: ABT Books.

Bell, Daniel (1987) 'Modernism Mummified', *American Quarterly* January.

Berman, Marshall (1982) *All That is Solid Melts into Air*. New York: Simon and Schuster.

Brick, Howard (1986) *Daniel Bell and the Decline of Intellectual Radicalism: Social Theory and Political Reconciliation in the 1940s*. Madison: Wisconsin University Press.

Eagleton, Terry (1986a) 'Capitalism, Modernism and Postmodernism', in *Against the Grain: Selected Essays*. London: Verso.

Eagleton, Terry (1986b) 'Fredric Jameson: The Politics of Style', in *Against the Grain: Selected Essays*. London: Verso.

Foster, Hal (1985) '(Post)Modern Polemics', in *Recordings: Art, Spectacle, Cultural Politics*. Port Townsend: Bay Press.

Habermas, Jürgen (1985) 'Modernity — an Incomplete Project', in H. Foster (ed.) *The Anti-Aesthetic: Essays on Postmodern Culture*. Port Townsend: Bay Press.

Jameson, Fredric (1971) *Marxism and Form*. Princeton: Princeton University Press.

Jameson, Fredric (1981) *The Political Unconscious: Narrative as a Socially Symbolic Act*. Ithaca: Cornell University Press.

Jameson, Fredric (1983) 'Postmodernism and the Consumer Society', in H. Foster (ed.) *The Anti-Aesthetic: Essays on Postmodern Culture*. Port Townsend: Bay Press.

Jameson, Fredric (1984) 'Postmodernism or the Cultural Logic of Late Capitalism', *New Left Review* 146.

Jameson, Fredric (1985) 'Baudelaire as Modernist and Postmodernist: The Dissolution of the Referent and the Artificial "Sublime"', in C. Hosek and P. Parker (eds) *Lyric Poetry: Beyond New Criticism*. Ithaca: Cornell University Press.

Lasch, Christopher (1979) *The Culture of Narcissism*. New York: Norton.

Lyotard, Jean-François (1974) 'Le désir nommé Marx', in *Economie libidinale*. Paris: Editions de Minuit.

Lyotard, Jean-François (1984) *The Postmodern Condition*. Minneapolis: Minnesota University Press.

Marcuse, Herbert (1962) *Eros and Civilization: A Philosophical Inquiry*. New York: Vintage.

O'Neill, John (1972) 'Public and Private Space', in *Sociology as a Skin Trade: Essays Towards a Reflexive Sociology*. New York: Harper and Row.

O'Neill, John (1982a) 'Introduction', *For Marx Against Althusser, And Other Essays*. Washington, D.C.: University Press of America.

O'Neill, John (1982b) 'Marxism and Mythology', in *For Marx Against Althusser, And Other Essays*. Washington, D.C.: University Press of America.

O'Neill, John (1982c) 'Naturalism in Vico and Marx: A Discourse Theory of the Body Politic', in *For Marx Against Althusser, And Other Essays*. Washington, D.C.: University Press of America.

O'Neill, John (1983) 'Television Ergo Sum: Some Hypotheses on the Secular Functions of the Media', *Communication* 7(1): 221–40.

O'Neill, John (1986) 'The Disciplinary Society: From Weber to Foucault', *British Journal of Sociology* 37(1): 42–60.

Toffler, Alvin (1980) *The Third Wave*. London: Collins.

John O'Neill is Professor of Sociology at York University, Toronto. His latest books include *For Marx Against Althusser, And Other Essays* (University Press of America), *Essaying Montaigne* (Routledge and Kegan Paul) and *Five Bodies* (Cornell University Press).

Nostalgia, Postmodernism and the Critique of Mass Culture

Georg Stauth and Bryan S. Turner

Most sociological explorations of mass culture, especially those undertaken within a Marxist or critical theory perspective, tend to be elitist in their cultural and political assumptions. This cultural elitism furthermore rests upon a position of high culture, requiring discipline and asceticism which can only be acquired by the professional intellectual through years of withdrawal from everyday labour and everyday realities. More importantly, an elitist criticism of mass culture presupposes, not only the distinction between low and high culture, but also the availability of some general or absolute values from which a position of critique can be sustained. Following Alasdair MacIntyre's justifiably influential study *After Virtue* (1981), we can argue that a coherent system of values as the basis of criticism presupposes a relatively coherent community as the underlying social fabric of moral systems and ethical arguments. Since in contemporary society the underlying communal reality of values has been shattered, there can be no clear position of values in order to establish a critique of mass culture. In any case, the consequence of postmodern cultural pluralism is to undermine the basis for the privileged claims of high culture to be the criterion of aesthetic supremacy (Featherstone, 1987a; Lyotard, 1984). Therefore, the predominant metaphor or mode of thought in contemporary critical theory is necessarily nostalgic, since critical evaluation must be backward looking.

In an earlier treatment of nostalgia (Holton and Turner, 1986; Turner, 1987), it was shown how the nostalgic metaphor was the leading motif of classical sociology and the Frankfurt School, especially in the cultural critique of Theodor Adorno. Nostalgia is historically speaking a primary disease of 'melancholic scholars'. It is well-known that the critical theorists were, in their attitude towards contemporary capitalism, typically melancholic in their eva-

Theory, Culture & Society (SAGE, London, Newbury Park, Beverly Hills and New Delhi), Vol. 5 (1988), 509–26

luation of modern culture and contemporary capitalism (Rose, 1978). While we focus on Adorno and critical theory, the Frankfurt School did not, of course, invent the notion of a revolt of the masses. Critical evaluation of 'the masses' can be traced back into the whole conservative tradition, especially the German rejection of the 'levelling', apathetic world of the mass (Giner, 1976). While the critique of mass culture is not peculiar to the German intellectual tradition, it did play an important role in the whole development of *Kulturpessimismus* (Kalberg, 1987). In this particular paper, we shall utilize the notion of a nostalgic paradigm as a method of examining the underlying assumptions of the critique of mass culture. Furthermore, it is argued that with the rise of postmodernism we need a new perspective on mass culture because the elitist framework can no longer be maintained; unfortunately it may be the case that academics are, as it were, congenitally committed to ontological nostalgia.

We may identify two primary criticisms of contemporary mass culture. First, there is the pervasive view that mass culture is essentially artifical because it is necessarily manufactured. For Walter Benjamin, we cannot understand a work of art extracted from its historical and productive basis. In an age of mechanical reproduction, art is extracted from its cultic and ritual location to become a commodity on a mass market. The modern cults of the cinema screen do not adequately replace or resemble their historic predecessors which enjoyed a religious aura. For example

> the film responds to the shriveling of the aura with an artificial build-up of the 'personality' outside the studio. The cult of the movie star, fostered by the money of the film industry, preserves not the unique aura of the person but the 'spell of the personality', the phony spell of a commodity. (Benjamin, 1973: 233)

In these terms, premodern art had an organic relationship to the community expressing ritualistically its natural forms of production and social relationships. Art and habitus were one. While in this quotation, Benjamin employed the language of Marxism to criticize contemporary art forms as a commodification of artistic activity, the underlying theme of Benjamin's critique depended also upon a classical Jewish opposition to all forms of human idolatory (Rabinbach, 1985; Scholem, 1981).

The second criticism of mass culture suggests that it should be regarded as an element within an incorporationist ideology or institution which has the effect of pacifying the masses through the stimulation of false needs via the 'culture industry' (to employ the language of Adorno). In his *Aesthetic Theory*, Adorno (1984: 24–5) had argued that

> duped by the culture industry and hungry for its commodities, the masses find themselves in a condition this side of art. In so doing they are in a position to perceive the inadequacy though not the untruth of the present life process of society more nakedly than those who still remember what a work of aŕt used to be. . . . This is all the more true in an age of over-production, where the material use-value of commodities declines in importance, where consumption becomes vicarious enjoyment of prestige and a desire to keep up with the Joneses, and where, finally, the commodity character of consumables seems to disappear altogether — a parody of aesthetic illusion.

In a similar argument, Herbert Marcuse in *One Dimensional Man* (1964) argued that mass production and mass consumption were essential features of the assimilation of subordinate groups to the dominant values and practices of the ruling class within capitalist society. For Marcuse, the potentially radical character of hedonism had been stunted by the development of contemporary production-processes which had restricted hedonistic happiness merely to the sphere of private consumption (Marcuse, 1968). In order to sustain this critical position, however, Marcuse was forced to develop a sharp contrast between true and false needs which remains theoretically problematic and unsatisfactory (Alexander, 1987: 366–7).

In developing a critique of critical theory's response to mass consumerism, we largely follow a position originally developed by Douglas Kellner (1983) in the special issue on consumer culture originally published by this journal. Firstly, we need a dialectic view of the contradictory features of all culture (both high and low), since mass culture contains the potentials of an egalitarian ethic in sharp contrast to the rigid hierarchical divisions embodied in traditional elite culture (Gellner, 1979). Secondly, we need a more positive view of consumption, as a real reward for the deprivations of production, which would avoid the implicit puritanism of the critique of mass culture, an argument which was developed in *The Body and Society* (Turner, 1984). To these responses to the tradition of the Frankfurt School, we shall add an account of the metaphor of nostalgia as a profoundly anti-modern location of cultural criticism in order to take note of the radical implications of postmodernism.

Critical theory involves implicitly a nostalgic appeal to the past (that is, to a situation where community and values were integrated) in order to develop an anti-modern critique of mass culture, the cultural industry and modern forms of consumerism. It is useful to identify two rather separate traditions in the western treatment of nostalgia. First, there is a medical tradition whereby nostalgia was associated with melancholy and the theory of the four humours. It is of some interest that nostalgic melancholy was a condition closely associated with intellectuals and religious, in particular with the dryness and withdrawal of intellectual and spiritual vocations. In classical times, this combination of nostalgia and melancholy came to be regarded as the occupational condition of the intellectual class (Klibansky et al., 1964). There was a second tradition of analysis, which from the seventeenth century regarded nostalgia as a positive moral value of the sensible and the intelligent person who, in response to the horrors of the world, withdrew into melancholic despondency. In this argument we are treating nostalgia as a particular form of the more general problem of melancholy. Melancholy had been for a long period of European history closely associated with intelligence, wit and foresight. For example, Aristotle in the thirteenth book of the *Problems* had claimed that all geniuses were melancholic. This tradition was subsequently elaborated by Erasmus who attributed profound spiritual powers to all melancholic maniacs (Screech, 1985). It was Kant in *Observations on the Sense of the Beautiful and Sublime* in 1764 who associated melancholy, nostalgia and sympathy with moral freedom and sensitivity. People become melancholic and nostalgic precisely because of their profound awareness of death and history. The Fall created a condition of ontological nostalgia (Fox, 1976).

Putting these traditions within a sociological context, we can argue that there is an ontological problem of nostalgia, which expresses the alienation of human beings in society as a consequence of their consciousness of their own limitations and finitude. In *On the Advantage and Disadvantage of History for Life*, Friedrich Nietzsche expressed the view that human beings must be necessarily melancholy because only human beings are self-consciously aware of the passage of time; human beings are essentially historical animals. This idea concerning the unhomelike quality of human life was taken up by Heidegger who regarded human beings as primarily uncomfortable in their being. There is a second meaning to the nostalgic metaphor which we have identified with an elitist critique of modernity which trades upon the myth of premodern stability and coherence. The elitist critique of mass culture nostalgically presupposes a world in which there was a unity of art, feeling and communal relations. This elitist form of nostalgia we may regard as simply a version of the Gemeinschaft/Gesellschaft distinction.

More precisely still, we can argue that the nostalgic paradigm has four principal components. First there is the notion of history as decline and fall, involving a significant departure from a golden epoch of homefulness. Secondly, there is the idea that modern social systems and their cultures are inherently pluralistic, secularized and diverse; this pluralization of life-worlds brings about an intense fragmentation of belief and practice. Thirdly, there is the nostalgic view of the loss of individuality and individual autonomy, since the autonomous self is trapped within the world of bureaucratic regulation under the dominance of a modern state. Finally, there is the sense of the loss of simplicity, authenticity and spontaneity. The regulation of the individual within a bureaucratic and administered world prohibits genuine feeling and emotion. The process of civilization thereby involves the taming of savage feeling.

This nostalgic paradigm was of great significance in the development of German social theory from Marx to the Frankfurt School. We can regard nineteenth-century social thought as a response to the loss of communal relations, the emergence of associational patterns of interaction and the development of a market which maximized the naked economic tie between human beings. Marxism with its emphasis on the cash nexus thereby shared a view articulated by Sir Henry Maine in *Ancient Law* under the slogan 'from status to contract'. Economic exchange destroyed the hierarchy of tradition in which conventional forms of distinction in taste and culture clearly demarcated the separate ranks of the social order. Economic capital became the major resource of excellence, thereby demoting conventional forms of inequality under the formal relations of exchange.

While social theory shared a common problematic which was the emergence of exchange relations in a market free from traditional regulations, we may detect quite distinctive patterns of critique and response. Marx following Feuerbach developed a materialistic theory of praxis which in its political form promised a revolutionary alternative to capitalism. Marx was characteristically ambiguous about the problem of time; he was outspoken in his critique of village life and peasant culture, regarding it as merely the garbage of history. Marshall Berman in *All That is Solid Melts into Air* (1982) has correctly identified Marx's commitment to modernity as an historical project, since Marx regarded capitalist production as a revolutionary system which liquidated all previous cultural forms. However, Marx's description of a future socialist society looks profoundly nostalgic, since this socialist utopia involved the absence of differentiation, of the division of labour and ultimately of human inequalities. Marx's description of the activities of future socialist man might be regarded, so to speak, as a forward-looking nostalgia, as a description of the homelikeness of socialism. Socialism undermines the alienation of human beings who are committed to nostalgia by virtue of a troubled consciousness.

If we can regard Marxism as a materialistic version of Hegel's teleology, then we can consider the leading thinkers of the nineteenth century as critics of the Hegelian system which sought to reconcile human beings to history, that is to reconcile men to the State. In this perspective, Kierkegaard's existentialist version of anti-system nostalgia developed a theological view of alienation in which against Hegelian reason Kierkegaard insisted upon the absurdity of faith. In a similar fashion Schopenhauer, against Hegelian historical optimism, asserted the centrality of the pessimism of will as the essential condition of human beings. Schopenhauer's solution was a form of Buddhist reconciliation with the world, involving a secular nirvana. It is within this intellectual movement that we can best understand Nietzsche's rejection of nostalgia, his proclamation of the emergence of modernity and the commitment to a pessimism of strength. Kierkegaard, Schopenhauer and Nietzsche are philosophers of the will who laid the philosophical basis for the emergence of a nineteenth-century sociology in Germany which was itself a sociology of the will, that is an analysis of action. The theme which linked together Tönnies, Simmel, Weber, Lukàcs and finally Adorno was the notion that we constantly create life-worlds which through alienation and reification negate the spontaneity and authenticity of the will and its conscious subject, Man.

Therefore to understand the problem of modernity, we need to turn specifically to the arguments of Nietzsche concerning the characteristics of the time in which we live. The argument here is that Nietzsche is primarily a prophet of modernity. The single element of nostalgia in his theory was a strong commitment to the classical world of Greece through his theory of tragedy. In *The Birth of Tragedy*, Nietzsche lamented the loss of the unifying and generative experiences of the ancient Greek cults which through the god Dionysus provided a healthy outlet for the violent passions of Greek actors. Dionysus combined with Apollo represented a dynamic component within Greek society which was ultimately swept aside by the emergence of a new culture, namely that represented by Socratic rationalism. This was the genesis of nihilism and human pessimism, since it involved an individuation of persons, the loss of innocence and the collapse of strong emotions. Civilization required the sublimation of feeling and violence in the interests of an orderly society which celebrated the values of the mediocre. This resentment in history found its final expression in the Christian culture of the West which turned the moral world of Greece upside down, disguising resentment behind the theory of brotherly love.

Nietzsche perceived various forms of nihilism in modern society; these included the negative effect of the German state and its ideologies, the continuing life-denying philosophy of Christianity, the ideal of asceticism, and the emergence of decadence in art and culture represented primarily by Wagner and Baudelaire (Mann, 1985). Nietzsche's philosophy was turned against the reactive forces in society, namely against resentment, the ascetic ideal and nihilism as modern forms of cultural and human sickness (Deleuze, 1983). His solution involved the revaluation of values, the reintegration of life against individuation, the assertion of the body as a value against rationality, the refusal to replace 'God' by 'society', and finally by aesthetics. For Nietzsche, the only justification for life was art (Nehemas, 1985). In addition, Nietzsche sought to condemn the separation between feeling and thinking, between mind and body, between the world of experience and the world of cultural distinction as expressed in the life of the professional philosopher and academic. Nietzsche saw rationalization and reason as life-denying processes insofar as professional life had become separated from the dominance of the everyday world. In *Ecce Homo*, Nietzsche argued that the men of culture had ignored the 'little things' of everyday life such as taste, place, food, climate and recreation in favour of entirely artificial properties such as 'God', or 'the soul' or 'virtue'. Nietzsche's response to the nihilism of professional culture was to assert the centrality of the everyday life-world in shaping the thoughts and emotions even of cultivated academic persons (Stauth and Turner, 1986).

Nietzsche's legacy in social science, and more generally in social philosophy, has only recently been fully recognized. It is now clear, following the Nietzsche revival in Germany and France, that Weber, Simmel, Horkheimer, Marcuse and Adorno were fundamentally influenced by Nietzsche's views and methods of analysis

(Dews, 1986; Stauth and Turner, 1988). This legacy may be summarized as follows: With the death of God, we are necessarily committed to perspectives, which we may regard as a form of value pluralism ruling out absolute ethical standards. This problem was particularly important in the development of Max Weber's philosophy of social science.

Since we live in a world of mere perspectives, the absence of stability in ethics and values results in a certain loss of direction which in turn leads to pessimism, disenchantment and melancholy. The world has become unhomelike, because we have lost all naivity and all certainty in values. The result was a profound cultural critique, especially of the pretentions of bourgeois values and culture. Nietzsche was particularly hostile to what he regarded as the idols of bourgeois culture and politics. The final legacy of Nietzsche was the idea that reason, far from being the liberating practice which frees us from unnecessary constraints, is in fact an essential component of the iron cage and the administered society.

While Weber's response to this crisis involved the ethic of responsibility (Roth and Schluchter, 1979), we shall argue that the critical theorists in their response to culture and the culture industry represented a return to Schopenhauer's pessimism of the will, namely a response involving resignation and nostalgia. In the absence of any genuine possibility of political reform let alone political revolution, Adorno and his colleagues turned to an aesthetic reflection on modernity which was largely pessimistic and elitist. The Frankfurt School was a response to the negative consequences of instrumental reason which had been institutionalized in a capitalist system of exploitation and found its final outlet in the gas chambers of fascist Germany. The project of enlightenment in history had turned in on itself through the rational imposition of knowledge in the administered society which ruled out the autonomy of the cultured and separate individual.

While these theorists drew overtly from the work of Marx, their project was in fact covertly a debate with the legacy of Nietzsche. While the presence of Nietzsche was generally muted in critical theory, the *Dialectic of Enlightenment* was clearly a debate with Nietzsche. The Frankfurt School sought within the enlightenment tradition a critical alternative to the norms of instrumental rationality which had become the dominant mode in the technical sphere of contemporary capitalism. However, for the critical theorists, the progressive enlightenment project was still a viable option as a model to stand against the emptiness of consumerism, the nihilism of the culture industry and the disguised predatory character of western democracy. The critical theorists therefore blocked off the possibility that even progressive enlightenment might be merely the resentment of politically marginal intellectuals who were in any case ultimately the servants of the state. From the perspective of Nietzsche, resistance to the world of capitalism based upon the enlightenment project still contained the perspectives and prejudices of reason which must assume unity, causality, identity, substance and being. Against this world of being, Nietzsche had always opposed the world of becoming. The critical theorists tended therefore to diminish the scope of Nietzsche's philosophy by treating his aphorisms as merely clever psychological insights into knowledge and reality. Furthermore, the critical theorists were essentially pessimistic with respect to the possibilities of radical change, whereas Nietzsche had always attempted to avoid the pessimism of will through a pessimism of strength. That is, Nietzsche had rejected Schopenhauer's solution in the resignation of the ideal of nirvana. In any case, Nietzsche regarded art, science and religion as ultimately merely illusions by which we attempt to comfort ourselves. In a world in which God is dead, Nietzsche proposed an entirely new platform, that is, the project of a revaluation of all values.

In summary then, we may identify four primary solutions to the problem of modernism. First, there is the aesthetic solution through artistic creation which Nietzsche regarded as a particularly powerful expression of all yes-saying practices, since art, especially in the pure form of music, was free of the immediate constraints of nihilism and resentment. It is in art that we appear to fully realize our abilities and potential to break through the limitations of our own circumstances. Secondly, there is the solution of the ascetic ideal which Weber embraced and developed into an ethic of personal responsibility. Within a world of polytheistic values, Weber attempted an orientation to modernity by developing the vocation of the men of science and politics. Thirdly, there is the genuinely nostalgic negation of the present in favour of some imaginary place constituted prior to the devastating consequences of urban industrial rational capitalism. Within this paradigm, the modern is totally rejected by a nostalgic reconstitution of communities. This nostalgic paradigm was particularly significant in the emergence of sociology as a nostalgic analysis of communal relations. Finally, there was Nietzsche's solution which was in two parts. Rejecting nostalgia,

Nietzsche argued that we have no substitute for 'God' and therefore we should develop new values which would express rather than deny the body, emotion and feeling. Secondly, we should abandon the ascetic ideal which must necessarily involve a nostalgic judgment of the world based upon a distinction between sacred and profane. This was Nietzsche's active reconciliation with necessity in the doctrine of *amor fati*. This doctrine in association with the notion of the eternal return was regarded by Nietzsche (1979: 68) as his greatest formula:

> that one wants nothing to be other than it is, not in the future, not in the past, not in all eternity. Not merely to endure that which happens of necessity, still less to dissemble it — all idealism is untruthfulness in the face of necessity — but to *love* it.

This doctrine asserts that the world should not be bifurcated into a world of superior intellectual values and inferior everyday values. The *amor fati* doctrine is against the domination of men of letters and cultured persons as employees of the state, as merely servants (*Beamten*) of an order of resentment. This separation between life and knowledge, feeling and art, was for Nietzsche expressed primarily in Kant's aesthetic doctrine that the aesthetic mode was entirely opposed to feeling, that is the aesthetic perspective was disinterested. For Nietzsche, life-enhancing art must express life not deny it or stand opposed to it. Nietzsche was therefore opposed to the new men of distinction, those bureaucrats of the German state who rendered service to the new bureaucratic domination in the world of culture.

The critique of contemporary culture, especially consumer culture on the basis of mass production and distribution, presupposed therefore an elitist position on culture, since the critique of mass society was grounded ultimately in a firm distinction between high and low culture. It has been argued that this critique of mass culture was both elitist and nostalgic, looking backwards towards a period in history when there was a greater integration between life and art, feeling and thought. The rejection of modernity in its consumer form can be regarded as a contemporary version of the opposition between Gemeinschaft and Gesellschaft. The critique itself presupposed a world of the conventional scholar and a secular ascetic whose vocation involved the production and reproduction of classical culture and knowledge. The world inhabited by the Frankfurt School had, in many senses of the word, been destroyed by the growth of consumer culture and responses to it.

In an important article by Fredric Jameson on 'postmodernism and consumer society', it was noted that the advent of a postmodern period brings with it the obliteration of precisely the distinctions upon which critical theory depended. He writes:

> The second feature of this list of postmodernisms is the effacement in it of some key boundaries or separations, most notably the erosion of the older distinction between high culture and so-called mass or popular culture. This is perhaps the most distressing development of all from an academic standpoint, which has traditionally had a vested interest in preserving a realm of high or elite culture against the surrounding environment of philistinism, of schlock and kitsch, of TV series and *Readers Digest* culture, and in transmitting difficult and complex skills of reading, listening and seeing to its initiates. (Jameson, 1985: 112)

While the concept of postmodernism has been much debated, Jameson employs it as an historical description of a particular stage in the development of modern capitalism. His argument is that modernism as such refers to the period which started with the postwar economic boom in the United States in the late 1940s and which brought with it the expansion of mass consumption, international travel, a new world order of economic relations and a new realm of cultural experiences for the masses. He goes on to argue that the 1960s was a transitional period involving the emergence of new forms of colonialism, the green revolution, the emergence of computerized systems of information, and the development of a global system of politics. The postmodern period therefore refers to the emergence of a new social order within late capitalism. One consequence of the development of a postmodern society, which brings with it a cultural egalitarianism liquidating the distinction between high and low culture, is the development of the 'nostalgia film' which through parody takes note of the absence of authoritative norms in aesthetic evaluation. Because we cannot achieve adequate aesthetic representation of our period, we are committed to nostalgic parody.

It is important to recognize that many of these features of the modernist/postmodernist debate were anticipated in the work of Daniel Bell, particularly in his essay 'Beyond Modernism, Beyond Self'. Bell, giving special emphasis to the importance of Nietzsche, noted that the modern period was ushered in by the secularization of culture, namely by the death of God, the loss of a sense of hell and the collapse of traditional systems of salvation. These developments were associated with other social changes particularly the growth of geographical and social mobility associated with the dominance of the city in social life. Bell noted that in the world of art this change was signalled by the disappearance of mythological creatures in artistic representation and the emergence of 'the promenade and the *plage*, the bustle of city life, and, by the end of the century, the brilliance of night-life in an urban environment transformed by electric light' (Bell, 1980: 277). This period of capitalism was also associated with a growing emphasis on the self and on individualism generally. However, people are still condemned by memory and consciousness to a sense of their own limitations and ultimately to their own death. Therefore one particular feature of the modernist culture of the late nineteenth century was a growing disenchantment with reason and rationality as adequate orientations to life.

Bell argues through an examination of the work of Gide, Dostoeveski and Nietzsche that central to modernism is the 'derogation of the cognitive' and an emphasis on the aesthetic experience as autonomous; against reason, there was a greater emphasis on emotion and desire. According to Bell (1976: xxv) 'in the culture, fantasy reigns almost unconstrained'. However, postmodernism against modernism rejects the aesthetic solution in favour of the instinctual so that pleasure becomes more important than artistic representation. Therefore 'in a literal sense, reason is the enemy and the desires of the body the truth' (Bell, 1980: 288). Like Jameson, Bell also recognized the decline of the high/low distinction in culture:

> What is most striking about post-modernism is that what was once maintained as esoteric is now proclaimed as ideology, and what was once the property of an aristocracy of the spirit is now turned into the democratization of the cultural mass. (Bell, 1980:289)

In short, bourgeois society which was the social and cultural manifestation of early capitalism is exhausted and with that exhaustion we are witnessing the disappearance of the possessive self and rugged individuality. As a result, nostalgia is a very potent mode for a moribund intellectual elite adrift from its traditional culture and institutional setting.

As a conclusion to this commentary, we shall turn finally to a modest defence of mass culture through a consideration of the egalitarian feature of mass consumption which is associated historically with the democratization of the mass. The imposition of taste involves necessarily the cultivation of distinction which is an expression of cultural and class superiority, as Pierre Bourdieu (1984) has so profoundly shown in his book on the judgment of taste. In modern industrial capitalism, there is, in addition to the constant reproduction of social classes, also a certain drift towards an egalitarian lifestyle. Modern societies are characterized by a relatively high degree of social mobility (by comparison with feudal and premodern societies) which makes the enforcement of conventional systems of rank difficult to achieve. Modern occupational mobility is therefore incompatible with a social system grounded in the notion of hereditary rank. Both social and geographical mobility make the imposition of hierarchical authority problematic in a society committed, at the level of political constitutions, to the principle of equality of opportunity. In addition, the mass media and modern forms of consumerism have created a leisure society where conventional principles of tastes and systems of cultural inequality have been threatened and challenged. The capacity for the working class to benefit from these new commodities has been enhanced by the growth of hire purchase systems and other loan facilities. The growth of a consumer society is therefore closely associated with social embourgeoisement. There has been a levelling of culture which necessarily involves a deterioration of elite standards. The emergence of a mass consumer culture was closely associated with the development of mass education and systems of uniform training providing again a certain levelling of national culture and experience.

We can also argue that the growth of mass transport systems brought about a democratization of geographical movement so that the ownership of a motor car became, along with the ownership of a home, a basic objective of modern democracies. While mass culture may involve, from the point of view of an elite, the trivialization of culture, there is nevertheless embedded in these new systems of culture a certain egalitarian standard which calls into question the conventional hierarchies of traditional society (Gellner, 1979; Turner, 1986). Modern systems of communication and commodity production have of course made the interaction between elite, avant-garde culture and mass culture especially complex and dynamic. Punk was transformed from oppositional/low culture to haute couture within the space of a few months (Featherstone, 1987a; Martin, 1981).

This view of the egalitarian implications of mass culture has been challenged by Bourdieu, who through a discussion of cultural capital, has shown how there is a profound relationship between the continuity of economic inequality and cultural inequality. Each social class location has its own habitus which is a bundle of dispositions which incline us towards particular forms of taste and particular appreciations of cultural social and other objects. Distinction is constantly reproduced in the competitive struggle between different classes and different fractions of classes. While Bourdieu's argument is clearly supportable and important, we should see the relationship between egalitarian mass cultures and the inegalitarian implication of dispositions as an unstable cycle of processes, or as a dynamic confrontation between different principles; we can see cultural artefacts as constantly transformed in the direction of both egalitarian and inegalitarian consequences. As social classes adopt the culture of their superiors so their superiors develop and adopt new patterns of cultural life. Both distinction and equality are thereby reproduced in the relationship between social groups and social classes.

One problem with Bourdieu's position is that it entails a total commitment to a dominant ideology thesis which largely rules out any significant possibility of resistance, change or transformation in cultural systems. Bourdieu sees the domination of cultural capital as largely unchallenged and complete in its penetration of the whole system. For example, he argues that

> there is no realistic chance of any collective resistance to the effect of imposition that would lead either to the valorization of properties stigmatised by the dominant taxonomy (the 'black is beautiful' strategy) or to the creation of new, positively evaluated properties. Thus, the dominated have only two options: loyalty to self and group (all liable to relapse into shame), or the individual effort to assimilate the dominant ideal which is the antithesis of the very ambition of collectively restraining control over social identity (of the type pursued by the collective revolt of the American feminists when it advocates 'the natural look'). (Bourdieu, 1984: 380)

While Bourdieu is often critical of the Frankfurt School, this view of the total domination of culture and the limitations of alternative strategies is largely compatible, at least in analytical terms, with the position adopted by writers like Marcuse and Adorno. By contrast, the analyses of the Birmingham Centre for Contemporary Cultural Studies point to the importance and presence of resistance within popular and mass culture, through, for example, the development of youth subcultures, to the dominance of the central cultural tradition (Hall and Jefferson, 1976). It is not clear that modern capitalist societies either require or can achieve such overall dominance of a central cultural tradition largely owned and fostered by the upper classes. The arguments against the dominant ideology thesis are relatively well developed in this area (Abercrombie et al., 1980). At the very least, we should see a tension or conflict between mass cultural systems, the cultural industry and the cultural elite, since this relationship of conflict in culture simply expresses underlying tensions which are political and economic in character. The existence of mass culture does not necessarily lead to mass incorporation in a dominant culture, since many aspects of mass culture are oppositional. Indeed in a postmodern era, it is somewhat difficult to know what would count as 'dominant' against which culture could be 'oppositional'. The world against which Nietzsche and Freud protested is now largely obsolete. It is difficult to know which cultural tradition or which cultural groups are in fact the defenders of a dominant tradition. As Bell has eloquently noted,

> the traditional bourgeois organisation of life — its rationalism and its sobriety — has few defenders in the serious culture; nor does it have any coherent system of cultural meaning or stylistic forms with any intellectual or cultural respectability. (Bell, 1980: 302)

This cultural dilemma (the disjunction between culture and social structure) creates a particular set of problems for the existence of an elite culture and for the social role of the intelligentsia. Are they to become merely the reactionary guardians of collective nostalgia, defending Wagner against the Beatles, Jane Austen against *Dallas*, or George Eliot against *Dynasty*?

In other respects Bourdieu's analysis of culture would be compatible with these reflections on the role of the myth of nostalgic communities in the division between high and low culture. Bourdieu has shown that in many respects high culture and low culture are deeply embedded one in the other. He argues that the high culture of intellectual class is ultimately rooted in 'the primary primitive dispositions of the body, "visceral" tastes and distastes, in which the group's most vital interests are embedded, the things on which one is prepared to stake one's own and other peoples' bodies' (Bourdieu, 1984: 474). We would argue that this is what Nietzsche intended by his doctrine of the little things, that is Nietzsche's argument that intellectual life was a resentful response to the everyday world of taste, emotion, feeling and reprocity. The cultural life of intellectuals involved both distinction and resentment. Bourdieu also goes on to note how the 'pure taste' of the intellectual class and its rejection of mass culture involves a profound disgust with the mass and the vulgar:

> what pure taste refuses is indeed the violence to which the popular spectator can sense (one thinks of Adorno's description of popular music and its effects); it demands respect, the distance which allows it to keep its distance. It expects the work of art, a finality with no other end than itself, to treat the spectator in accordance with the Kantian imperative, that is, as an end, not a means. Thus, Kant's principle of pure taste is nothing other than a refusal, a disgust — a disgust for objects which impose enjoyment a disgust for the crude, vulgar taste which revels in this imposed enjoyment. (Bourdieu, 1984: 488)

The cultural elite, especially where it has some pretention to radical politics, is thus caught in a constant paradox that every expression of critique of the mass culture of capitalist societies draws it into an elitist position of cultural disdain and refrain from the enjoyments of the everyday reality. To embrace enthusiastically the objects of mass culture involves the cultural elite in a pseudo-populism; to reject critically the objects of mass culture involves distinction, which in turn draws the melancholic intellectual into a nostalgic withdrawal from contemporary culture. Since in postmodern times probably all culture is pseudo-culture, it is invariably the case that all intellectuals are melancholics. The thesis of Erasmus (that spiritual powers of distinction belong exclusively to melancholic maniacs) appears to have been validated among middle-class intellectuals in postmodern times.

References

Abercrombie, N., Hill, S. and Turner, B.S. (1980) *The Dominant Ideology Thesis*. London: George Allen and Unwin.

Adorno, T.W. (1984) *Aesthetic Theory*. London: Routledge & Kegan Paul.

Alexander, J.C. (1987) *Twenty Lectures, Sociological Theory Since World War II*. New York: Columbia University Press.

Bell, D. (1976) *The Cultural Contradictions of Capitalism*. London: Heinemann.

Bell, D. (1980) *The Winding Passage, Essays and Sociological Journeys 1960–1980*. New York: Basic Books.

Benjamin, W. (1973) *Illuminations*. London: Collins/Fontana.

Berman, M. (1982) *All That is Solid Melts into Air*. New York: Simon and Schuster.

Bourdieu, P. (1984) *Distinction. A Social Critique of the Judgement of Taste*. London: Routledge & Kegan Paul.

Deleuze, G. (1983) *Nietzsche and Philosophy*. London: The Athlone Press.

Dews, P. (1986) 'Adorno, Post-Structuralism and the Critique of Identity', *New Left Review* 157: 28–44.

Featherstone, M. (1987a) 'Lifestyle and Consumer Culture', *Theory, Culture & Society* 4(1): 55–70.

Featherstone, M. (1987b) 'Consumer Culture, Symbolic Power and Universalism', pp. 17–46 in G. Stauth and S. Zubaida (eds) *Mass Culture, Popular Culture and Social Life in the Middle East*. Frankfurt: Campus Verlag.

Fox, R.A. (1976) *The Tangled Chain. The Structure of Disorder in the Anatomy of Melancholy*. Berkeley and Los Angeles: University of California Press.

Gellner, E. (1979) 'The Social Roots of Egalitarianism', *Dialectics and Humanism*, 4: 27–43.

Giner, S. (1976) *Mass Society*. London: Martin Robertson.

Hall, S. and Jefferson, T. (eds) (1987) *Resistance Through Rituals, Youth Sub-Cultures in Post-War Britain*. London: Hutchinson.

Holton, R.J. and Turner, B.S. (1986) *Talcott Parsons on Economy and Society*. London: Routledge & Kegan Paul.

Jameson, F. (1985) 'Postmodernism and Consumer Society', in H. Foster (ed.), *Postmodern Culture*. London and Sydney: Pluto Press.

Janz, C.P. (1981) *Friedrich Nietzsche*. München: DTV. 3 vols.

Kalberg, S. (1987) 'The Origin and Expansion of Kulturpessimismus: the Relationship Between Public and Private Spheres in Early Twentieth Century Germany', *Sociological Theory*, 5: 150–65.

Kellner, D. (1983) 'Critical Theory, Commodities and the Consumer Society', *Theory, Culture & Society* 1(3): 66–84.

Klibansky, R., Panofsky, E. and Saxl, F. (1964) *Saturn and Melancholy. Studies in the History of Natural Philosophy, Religion and Art*. New York: Basic Books.

Lyotard, J.-F. (1984) *The Postmodern Condition*. Minneapolis: University of Minnesota Press.

MacIntyre, A. (1981) *After Virtue. A Study in Moral Theory*. London: Duckworth.

Mann, T. (1985) *Pro and Contra Wagner*. London: Faber and Faber.

Marcuse, H. (1964) *One Dimensional Man*. London: Sphere Books.

Marcuse, H. (1968) *Negations*. London: Allen Lane.

Martin, B. (1981) *A Sociology of Contemporary Cultural Change*. Oxford: Basil Blackwell.

Nehemas, A. (1985) *Nietzsche. Life as Literature*. Cambridge, Mass.: Harvard University Press.

Nietzsche, F. (1979) *Ecce Homo*. Harmondsworth: Penguin Books.

Rabinbach, A. (1985) 'Between Enlightenment and Apocalypse: Benjamin, Bloch and Modern German Jewish Messianism', *New German Critique* 34: 78–124.

Rose, G. (1978) *The Melancholy Science. An Introduction to the Thought of Theodor W. Adorno*. London: Macmillan.

Roth, G. and Schluchter, W. (1979) *Max Weber's Vision of History, Ethics and Methods*. Berkeley: University of California Press.

Scholem, G. (1981) *Walter Benjamin. The Story of a Friendship*. Philadelphia: The Jewish Publication Society of America.

Screech, M.A. (1985) 'Good Madness in Christendom', pp. 25–39 in W.F. Bynum, R. Porter and M. Shepherd (eds), *The Anatomy of Madness, People and Ideas*, Vol. 1. London: Tavistock.

Stauth, G. and Turner, B.S. (1986) 'Nietzsche in Weber oder die Geburt des modernen Genius im professionellen Menschen', *Zeitschrift für Soziologie* 15(2): 81–94.

Stauth, G. and Turner, B.S. (1988) *Nietzsche's Dance. Resentment, Reciprocity and Resistance in Social Life*. Oxford: Basil Blackwell.
Turner, B.S. (1984) *The Body and Society. Explorations in Social Theory*. Oxford: Basil Blackwell.
Turner, B.S. (1986) *Equality*. Chichester: Ellis Horwood and London: Tavistock.
Turner, B.S. (1987) 'A Note on Nostalgia', *Theory, Culture & Society* 4(1): 147–56.

Georg Stauth teaches Sociology at the University of Bielefeld. He is co-editor of *Mass Culture, Popular Culture and Social Life in the Middle East* (Campus) and co-author of *Nietzsche's Dance* (Blackwell forthcoming).

Bryan S. Turner teaches Social Science at the University of Utrecht. His latest book *Status* will shortly be published by the Open University Press.

The Art of the Body in the Discourse of Postmodernity

Roy Boyne

Introduction

It has been suggested that postmodernism can be described as a culture of ontological doubt, and that therefore the key shift from modernism has been the replacement of the plurality of interpretation by the exploration of multiple realities, each one as inherently meaningless or meaningful as any other. We may also refer here to Lyotard's (1971) parallel distinction between discourse and figure. Even though such views may be too simple — for we are not yet beyond discourse, nor beyond the conflict of interpretations — the notion that the postmodern sensibility involves a shift of emphasis from epistemology to ontology, if it is understood as a *deprivileging* shift from knowledge to experience, from theory to practice, from mind to body, is one that is, as far as any such notion can be, broadly correct.

I do not wish to say that the art of the body is the art of postmodernism, nor do I wish to label Francis Bacon as *the* postmodern artist, nor, finally, am I centrally concerned with distinguishing the modernist and postmodernist moments in his work — although, inevitably, there will be something of the latter in what follows. What I want to argue is that the postmodern sensibility and the art of Francis Bacon have a certain affinity, and that the work of Francis Bacon can reveal certain facets of our contemporary culture *in a much more persuasive way than even the best sociological commentaries because his work encourages experience rather than 'mere' knowledge of the world he depicts*.

With its suspicion of any notion of a single objective world the postmodern sensibility will tend to be exercised on the past as well as the present (notions which the postmodern sensibility will place, as Derrida would say, *under erasure*), on Goya or Baselitz, Hegel or

Theory, Culture & Society (SAGE, London, Newbury Park, Beverly Hills and New Delhi), Vol. 5 (1988), 527–42

Baudrillard, Silicon Valley or the Greek city state. In the space of a single essay, I cannot hope to do anything but exemplify this thesis, and I do this in the realm of painting by presenting a practical exercise with a work by Mondrian.

The fact that the postmodern aesthetic sensibility is with us, however, means that it also has its effect on cultural production in the widest sense. Although I am concerned almost exclusively with art, in this paper, some mention has to be made of the social condition that supports the postmodern aesthetic. The key sociological concept is that of *progress*. The key social event was World War II, which for millions of people was the ultimate illustration of the death of God. The postmodern condition derives from the desperate search for the meaning that will validate the effort and striving to progress, which still defines the Western socialization process from start to finish, combined with the knowledge or feeling that all findings are bogus, all results falsified, all products disposable.

I explore this, only at the edges, by fastening onto the work of Francis Bacon. Bacon is taken as an icon *only within this essay*. Although his work is highly susceptible to the postmodern aesthetic sensibility, a definitive characterization of his work as postmodern is not possible: to attempt this would be a category mistake not least because the postmodern sensibility rejects epistemological certainty.

The Interpretation of Art

From a formal point of view, there are three principal ways in which a modern artwork may be understood. The first of these ways locates the work within the history of art. Reference here will be made to genres and predecessors. Such reference may be either positive or negative, affirming continuity or rejection. Postmodern architecture is exemplary in this respect. It rests upon an aesthetics which combines homage and historical disrespect. A comment from Charles Moore, on his Piazza d'Italia in New Orleans, illustrates the simultaneous working of both attitudes:

> I remembered that the architectural orders were Italian, with a little help from the Greeks, and so we thought we could put Tuscan, Doric, Ionic and Corinthian columns over the fountain, but they overshadowed it, obliterating the shape of Italy. So instead we added a 'Delicatessan Order' that we thought could resemble sausages hanging in a shop window. (Moore in Jencks, 1980: 20)

A focus on genres also opens the way to grammars of art, to a structuralist approach which would work toward an *explanation* of works of art, construing an individual work as a statement within a discursive system. Such an approach might be seen as having the potential to solve the question of what successful art is, in the same way that the grammar of a language, if fully specified, would unambiguously determine the systemic propriety of any statement. The disadvantage of the internally systemic approach, whether of the historicist or structuralist kind, is that questions meaning and ideology become, at best, peripheral.

The second way in which the modern artwork may be understood looks to its place within the present conjuncture: what is the *function* of the work within the culture? The link between the artwork and the cultural totality brings both normative and referential questions to the fore. Questions of meaning and socio-political acceptability arise. The debate between Kandinsky and the Constructivists, which took place in Russia in the early 1920s, shows just how central the interconnected issues of function, meaning and artistic obligation may become. Kandinsky was the champion of the spiritual purity of the individual artist, against the Constructivist demand for social relevance, but he nevertheless spoke the language of meaning and duty:

> The artist has a triple responsibility to the non-artists: (1) he must repay the talent which he has; (2) his deeds, feelings and thoughts, as those of every man, create a spiritual atmosphere which is either pure or poisonous. (3) These deeds and thoughts are materials for his creations ... (Kandinsky, 1977: 54–5)

Kandinsky's inner-directed asceticism, and the materialism of the Constructivists, are different variations on the same logical structure of duty, function and meaning. In both cases, the artistic imagination is stamped on the world in the terms of a particular ideology. It is the relation between art and politics that is at stake in apparently rational debates over function and meaning.

To be precise, it is only to the second way that the term 'understanding' can be properly applied, for it is here that the intellect strives to grasp the whole under the deceptive sign of objectivity and truth. The power of the first way rests on the reassurance of the familiar, the force of convention and the supremacy of the idealized standard.

The third form of understanding is, correctly speaking, not understanding at all. For it is not the intellect that is engaged, but the body, with its more or less repressed sensual faculties, and along its more or less compressed emotional range. The sculptor has fabulous potential here, producing work that would never be released: at the limit, the artist's experience of touching, holding, moulding would not be relinquished. We are speaking here, not of what the work means, nor about how it measures up to some Platonic ideal, but rather about what it does: the embodied reaction that it summons up for both artist and audience. Psychoanalysis has been of particular importance in understanding this dimension of art. But the theorization of the psychic and sensual aspects of art can effect a withdrawal, into discourse, from these aspects. For example, the psychoanalytically grounded explanations of Jackson Pollock's work engender an intellectual rather than an embodied reaction to it. They function as devices of distantiation, raising questions of meaning and making the work something to be understood as well as experienced. But the general western presumption of the superiority of mind over body may result in the eclipse of the embodied reaction by the intellect.

Kaiser and Mondrian

Can there be a discourse on art which is not obstructive of the embodied experience of art, which on the contrary, can help to elicit that form of involvement in the artwork? Or should we banish all but the children from the galleries of the West?

The argument of this paper is that discourse can be deployed in such a way as to allow the embodied experience of art to take its place as one of the most valuable ways of 'understanding' art. This argument will not depend upon logically compelling demonstrations of this or that truth, but rather upon (and in the nature of the case there can be no guarantees here) the disclosure of existentially significant effects arising out of an interplay between art and text.

Much of what follows will be concerned with the work of Francis Bacon, and with the commentaries on that work by Bacon himself, and by Gilles Deleuze. But it may be thought that Bacon's work is so much of the body that to take it as the only example would be just a little too easy, So, first of all, I want to suggest the possibility of experiencing the work of Piet Mondrian — geometric artist and theorist of abstract art, whose work was seen by, for example, Pollock and de Kooning as uninvolving and cold — in a psychic-sensual kind of way. This will be done by placing some of his work in apposition to an extract from *Gas II*, a play, published in 1920, by Georg Kaiser.

It need not be a question of looking to see if the meaning behind the text can illuminate the meaning behind the paintings; it can be a question of *slipping inside* the one (in this case the text may be more accessible) and then across into the other. With what result? The situated experience of monotony and linearity within the factory facilitates a movement into the painting itself, makes possible travel along its lines. Once there, one experiences a sequence of elation and despair, promise and fear: the safety of the line versus the threat of the space, the exhilaration of turning a corner into a different colour; but soon the exhaustion, the insufficiency, and the first steps away from the line and into the void (steps which ineluctably led the body rather than the mind in the direction of colour field painting). How else, but from being enclosed within the paintings themselves, could Mondrian cry, 'Oh the work, it is so hard'? (Carmean, 1979: 38). Why else would Rothko end his life, if not from the realization that the field is empty? And how prejudicial and narrowly intellectual a statement is the following from van Doesburg seen to be: 'It is alright for [Mondrian] to use the diagonal. It means, however, he has not understood neo-plasticism' (Carmean, 1979: 35).

There are two particularly important differences between the embodied experience of an artwork and the other two forms of understanding. In the first place, the question of representation is absolutely central to any theory of art which is within the horizon of the first two forms of understanding. Where the emphasis is on genre, the quest is for the perfect representation of the generic ideal; where the emphasis is placed upon function and meaning, the quest is for representations of the world, whether in its surface detail or in its deep structures (in this respect the work of Goya and Rothko, for example, is strictly comparable, the difference between them being that the latter seeks to represent the ineffable depth of the world, while the former will lead us along its damaged surface). Secondly, and following from the centrality of representation, the first two forms of understanding are judgmental.

Paradigmatically, then, the art critic is a judge of representations for whom the embodied experience of art will be at best peripheral. Although it is not being claimed that the three different forms of understanding correspond strictly to three types of art, and, indeed, the point of the brief examination of Mondrian was partly to show that this claim is not being made, different artworks do incline themselves in one of the three directions rather than another. So far

Act One

Concrete hall. Light cascading from arc-lamps. From the hazy height of the dome a cluster of wires vertically down to the iron platform and thence distributed to small iron tables — three right, three left. The wires coloured red to the left — green to the right. At each table a BLUE FIGURE – *sitting stiffly in uniform staring at a glass panel in the table, which — red left, green right — colours the face as it lights up. Slantwise across the front of the stage a longish iron table with a chequered top, in which green and red plugs are being manipulated by the first* BLUE FIGURE. *Silence.*

SECOND BLUE FIGURE: (*Before red-glowing panel*) Report from third battle sector: enemy concentration growing.
(Panel-light fades. FIRST BLUE FIGURE crossplugs red contact)
FIFTH BLUE FIGURE: (*before green-glowing panel*) Report from third workshop: production one point below quota.
(Panel-light fades. FIRST BLUE FIGURE crossplugs green contact)
THIRD BLUE FIGURE: (before red-glowing panel) report from second battle sector: enemy concentration growing.
(Panel-light fades. FIRST BLUE FIGURE crossplugs red contact)
SIXTH BLUE FIGURE: (before green-glowing panel) Report from second workshop: production one point below quota.
(Panel-light fades. FIRST BLUE FIGURE crossplugs green contact)
FOURTH BLUE FIGURE. (before red-glowing panel) Report from first battle sector: enemy concentration growing. (Kaiser, 1985: 245–6)

* * *

FIGURE 1

Piet Mondrian, *Composition with Red, Yellow, and Blue* (c. 1937–42)

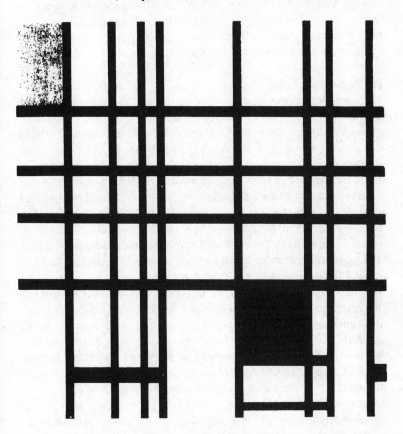

Reproduced by kind permission of the Tate Gallery, London.
© DACS 1988.

*   *   *

as painting is concerned, I wish to describe those works that tend toward the body and away from the intellect as postmodern. This is a usage that, in some ways, differs from the pronouncements of Jean-François Lyotard who seems to find the categories of judgment and representation (even though given a new twist by subordinating them to a reinterpreted notion of the sublime) unavoidable.

The Body of the Other

The term 'representation' is hard to avoid; the experience and knowledge of one thing standing for another is central to much of western culture. There are lacunae, however. Foucault (1967) found such a hiatus in his work on madness: the discourses on unreason fail to capture the experience of madness itself. Foucault, of course, argued that this was never their intent. Science did not subject madness to the bright light of reason; it denied madness as valid experience, and set free the minds which had passed through the Otherness of madness only when they also would live that same denial. It may have been possible to summon madness, without simultaneously denying it (and thereby repudiating the task of implicating in madness anyone who could not resist the journey), in the time of Hieronymous Bosch. But today such presentation of the thing itself is much harder, we do not think in such ways. We tend, as Baudrillard (1983) has explained, to look at one thing in terms of another; and this process never stops. Nothing is granted reality. All is simulation, with no ground or stopping place for ultimate value. There is no Other, and social process is infinite deferment and ubiquitous deference. In such circumstances, is not representation the heart of it? How can we avoid such a force, if it is *the* organ which must not cease to beat. The notion of representation, however, invites the question, 'If this is secondary, what is first?' Thus ordinal matters are invoked from the start. Because, in the present era, *all* is representation (a Sophistical position whose unassailability led Plato to repudiate art itself), the answer to the question, 'What is first?' can only be evasive. Thus, if we wish to avoid complicity with the culture of evasion which we inhabit, we have to stop asking the question. We must finish with representation and the political cowardice that it now connotes (which brings up the question of *real* democracy, which cannot be pursued here). So let us return to art and the body.

Consider Expressionism. It was, we may say, concerned with the Other. Its desire was to move aside the curtains of a seductively velvet but synthetic objectivity, and so to expose a view from which we are normally screened. In a world of deceptive appearance, however, such a view is hard to attain. It will not be a question of seeing it, but rather of being oneself through it, of abolishing the difference of quiddity in an expanded subjectivity. The entry in Kafka's (1972) diary, 4 May 1915, can be taken as an illustration:

> In a better state because I read Strindberg (*Separated*). I don't read him to read him, but rather to lie on his breast. He holds me on his left arm like a child. I sit there like a man on a statue. Ten times I almost slip off, but at the eleventh attempt I sit there firmly, feel secure, and have a wide view.

A representational understanding of that passage from Kafka would be similar to a naively objectivist interpretation of a Magritte canvas, echoing the child who asks, 'What's that train doing in the fireplace?' We are dealing, then, with experienced conditions of being, rather than statements of fact. So, contrary to what might first be thought, a certain naivete is necessary, in particular a certain prerational kind of co-existence with the world. A child reading Kafka's (1961) *Metamorphosis* becomes the beetle, feels the hard shell, and wakes in the night, shivering and frightened with the horror of it. A sophisticated intelligence has already developed the means of repressing this physical involvement; it is sufficient to ask what the text means, or to assign the text to some literary genre.

There are certain traditions in which one finds a determined refusal to name the Other. Judaism is one example; the tradition of Enlightenment rationalism is another, although in the latter case the motivation for the refusal is rather different. In an age of pluralization where suspicion of metanarratives has become an increasingly dominant cultural characteristic, prohibitions against the specification of the Other grow weak. This is understandable since the field of the Other unless dispersed through a process of multiple specification remains a site of totalizing potential and metanarrativistic desire. One of the current specifications of otherness today pertains to the body. In certain of Francis Bacon's paintings, otherness is meat.

The Architecture of Butchery

In 1966, Bacon wrote: 'We are meat, we are potential carcasses. If I go into a butcher's shop I always think it's surprising that I wasn't there instead of the animal' (Sylvester, 1980:46). What is the difference between animal meat and human flesh, between the twist of the spine in a Degas painting and the bones on the plate at the end of a meal? For the rational mind this is an absurd and even disgusting question, the spectres of cannibalism and mass slaughter confirm the greatest possible moral divide. But beyond the rules of division between human and beast, and beyond the meaning of life, is there difference? Is there not a profound parallel between the regime of the abattoir and the ritual of the crucifixion? The similarity works both ways, as the suffering animals take on a human and moral identity. The idea that suffering is a basic form of Being is hardly a new one, but the innovation wrought by Francis Bacon is to communicate this directly through and to the body by focusing on the body as meat and bone. Deleuze puts it like this: 'Have pity for meat! . . . Meat is not dead flesh, it has preserved every torment and assumed the colours of living flesh . . . Bacon does not say, "Pity the beasts", but rather everyone who suffers is meat' (Deleuze, 1984, Vol.2: 20).

If poststructuralism turns on the principle of undecidability, as Derrida's critique of structuralism might indicate, then, for Deleuze, Bacon is *the* poststructuralist artist, for he paints in that area of indeterminacy between life and death, between flesh and meat, between human being and the beast. There is even something more profound about such a Deleuzian-Baconian delineation of poststructuralism than the Foucaultian emphasis on the body. Foucault will speak of the distribution and redistribution of bodies, of the refinement, development and focusing of their powers, and of their medical and neurological redefinition, which all amounts to a sociologization of the body. Bacon, on the other hand, through a pulpy deconstruction of language will direct us to the mouth, a side-to-side slash in a mass of suffering meat, bone, blood and nerve:

> What, personally, I would like to do would be, for instance, to make portraits which were portraits but came out of things which really had nothing to do with what is called the illustrational facts of the image; . . . if the thing seems to come off at all, it comes off because of a kind of darkness which the otherness of shape which isn't known, as it were, conveys to it . . . you could draw the mouth right across the face as though it was almost like the opening of the whole head, and yet it could be like the mouth. (Sylvester, 1980: 105–7)

Bacon himself does not fully understand how such effects are achieved. His image of the process is of a tightrope walk between

FIGURE 2

Francis Bacon, *Triptych August 1972* (left panel)

Reproduced by kind permission of the artist.
© Tate Gallery, London.

FIGURE 3

Francis Bacon, *Triptych August 1972* **(centre panel)**

Reproduced by kind permission of the artist.
© Tate Gallery, London.

figuration and abstraction, and this poorly defined area is seen as a part of the territory of the nervous system. When we say that someone is 'on edge', or, more dramatically, that someone is 'on the edge', a particular range of bodily states is conjured up. Bacon will ask us to consider these, not as abstractions or theorizations, nor as images or symbolizations, but as specimens of embodied nervousness. On edge while he paints, Bacon will link his nerves to ours. As he said in a recent interview, 'each artist . . . works according to his own nervous system' (Gilder, 1983: 18).

Perhaps a view of reality as tunes on irritated nerves is defensible. It would certainly make sense for the victims of the dental disorders pictured in a medical text which was one of Bacon's formative influences. But, of course, he is not unaware of other visions of reality. The following is not uninstructive in this respect:

> I've lived through two world wars and I suppose those things have some influence on me. I also remember, very well, growing up in Ireland, the whole thing of the Sinn Fein movement. I remember when my father used to say — this is when people were being shot all around — 'If they come tonight, just keep your mouth shut and don't say anything.' And I had a grandmother who was married to the head of the police in County Kildare and used to live with windows sandbagged all the time, and we used to dig ditches across the road so the cars would go into them. (Gilder, 1983: 17–18)

The sociologist would normally seek to connect Bacon's painting to his politically spectacular upbringing (he even left Ireland to go and live in Weimer Berlin). But how can we connect such a personal history to the project of painting on our nerves, and to the aleatory painting technique which results in the communication of the feeling in the meat? There is no simple connection, such as the one found in the experience of Joseph Beuys, who saved from a frozen death by fat and felt, went on to work with these materials as an artist. We can, no doubt, attain a high degree of understanding of Bacon's work by documenting his homosexuality, the influences upon him, and his realization (in common with millions of others) that the world is a place of pain and butchery. Such understandings can help us to become a part of the work that Bacon creates, but they can also get in the way of sensation, obstructing the connection which makes for temporary coalescence of art and audience, of object and subject.

Bacon has often remarked that narration gets in the way of sensation. For this reason, the catalogue of his 1985 exhibition at the Tate Gallery contained no explanatory commentary upon the pictures which were reproduced there. For Bacon, that way lies boredom. His refusal of narration goes much further, extending to the subjects of all his work: faces, single figures, couples locked in a kind of presocial embrace. None of these pictures is meant to tell a story, for stories are evasions. So it is that Bacon claims that the violence of war is not represented in his work. Although he accepts that his work is about violence, and that it is produced in search of a certain truth, that truth and that violence lie within the image, within the paint, rather than in the events or characters which might be taken as forming the subject of the work. But there is little doubt that Bacon is the most illuminating commentator on his own work, and therein lies the paradox. At its simplest, it can be put like this, that those few paintings which are given informative titles (consider, for example, *Three Studies for Figures at the Base of a Crucifixion* or *Triptych Inspired by T. S. Eliot's Peom 'Sweeney Agonistes'*) owe part of their power to generate sensation in the viewer to the narrative effect of the title. The effect of that minimal narration is to deepen the physical response. It can be argued that the same is true for Bacon's portraits, that some of the profoundest physical response will be found in viewers who have listened to the pertinent elements of the story of Bacon's struggle with the head. The pictures themselves cannot constitute a self-sufficient language; that modernist dream was never realized. This is not to say that Bacon's words form the only mechanism for channelling and forming the physical response, but it is to say that some mechanism is necessary, some discursive complement to the pure figure, because the pure figure does not exist: Bacon's work as a whole attests to the realization of that fact.

If explicit narration will obstruct the process of sensual communcation, some less explicit mechanism is required: suggestions rather than didacticism, experience rather than logical plot. The personal world of a viewer of Bacon's paintings may be constructed in such a way that it may fulfil the supplementary discursive function; then the paintings, freed from titling, authorship, narrative accompaniment, will have their effect. Bacon's art may aspire to a universal communication (a residual modernism does have its place in his body of work), but such aspirations are no longer tenable. If the paintings are to provide a temporary completion of the partial and decentred subjectivity of the viewer, it is necessary that there be a junction. If such a locking device is not pregiven within the

FIGURE 4

Francis Bacon, *Three Studies for Figures at the Base of a Crucifixion 1944*
(right panel)

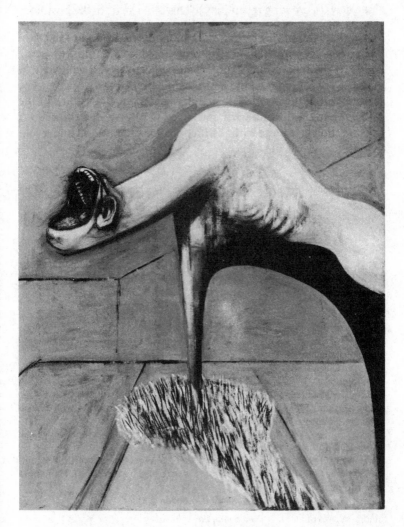

Reproduced by kind permission of the artist.
© Tate Gallery, London.

viewing subject, then it has to be created (the ambience of an exhibition space, the persuasive rhetoric of the artist, an unexpected juxtaposition between picture and text, these are just some of the ways of creating receptivity). This is the heart of the postmodern condition, that the subject needs to be processed to completion.

Another side of this rather more humble conception of the subject is our corporeality, our untranscendable condition of being edible. If the separation of subject and object was the achievement of the age of reason, and the desubjectification of the world was the secret of modernism, then postmodernism marks the return of the subject, but cut down to size, packaged in plastic, and offered for consumption complete with instructions for preparation and a sell-by date.

Note

The illustrations which appear here are reproduced by kind permission of The Tate Gallery.

In order of appearance, they are:

Figure 1. Piet Mondrian, *Composition with Red, Yellow, and Blue*
Figure 2. Francis Bacon, *Triptych August* 1972 (left panel)
Figure 3. Ibid., (centre panel)
Figure 4. Francis Bacon, *Three Studies for Figures at the Base of a Crucifixion 1944* (right panel)

References

Baudrillard, Jean (1983) *Simulations*. New York: Semiotext(e).
Carmean, E. A. Jr. (1979) *Mondrian: the Diamond Compositions*. Washington: National Gallery of Art.
Deleuze, Gilles (1984) *Logique de la sensation*. (two vols), Paris: Editions de la Différence.
Foucault, Michel (1967) *Madness and Civilization*. London: Tavistock.
Gilder, Joshua (1983) 'I Think about Death Every Day'. Interview with Francis Bacon, *Flash Art* 112 (May).
Jencks, Charles (1980) *Post-Modern Classicism*. London: Architectural Design and Academy Editions.
Kafka, Franz (1961) *Metamorphosis and Other Stories*. Harmondsworth: Penguin.
Kafka, Franz (1972) *The Diaries of Franz Kafka* (edited by Max Brod). Harmondsworth: Penguin.
Kaiser, Georg (1985) *Plays Volume One*. London: Calder.
Kandinsky, Wassily (1977) *Concerning the Spiritual in Art*. New York: Dover.
Lash, Scott (1985) 'Postmodernity and Desire', *Theory and Soceity* 14 (1).
Lyotard, Jean-François (1971) *Discours, figure*. Paris: Klincksieck.
McHale, Brian (1987) *Postmodernist Fiction*. London: Methuen.
Sylvester, David (1980) *Interviews with Francis Bacon, 1962-1979*. London: Thames and Hudson.

Roy Boyne teaches Sociology at Newcastle Polytechnic.

Beyond Progress: The Museum and Montage

David Roberts

Reflexions on Postmodern Art

Let me by way of introduction make it immediately clear that by *postmodern* art I mean art since the First World War, since the revolt of the avant-garde movements against bourgeois art and society. By *modern* I mean European art since the Renaissance, whose last stage is bourgeois art proper from the middle of the eighteenth century on, the epoch of the emergence of art (and aesthetic theory) as an autonomous sphere. The most obvious index of the limit of the art of the modern European age is the dissolution of the system of tonality in music and of the frame of illusionism for painting in the first decade of this century. The thesis of a basic, indeed radical separation between modern and postmodern art serves to focus attention on the new situation of art after the disintegration of the binding force of European tradition. The new situation of emancipated art, itself the product of aesthetic progress, is analysed in this paper (part of a longer study) from the related aspects of the emancipation *from* and *of* tradition beyond the idea of progress.

Habermas sees historicism as the Janus-faced legacy of the Enlightenment. It defines the conditions of modern identity and offers at the same time the possibility of flight from the present into borrowed costumes. In both senses it reflects the problematic of modernity. The idea of progress and historicism are the two faces of the nineteenth century. We could call historicism the decadence of progress. Retrospectively, however, progress and decadence appear as complementary interpretations which meet in the indifference which signifies the end of the modern age. This is the crisis, emphatically underlined by the oubreak of war in 1914, which was registered in various forms: for Spengler and Adorno as the end of Europe's time, of the time of music. But it was also for Lukács and for Ernst Bloch, and here precisely in the form of a philosophy of

Theory, Culture & Society (SAGE, London, Newbury Park, Beverly Hills and New Delhi), Vol. 5 (1988), 543–57

music (*Geist der Utopie*), the dawn, the advent of a new chiliastic time. At the border between the old and the new, between ends and beginnings, the end of tradition, the end of a world announces itself in contradictory constellations. When we turn to painting and music, we see in the eruption of primitivism — Picasso's African masks and Stravinsky's *Rite of Spring* — the signal of the break, which opens up a new relation between the old and the new beyond tradition. It prompts Gadamer (1983: 459) to the following reflection:

> The art precisely of our century has shown us how a changing world can liberate new possibilities of form and how in particular the general bringing closer of all distances expresses itself in new productive possibilities. What would artists such as Giacometti or Henry Moore or Bissier be without such new stimuli, and what would our music be without the challenge of the exotic impact of rhythm on our musical sensiblity. Where the limits of language create barriers the situation is not so evident. There can be no doubt, however, that here too as everywhere the break in tradition, accomplished in our century, has blocked off the false historicising escape routes of our grandfathers and opened our ears to the voices of remote traditions.
>
> It could be argued that this was always the case ... It is nevertheless a new situation. Formerly it was the inheritance of a single culture, its religion, philosophical and artistic tradition, into which the foreign was assimilated as the new which was yet like the old — with the same self-evidence as that which allowed Altdorfer for instance to represent Persians and Macedonians in his Battle of Alexander in the costume of the German Renaissance.
>
> Such a power of assimilation, such self-evident subsumption of the old under the new, of the new under the old exists nowhere any longer, not in our little Europe, not in the great Europe of today's world civilization. The world in motion challenges all closed historical traditions and confronts them with the question of self-identity.

The art of our century articulates the new historical consciousness which follows from the collapse of the defining and confining structures of a single culture, prepared of course within the confines of the culture of 'Faustian' transition by the tradition of the modern since the sixteenth century, since the Enlightenment. The new historical consciousness of our century transforms historicism into something qualitatively different, for which following Malraux (1967) we propose the term Museum. The museum without walls is the final radicalization of the Enlightenment which universalizes historicism and defines the conditions of identity of postmodern art. The Museum is the product of progress. That is to say, the legacy of the exhaustion, the self-destruction of the idea of progress is the emancipation of the past. The temporal hierarchy of modern art (progress/decadence) issues into the simultaneity and presence of the museum without walls. In this sense we can say that the end of Progress (the grand narrative of History) is also the end of the Future, which brings the past increasingly into focus. Beyond tradition the arts enter into a continuum of past and present, in which a universal historicism responds to the situation of contingency (the loss of the pregiven of tradition) for which everything can be potentially material and model, irritation and inspiration.

The museum without walls thus expresses a new relation of the old and the new, no longer under the organizing hierarchy of progress. It involves a transposition and reversal of signs, a revision of perspectives which take us from the hypertrophy and atrophy of the *present* — the fetish of the Contemporary — to the complex simultaneity of *presence*, whose paradoxical 'progressive' formulation is the synchrony of the non-synchronous. This formulation does indeed apply in terms of the logic of economic development. For postmodern art, however, this synchrony represents a conjunction which signifies disjunction, the uncoupling of aesthetic rationality from technological rationalization. The synchrony of the non-synchronous — which so disturbed Adorno (1973) in Stravinsky's music that he could only account for it negatively as the absence of developmental logic, as a succession of inauthentic masks, as schizophrenic dissociation, as time travel — can only be considered the Alexandrian world of quotation as long as we think in terms of a 'progress' which lives from tradition, and identify present art as the parodistic parasite of the past, the product of 'organic' dissolution. The verdict of decadence, however, not only fails to escape the paradigm of progress, it fails above all to recognize the new more complex level of the self-reflection and the self-problematization of identity which characterizes the art of our century, which in turn has called forth the charges of arbitrary eclecticism and linguistic chaos. Both charges fail to recognize or rather accuse the fact that neither producers nor recipients can situate themselves in *one* historical tradition, let alone any single functionally differentiated sphere. The 'world of quotation' and 'linguistic chaos' are rather to be seen in the light of a universalized historicism as the complementarity of the open, indeterminate possibilities of the system of the arts and a corresponding expansion and differentiation of the past, whose necessary corollary is the task of selection: the task of self-definition effected by the respecification and recombination of materials and codes. Auden (1975: 79) defines clearly the consequences for the artist of the Museum, that is, the 'consciousness of the whole of the past as present':

> Further, the fact that we now have at our disposal the art of all ages and cultures has completely changed the meaning of the word tradition. It no longer means a way of working handed down from one generation to the next; a sense of tradition now means a consciousness of the whole of the past as present, yet at the same time as a structured whole the parts of which are related in terms of before and after. Originality no longer means a slight modification in the style of one's immediate predecessors; it means a capacity to find in any work of any date or place a clue to finding one's authentic voice. The burden of choice and selection is put squarely upon the shoulders of each individual poet and it is a heavy one.

The burden of options applies no less to the recipient.

Not only production but also reception is emancipated from tradition. We must all construct our own individual contingent 'traditions' from the Museum in the form of a montage of juxtaposed preferences which combines the nearest and the most distant. We may recall here Constance Lambert's (1948: 53) pejorative but prescient observation in 1934 that modern taste is represented far more by the 'typical post-war room, in which an Adam mantlepiece is covered with negro masks' than by the austerities of Corbusier. Aztec sculpture, Balinese music, Polynesian masks, Japanese theatre and so on co-exist in a continuum with postmodern art.

All this was prepared by historicism, the first *self*-comprehension of the specificity, the identity of a culture, whose complement was the recognition of the immanent developmental logic of autonomous, differentiated spheres. The emergence of historicism and of autonomous spheres marked the point of the highest fusion of organic time and the developmental time of progress, of the synthesis of *self*-differentiation (Goethe, Beethoven, Hegel) on the threshold of modernity, whose outcome is the decentred relationism of fully differentiated functional society. The nexus between historicism and the differentiation of art as an autonomous sphere, which leads to the transformation of the museum (tradition) into the museum without walls, is Malraux's (1967) point of departure. Up to the nineteenth century the work of art was essentially a representation of something, real or imaginary. Only in the artist's eyes was painting specifically painting (Malraux, 1967: 10). The self-reference of art — what Malraux (1967: 66) calls rendering and execution — can only emerge when painting has become *a* supreme value in the vacuum left by the disappearance of the supreme value of society. With the loss of a patron class and a public, painting abandons the fiction of three dimensional *illusion* i.e. the conception of painting as narrative, and turns to two-dimensional colour (Malraux, 1967: 36, 46). Autonomous art found its cathedrals in the museum and as the museum expanded the non-European arts revealed to artists their freedom (Malraux, 1967: 71). The walls of the museum fall — European art is no longer the whole history of art — opening the way to the resurrection of the past.

For Adorno (1984) the new in art remained an unquestioned, if tragic, value which annihilated the past. The one crucial criterion was the dialectic of the age and the work. It was the irreversibility of this dialectic which lent necessity and dignity to the work, even if it only mirrored the progress of art to unfreedom. However problematic the new, the real paradox from the standpoint of progress resided in the old: how could the art of the past survive the ravages of time? This was the question *progress* posed and could not answer, as Marx's (1979: 110–11) famous Homer conundrum testifies. Marx's answer — the presumably eternal appeal of departed conditions, the youth of Greek culture — hardly satisfies. The conundrum remains caught in the ambivalence of the interfering perspectives of progress and historicism. It is here that we can situate Benjamin's (1970) 'Theses on the Philosophy of History' for *his* version of historical materialism is defined by the rejection of both the legacies of the nineteenth century: progress and historicism. But at the same time we must resituate the 'theses' in relation to the museum without walls, for the Museum alone cancels the irreversibility of time in the synchrony, the presence of the contemporaneous. This presence can be seen as the *secular* meaning of Benjamin's messianic 'Jetztzeit': the revolutionary revolution of time which redeems the past. In this third thesis Benjamin (1970) writes:

> To be sure, only a redeemed mankind receives the fullness of its past — which is to say, only for a redeemed mankind has its past become citable in all its moments. Each moment it has lived becomes a *Citation à l'ordre du jour* — and that day is Judgement Day.

However, we wait in vain for the messianic-revolutionary redemption of mankind. Past suffering cannot be redeemed, but mankind's past *is* citable in the 'lived moments' of its art. Moreover, it is a past which cannot be touched by Benjamin's storm of progress which piles ruins on ruins (Thesis IX), because it is not the past of the past but our past, our creation. That is to say, the Museum is the true legacy of the convergence of progress and historicism, which has emancipated the past and brought it close to us. Above all this past cannot be touched because it is the antithesis to the 'homogenous and empty time', which Benjamin identified as the common denominator of all the conceptions of mankind's (endless) progress. If the art of the past is present as presence, that is, citable, it is because it contains the filled time of 'Jetztzeit', emancipated from the continuum of history. The Museum is thus the repository of all the times of the past which speak to us across time. Benjamin's concept of a present, which is not transition but the standstill of time in a constellation imbued with tensions, crystallized by shock into a monad (Theses XVI, XVII), can therefore be reconceptualized as the 'Jetztzeit', latent in the work of art, which is actualized by the shock of reception. '*Mona Lisa* is of her time, and outside of time. Our reaction to her is not on the level of knowledge but of *presence*' (Malraux, 1967: 233).

In the face of the fragmented — differentiated and mutually indifferent — times of functional society, the aesthetic experience of filled time — and here we could define aesthetic experience as fulfilled time — becomes more significant than ever. It is the presence of the past which now beyond progress conquers time and answers Marx's conundrum. The works of art of the past are 'timeless' because they are filled with time, with the time of their culture. The discovery of the past was the achievement of the modern age, it was subsumed, however, under the progressive perspective of universal history. From a postmodern perspective this universal history can also be grasped as the universality of an emerging world tradition, which also calls into being the balance of the old world against the new, the horizon of the past against the horizon of the future. The past becomes the cultural counterweight to a progress which unfolds the hybris of the domination of nature. The new sense of solidarity with human culture in all its particularistic manifestations is now more than ever the protest of a living past against the dead hand of progress and the homogeneity of a world civilization which destroys the particular. With the end of Progress the Other of the contemporary world has become the past and not a future endlessly deferred by the progress of modernity. After the end of tradition we live from the emancipated past. As Malraux (1967: 231) puts it, we live in a world 'in which each masterpiece is supported by the testimony of all others, and becomes a masterpiece of a universal art whose values, still unknown, are even now being created from the assemblage of all its works'.

The emancipation of the past signifies, however, that our 'tradition' stands outside tradition. The result is a historical consciousness, a dialectic of the old and the new, more complex than that of the modern age, for the condition of the emancipation *of* the past is the emancipation *from* the past. This is the double meaning of the explosion of Progress effected by the avant-garde movements. The effects of the explosion — the acceleration and inflation of the new — were long mistaken for progress. The shock of the new, released by the radical rupture of the break out from tradition (the museum of the one culture), was transformed into the ideology of avant-gardism: the celebration of the new for its own sake, whose outcome was the symbiosis of art and fashion which reduced the most advanced to the eternal return of the new. Just as progress culminated in the revolt of the avant-garde in the name of progress against the self-consuming progressive differentiation of aesthetic rationality in bourgeois art, so in turn the fetishization of the new in avant-gardism — this last shock wave of the explosion — led to the emptying out of the contemporary moment, the moving point of the new. Avant-gardism's abstract cult of innovation provoked in its turn the critical reflexions of 'postmodernism' on the progressive spirit of 'modernism', Only the collapse of the pathos of the Contemporary brought to full, belated consciousness the explosion of Progress and led the way to the 'postmodernist' reaction and behind 'postmodernism' to the recognition of the secular rupture, the new time of postmodern art.

It is this *new time* which Benjamin (1970) sought to articulate in contradictory fashion in 'The Work of Art in the Age of Mechanical Reproduction' and in his 'Theses on the Philosophy of History'. For Adorno no less than for Lukács the new time is schizophrenic and dissociated, for Bloch it is the synchrony of the non-synchronous, with Benjamin it manifests itself in the unreconciled ambivalence of nihilistic progress and messianic restoration, emancipation from the past and emancipation of the past. That the two belong together is what we must disengage from Benjamin's opposed 'theses. Benjamin proposes two contradictory versions of the emancipation of the past: secularization and redemption. In 'The Work of Art' the argument is this: technical reproduction destroys the unique aura of the art of the past by alienating the reproduced from its context, by breaking it free from the matrix of tradition. Reproduction thus emancipates for the first time in world history the work of art from its parasitic existence in and as ritual, whose final expression was the theology of art for art's sake. The whole function of art is thereby revolutionized. The liberation of the art of the past from the alienating function of magic and religious representation (cultic value) and aesthetic self-representation (authenticity) frees art for its new function. Mass reproduction together with the new techniques of reproduction in the film destroy the auratic distance of cult and bring art close to the masses. Against the secularization stands, as we have seen, the contrary redemption of the past in the 'Theses on the Philosophy of History'. The destruction of aura is reversed into the redemption of aura through the act of revolutionary reception which constitutes the *nunc stans* of 'Jetztzeit'. This reversal (and our comparison) is only possible because the *one* avant-garde operation of *montage* underlies both constructions: the breaking of the monadic constellation — the work of art but equally a specific epoch, work or life (Thesis XVII) — out of the homogenous course of history.

In order to go beyond the contradictions of Benjamin's emancipation of the past we must redeem his secularization of auratic art and secularize his redemption of the past. The only redemption of the past which is possible is the presence of the past in the museum without walls, and the means of this redemption of the past is technical reproduction. In this sense Malraux's (1967) *Musée Imaginaire* is the answer to Benjamin's version of the secular transmutation of the work of art in the age of reproduction, just as 'Jetztzeit' is the messianic version of Malraux's Museum. The reconciliation of the contradiction requires, however, that we distinguish clearly between the effects of technical reproduction. Benjamin's uncritical faith in the politically emancipatory powers of technology in 'The Work of Art' — Brecht's influence is unmistakable here — is a simplistically 'revolutionary' response to the end of the age of print and the revolutionary impact of the media age. Against Benjamin's argument technical reproduction is on the one hand the medium of the Contemporaneous, the time and space travel which brings the distant near, on the other hand it is also the medium of the Contemporary manufactured by the culture industry. For Benjamin the destruction of aura was the signature of a new perception, whose 'sense for the similar in the world' imposes itself on the unique. But this sense of the similar (the 'scientific' perspective of Brecht's method of estrangement) is also the Midas hand of the culture industry, which 'magically' alienates the world into exchange value. The emblem of this alienation is the image (Boorston, 1972). The image, we may say, is the true 'parodic work of nothing' (Lyotard, 1974) which reduplicates the cynicism of capitalism in the blank face of the fetish. We buy not the commodity but its image, whose function is the enchantment of mass production. The image is thus the aura of the culture industry, the signature not of the unique but of the eternally same which imprisons art in the vanishing moment of the contemporary, in the timeless present of repetition. It is this which paradoxically but necessarily makes technical reproduction also the medium of the redemption of the past.

'The fact that we now have at our disposal the art of all ages and cultures' (Auden) presupposes the qualitatively new situation of the manifold possibilities of technical reproduction. They are the precondition for what Gadamer calls the general bringing nearer of all distances. And so just as we must reverse Benjamin's 'progressive' thesis so we must reverse his definition of aura. Instead of the 'unique appearance of distance, however near' of the traditional work of art, which is destroyed by reproduction, aura in the age of technical reproduction is the *unique appearance of nearness, however distant*, manifested in the presence of the Museum. Through technical reproduction William Byrd is as much our contemporary as Berio or Boulez, and Beethoven is more our contemporary than he was for the Vienna of his time. The wall paintings of Lascaux stand side by side with Michelangelo's *Last Judgement* and twentieth-century Mexican murals. Now that the Imaginary of the Future fails us and the utopia of possible worlds has turned into dystopian visions of horror, the art of the past increasingly becomes the only dimension of time available to us to escape the prison of the present. To quote Auden again:

> the wonderful, the other nice thing about the arts, the invaluable thing about them, is that they are almost the only means we have of breaking bread with the dead. That is to say, all right, Homer is gone, his society is gone, but you could still read the Iliad and get a lot from it. And I do. I personally think that, without communication with the dead, we'd be entirely enclosed in the present, and that is not a fully human life. (quoted in Osborne, 1982)

The museum without walls has replaced the museum of a single culture. It is the move from the European to a world tradition which has brought with it an enormous expansion of horizons and a corresponding openness and indeterminacy of the boundaries of the system of art. The museum without walls is the correlate of our tradition without walls, whose conditions of identity are given by the emancipation from the past which is at the same time the emancipation of the past. From this explosion of Progress — the end of the European tradition — postmodern art emerges in all the contingency of its freedom and the freedom of its contingency, which confronts it as the burden of options. Thus Adorno's (1973) desperate opposition of Schoenberg and Stravinsky in *Philosophy of Modern Music* only confirms that the new music seeks in vain to restitute identity (appearance, authenticity). Adorno's self-defeating endeavour to restore the boundaries of identity ends in the paradoxicality of endless negativity. It is dialectics' finale which opens up the problematic of the postmodern, in which the exclusive alternatives of authenticity and inauthenticity come to rest in the unity of (the difference between) identity and non-identity, which we have attempted to relate to the universalizing of contingency and historicism. The Janus face of our historicism is that of identity grounded in difference, which is not the indifference of nihilism, of progress but the difference of our tradition beyond tradition and progress.

This difference emerges sharply in the contradictions of Benjamin's 'historical materialism', but it also underlies Malraux's resurrection of the past, for the standpoint of both is the new standpoint of relativity, of estrangement, whose instrument is technical reproduction. Just as for Benjamin the photograph contains virtually the film, so too Malraux's vision is that of the film age. What this means is that space and time travel, in all the forms given by technical reproduction, brings about a *twofold estrangement* of the unifying perspective of tradition, of the hierarchizing vision of a single culture. This twofold estrangement we may call the Museum and Montage. The space and time travel of the Museum, the general bringing nearer of the most distant, is dependent on technical reproduction. Technical reproduction, however, is not simply the medium of the Museum, it is itself the instrument of a qualitative change of perception through its sovereignty over time and space. Perception is differentiated and relativized through the expansion and contraction of space and time, the alteration of relations and dimensions made possible by photographic enlargement and the changing speeds, focuses and positions of the camera (slow motion, the close up, long shots, perspectives from all angles, etc.). The techniques of cutting, the assembly of sequences in the film mark the end, as Brecht and Benjamin saw, of the unitary perspective of the *camera obscura*, the box-frame of *illusion* in drama and painting, and inaugurate the multi-perspectivism of *montage*.

The estrangement of perception is one with the estrangement of the object reproduced. Benjamin, however, interpreted this emancipation of the work of art too reductively. It is for this reason that we turned to the 'Theses on the Philosophy of History' not only to redress the balance but also to reinterpret both 'The Work of Art' and the 'Theses'. We no more need to see the secularization of art as the destruction of aura any more than we need deny that the redemption of the past, of which Benjamin dreamed, remains quotation and not identity. If the fruit of historical comprehension of Benjamin's (1970) historical materialist carries the seed of time within it (Thesis XVII), then the secularization of art effected by technical reproduction can also be understood as the emancipation of aura. The estrangement, which transforms the use-value of all closed cultures into the exchange-value of 'art' — the context free material of our 'tradition' — releases in the process its surplus value from its original bonding: aura as the seed of time. Malraux grasped the implications of this epochal secularization far more profoundly. Technical reproduction enables us not only to gather together the arts of different cultures, it permits us to analyse and compare whole corpuses of art (Malraux, 1967: 79). Just as timelapse photography animates the growth of a plant so the reproduction of a whole corpus of art animates style (Malraux, 1967: 160). Reproduction is thus one of the most effective tools of the intellectualization of art which reveals a style in its entirety (Malraux, 1967: 80). As a consequence all European art becomes one style compared to non-European art: 'The past of art, which to Europe had been only the past of one style termed art, appears to us a world of styles . . .' (Malraux, 1967: 182). Not until the twentieth century did we discover that style is the resurrected expression of other cultures: now 'we think of every great style as the symbol of a fundamental relationship between man and the universe, of a civilization with the value it holds supreme' (Malraux, 1967: 162).

Nevertheless, Malraux's resurrection is possible only as secularization. The gods we resurrect are no longer divine, all that is *sacred* has been metamorphosed into *art* (Malraux, 1967: 180). We can only admire the amazingly different heritage of the world's cultures because we have transformed it into art. Picasso did not see African masks with the same eyes as those for whom they were intended (Malraux, 1967: 208–9). Picasso's use of African masks in *Les demoiselles d'Avignon* can now be seen as *the* symbolic art of montage which opens the museum of world art. The Museum and montage are thus the twin aspects of the end of tradition: the emancipation of art from its organic context. The new time of montage is thus reflected in the grandiose montage of the art of all times *and* all the times of art in the presence of the Museum.

All this, we may say, is contained in the fundamental configuration of Benjamin's thought in *The Origin of German Tragedy* (1977), in 'The Work of Art', in the 'Theses on the Philosophy of History'. Whether allegory, destruction of aura or redemption of the past, the one fundamental idea returns as the ambivalence of secularization and redemption: *only that which is dead can be resurrected*. This is Benjamin's theological version of the Museum and montage. If Benjamin is the Janus face of the postmodern paradigm, Adorno is the death mask of the modern paradigm. Adorno held fast to the Devil of unending progress because he feared the Devil of endless possibilities, the transformation of the *time* of progress into the *space* of seemingly meaningless juxtapositions. He (1984) thus clings to the idea of the paradigmatic work even if the authentic work of emancipated art (Schoenberg) is possible only as its own negation. Adorno's attempt to hold fast to the limits of the modern paradigm but also to transcend these limits leads his aesthetic theory into irresolvable aporias. The question of the paradigmatic work requires rethinking.

The question of the paradigmatic work is by definition a question of the paradigm. The paradigmatic work is the replication, the microcosmic expression of the paradigm, which excludes most actual works to concentrate on the representative work, which is the highest realization of the idea of the paradigm. Thus for the *modern* paradigm the normative work is for Adorno the organic-teleological work, which gives form to dynamic time. The modern paradigm is grounded in the subject, its values are expression, creativity, subjectivity, originality, its form is the inner form of the unfolding of essence in time: the self-differentiation of identity realized through the dialectic of subject and object, freedom and necessity, form and content. Microcosm and macrocosm correspond in the self-realization of the subject as humanity and of humanity as subject. The microcosm is the *totality given form*: the definition of identity and the self-definition of the paradigm.

In what sense can we speak of self-definition, of the paradigmatic work in relation to the indeterminate boundaries of the postmodern paradigm? The answer is logical — here too the microcosm reflects the macrocosm — and paradoxical, for we have to think of the possible and the paradigmatic together, that is to say, the indeterminate (contingent) system demands an indeterminate number of possible paradigmatic works. A paradigm grounded in difference can have no one exemplary and hierarchizing norm of self-definition. The post-teleological work articulates and masters contingency, and this means for instance that the attempt to master contingency through aesthetic closure (as in realism) may well fall short of the possibilities of the system through the failure to reflect the relationship between individual work and the system. Instead of the concrete dialectic of form and content of the modern paradigm we move to the more abstract level of the relation of relations both as self- and system-reference, the self-consciousness, that is, of the work as a 'possible world'. It presupposes the arbitrary relation of sign and signified, the contingent relations of form and content (whether this finds open or closed expression). Where originality originally meant inner substance, the self-differentiation of the origin, originality now means something completely different, namely difference: the awareness and exploration of alternative possibilities. What is important here is not so much the endless range of possibilities as this consciousness of difference. It is the break with the organic work as self-expression and its replacement by a concept of the work not as necessary but hypothetical — and of course all methods of strict organization only confirm this, for they define the rules of the game, delimit the possibilities of permutation and combination. The hypothetical work derives its cognitive and pleasurable surplus from the *use* of contingency, from the difference of form and content.

Just as the privileging of individuality and creativity in the organic work excluded the conception of the work as experiment and construction (montage) so the identity based on temporal hierarchization precluded the mixture of past and present styles (the Museum). Leonard Meyer (1967) has well expressed the consequences of this paradigm change: in place of the unique organic work we now conceive of the work as an objective construction, whose creativity pertains to the organization of the materials. Creativity (originality) has become a species of problem-solving for which any style or combination of styles can constitute the basis of construction. Form and technique have thus taken the place of inspiration and self-expression (Meyer, 1967: 188), correspondingly the primacy of materials and forms tend to subsume ends under means, so that content and material converge in aesthetic self-representation (Meyer, 1967: 214). This move to formalism is reinforced by the pluralism of taste because formalism is itself inherently relativistic and pluralistic (Meyer, 1967: 232), since it operates with the awareness of the possibility and validity of alternative selections and solutions.

The plurality of styles and tendencies as the presence of alternatives, as the simultaneous exploration of differing possibilities so characteristic of the situation of the arts this century cannot be grasped progressively, it lies beyond progress. Here too we can follow Meyer (1967: 146), who has sought to clarify the consequences for the arts of the 'demise of the idea of Progress'. His thesis is this: 'The paradigm of style history and cultural change which has dominated Western thought since the seventeenth century does not seem able to illuminate or make understandable the situation in the arts today.' If we accept that the present pluralism of co-existing styles 'represents not an anomalous, transient state of affairs, but a relatively stable and enduring one', then our understanding of the present age as a time of crisis is a misunderstanding (Meyer, 1967: 171–2). Meyer argues instead that art since the First World War has brought to an end the preceding 500 years of ordered sequential change. We have entered 'a period of stylistic stasis, a period characterised not by the linear, cumulative development of a single fundamental style, but the coexistence of a multiplicity of quite different styles in a fluctuating and dynamic steady-state' (Meyer, 1967: 98). The end of the idea of Progess is thus a new *secularization*, which brings with it the realization of the artificial nature of style. As a result 'the past, whether recent or remote, has become as available as the present' (Meyer, 1967: 149). 'Past and Present are chronologically separate but epistemologically equal' (Meyer, 1967: 151). Hence the fluctuating steady state of the arts since 1914, in which all styles continue to co-exist (as opposed to the illusory temporal sequence of modernism and postmodernism) and the repertory of available styles grows to include earlier western art and the art of non-western civilizations. Artists may work in one style or shift from style to style (Meyer, 1967: 173–4). The pluralism of styles reflects the pluralization of reception and taste, the loss of a cohesive audience for serious art, music and literature since 1914. Meyer does not lament the loss of stylistic consensus since he regards unity of style as incompatible with the values, freedom and world scope of our culture. Moreover, technical reproduction and communication have made pluralism inescapable (Meyer, 1967: 175–9).

If this situation of postmodern art is 'normal' and not one of crisis, if the 'norm' is the fluctuations of the steady state, what consequences does this have in turn for aesthetic theory? What replaces the ahistorical prescriptive classification of traditional society, the historical-normative aesthetics of the modern age? It is, inevitably, I suggest, the standpoint of relativity. The pluralization of production and reception, the paradox of possible paradigmatic works have as their necessary corollary the pluralization of aesthetic theory. The contingent self-referential system of art is a differentiated subsystem of functional society, the product of a specialized social group, intellectuals, and its counterpart is the multiplication of theoretical descriptions and definitions. The steady state (which is perceived temporally as the sequence of styles and fashions) allows space for the awareness of the *latency of alternatives* in any given structure or selection, in any given work or theory. The definition of the paradigmatic works of postmodern art must therefore remain abstract, can offer only an indeterminate framework, can register only possible not necessary solutions. Theory must validate itself through concrete analyses, which seek to relate the individual work, style or method to the paradigm. We must be clear, however, that the postmodern paradigm has many highest realizations.

References

Adorno, T.W. (1973) *Philosophy of Modern Music*. London: Sheed and Ward.
Adorno, T.W. (1984) *Aesthetic Theory*. London: Routledge & Kegan Paul.
Auden, W.H. (1975) *The Dyer's Hand*. London.
Benjamin, Walter (1970) *Illuminations*. London: Cape.
Benjamin, Walter (1977) *The Origin of German Tragedy*. London: New Left Books.
Boorstin, Daniel (1972) *The Image*. New York.
Gadamer, Hans-Georg (1983) 'Das Rätsel der Zeit über Altes und Neues', *Universitas*, 444 (May).
Lambert, Constant (1948) *Music Ho! A Study in the Decline of Music*. London.
Lyotard, Jean-François (1974) 'Adorno as the Devil', *Telos* 19: 127–37.
Malraux, André (1967) *Museum without Walls*. London.
Marx, Karl (1979) *Grundrisse*. Harmondsworth: Penguin.
Meyer, Leonard B. (1967) *Music, the Arts and Ideas*. Chicago.
Osborne, Charles (1982) *W.H. Auden, the Life of a Poet*. London.

David Roberts teaches German at Monash University, Melbourne.

Nr. 2, Fall 1987

Brian V. Street: Orality and Literacy as Ideological Constructions. **Jesper Svenbro:** The "Voice" of Letters in Ancient Greece. **Michael Chesnutt:** Minstrel Reciters and the Enigma of the Middle English Romance. **Peter Burke:** The Art of Insult in Early Modern Italy. **Frans Gregersen:** The Conspiracy against Letters. **Mogens Trolle Larsen:** Orientalism and the Ancient Near East.

Nr. 3, Spring 1988

Masao Miyoshi: The "Great Divide" Once Again: problematics of the novel and the Third World. **Martin Zerlang:** Juan Rolfo's lonely Storyteller. **Christopher Miller:** Orality through Literacy: Mande Verbal Art after the Letter. **Howard Bloch:** The Voice of the Dead Nightingale: Orality in the tomb of old French Literature. **Anne Knudsen:** Men Killed for Women's Songs. **Martin Bernal.** The British Utilitarians, Imperialism and the Fall of the Ancient Model for Greek Origins.

Prices subscription for one year/two issues dkr. 220 single issues nr. 2 dkr. 130.

Culture & History is a new interdisciplinary journal dedicated to the study of historical anthropology and intellectual history. It is published by the Centre for Research in the Humanities, Copenhagen University.

Museum Tusculanum Press
University of Copenhagen
Njalsgade 94
DK-2300 Copenhagen S
Denmark.

NEW GERMAN CRITIQUE

Fall 1987
No. 42

Special Section on Lukács

Istvan Eörsi: The Unpleasant Lukács
Michael Löwy: Naphta or Settembrini? Lukács and Romantic Anticapitalism
Peter U. Hohendahl: Art Work and Modernity: The Legacy of Georg Lukács
Pauline Johnson: Jauss's Dispute with Adorno
Hendrik Birus: Hermeneutics Today
Winifred Woodhull: Fascist Bonding and Euphoria in Michel Tournier's *The Ogre*
Paul Coates: Karol Irzykowski: Apologist of the Inauthentic Art
Karol Irzykowski: The Tenth Muse
Heinz D. Osterle: Interview with Enzensberger

REVIEW-ESSAYS

Florindo Volpacchio: The Early Lukács
George Mosse: Anatomy of a Stereotype

Individual one year subscriptions are: $18.00 in the U.S. and $20.00 elsewhere. One year institutional subscriptions are $36.00 in the U.S. and $40.00 elsewhere. Make checks payable in U.S. funds, drawn upon U.S. Banks. Back issues are $7.00 each. Send all correspondence to: **Telos Press, 431 E. 12th St., New York, N.Y. 10009.**

Review Article

Postmodern Politics

Michael Ryan

Postmodernism is to art what poststructuralism is to philosophy and social theory. The two came into being at about the same time, with postmodernism emerging in the late 1960s, as structuralism was moulting into poststructuralism. It is the name for a movement in advanced capitalist culture, particularly in the arts — literature, the pictorial and plastic arts, music, performance and video art, etc. — that emphasizes reflexivity, irony, artifice, randomness, anarchy, fragmentation, pastiche and allegory. Cynical regarding the progressivist dreams of modernism, which hoped to shape the cultural world in the image of technology, industry and science, postmodernism is resolutely ironic regarding the enabling myths of art, culture, society and philosophy. In philosophy, it exposes the concealed mechanisms that produce conceptual meaning, and in art, it puts on display the hidden workings of artistic production, demystifying its pretensions to expressive truth. As a result, in postmodernism the emphasis shifts from content to form or style. The metaphoric substitution of a meaning or content for signs gives way to the sheer contiguity, random and unpredictable, of forms.

One of the central objects of critique in postmodern philosophy, therefore, is the classical theory of representation, which held that meaning or truth preceded and determined the representations that communicated it. This theory is associated in postmodern philosophy with social normativity, so that the critique of representation comes to have a political value. The argument for the rhetorical power of material effectivity of representation is also an argument against classical patriarchal and capitalist ideologies that secured legitimacy by grounding social institutions in truths or ideas of substance held to be outside representation altogether.

Theory, Culture & Society (SAGE, London, Newbury Park, Beverly Hills and New Delhi), Vol. 5 (1988), 559–76

The postmodern rejection of the traditional epistemological frameworks out of which such modern progressive movements as Marxism emerged has provoked a negative reaction on the part of some Marxists to the movement. Jameson (1984), for example, in a classicist Marxist gesture, declares it to be the cultural expression of late capitalism. This judgment presupposes that culture can still be directly expressive of economic phenomena, an example, in other words, of the theory of representation that is under critique in postmodernism. What postmodernism suggests is that late capitalism has the effect of creating cultural possibilities that become detached from the realm of economic necessity and with that from the logic of extradiscursive determination by a precultural substance. Those possibilities overturn the logic of representational expression and material overdetermination that restrains previous cultural forms and that shapes Jameson's argument.

What postmodernism as a movement has discovered is that what were thought to be effects in the classic theory of representation can be causes; representations can create the substance they supposedly reflect. This can be looked at in two ways — either as a movement toward artifice, informationalism and a techno-culture of entirely simulated realities that supports capitalist ideology by further distancing the realm of raw, dirty production, or as a movement with progressive possibilites that signals the ability to reshape the supposedly immovable material universe that can no longer be thought of as external and determining in relation to culture. It has been subsumed to the realm of human invention and collective social creativity. In the cultural scene that high capitalism admittedly makes possible, therefore, the positive lineaments of a post-capitalist world can be glimpsed. Capitalism also digs its own grave on the cultural level.

To derive an analogy from Marx, just as capitalism at its furthest reaches is also the first indication of the possibility of communism, so also, one could say, capitalist culture at its furthest reaches (where culture or simulation subsumes reality entirely) becomes the instrument for fabricating a post-capitalist culture. The crucial reversal in this equation is that of sign and thing, culture and the social, or the political, or the economic. It is this reversal that allows one to grant culture a power it could not possess when it still was accountable to a determining materiality. Rather than being expressive representations of a substance taken to be prior, cultural signs become instead active agents in themselves, creating and evoking new substances, new social forms, new ways of acting and thinking, new attitudes, reshuffling the cards of 'fate' and 'nature' and social 'reality'. It is on this margin that culture, seemingly entirely autonomous and detached, turns around and becomes a social and material force, a power of signification that discredits all claims to substantive grounds outside representation, and this discrediting applies to political institutions, moral norms, social practices and economic structures. Detached from the ontologica!, natural and moral foundations that give political, social and juridical institutions their meaning as representations of a prior referent or truth, the expressions of an inherent or already established moral or social order, cultural signs instead are revealed to be the instruments of the creation of new grounds, new meanings and new institutions.

Consequently, although it is true that late capitalism makes postmodernism possible, this does not necessarily mean that postmodernism expresses late capitalism. The figure or trope of external material determination (like the figure of necessary economic development) posits an authority of extracultural substance that results in the characterization of the field of culture as nothing more than a secondary representation. The real issue, the truth of the matter, lies outside, over there, in materiality. Just as the capitalist economy moves necessarily and inevitably toward communism, so also anything that emerges in capitalist culture is given meaning inevitably by a determining material context. The common feature of these descriptions is the idea of a precultural materiality that is the bearer of an inherent power and that expresses itself in incontrovertibly determining ways. These tropes distinguish classical Marxism from modern Marxism of the variety associated particularly with the work of autonomists like Negri or feminists like MacKinnon.

The political valence of postmodernism is therefore at least undecidable, rather than being decisively conservative, as Jameson would have it. The reasons for condemning a cultural and social movement must come not from the fact that it was made possible by a certain stage of capitalism (so were universities and literary critics after all) but from an assessment both of its internal values and of its probable effects. Cultural movements are themselves multiple, and they can have multiple meanings. Parts of postmodernism may indeed fulfil the imperatives of late capitalism, may even express its values, but the same features of the movement can be interpreted as

signalling the availability of a high enough level cf social development to make possible the building of an alternative world (Marx's
reading of automation, for example), and other parts of the movement can use the same postmodernist instruments for progressive
ends or to create radical effects.

Indeed, postmodernism is in many respects the philosophy of
such malleability or rhetoricity. It suggests that capitalist economic
necessity can be transcended; play, with its logic of contingent
connection, can replace work, which is shaped by the rhetoric of
capitalist efficiency that subordinates needs and desires to the rules
of symbolic and material accumulation. The postmodern questioning of the substance of social reality and of the determining power of
material necessity is not only a troubling, and obviously frightening,
philosophical possibility; it is also an important political opening
that deprives those in social power of the grounds (material necessity, social reality) for imposing austerity, efficiency and subordination on the large majority of people.

I will be primarily concerned with political, rather than aesthetic
postmodernism. My argument will be that postmodernist insights
need to be radicalized and pushed beyond the points achieved by
such thinkers as Lyotard and Baudrillard. I will concentrate on the
translations published in the Foreign Agents Series by Jim Fleming
and Sylvere Lotringer at *Semiotext*.

*   *   *

Lyotard's (1982) *Driftworks* consists of essays written for the
most part in the early 1970s, and they bear traces of 1968 and of all
that it represented in regard to a reconsideration of traditional left
politics. Lyotard identifies political repression with reason and with
the way semantic content or meaning implies the repression of the
syntactic play of language. In this, he follows in the path of thinkers
like Derrida and Kristeva, who also argued against the privilege of
reason over rhetoric, abstract ideality over the materiality of language. Reason, Lyotard contends, is trapped because it requires
language, yet its concepts are seemingly metarhetorical. It cannot
be the ordering operation it claims to be so long as it is constitutively
attached to language, whose materiality and productivity contain
the potential for generating meaning effects that are quite dis-
orderly and unreasonable. Consequently, Lyotard locates a radical
political potential in aesthetic strategies of language, form and figura-

tion that undermine rational order and the order of meaning that sustain communicational efficiency and scientific operationalism (the translation of words into things).

This is in some respects a classic preformulation of postmodernist aesthetics. Lyotard extends these insights to the question of political organization. Like many other leftists of the time, Lyotard points out that political organizations merely reproduce the order of power against which they are directed. As the deconstruction of power discourse concerns not what is said but how it is said, the way discourse is laid out or deployed, so also the deconstruction of traditional politics means leaving aside large organizations and attending to the places and institutions of everyday social practice. Dealing with traditional political discourse in its here and now, its time and place, instead of in terms of its contents, reveals the repression in the system. In this programme, one finds an outline of the molecular politics of everyday life that characterized the new social movements of the 1970s and 1980s in western Europe.

Another way of stating Lyotard's point would be to say that those whose psychological training leaves them intolerant of the material, situational and socio-historical character of language, of its open-ended semantic possibilites, and of the socially negotiated and contractual quality of meaning, are likely to be matched by those in political life who refuse to reflect on the politics of organization and who reject democratic forms as being anarchic. Both forms of rationalism are justifiably contested by Lyotard, but his alternative (like that of Irigaray in another register, which veers into religion) risks being a kind of mysticism that merely confirms the worst fears rationalists have regarding the irrationalist destiny of poststructuralism. For Lyotard, capitalism, the family and personal identity form an alliance against the unconscious and desire. One must combat it by freeing up one's libidinal drives, decathecting from capital, and releasing oneself into the plurality of singularities Lyotard calls 'driftworks'. The trick is not to seek power over anything, but to dissolve oneself into libidinal 'workings'. This kind of zen Marxism applies to discourse as well, since any consistent discourse ultimately will serve the ends of power. One must seek a level prior to discourse, abstraction and logic.

All very well and good, but this critique fails to distinguish varieties of rationality or genres of use of reason, and it takes for granted that libidinal freefall will have a happy, rather than a tragic result. It operates with the unarticulated assumption that reason is so embedded in western culture that release from its authoritarian aspects will give rise to a better world rather than to violence, brutality and domination — all former stars of earlier rejections of liberal reason. This can be understood in two ways, either as a temper tantrum of release directed against a bad father that presupposes the overarching presence of a good father, or as a kind of advanced experiment in release from constraints that must operate elsewhere in less developed contexts where irrationalist violence is a real threat. The latter possibility is the more generous, and it seems more in keeping with the opening Lyotard promotes to run with it.

In that frame, Lyotard's project, like Irigaray's, consists of moving to the other side of what reason requires — order, consistency, predictability, etc. Reason presupposes that the same rules must apply in the same way everywhere; this is the blindspot of rational universalism. On the other side of this rationalism is the material reality of difference which requires that each situation elicit its own understanding, its own appropriate level of reason or feeling. From this perspective, living reasonably requires less consistency than flexibility, less the ability to remain the same in different situations, than the capacity to change and to assume distinct roles according to the requirements of each new context. Feeling one's way, in other words, rather than applying the same rigid formulae all the time. A just society would as much require this skill, this ability to 'drift', as Lyotard puts it, as it would require the ability to participate in discussions of rational norms like 'let's not kill each other'. Norms which will always be a matter of desire and feeling, as well as of material contexts and intersubjective structures. If libidinal release always presupposes an implicit norm of a reasonable world that will safeguard against violence, reason itself must always presuppose feeling and desire, those others with whom it seemingly has no commerce. For reasonable norms and rational laws ultimately come down to how people feel about each other, and the killing won't stop until the kind of libidinal release Lyotard proposes can occur without murder resulting. That is the stake, the hope, of his version of postmodernism. It contrasts with a conservative reason that would seek order through restraint rather than through a material reconstruction that sees in the ability to express feelings without violence, the ability to drift, a positive therapy that builds reason from below, as part of a materiality that ultimately would not require external laws.

The French postmodern critique of reason can thus be said to have a certain reasonableness about it. But it can also tend toward mysticism. In general the critique is directed at the kind of reason found in patriarchal capitalist culture, a principle of order that reduces the domains of indeterminacy, contingency, and democracy for reasons of efficiency, domination and power. In the work of Jean Baudrillard, it begins to veer into nihilism. In *Simulations* and *In the Shadow of the Silent Majorities*, Baudrillard (1983a, b) applies deconstructive insights to social phenomena, but his conclusions, rather than being affirmative, lapse into 'asemism', a celebration of meaninglessness and a despairing assessment of the uselessness of all political action.

In *Simulations*, Baudrillard (1983a) takes ideas from Derrida and expands them into a social theory. Those ideas are:

1) The referents of representational systems (especially of language) cannot be determined outside representational systems. At no point does a sign exchange itself for a referent or a meaning that is not itself in some way bound up with representation.

2) Representation does not come after objectivity or meaning as something added on. The designation by the human mind of a domain of objectivity itself requires representation, and equally, the condition of ideality or meaning is representation.

3) Because linguisitic representation is made up of a system of differences whereby each substantive term is constituted through its interrelations with all other terms in the system, and because language is inseparable from its pragmatic context, the possibility of indeterminacy in the designation of objectivity and the communication of meaning can never be fully purged. Language units refer to each other, and it is this which allows them to function as referring to things or ideas. Thus, in reality, there is a circulation of signs rather than a one to one correspondence between signs and things.

Baudrillard gives these ideas a social, political, and historical bent in the following ways. Models, he argues, are now more determining of reality than they are representations of reality. Watergate, for example, consisted of a manipulation of representations on all sides. It was a simulacrum of scandal for regenerative ends. By falling for the lure by engaging in a moral critique of the events, the left ended up doing the work of the right. It took a simulacrum for something real and thereby lent it a credibility it didn't merit. More generally, Baudrillard asserts that stable positions of power or of discourse can no longer be determined; all is merely a vertigo of interpretation. The power of the media now means that the real no longer exists. Images or simulacra determine what 'is' as a constantly circulating play of representations. Order consists of reducing this play to a supposed reality. Even revolutionary discourse is guilty of this operation. Nuclear deterrence serves as an example in that it is a simulacrum that reduces all chance in society to a nuclear order, a balance of terror that amounts to a terror of balance. Because both capitalism and communism are forms of domination, the possible war is merely a feint that maintains power for both sides. Baudrillard concludes that all politics is a form of manipulation, even democratic forms, since they feign equality of participation.

In the second part of *Simulations*, Baudrillard periodizes modern history in terms of semiotics. The contemporary period is the age of simulacra, of endlessly circulating signifiers or representations that nowhere touch a reality. Production has given way to reproduction, and simulation is now determinant. For example, opinion polls predetermine results; the medium controls the message; and the image anticipates the real. There is no real which is not 'always already' reproduced. The 'discontinuous indeterminism' of genetic codes now operates in society itself as the montage logic of the media, which allows no distinction any longer of true and false. The false image is as true as any supposed truth.

In the Shadow of the Silent Majorities is a polemic against the socialist left (Baudrillard, 1983b.) The silent majority or masses are privileged for rejecting all attempts to impose a meaning, a reason, or an order upon them. Baudrillard's populist neo-romanticism comes to the fore here. The masses reject all rational communication, but in their pre-articulateness, they are radical in a way that left intellectuals and revolutionaries cannot grasp; they block the economy in its attempt to administer a rational balance of behaviour and goals. They know there is no liberation and that the system can only be destroyed by pushing it into 'hyper-logic', an implosion that is centripetal, plural, anti-authoritarian, and non-representational. The silent majority, along with terrorism, carries out a rejection of all representational systems, of all traditional political meaning. They are therefore immune to revolutionary calls for expansion and liberation. (The translation leaves out an essay in the original French edition which carries the anti-left argument further in a critique of the French socialist government that originally appeared in the rightwing *Le Figaro*.)

Baudrillard probably represents the apotheosis of the post-1968 critique of the traditional left that gave rise to the slogan 'the end of politics'. Yet whereas that critique of statist socialism and Leninist vanguardism led others to seek alternate social models in the 'area of autonomy', it leads Baudrillard to a sort of 'tactile mysticism' that mixes McLuhan with Castaneda. Nevertheless, there is an autonomous dimension to Baudrillard's work in that it posits a non-Leninist political potential amidst the mass of people.

More problematic from a political perspective is his contention that the advent of the Information Age in the advanced capitalist countries implies that reproduction has replaced production. Those computer chips are still produced by factory labour in third-world countries like Malaysia, the material basis of the first world's Information Age. And that labour is predominantly female, since women workers are more 'pliant' and less likely to unionize. Baudrillard's theory thus in some respects replicates the capitalist displacement of work away from the white centre to the nonwhite periphery in that it obliterates the reality of peripheral labour in an analogous gesture of intellectual gentrification. By accepting the premises of capitalist modernization (which does indeed strive to replace a first world production economy with one based on tertiary or reproduction activities like information and entertainment, as it shifts production to the third world), Baudrillard's theory participates in the imposition of exploitative production on the nonwhite and the nonmale.

In addition, to claim that the Information Age has replaced production with simulation overlooks the fact that the information that most corporations rely on has to do with such things as accounting, which is to say, with the tracking of efficiency based in wages paid and prices extracted, with in other words the very material world of production that informationalism supposedly displaces. This is not to claim that the world of economics stands outside representation. Women workers in Malaysia are lured to factories by the promise of money for cosmetics that allow them to refashion themselves according to prevailing advertising images of female beauty, and they are ideal workers because of the internalization of representations from the culture that induce in them social attitudes of obedience and conformity. Even the materiality of work itself is representational, since it consists of looking through microscopes at microchips all day long, a labour that ultimately results in semiblindness, a deprivation of representational power. So it is true:

capitalism is simulational, but the execution of an efficiency model (by the International Monetary Fund, for example, in the third world) can be as murderous as a death squad, and informationalism only seems to change the language in which power speaks.

Baudrillard's despair over capitalist culture also overlooks contradictory impulses, tensions and embedded resistant potentials. Much like Adorno, who was translated into French in the mid-1970s, Baudrillard's early 1980s reading of capitalist culture is excessively one-sided and pessimistic. Things that he reads negatively can be given a positive inflection. The power of simulation is also a power to produce models of alternative worlds; it can be turned against its capitalist use. But that turn requires a sense of the semantic plasticity, the polysemous character of social instruments. To envision an alternative use for simulation, one must see seemingly univalent social phenomena as being capable of giving rise to multiple semantic effects. The media, rather than being only a source of domination, must come into focus as sites of contestation, where meanings derived by audiences might be entirely at odds with the intention of domination.

Still, Baudrillard's description of the resistant quality of daily mass life opens up the possibility of alternative meanings to the dominant left one for that phenomenon. It suggests that simply because left revolutionary intellectuals have failed to connect their fairly abstract concepts to the everyday material concerns of the people they supposedly address, it is not necessarily true that there is no counter-hegemonic power in the preconceptual needs and desires that seem to be the blind preoccupation of those people. Baudrillard is right to suggest that revolution is a matter of such needs and desires, not only right ideas, although the poststructuralist resistance to reason prevents him from seeing or working out the necessary mediation of those two sets of terms. Can revolution be blind need–satisfaction alone without any reasonable, which is to say, principled and equitable, mechanism for distributing resources?

His theory of the power of mass resistance therefore threatens to lapse into a populist metaphysic that is the mirror image of his intellectual cynicism regarding culture. It is as if the theory of simulation carried embedded within it a hidden yearning for authenticity or genuineness that seems ultimately to be fulfilled by the silent majorities. Capitalist culture is bad because it has replaced the real with simulation, and what is real is to be found outside that culture amidst the undifferentiated *populo*, in a sort of preverbal realm of nonreflexivity. The positing of such an outside is one of the characteristic tropes of romanticism. The gesture suggests the existence of another that is genuine, a presimulational ground whose transcendental meaning resides precisely in that it is external to all syntactic figuring and semantic coding. Such is the silent majority, outside language altogether.

Had he wished to move more consistently within the categories that initiate his critique of capitalist culture, Baudrillard would have been obliged to describe the simulational character of even this supposedly extrasimulational reality, the extent to which its 'outsideness' or otherness is shaped by a representational power that expels such majorities into an undemocratic silence. The contouring of social positions is itself a rhetorical or simulational procedure, and it is necessary to describe the shape societies assume in rhetorical terms. Banished from a democratic determination of what their culture will be, the silent majorities of Baudrillard are the victims of a metaphoric substitution, a displacement that obliges them to relate in a part to whole or synechdochic way to a society whose shape should be wholly theirs to determine. As in psychology, the shapes given by rhetoric constitute social reality as a form of perversion, or to put it differently, as a formal skewing of what might be a more fulfilled existence into a shape that turns away from or misshapes that potential fulfilment. The life of the silent majorities is a rhetorical misshaping of certain other possible life shapes or forms. In this way, simulation can be located at the root of even those seemingly presimulational realities that Baudrillard places outside the culture of simulation as its other.

Similar problems turn up in Arthur Kroker and David Cook's (1987) *The Post-Modern Scene*, an important application of Baudrillard. Kroker and Cook convincingly thread together contemporary art and social theory, showing how infirm the boundary is between the aesthetic and the political. Yet, like Baudrillard, Kroker and Cook emphasize domination effects in culture at the expense of other possibilities. Culture is not conceived as a terrain of struggle or difference; it contains no inherently progressive potentials, no radical lines of tension that outline alternative possibilities to the identity of power.

One of Kroker's major arguments is that Nietzsche represents the negative side of what Marx presented positively as his analysis of the capitalist commodity form. Yet one could, as indeed Negri does, read the description of the commodity in Marx as nothing but political force disguised as economic calculation. The commodity is merely a metaphor for command. Moreover, it is difficult to accept that the commodity form is now no longer a matter of production but instead entirely given over to semiosis when standing armies all over the world seem to indicate that although commodities depend increasingly on marketing signification, they are always also a matter of enforcement, the imposition of work, through the implicit threat of the infliction of bodily harm, on large, generally unseen and certainly unrepresented populations. And even though that threat is representational and pain is nothing more than a signal to the brain, what this suggests is that a recharacterization of reality (from substance to simulation, for example) does not affect the ethical modes of judgment applied to that reality. A painful simulation is just as bad as a painfully real thing.

Kroker, like Baudrillard, uses turns of phrase ('the disappearance of the real', 'the triumph of signifying culture') that suggest that culture has become increasingly simulational and that there might be or might have been at some point an outside to simulation. But one could argue that simulation always has been the case, from Plato and the sophists down to Reagan and prime time TV. All societies rely on ruses to maintain legitimacy, rituals to position subjects, and rhetoric to stabilize a communal representational world that assures the continuity of a shared phenomenal reality. Images have always sustained and produced power, and it is doubtful there has ever been a genuine or authentic sociality of the sort implied by Kroker's metaphors of artificiality and decline. As with Baudrillard, one could perhaps attribute to Kroker a nostalgia, a desire for a world prior to technology, cosmetics, mediascaping and commodification, a world akin to that of religious faith, before the fall into doubt and rationality.

Baudrillard has been accused of sexism for his use of metaphors of seduction to describe simulated culture. Kroker seems less susceptible, but there is nevertheless something troubling about the idea that culture has become 'cosmetic' (a metaphor with unfortunate gender presuppositions) in the age of the mediascape. Perhaps it is a similar gender unconsciousness that motivates him to read an Alan Parsons song, 'Eye in the Sky', which is about male power over women played out through a power of surveillance, as a radical postmodern text about surveillance in general ('I ain't gonna take any more ... The sun in your eyes/ Made some of the lies worth

believing/ I am the eye in the sky/ Looking at you/ I can read your
mind/ I am the maker of rules/ Dealing with fools/ I can cheat you
blind ... Don't cry cause I ain't changin' my mind'). Bearing in
mind that it is a male persona speaking to a woman, the song's
gender-political inflection seems fairly clear.

Baudrillard and Kroker together practise the male intellectual
genre of discourse (as I myself do here), a genre that permits us to
describe world truths without marking the fact that we speak from a
singular perspective that only pretends to generality. If postmodernism teaches anything, it would seem to be that reality is fractured
and plural; it has different versions, and no version is complete. The
white male position is a particularly privileged one, and there is
nothing wrong, I suppose, with its having its day. But one must at
least pose the question of the other, of the other's perspective and of
the other reality it creates. Is the 'fun mood of America in ruins'
really shared by those blacks who have been the primary victims of
the Reagan era? Or would they describe the ruins slightly differently, as bodily pain or the denial of a sense of worth or the absence
of pleasure? I make these remarks not in a spirit of moralistic high-
handedness but rather in the hope of underscoring the limits we
ought to place on our own discursive presumption. We white male
intellectuals, that is.

It would seem from Baudrillard's work that there is no reconciliation possible between postmodernist political thinking and Marxism. But that is to assume that Marxism is as it has been traditionally
constituted a philosophy of totality. Another book in the Foreign
Agents Series, *Anti-Power*, by Guattari and Antonio Negri (1988),
the exiled former theorist of the autonomy movement in Italy,
suggests that Marxism need not be defined in those terms exclusively. The tract brings together Guattari's molecular political and
psychoanalytic concerns with Negri's Marxist macro-political outlook. Thus, they begin by redefining communism as comprising
both molar struggles against exploitation and molecular struggles
for singularity and liberation. The liberation of work and the generation of new modes of subjectivity are both necessary for the
communist project. The political aim of the book is therefore also
very much a reflection of the collaboration that produced it.

1968, the authors argue, saw the end of traditional left parliamentary and party politics and the relaunching of revolution as a form of
struggle. Because capital had spread productive command throughout society and the sphere of reproduction, to the extent of coloniz-

ing the unconscious, the new revolutionary movement combined for the first time the molecular and the molar, addressing issues of everyday life as well as the traditional class struggle. The women's movement was a token of this, as was the new importance given to marginal sectors (the unemployed). State administered work as a model of socialism was rejected, and a new emphasis was given to the bodily character of liberation. Human ends and values of desire were now projected as what should orient production.

What Negri and Guattari call Integrated World Capitalism, which includes both capitalism and socialism, was the determining force of the 1970s, superseding the nation state. The nuclear state is its central figure. The law of value ceased to function; intimidation spread throughout society; and hunger was used as a weapon to turn the third world into the new reserve army of labour. Nevertheless, Negri and Guattari see new revolutionary subjects emerging in the underemployed sectors, in areas of management whose life is rendered precarious by crisis, and in the various new social movements around feminism, ecology, and peace. They condemn terrorism, and argue that Leninist and statist models of organization are incompatible with the new composition of revolutionary subjectivities. They call for a 'functional multicentrism' that would in a new organization establish a plurality of relations between a multiplicity of singularities or movements, a plurality geared toward collective objects that would be beyond bureaucratic control. The principle task is to reunify the traditional components of class struggle against exploitation with the new movements for liberation. One important element of the new strategy is 'work on oneself', as a singular collective, thus renewing the 'human roots' of communism.

They conclude with a list of tasks and diagrammatic propositions. The first task is the development, definition and expression of the new productive subjectivities, dissident singularities, and new proletarian arrangements. They call for struggle around welfare, rent and the imposition of life-oriented time arrangements on work. The second task is the redefinition of work independent of the 'capitalist and/or socialist' ways of organizing it, and they point to the necessity, of addressing issues of workday legislation. The third task is to break with the State form. The fourth is that the anti-nuclear and peace movements have to be made a priority. And finally, the question of a new mode of non-Leninist organizing has to be addressed. The three propositions are that the North/South axis should replace the East/West axis as a primary focus of attention.

The movement should promote alliances between the proletariats of the North and the South against East/West nuclear terror. The second proposition is that Europe needs to be reinvented as a political terrain. And in conclusion, they propose that peace must be seen as a primary condition for overturning the North/South power structure.

Anti-Power is an important amalgam of political strains of thought and action that till now have seemed at least disparate if not altogether incommensurable. The term 'alliance' in their vocabulary is well-chosen for this reason, since it implies difference within unity, and Negri and Guattari are wise to argue that there is no reason why different movements should have to be collapsible into each other in order to work together. The question of what the concrete form such alliances might take is, however, not engaged. At times, Negri and Guattari seem to be suggesting that the alliances are material and unconscious, rather than deliberate. For example, the Latin American proletariats are placed in material alliance with those of the first world when they provoke their national governments to threaten to refuse to repay debts. Even in this regard, the material connections are sometimes drawn, sometimes left to guess. The logic of the necessary link between the anti-nuclear movement and the proletarian movement is made evident; nuclear terror is spread throughout society in a way that neutralizes class struggle. But the relations between the women's movement and the other movements in terms of the linkages between patriarchal sexual power, the hyperbolic aggressivity of the military institution, and the power drive of either the capitalist market or statist administration are not addressed. Without the establishment of such material linkages, the call for alliances can seem organizationally opportunistic or merely tactical. It would seem that truly effective alliances should be forged on the basis of an understanding of the necessary material connections between movements.

Nevertheless, the collaboration between Guattari and Negri indicates the possibility of certain catalytic combinations, of postmodern political collages that need not necessarily be beholden to material necessity or to historical determination for their validation and that still enrich, rather than deplete, the traditional 'metanarratives' like Marxism. Even if the connections are contingent, their very making overrides any weakness that might result from leaving behind the old anchors. In this sense, postmodern politics would ultimately mean the evolution of a greater sense of leverage regarding what can be done, what can be created from the available political materials. A new political rhetoric emerges to the extent that metaphoric political forms, which stressed the subsumption of diverse subordinate movements to semantically more significant, higher-order ideals of unity and identity, give way to metonymic forms that stress the greater variety of contingent connections, contiguous links that are not in the order of subordination but instead of coordination in an equal and diverse field of possibilities. Rather than discard the metanarratives (as much a male socialized gesture of exclusion and subordination as the metanarratives themselves), they are preserved, deepened, made more complex and differentiated. It amounts to adding detail and colour to a rough sketch, rather than destroying the sketch and claiming that only the detail is true.

The postmodernist and poststructuralist critique of representation thus has a political corollary. The belief that rhetoric is attached to reason as a secondary and dispensable appendage that has no productive power of its own creates a hierarchy that places semantic ideals over syntax or meaningful content over mere rhetoric or form. The theoretical hierarchy resembles the practical one in capitalist societies that places political ideals (freedom) over everyday materialities or that places economic fetishes (the free market) over the everyday forms of need and desire. On the left particularly, such semanticism (the assumption that social principles like communism are teleological ideals or contents rather than rhetorical procedures of democratic, material social constitution that are concerned with everyday forms of existence) allows the question of the rhetoric of everyday life — the forms it assumes — to be subordinated. It also places institutions like the patriarchal family and the workday in a secondary realm of social rhetoric that does not bear importantly on the more significant issues of the 'socialist' content of society. But that content is itself constituted and shaped by those 'secondary' forms.

A shift toward an understanding of how the procedures of political rhetoric constitute the ideational and institutional world they supposedly represented necessarily brings with it a shift toward an understanding of how the rhetorical procedures of everyday life, the shapes and forms of the workday, sexual relations, and so on, constitute the supposedly metatheoretical or extrarepresentational reality or content of social existence. What postmodernism suggests is that there is no content of society apart from the rhetoric of forms, procedures, modes, shapes and genres that constitutes the embodiment in everyday life of that content.

The critique of representation can therefore be said to bear on left politics in crucial ways. The reversal of sign and thing also reverses certain polarities or hierarchies, the one that placed the form of the workday second in relation to the content of the state plan, or the one that placed the form of gender relations second in relation to a more primary non-sexual concern (one usually associated with male socialized forms of reason) like rational organization. This is a politics that addresses the formal dimensions of social life as much as its materiality. Its orientation is horizontal and egalitarian rather than vertical and hierarchic. It privileges lateral connections between different political dimensions and refuses to subordinate one to the another. The authority that traditional political representational systems sanctify melts into an entirely democratic and levelling movement. Subordination ceases to be the principle of political life, and conjugation takes its place. Aware of its own status as a rhetoric, such a politics seeks to posit new worlds through representation, to develop models of alternative forms of social existence. Rather than being beholden to a spurious ideal of extradiscursive substance or prerepresentational truth, it works to create new forms, and in so doing to give rise to new substances, new meanings, new realities.

What one gains from this insight is the conclusion that social power and social politics are forms, malleable shapes, particular dispositions of mouldable elements, configurations given over constitutively to reformulation. From a postmodern perspective, politics comes into focus as a radically contingent arena of imagination, strategy and creative manoeuvre around stakes that are at once material and representational. For the purpose of power is to secure the accumulation of the goods of desire, the commodities that are as much factors of material need as of psychological cathexis. If they are things, they are also signs. In Mystic, Connecticut, where I live, the signs of power are large lawns, high trees enclosing hermetic estates, beautiful large buildings — space, quiet, beauty, exclusion. These things are all quite material, linked to desire both as the fulfilment of psychological images and as felt pleasures. And they are linked to the normalized brutality of wage labour elsewhere in the world, the source of the power to buy estates.

But materiality can no longer be taken as the term for necessity or for what is outside simulation and contingency, or for what is true in an extratheoretical sense. A rhetorical (that is, a poststructuralist or postmodern) theory of social politics sees materiality as inseparable from the shapes given it by social construction. To embrace politics in a postmodern sense is to place a stake on contingency, on the insight that power, no matter how grounded in 'reality', how seemingly bound to 'material' necessity, is up for grabs, movable and therefore removable. This is why the anti-political strain of postmodern theory does not take its insights far enough, far enough to see that society is not a real that can become simulational, but an arrangement of rhetorical forms and materialized tropes that has never been anything but simulational. And it is precisely at that point, with that insight, that a postmodern politics should begin.

References

Baudrillard, Jean (1983a) *Simulations*. New York: Semiotext(e).
Baudrillard, Jean (1983b) *In the Shadow of the Silent Majorities*. New York: Semiotext(e).
Guattari, Félix and Negri, Antonio (1988) *Anti-Power*. New York: Semiotext(e).
Jameson, Frederic (1984) 'Post-Modernism, or the Cultural Logic of Late Capitalism', *New Left Review* 146: 79–146.
Kroker, Arthur and Cook, David (1987) *The Post-Modern Scene*. New York: St. Martin's Press.
Lyotard, Jean-François (1982) *Driftworks*. New York: Semiotext(e).

Michael Ryan teaches Politics at Northeastern University, Massachusetts. His latest book, *Culture and Politics* has just been published by Macmillan.